Praise for *Black Trumpet*

"A wonderful culinary tour, both through the seasons and through an endlessly inventive and particularly New England kind of sense and sensibility."

—**PAUL GREENBERG**, author of *Four Fish* and *American Catch*

"Rare is the book that can both deepen your appreciation of tradition and open your mind to innovation, yet *Black Trumpet* seems to accomplish this on nearly every page. You think it's all been done, and then Evan Mallett shows you it hasn't. In a region swimming with farm-to-table chefs, Mallett has managed to break free and create something truly new—an original cuisine that tells the story of modern coastal New England in words, images, and an extraordinary palette of flavors."

—**ROWAN JACOBSEN**, author of *American Terroir* and *The Essential Oyster*

"The only complaint I've ever had about Evan Mallett's acclaimed Black Trumpet restaurant is that it's too far from where I live for me to dine there as often as I'd like. With this book, I'm finally able to enjoy Mallett's imaginative, seasonal, and ultra-tasty food at home any time the urge hits—and it will hit often."

—**BARRY ESTABROOK**, author of *Pig Tales: An Omnivore's Quest for Sustainable Meat*

"From the very first chapter, I was captured by Evan's knowledge of stocks, dressings, aioli, butters that have been browned, and all the necessary beginnings for the magical dishes this wonderful cook has fashioned. All through the book, from one season to the next, I was profoundly impressed by Evan's understanding of ingredients that bring more than one taste to your delighted mouth.

"There are three classic books for cooking: *The Joy of Cooking*, Julia Child's *Mastering the Art of French Cooking*, and *The New York Times Cookbook*. You only need to add one other now—Evan Mallett's *Black Trumpet*."

—**JAMES HALLER**, founding chef/owner, Blue Strawbery; author of *Salt & Pepper Cooking*

"Evan Mallett is a well-respected food hero who lives and cooks in an edge of North America known more for its trying climate than for its bounty: harsh winters, short seasons, thrifty New England ways. And perhaps it is that very element that makes *Black Trumpet* so inspiring: the creative use of what's available in a part of the world where land meets sea; where eaters are only beginning to learn how best to orient their passion for the familiar with the wild offerings of the seasons.

"Evan's book is both a fascinating read and marvelously useful: Beautifully adorned with Enna Grazier's photographs, *Black Trumpet* serves as an inspiration and resource for the home cook who seeks practical tools for entertaining. While Evan's commitment to sustainability and cultivating leadership in the food community via Chefs Collaborative and Slow Food makes him a chef's chef, this book illustrates how, more than anything, Evan is a teacher and guide for cooks who create in their home kitchens."

—**RICHARD MCCARTHY**, executive director, Slow Food USA

"Evan Mallett stealthily and humbly creates our regional culinary identity. His dishes honor our seasonal ingredients but also give us a sense of adventure in exciting flavors and traditions from Morocco, Mexico, and India. This is the new, true New England cuisine. I'll make these delicious dishes season by season, but there are beautiful stories here, too, about farmers and fishermen, family and loyal staff—all part of the bigger story behind Evan's dedication to our Good Food Revolution."

—**RACHEL FORREST**, food writer and restaurant critic

BLACK TRUMPET

BLACK TRUMPET

A CHEF'S

JOURNEY

THROUGH EIGHT

NEW ENGLAND

SEASONS

Evan Mallett

PHOTOGRAPHS BY ENNA GRAZIER

Chelsea Green Publishing
White River Junction, Vermont

Project Manager: Patricia Stone
Project Editor: Benjamin Watson
Copy Editor: Laura Jorstad
Proofreader: Eileen M. Clawson
Indexer: Shana Milkie
Designer: Melissa Jacobson

Printed in the United States of America.
First printing September, 2016
10 9 8 7 6 5 4 3 2 1   16 17 18 19

green
press
INITIATIVE

Chelsea Green Publishing is committed to preserving
ancient forests and natural resources. We elected to
print this title on paper containing at least 10% postconsumer recycled paper, processed chlorine-free. As a
result, for this printing, we have saved:

24 Trees (40' tall and 6-8" diameter)
11,610 Gallons of Wastewater
12 million BTUs Total Energy
777 Pounds of Solid Waste
2,140 Pounds of Greenhouse Gases

Chelsea Green Publishing made this paper choice
because we are a member of the Green Press Initiative, a
nonprofit program dedicated to supporting authors,
publishers, and suppliers in their efforts to reduce their
use of fiber obtained from endangered forests. For more
information, visit www.greenpressinitiative.org.

Environmental impact estimates were made using the
Environmental Defense Paper Calculator. For more
information visit: www.papercalculator.org.

Our Commitment to Green Publishing

Chelsea Green sees publishing as a tool for cultural change and ecological stewardship. We strive to align our book manufacturing practices with our editorial mission and to reduce the impact of our business enterprise in the environment. We print our books and catalogs on chlorine-free recycled paper, using vegetable-based inks whenever possible. This book may cost slightly more because it was printed on paper that contains recycled fiber, and we hope you'll agree that it's worth it. Chelsea Green is a member of the Green Press Initiative (www.greenpressinitiative.org), a nonprofit coalition of publishers, manufacturers, and authors working to protect the world's endangered forests and conserve natural resources. *Black Trumpet* was printed on paper supplied by QuadGraphics that contains at least 10% postconsumer recycled fiber.

Library of Congress Cataloging-in-Publication Data
Names: Mallett, Evan, author. | Grazier, Enna, photographer (expression)
Title: Black Trumpet : a chef's journey through eight New England seasons / Evan Mallett ;
    photographs by Enna Grazier.
Description: White River Junction, Vermont : Chelsea Green Publishing, [2016] | Includes index.
Identifiers: LCCN 2016022941| ISBN 9781603586504 (hardcover) | ISBN 9781603586511 (ebook)
Subjects: LCSH: Cooking, American—New England style. | Seasonal cooking—New England.
    | Black Trumpet (Restaurant) | LCGFT: Cookbooks.
Classification: LCC TX715.2.N48 M36 2016 | DDC 641.5974—dc23
LC record available at https://lccn.loc.gov/2016022941

33614057793878

Chelsea Green Publishing
85 North Main Street, Suite 120
White River Junction, VT 05001
(802) 295-6300
www.chelseagreen.com

MIX
Paper from
responsible sources
FSC® C084269

To Evan
Thanks for Your
Support
Through
the Years. I
Could not have
done it without
You

GH

I n 1999, I told my local heirloom tomato farmer, a former chef himself, that I loved his tomatoes, but that I cherished the antique wooden box he delivered the tomatoes in even more. I pestered him for over a decade, including two winters when he worked in my kitchen, to give me the box when he was ready to retire it. Sure enough, fifteen years later, he brought me this sacred box with a thoughtful inscription on the bottom. Now, when it is not housing packets of heirloom seeds we have saved from our garden, it is used as a prop in photo shoots for this very book. The farmer's name is Garen Heller, and he was my first local farmer connection.

CONTENTS

Clockwise from the top left: Rebecca Colcord, Jon Plaza, Carrie Dahlgren, Monica Briselden, Gabriel Balkus, and John Flintosh

ACKNOWLEDGMENTS

I have shared with my staff over the years these simple observations: Most restaurants' wait staffs are in the business for the cash to support another, less lucrative career path. The majority of Black Trumpet's front-of-house staff members have chosen hospitality for the long haul. Black Trumpet guests experience this distinction the moment they walk in the door. As business owners, Denise and I understand the value a staff that cares about their work can bring to the guest's experience. How can restaurant guests be happy to dine where the staff isn't happy to work?

To my cherished kitchen staff past and present, whose desire to grow and learn and support what Black Trumpet stands for, I have been known to unironically (and cornily) say, "Most restaurant cooks work for a living, but Black Trumpet cooks work for a *loving*." Their patience during the making of this book has been a testament to that love.

I believe these are the traits that make our staff invaluable and unique in an industry that doesn't always treat workers with the respect they deserve. This book is as much a compendium of their stories as it is a chronology of mine.

My love Denise—for raising me and our kids right, for her wisdom and scrutiny, and for always believing I had at least one book in me.

Enna Grazier and Steph Deihl—for endless hours of egoless collaboration.

Chef de Cuisine John Flintosh—whose second tour of duty at Black Trumpet made this book possible.

Kathy Gunst, Sally Ekus, and Ben Watson—for helping me navigate the publishing world.

Eleanor and Cormac—the best, brightest, most patient (and adorable) guinea pigs a chef could hope for.

My parents, Charles Mallett and Beverly Collymore.

INTRODUCTION

You can taste passion. I believe that, and when any restaurant is at its best, the rhythmic pulse of passion issues from the kitchen and seasons every aspect of the guest's experience, traveling with each plate in a seamless ballet, from the kitchen to the table, in the hands of wait staff who share the untamed fire of the kitchen yet have the ability to gracefully harness it. Passion is the blood that runs in a great restaurant's veins. Without it, the guest tastes just another dish in just another restaurant. Black Trumpet has always been about surpassing that expectation.

As the chef behind Black Trumpet, I have put the passion that sparks my intellectual and creative juices into each menu. I won't pretend here that every dish has been a flawless success, or even a reflection of my good intentions. There have been abject failures. And then there have been the anomalies: dishes that won the hearts of critics, appeared in magazines, and solidified our reputation as an outside-the-box dining destination, but that were ordered by only a scant few guests.

As I sat down to write this book, I had to put Black Trumpet in the context of my own career, which was easy. But I also had to circumscribe roughly how Black Trumpet the restaurant fit into the protean mosaic of American food and dining in this era I have come to refer to as the Good Food Revolution. That was hard. In the end, I guess it is safe to say that, like the prototypes that built the local food foundation decades ago, and like the brave new menus that will (hopefully) continue to enrich our culinary landscape for generations to come, Black Trumpet has made an impact by setting an example of how to make people happy while doing what we believed to be the right thing. In order to succeed in that messaging, the food has had to be delicious, or else people would have dismissed the meaning behind it.

When we first opened the doors of Black Trumpet during a blizzard on the Ides of March, 2007, our food community had no clear identity. And although local organizations were working on developing initiatives to support our immediate foodshed, our independent businesses, and a robust farmers market, there was no obvious path to the uniquely galvanized community that exists today.

Nearly a decade later, we now have a synergistic cross-pollination of volunteer armies that include local university organizations, a thriving Slow Food chapter, a local chef network that is the pride of Chefs Collaborative, a series of indoor winter farmers markets that have inspired many other regions around the country, and emerging food hubs and distribution systems dialed in to bring more local food to the masses. So why have Portsmouth and the Seacoast region of New Hampshire been so effective in creating this web of food-based organizations? I say it's the determination, humility, and ego-free passion of the personalities behind the local food movement in our area.

Black Trumpet is viewed today as one of the key local progenitors of this movement. In the 2011 novel *Maine*, author J. Courtney Sullivan (whom I have never met) writes, "She had read about a place in Portsmouth called the Black Trumpet . . . located in an old shipping goods warehouse, and the chef cooked with organic ingredients from local farms." When someone brought me a copy of that book and showed me the quote, I thought for perhaps the first time that I could sum up the meaning of Black Trumpet in a single sentence. Yet so many other components and values are missing from this description. I still don't have an elevator pitch that can answer the oft-asked questions, "What kind of food do you serve?" and "What type of

Clockwise from the top left: Alison Magill, Denise Mallett, Josh Jennings, Karen Marzloff, Jean Pauly, Debra Kam, Abigail Wiggin, Brendan Vesey, and John Forti

restaurant is it?" I continue to let people form that opinion for themselves.

To better understand Black Trumpet's identity, one must first be acquainted with the legacy of its forebears.

Black Trumpet occupies a charmed and charming address—29 Ceres Street—whose history boasts three successful restaurants spanning four and a half decades. The neighborhood's working-class history begins with the city of my mother's childhood—one known for stevedores, warships, prostitutes, and prisoners—and ends with the ultimate makeover. The wharf-side neighborhood once known as Merchants' Row, running alongside photogenically huddled tugboats and megaton cargo ships, has evolved—over the course of almost four hundred years—from a humble, hardscrabble fishing port into the charming mini city it is today.

In November 1970, an out-of-work actor named James Haller and his friends stumbled (quite literally) upon a dilapidated old brick warehouse building in the red-light district by the city's working pier. In this building, they saw a promise so far-fetched that it would have taken an indomitable, indefatigable visionary to pull it off. Haller was that visionary, and like so many visionaries he was erratic, obdurate, louche, and sometimes maniacal, according to many of the cooks who have worked with him. Of course, his personality was also a magnet to his employees. Into this surreal, dichotomous world was hatched the formidable and unforgettable Blue Strawbery. (For any out-of-town readers, *Strawbery* with one *r* is the appropriate spelling, since it matches the colonial spelling of Portsmouth's historic Strawbery Banke district.)

Chef Haller, who—like me—had no formal training as a chef, was by all accounts a pioneer who began cooking his dazzlingly innovative and whimsical style of food at a time when the modern American culinary era was in its infancy. The American restaurant landscape in 1970 was a bleak wasteland of steak houses, stodgy Francophilic hotel dining rooms, and "Continental cuisine" institutions, the collective chefs of which could be credited with a handful of original ideas at best.

Interestingly, original thinking and creative cuisine had no cachet in the restaurant industry until the last few decades. Haller is one of the unsung chefs who built

this new paradigm, changing the face of dining in America once and for all. It is important to remember that Haller came before the monumental game changers of Modern American Cuisine. Alice Waters opened Chez Panisse the following year. Down the road a piece in Boston, legends Jasper White and Lydia Shire were almost a decade away from opening their own landmark restaurants. Sam Hayward of Portland, Maine's vaunted Fore Street was three years shy of his first job on nearby Appledore Island, which began a forty-three-year local food odyssey that ultimately rebranded Portland as a culinary destination. Given all those landmarks yet to come, it is safe to say that there was nothing like Blue Strawbery in the Northeast, or even in America, in 1970.

It is not hyperbole then to suggest that Blue Strawbery—along with the art and theater community that was emerging at the same time—inspired the gradual gentrification of Portsmouth while also laying the groundwork for what would later become the Good Food Revolution. Buddy, as Chef Haller is known to his friends, tells of the day that two Bentleys pulled up in front of his new restaurant. That was the day he knew his vision had paid off. More than one local historian has told me that the opening of Blue Strawbery on the busy, squalid wharf was a turning point in the history of Portsmouth.

Chef Haller's style was at once innovative and desperate. There was not, at the time, a centralized food system that could distribute "exotic" foods to Portsmouth. So when Haller, who hailed from Chicago originally, wanted to put rabbit on his menu, he had to go out and find a rabbitry. Miraculously, he did. When he wanted to serve a good Jewish rye bread in his restaurant, he had to teach the local baker how to make what he wanted. Chefs today, including me, have it so easy!

In 1996, Blue Strawbery closed its doors, ending a twenty-six-year journey into the modern era of American dining. The restaurant was purchased by three young men, each with some restaurant experience, two of whom had been pilots in Operation Desert Storm.

The result was Lindbergh's Crossing, a bistro and wine bar dedicated to simple, country French-inspired cuisine. At the magical address they inherited,

Lindbergh's owners and young chef Jeff Tenner found a devout audience for their business model, instantly aggregating a following of fiercely loyal regulars.

My fiancée and I sat down at a window table upstairs at Lindbergh's Crossing in 1998 and, while swooning over rabbit and pappardelle, decided to pack up and move to Portsmouth. That memorable meal was part of the city's allure. At the time, I was struggling as a freelance food writer. The meal at Lindbergh's had that kind of power over us: It inspired us to relocate our lives and rethink our careers.

Once we settled in Portsmouth, it was only a matter of time before I applied for a job at Lindbergh's Crossing. Chef Tenner hired me despite the seven-year gap in cooking jobs on my résumé. And so began my tenure in the storied kitchen at 29 Ceres Street.

After a few months, Lindbergh's owners—Tom Fielding, Louis Hamel, Chef Jeff, and Scott O'Connor—opened a sister restaurant, Ciento, around the corner from Lindbergh's. After working the garde-manger and grill stations for a few months, I was named sous chef. Unfortunately, Ciento—a risky (at the time) Spanish-tapas-inspired concept, closed its doors after just a year and a half. This was my first taste of failure, one that would inform many of my later decisions as a business owner.

Through a connection with a flamenco guitarist who had played at Ciento, I accepted an offer to consult on the opening of a restaurant in San Miguel de Allende, a preposterously charming mountain village in central Mexico. Almost two years in Mexico, running the kitchen of a Cajun restaurant and an adjacent "gourmet" market, spawned an arsenal of unbelievable stories, some of which are laid out in the pages that follow.

From Mexico I returned to Portsmouth, young family in tow, at the behest of Lindbergh's owners Tom and Scott. Chef Jeff was leaving for Boston, and they wanted me to take the helm of the kitchen. So with toddler Eleanor in a car seat and her baby brother Cormac in the womb, we came home to Portsmouth slowly, traveling through Mexico and camping along the way over a period of two months. Back in Portsmouth, I transitioned into the role of executive chef of Lindbergh's Crossing, inheriting a much-loved menu along with a gorgeous restaurant run by good friends of mine. Three years later, over dinner at their house, Tom and Scott announced they were going to sell the restaurant, and they wanted Denise and me to take it over. This kind of transition is not always easy to pull off, but part of me wishes every restaurant sale could be awarded to those employees who have moved up through the ranks and earned the privilege.

Today the city of Portsmouth boasts an improbably vast number of restaurants. According to one survey published in the summer of 2013, Portsmouth now has more seats in eateries than it has people. With over twenty-one thousand people, that's a whole lot of seats. I do know that Portsmouth's ever-growing restaurant community will continue to attract the masses because the city exudes charm and invites people to admire its idyllic network of one-way streets and quaint shops, its nearby beaches and mountains, and—of course—its bustling restaurant scene that caters to pretty much every taste and type of person under the sun.

It was in 2008, one year into the life of Black Trumpet, that the mortgage crisis crippled our nation's economy for a harrowing couple of years. (One local retailer I know, who also happens to be a former banker, believes the 40 percent decline in consumer spending that began that year has made a permanent change in buying habits.) In addition, 2008 was the year when the local food movement in Portsmouth came into its own, whether as a product of many individuals' hard work, or out of necessity, or both. Portsmouth was hit like everywhere else. Our business was certainly adversely affected. But when I reflect on the economic "bubble" so often referenced during that time, I recall that Portsmouth and the surrounding Seacoast area were somehow insulated from the worst of the burst. Advocates of a strong local economy point to the cooperative nature of our independent shopkeepers, innkeepers, and restaurateurs during the Great Recession as an example of how a local economy can persevere through a global crisis.

Portsmouth is a well-preserved historic city pregnant with promise. The city's civic leaders remain committed to preservation but also see the great potential in expanding its commerce responsibly and sustainably. Housed in a six-story, 230-year-old brick building, Black Trumpet truly occupies part of the bedrock of the city. In this sometimes congested landscape, Black Trumpet continues to do its part to stretch boundaries and educate its guests while serving creative food that veers from the mainstream just enough to make the menu and the experience stand out in a crowded restaurant market.

This book represents my attempt to capture the high points of Black Trumpet's wild ride from start-up to dining destination. In one decade, it has been said,

Black Trumpet has given the ship of sustainability plenty of horsepower, moving the dial of good and healthful local food in a positive direction. I hope this book will have an appeal beyond New England, beyond this small corner of our nation, in part because our heritage, our ingredients, and the Black Trumpet recipes that celebrate both should serve as a reference for cooks and historians everywhere.

The restaurant business, by its very nature, is a labor of love. Without the love, there are few reasons mere mortals would endure the long hours, sometimes brutal conditions, and unwarranted attacks that come with restaurant ownership. Black Trumpet has thrived on the love of its owners and staff, as well as that of its guests, through the dawn of the Good Food Revolution. I look forward to someday sitting at the table we call Window 2, upstairs on the right, overlooking the harbor and the tugboats, with my wife and partner, reflecting on the years that transpired between milestone meals at that table. We might feel wistful, nostalgic, a little sad about the passage of time, but we will certainly feel a great sense of pride in the Black Trumpet story. It is a beautiful story of hard work and passion, intermingled with heartbreak and loss, that could easily fill the pages of a novel. But it is a real story of real people, and that makes our journey even more compelling, albeit complex, personal, and at times difficult to recount; but throughout, our growth has revolved around a deep passion for flavor and hospitality, and the glorious stories behind the constituents that have contributed to both.

On behalf of Black Trumpet; my patient and dedicated partner, Denise; and our wonderful staff over the years, I hope you—the reader—enjoy the journey that this book represents. For those who will be dining at Black Trumpet in the future, I look forward to meeting you and including you in the story as it continues to unfold.

WILD CARD DITTES

2 qts WATER
3 C SUGAR
3 T MUGWORT
1 T CHAMOMILE
1 T ANGELICA

Duck Confit Cure

Cinnamon
Cloves
Ground Mace
Ground Allspice
Pepper
Anise
garlic
Sugar

HOW TO USE THIS BOOK

I f one were to map the way my mind works, the result would probably look like a fractal geometry equation interrupted by a catchy song and a flock of migrating waterfowl. So organizing this book has posed many challenges, not least of which is where to fit in thoughts, rants, and experiences that might give recipes context, but also stand on their own as evocative anecdotes. Using the same fractal rationale, I have employed all manner of tropes—sidebars, headnotes, endnotes, profiles, and even the bodies of recipes themselves—to fit words in edgewise wherever possible. The indices at the back of the book should serve as a consistent go-to for navigating these sometimes disembodied thoughts.

Over the years, Black Trumpet menus have fallen into eight seasons a year (early spring, late spring, early winter, et cetera). Although that is no longer a strict guideline, the idea remains that those half seasons more or less encapsulate and harness the peaks of locally available ingredients. At the very least, the delineation of those six-week periods serves to discipline me and my staff to stay on top of what's coming and going. In attempting to organize this book, I have created chapters based on that chronology, beginning with early winter.

There is little question that something cataclysmic has befallen the Earth's climate—fish and other aquatic species have migrated north, growing zones have shifted, ice caps are shrinking—so our regional delineation of seasons will surely also be impacted in the generations to come. Having said that, we are all of us rooted in agricultural tradition, and whether we are accustomed to growing sugarcane or balsam fir trees, and despite a century of research and technology, we remain at the mercy of our climate.

For all you home cooks using this volume as a cookbook, I encourage you to engage the four *F*s—farmers, foragers, fishermen, and friends—to help you source hard-to-find ingredients. That said, substitutions are a necessary fact of life in the sustainable food world, so I have tried to indicate where those might be applied to the recipes in this book.

The downside of sticking to a seasonal menu-planning philosophy is that we often don't have time to thoroughly perfect a dish before its time is up on our menu. Other restaurants settle on tried-and-true dishes, and some places that boast seasonal menus will circle back to dishes that were "in season" from past years. That makes good business sense, and it builds reputations based on signature dishes. Yet I remain stubborn about avoiding repetition. This may be the hallmark of a foolish businessman, but it is also one reason I have stayed in the kitchen as long as I have. I am always learning, always reaching for new ingredients and flavors, and always trying to inspire my cooks to do the same. I think it is a healthy way to run a kitchen, and a restaurant, as long as there is a shared energy to support it.

So in the pages that follow, seasons are used as temporal reference points, but within each season lies a fixation on an ingredient or two that have inspired Black Trumpet menus year after year. I encourage readers to find inspiration from these ingredients as I have, and perhaps find either solace or further inspiration in the tales that accompany each chapter.

As a final note of encouragement, in the back of this book I have written a compendium of ingredients, equipment, and techniques and where to source them. I have also included proposed menus that home cooks can put together from recipes in the book to recreate something of the Black Trumpet experience in peak season.

BLACK
TRUMPET
BUILDING
BLOCKS

BUILDING BLOCK
RECIPES

While our menus may morph constantly, there are a few elements of the Black Trumpet repertoire that keep popping up. These items serve as building blocks that are helpful to have on hand for quicker (and tastier!) cooking, Black Trumpet style.

Clarified Butter and Olive Oil Blend (CBOOB)

If culinarians in the know now refer to extra-virgin olive oil using the acronym EVOO, I can also call our unique ratio of clarified butter to olive oil CBOOB, right?

We use this as our cooking fat for just about everything. It is the secret that turns our elemental Fried Almonds, Olives, and Garlic dish (page 124) into something otherworldly. To make this blend, simply heat butter in a heavy-bottomed saucepan over low heat until the milk solids separate out of the butter and leave a clear golden liquid. Some of the solids rise and float, and others encrust the bottom of the pot. Skim off the floating white solids with a ladle or spoon, and pour the butter through a mesh strainer into a vessel, leaving room to add oil. We use pure olive oil—not extra-virgin—at a ratio of half the amount of oil to clarified butter.

Mirepoix

Most classic French sauces and soups begin with the archetypal threesome of carrots, onions, and celery. Spain and Italy each have versions of this idea called *sofrito* and *soffritto*, respectively. The Cajun "trinity" substitutes bell pepper for carrot, and we will use that at Black Trumpet in Cajun and Creole dishes from time to time. But more often than not, we keep a few pounds of mirepoix on hand to lend soups, stews, braises, and sauces that extra depth they so richly deserve.

Stocks

Stock is a chef's best friend. It not only fortifies the flavor of everything it touches but also builds flavor as it reduces, yielding a concentrated amalgam of its myriad components—to say nothing of the well-known health benefits stocks contribute to our diets.

In order of complexity, here are the stocks Black Trumpet has to have on hand at any given time, with suggested cooking times. At home, pour them into resealable bags, zip them up tight with as little air as possible, label them, and freeze them. They can be microwaved in no time, giving the home cook a healthy version of instant cup-a-soup.

Vegetable Stock

SIMMER 40 MINUTES

In my world, I am never more than a couple of degrees of separation away from a vegetarian, so it's always a good idea to have what we call veg stock on hand. We use scraps from a busy prep day in our veg stock, but if I'm starting from scratch, here is my recipe:

2 carrots, diced
1 red, yellow, or orange bell pepper, top and tail, chopped (reserve sides for other recipes)
2 stalks celery, diced
1 large Spanish onion, chopped
6 cloves garlic, bruised with the side of a knife
¼ cup (15 g) chopped fresh basil
3 sprigs thyme
½ cup (85 g) tomato paste
1 bay leaf
16 black peppercorns
2 quarts (1.9 L) water

Boom Stock

SIMMER 1 HOUR

Husks from 2 ears corn
½ cup (15 g) dried mushrooms
Any fresh mushroom stems, trimmings, or even whole mushrooms kicking around
½ cup (125 g) mirepoix
1 bay leaf
1 thumb gingerroot, peeled and sliced
10 peppercorns
2 quarts (1.9 L) water

Fish Stock

SIMMER 90 MINUTES

When we fillet whole fish, we put the heads and bones in a pot and cover them with white wine and water. Celery, onion, fennel, and sometimes saffron go into the pot as well, along with some aromatic herbs and peppercorns.

Rabbit (or Poultry) Stock

SIMMER 2 HOURS

One of the stranger things about Black Trumpet is that we often have rabbit stock on hand but rarely chicken stock. When we do have local chickens on our menu, we use the same recipe, substituting birds for bunnies. Duck makes an even more delicious stock, and therefore no duck carcass should ever go into a trash can until it has yielded a stock.

2 tablespoons olive oil
Carcass and bones remaining from 3- to 4-pound
   (1.4–1.8 kg) rabbit (see "Rabbit Butchery," page 72)
1 stalk celery, large dice
½ onion, large dice
2 medium carrots, peeled, large dice
4 cloves whole garlic
1 cup (235 ml) white wine
2 sprigs thyme
2 bay leaves

Coat a roasting pan with the olive oil and add the rabbit carcass to the pan. Roast for 40 minutes at 425°F (220°C). Add the celery, onion, carrots, and garlic and return the pan to the oven for 10 minutes. Making sure ventilation is good, put the pan on the stovetop over a low flame, add the white wine, and cook, scraping up

the browned bits, until the scent of alcohol wears off, 2 to 3 minutes.

Remove the carcass to a small stockpot. Scrape in the vegetables and wine, and add the thyme and bay leaves. Barely cover the carcass with cold water and set it on the stove over medium-high heat. When the mixture just barely comes up to a boil, reduce the heat to the lowest setting and simmer 2 hours. Remove the pot from the heat and strain into a large container. Let it cool to room temperature and refrigerate until you're ready to use it.

Head and Foot Stock

SIMMER OVERNIGHT

The best-tasting stock I have ever made was a white stock (made from bones that were not roasted first), as opposed to a brown stock (typically made from roasting bones and vegetables). This flies in the face of popular chef thinking, because roasting intensifies the flavor of stocks, but this was an exception. Jim Czack, my goose farmer friend at Élevage de Volailles, raises a few Embden geese for me every year. The birds take ten months or so to grow to a perfect weight for our Christmas Eve ritual (see "The Holiday Goose Tradition" on page 66), and they always warm hearts on that occasion with their rich and satisfying flavor. One year, Jim brought me the necks, heads, and feet of the geese in a separate parcel. They were so clean and meaty, I set them in a huge pot with mirepoix and aromatics and simmered the stock for about 16 hours. The result made me think that every stock should contain heads, necks, and feet. That same year, at the Beer & Game Dinner, I replicated this stock with squab. I remain convinced that it was the most spectacular flavor a stock has ever achieved.

Whenever whole quadrupeds come our way, their bones get roasted for about an hour at 400°F (200°C), then are painted with tomato puree and roasted for another 15 minutes. We deglaze the pan with mirepoix and red wine; add bay leaves, peppercorns, rosemary, and bay leaves; and then simmer everything in a stockpot, covered with water, for 14 hours. We skim and strain the stock, let it cool, and skim the fat again. To turn it into pure culinary magic, boil the stock over a medium flame for several more hours, or until the volume is reduced by more than half, skimming periodically. The result is demi-glace, the French *grandmère* of all bases for soups and sauces.

Harissa

MAKES 3½ CUPS (795 G)

My gateway drug into the cooking of the souks and bazaars of North Africa's ethnoculinary region known as Maghreb, harissa possesses a spicy, zesty flavor punch that adds a perfect piquant dimension to any pedestrian condiment. And it is also the flavor tie that binds many of the recipes in this book, such as Sautéed Calamari with Harissa, Celery, and Preserved Lemon (page 99), that graced our first couple of Black Trumpet menus.

4 red bell peppers
6 red Fresno (or jalapeño) peppers
2 tablespoons olive oil
Pinch plus 2 teaspoons salt, divided
4 ounces (115 g) ancho chiles, soaked in water for 24 hours
12 cloves garlic
3 tablespoons cumin seed, toasted and ground
¼ cup (20 g) coriander seed, toasted and ground
1 teaspoon caraway seed, toasted and ground

Preheat the oven to 400°F (200°C). Slice the bell peppers in half, removing the stems and seeds. Combine the pepper halves with the jalapeños, drizzle with the olive oil, and sprinkle with a pinch of salt. Place on a cookie sheet and roast on the middle rack of the oven for 10 minutes, then rotate the pan and turn the jalapeños. Roast another 10 minutes. The skin of the jalapeños should be blistered and split and the flesh soft. Remove the jalapeños from the oven and let them cool. Return the bell peppers to the oven and roast an additional 15 minutes, until the flesh is soft and the skin is blackened in spots.

While you're waiting for the peppers to cool slightly, remove the ancho chiles from the water, remove the seeds and stems, and scrape the flesh away from the skin. Discard the skin and reserve the flesh.

When the peppers are cool enough to handle, remove the skin and seeds from the bell peppers and the stems, skin, and seeds from the jalapeños.

Combine the garlic and spices in the bowl of a food processor. Spin until smooth, about 20 seconds. Add the ancho flesh and spin until smooth, another 20 seconds. Add the bell and jalapeño peppers and spin until smooth, about a minute. Add the remaining 2 teaspoons of salt and pulse until combined.

Use immediately or store in the refrigerator for up to 1 week.

Preserved Lemon

MAKES 12 LEMONS

Another North African ingredient, and an indescribably complex additive to any dish that needs a citric lift, preserved lemons are easy to make at home, and they store forever.

12 Meyer lemons
1½ cups (225 g) kosher salt
Water

Cut the lemons in half lengthwise, three-quarters of the way through. Make another cut at a right angle to the first cut, also three-quarters of the way through, so the lemon opens into four quadrants like a flower. Repeat with the remaining lemons.

Pack 2 tablespoons of the kosher salt into the cavity of each lemon and close the lemon quarters as tightly as possible. Force the lemons into a 1-quart (1 L) mason jar.

Cover the lemons with water, cover the jar tightly, and let it sit at room temperature for 3 weeks. Refrigerate indefinitely. The longer the lemons sit, the better they get.

Aioli

MAKES 1½ CUPS (355 ML)

I grew up feeling pretty excited about the idea of my mother (or grandmother) including with dinner (or on its own as a snack, usually on an unbreakable Corelle plate) a sliced fresh red tomato heaped with Cains mayonnaise. Just those two elements together were enough; they were everything I needed. I now realize that store-bought mayonnaise represents the perfect ratio of fat, sugar, and salt, and therefore makes the perfect condiment, dear to all Americans primarily as a sandwich spread. But for me, its perfect foil was a fresh tomato. In retrospect, at least, I think I (and the influences of my matrilineage) revered the tomato in its season. And for those who may wonder about the choice of brand, I actually didn't encounter the superior Hellman's, or the inferior non-mayonnaise competitor Miracle Whip, until I spent the night a few times at friends' houses and learned that Cains mayo, Colgate toothpaste, and Prell shampoo were brand-loyal family choices, and that there was a world of other, better consumer options out there.

Even today, in our house, we always have an emergency jar of mayonnaise—generally Spectrum or other "organic" takes on the big supermarket brands—for a quick-fire sandwich, slaw, or salad. But the truth is, no one in our house (except me) cares much for mayonnaise. I suspect this is because the aforementioned sweet and salty hydrogenated-oil-based goops are manufactured by multinational megacorporations that also dabble in shampoo and underwear. Or maybe it is just that, when mayonnaise is called for, we simply whip up an aioli in our mini food processor. Everyone should have a food processor for this very reason. Yes, aioli can be made with a whisk and a mixing bowl, too, but the processor boasts a higher rate of efficiency and success.

2 egg yolks (36 g)
½ teaspoon salt
3 cloves garlic
1 tablespoon Dijon mustard
Juice of 1 lemon (about 2 tablespoons plus 1 teaspoon)
1 cup (235 ml) olive oil
1 tablespoon very cold water

Combine the yolks, salt, garlic, and Dijon in the bowl of a food processor. Add the lemon juice and pulse to combine. With the motor running, add ½ cup (120 ml) of the olive oil in a slow and steady stream (this should take about 30 seconds). Stop the motor and scrape down the bottom and sides of the bowl with a spatula. Turn the motor back on and add the water in a slow, steady stream. Add the rest of the oil, counting to 30. Remove the aioli to a bowl and adjust the seasoning if necessary. Use immediately or refrigerate for up to 4 days.

Boiled Cider

MAKES 1 CUP (235 ML)

Relatively unheard of in most regions of the country, this unique northeastern syrup tastes like what it is: a sweet and tart concentrate of cider made from heirloom cider apples. If you can source this product from Wood's Cider Mill in Vermont, you should, but if you can't, it's easy to make yourself at home:

Reduce 5 cups (1.2 L) apple cider to 1 cup (235 ml) over low heat, occasionally skimming the foam off the top. Pour through a fine-mesh strainer and reserve the strained liquid.

Plain Pasta Dough

MAKES JUST OVER 1 POUND (455 G)

Having pasta dough in the freezer makes sense to me, although most home cooks consider rolling out fresh pasta an arduous and messy step during the already hectic dinner preparation process. Modern supermarkets' frozen-food sections offer a wide variety of microwavable, not-awful filled pasta dishes ready to go. *Not-awful* may be read as "mediocre," and—most of the time—that's no way to live. So when the family needs a project, make some dough and freeze it. At the restaurant, we often have scraps of cheese, braised meat, or other fun fillers that desperately want a second chance on a dinner plate in the form of filled pasta—agnolotti, tortelli, ravioli, cannelloni, tortellini, and anolini have all graced Black Trumpet menus over the years. Whether you are feeling courageous or just planning a more elaborate dinner party menu, try out this easy dough. Freeze what is left and roll it out whenever the fancy strikes.

3 cups (360 g) "00" flour, found in specialty stores (all-purpose flour can be substituted)
1 teaspoon salt
5 large eggs (250 g liquid egg), cracked into a bowl and lightly beaten with a fork

Combine the flour and salt in a large bowl and make a well in the middle. Add the eggs and stir to combine, slowly bringing flour from the sides into the center of the well to gradually incorporate it into the eggs. Once all the flour is combined with the eggs, turn it out of the bowl onto a lightly floured surface and, using a bench or bowl scraper, cut the mixture so the wet continues to be incorporated into the dry. Once the mixture resembles a craggy ball, begin kneading by pushing the top quadrant of the dough away from you with the palm of your hand. Flip the dough back onto itself, move a quarter turn, and knead again. Repeat, continuing to knead in quarter turns, until the dough is smooth and stretchy and bounces back about three-quarters of its original size when poked with a finger, about 6 to 8 minutes.

Form the dough into a disk, wrap tightly with plastic wrap, and let rest at least an hour in the refrigerator.

Cured Fatback

At Black Trumpet, we keep cured fatback around for a number of reasons. It is a key ingredient in charcuterie items like sausage and pâté, which we make with some frequency, but it also adds great flavor and depth to braised greens and other stews. Colonial times called for salt pork—a similar, albeit drier and denser additive.

So every month when Tom Hasty drops off half a hog from Breezy Hill Farm, we harvest the fatback and pack it in salt, garlic, herbs, and a small amount of sugar. After a few weeks in the refrigerator, we have a cured fat with intense flavor that only improves over time.

If you don't have access to fresh fatback, you can spend money on Italian lardo (which is what our recipe is based on) or you can opt for the less opulent, more intense salt pork still found in most New England supermarkets and butcher shops.

Brown Butter

The nutty flavor of brown butter (*beurre noisette en français*) knows no equivalent or peer. Over the years, when tasked with making clarified butter, almost every prep cook at Black Trumpet has, at least once, neglected the butter, transforming it into a warm, amber, nutty fat that makes winter a more delicious place to be. Surely this is how the French invented brown butter, and so we have also turned folly into golly.

HOT SAUCE 9/29

Hot Sauce

MAKES 1½ QUARTS (1.4 L)

Between my brief tenure in the world of barbecue competition and my time in Mexico, I have developed a lust for chiles that can only be quelled by that feeling of sweat on my scalp, numbness on my lips, and tens of thousands of Scoville units dancing on my tongue. In our garden one year, we had such a diverse array of chiles, I had to dehydrate, pickle, ferment, puree, and freeze more than I would ever use. That year, I learned that, when life gives you heat, you have to make hot sauce. The varieties we have grown over the years include Hinkelhatz, red cherry, Trinidad purple, poblano, Fish, Corno di Toro, Joe's Long Hot Cayenne, and the mild—but always robust—Jimmy Nardello.

When working with hot peppers like the ones in this recipe, do yourself a favor and prep them with gloves on. Even more important, cook them outside or in a well-ventilated kitchen. Failure to do so may create a potent home brew of tear gas, which can really put a damper on a dinner party.

6 dried pasilla chiles, seeds and stems removed
½ cup (12 g) dried chiles de árbol
1 tablespoon dried pequin peppers
2 meco chipotle chiles
½ cup (120 ml) olive oil
1 dried ghost chile
12 fresh red Fresno chiles, rough-chopped
1 Spanish onion, small dice
1 red bell pepper, rough-chopped
2 carrots, peeled, rough-chopped
1 tablespoon minced garlic
1¾ cups (415 ml) malt vinegar (or substitute cider vinegar)
2 cups (475 ml) water
1½ cups (355 ml) tomato puree
¼ cup (60 ml) agave syrup
1 tablespoon coriander seed, toasted and ground
1 teaspoon smoked paprika (sweet)
½ teaspoon salt

In a well-ventilated area, toast the first four chiles in a dry pan over high heat for 2 minutes. Lower the heat to medium and add the olive oil, ghost chile, Fresno chiles, onion, bell pepper, and carrots; cook 2 minutes, stirring. Add the garlic and cook 5 minutes. Add the vinegar and water, bring to a boil, reduce the heat to low, and simmer, covered, 40 minutes. Add the tomato puree, agave syrup, spices, and salt and stir to combine. Simmer, uncovered, for 20 minutes.

Puree everything in a blender while still warm, adding vinegar or water if necessary to achieve the optimal consistency, and more salt if desired. Let the sauce cool and can it in small jars or bottles. If properly canned, this sauce can last for years.

House Mustard

MAKES 2 CUPS (475 ML)

Like so many foods, this mustard improves over time. The sulfurous gases released by the seeds dissipate, as does some of the sharpness, over the course of a few days, so always keep some mustard on hand and make a new batch before the current one gets too low.

Perhaps counterintuitively, using a higher ratio of water to vinegar produces a sharper mustard.

½ cup (115 g) black mustard seed
½ cup (115 g) yellow mustard seed
1 cup (235 ml) water
1 cup plus 3 tablespoons (280 ml)
   Champagne vinegar, divided
3 tablespoons honey
1 tablespoon salt
1 tablespoon sugar
1 teaspoon ground turmeric
1 teaspoon mustard powder

Soak the black and yellow mustard seeds overnight in separate vessels, each with ½ cup (120 ml) of the water and ½ cup (120 ml) of the Champagne vinegar.

Combine the seeds, their liquid, and the remaining ingredients in the bowl of a food processor. Spin for 5 minutes, periodically scraping down the sides of the bowl with a spatula, until smooth. Refrigerate for up to 3 weeks or can forever.

House Pickle

MAKES ENOUGH LIQUID TO PICKLE
8 POUNDS (3.6 KG) VEGETABLES

Here I have to summon the lampoon from the popular *Portlandia* skit titled "We Can Pickle That" by disabusing people of the notion that only certain things can be pickled. Pickling as an acid preservation technique or a fermentation is an ancient craft that should itself be pickled or preserved for future generations. As *Portlandia* and our ancestors would exhort, "Pickle now, and pickle often!"

1 quart (945 ml) red wine vinegar
1 pint (475 ml) water
¼ cup (55 g) sugar
2 tablespoons salt
¼ stick cinnamon
1 teaspoon fennel seed
1 teaspoon mustard seed
1 teaspoon black peppercorns
1 teaspoon coriander seed
½ teaspoon pink peppercorns
6 bay leaves
8 cloves

Combine the ingredients in a 6- to 8-quart (6 to 8 L) pot over medium heat. Stirring occasionally, heat until the sugar and salt dissolve.

Pour the hot liquid over any combination of sliced or chopped vegetables, cover, and refrigerate for at least 1 day. This mixture can be canned, but it will also hold in a refrigerator for a week or more.

Tomato Puree

In the best of summers, there is a glut of tomatoes, and local farmers can't find outlets for the bounty. This is not necessarily the best of times for farmers, because supply far exceeds demand. One year, I remember standing at one farm's store before a wall of totes stacked to the ceiling with "excess" tomatoes, meaning that they were earmarked for compost or pig food.

When this happens, our incredibly collaborative community of chefs comes together, rising to the challenge to can and preserve, freeze and sauce as many lycopersicons as we can get our hands on.

Every chef I know swears by a brand of canned tomatoes (Muir Glen Organic has been my go-to over the years), but lots of chefs prefer the imported Italian San Marzano varieties that are picked and packed in their prime from the most respected Vesuvian volcanic tomato terroir in the world: Campania, Italy. These truly are the best-tasting canned tomatoes, and I don't dispute that, but I am also a fan of the flavor of domestic Muir Glen (out of California), and I tout the tomato puree we make at Black Trumpet as the pinnacle of tomato flavor, because this in-house tomato sauce is made from heirloom paste tomatoes we grow in our own garden. There is nothing like that puree made from slowly simmered varieties—like Amish Paste, Costoluto Genovese, Jersey Giant, Principe Borghese—with little else, in a covered nonreactive pot.

Herbs

As the season dictates, we keep a blend of fresh herbs on our sauté station all year round. Typically, one can find rosemary, oregano, sage, and thyme in the mix. This blend is instrumental in finishing paella and many other dishes.

Red House Pepper Blend

MAKES A LITTLE OVER 1½ CUPS (AROUND 400 ML)

2 tablespoons dried red pepper flakes
¼ cup (40 g) dried Aleppo chile flakes
 (available at stockandspice.com)
¼ cup (36 g) hot smoked Spanish paprika (*pimentón*)
¼ cup (36 g) chipotle powder
¾ cup (108 g) dark chili powder

Whisk the dried, ground peppers together in a bowl and store in any resealable, airtight container.

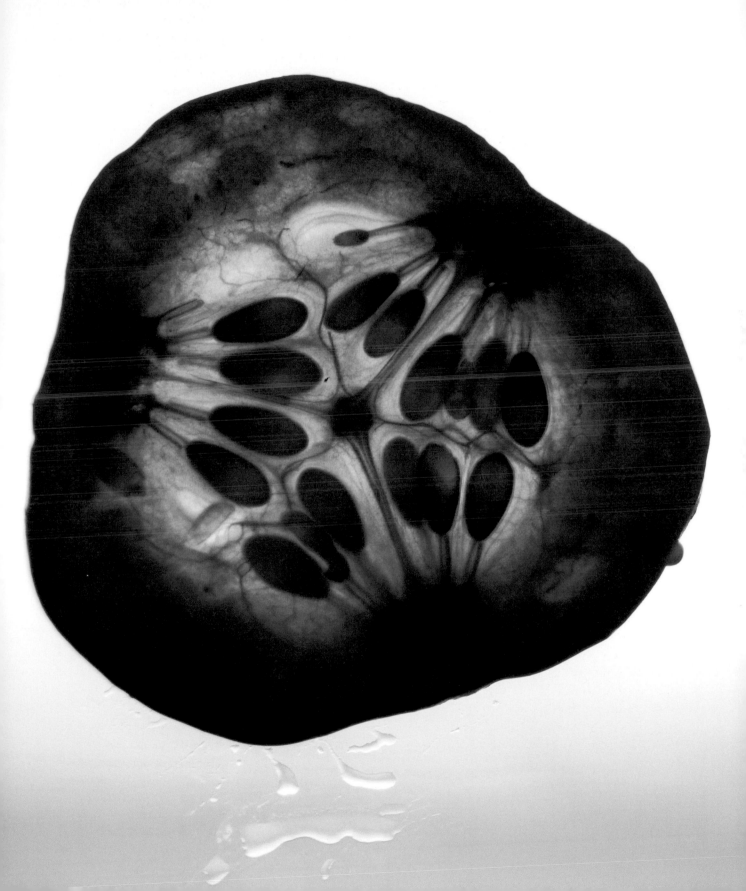

Bread Starter

At the restaurant, we have maintained a few of these alchemic wonders over the years, but none have lasted as long as the one I started at home with the skins of wild elderberries and grapes that my children and I foraged. For almost four years, I attempted to make a sour loaf every Sunday morning. The sour funk of those loaves evolved over those years, but my knack for bread baking didn't. Despite my repeated failures, my kids still wax nostalgic about those halcyon childhood Sundays when they could count on a loaf of sourdough with Daddy's weekly twist.

In his groundbreaking book *The Art of Fermentation*, Sandor Katz—the fermentation guru I share with scores of others—has simplified the recipe for maintaining a "sourdough," added a paragraph or two about the history of bread yeast, and boiled it down to this: Add a little rye flour to all-purpose flour and whisk in almost as much unchlorinated water, making a thin and runny dough. Let this dough sit in a vessel covered with cheesecloth or a clean dish towel overnight. For the next few days, stir the dough every day and look for bubbles. When the dough comes to life, it is time to start feeding it flour and water once a day, essentially making the dough a household pet, until there is enough to spare some for a loaf or boule. Once this process becomes second nature, your new pet will keep on giving back in return for your nurturing efforts.

Vital Tools: Vitamix and Robot Coupe

These two invaluable implements, whose names belong in a science-fiction cage fight, are the Black Trumpet kitchen's two best friends. We have eschewed lots of technological trappings in this, the age of food technology, but we have built menus that depend on the most loyal and indestructible electronic weapons in all of Culinaria: the Vitamix blender and the Robot Coupe food processor. Yes, a mortar and pestle, or a Mexican molcajete cast from cool magma, are far more romantic kitchen tools for making pastes, pestos, aiolis, and sauces, but there can be no disputing the efficiency of these two devices. I can't imagine cooking without them.

CHAPTER ONE

EARLY WINTER

Darkness into Light

EARLY WINTER RECIPES

Americans are rebels by nature. Our (C/c)onstitution shows that we will only take being pushed around for so long. In New England, the birthplace of the resourceful Yankee, weather gods may reign, but we persevere. Our farms suffer from every type of weather imaginable. Our seas—once so fruitful that we came to call our fishing grounds "banks"—give up far fewer fish nowadays, but the hazards of life at sea continue to imperil fishermen, particularly in the cold winter months. The ruddy-faced fishermen (and shovelers and snowblowers) that follow every winter storm prove that we New Englanders are, above all, survivors. We are hardy as parsnips, our wills stronger than the roots of the sugar maple, even in the "dead" of winter.

Whether it comes in like a lamb or a lion, early winter can be a season of pleasant surprises, from the sweet heirloom spinaches to the root cellar bounty and high tunnel greens, from holiday turkey and goose to wild game birds and venison, and from the sweet, meaty pearls we call bay scallops to the running of the smelts. Yes, the first half of winter still delivers plenty of inspiration for the seasonal chef.

While winter is by no means as rich in fresh flavors as the other three seasons, I am always thrilled to find our talented farmers' adaptations that introduce new ingredients previously unthought of. Hardier varieties of "winter spinach" stand out in this department.

The first year Josh Jennings and Jean Pauly grew winter spinach at Meadow's Mirth Farm, I made a quantum chef leap from darkness into light. My proverbial Popeye forearm had a whole new November muscle to flex in the form of Bloomsdale Longstanding spinach. This variety, which has been seed-saved in a single region of Delaware since the mid-1800s, has a balance of sweetness, textural crunch, and versatility that most spinaches lack. The signature squeaky astringency is still there, but subdued, and the flavor is so surprisingly sweet and nutty that most people ask if something was done to it when they taste it for the first time.

"Nope," I tell them. "That's just how sweet it is."

But spinach is just one example of the fresh winter bonuses farmers bring to Black Trumpet. It takes weeks, sometimes months, to cure a sweet potato to the point where its starches have converted to the sugars that give the tuber its dulcet name. In fact, most roots, by virtue of their design, spend the postfrost season building Brix (the measure of stored sugars and other solids) until they are bursting with sweet flavor.

When confronted by the inevitable seasonal decline in fresh produce, the chef's mind turns to slow-cooking techniques, richer sauces, and deeper, darker flavor combinations.

Each New England winter is different and brings its own set of vagaries and demands. The "living of winter," as opposed to the "dead of winter," describes the month and a half that surrounds the holiday season. For me, regardless of what station in life I am occupying, this season always represents joy, nostalgia, family, and love. Because my family tree looks more like a telephone pole, due to successive generations of only children, it is mainly through my adoptive in-law family that I fully appreciate the value of large holiday congregations. I can remember many childhood holiday dinners spent with one or two parents in restaurants that tried to emulate the family holiday experience. So depressing. My in-law clan, on the other hand, applies the "more the merrier" rule of holiday dining, and I can attest that this latter model makes for a superior family holiday experience.

Warm Spinach Salad with Clementines, Goat Cheese, and Pickled Shallots

SERVES 4

This was an extremely popular warm winter salad; so much so that I think we lost a few regular customers when I took it off the menu. This is a risk we run by changing the menu frequently. The good news, though, is that this is an easy salad to make at home.

Note that this salad can be made meatilicious with the addition of warm Bacon Lardons (page 281) or Duck Confit (page 111) on top, or made vegan by substituting crumbled walnuts for the chèvre.

½ cup (120 ml) red wine vinegar
2 tablespoons water
1 tablespoon sugar
1 teaspoon salt
2 large shallots, halved and sliced very thin
8 ounces (225 g) Bloomsdale Long-standing spinach (or substitute baby spinach), large stems removed
2 clementines, segmented and cleaned of pith
¼ cup (60 ml) Pomegranate Dressing (recipe follows)
4 ounces (115 g) crumbly chèvre (or goat feta)

Bring the vinegar, water, sugar, and salt to a boil, stir, and pour over the shallots in a heat-safe container. This pickle can be prepared well in advance if so desired.

When you're ready to serve the salad, form a big pile of spinach on each plate (the size will shrink when the hot dressing is poured on it). Arrange the clementine segments and pickled shallots around the spinach.

Heat the Pomegranate Dressing in a pan until it is bubbling hot. Pour over the salads, sprinkle goat cheese over the top, and serve right away.

Pomegranate Dressing

MAKES ALMOST A CUP (220 ML)

1 pomegranate, seeded
¼ cup (55 g) sugar
½ cup (120 ml) red wine vinegar
Juice of 1 orange
1 tablespoon pomegranate molasses (found in most Middle Eastern markets or online at stockandspice.com)
1 large shallot, minced
½ teaspoon salt
Pinch black pepper

Combine the pomegranate seeds, sugar, vinegar, orange juice, and molasses in a small heavy-bottomed pot over medium-high heat. Boil until the sugar dissolves and the mixture reduces slightly, about 20 minutes. Let it cool slightly and puree in a blender. Strain the mixture back into the same pot, add the shallot, and simmer 15 minutes longer, until the mixture thickens and easily coats the back of a spoon. Stir in the salt and pepper and adjust to taste.

If you're not using this right away, store for up to a week in the fridge.

Pork and Pistachio Country Pâté

SERVES 24

When I was eleven, my father brought me on an extended business sojourn that took us to Ireland, France, and Switzerland. It lasted about a month, and one of the highlights of the trip was, perhaps oddly, our return flight. Some poor schlep at Swissair had bungled our reservation, so my father groused loudly enough to warrant a free upgrade to first class. May I suggest that, if you ever travel first class, you do so with Swissair. On that flight, I tasted many firsts: Champagne, triple-cream cheese, and—most memorably—pâté. I fondly remember the feeling of being treated as royalty, complete with a tour of the cockpit and a giveaway packet of puzzles and games, but the taste of that pâté changed my food world for good.

I owe much of what I know about pâté to Jeff Tenner, who first taught me the basic foundation for making a *pâté de campagne*, country-style pâté. As the precocious and talented chef of Lindbergh's Crossing, Jeff brought the comforting flavors of country French cuisine to the New Hampshire Seacoast in 1996, when he was in his very early twenties. At Black Trumpet, threads of this cuisine and Jeff's influence remain in the storied kitchen, in both the recipes and the equipment (I still use a very old steel terrine mold he left behind when I have to make multiple pâtés). Although I have adapted Jeff's original recipe in a lot of different ways over the years, the backbone remains intact.

This recipe can be scaled down for the home cook, but why bother? Even a rustic pâté like this is a ceremonial food, to be enjoyed with friends, wine, cheese, pickles, mustard, and something sweet, and it lasts in the refrigerator for up to a week. Of course, any Frenchman would argue that pâté is everyday food to be smooshed into a torn chunk of crunchy baguette, but I would reply that, in France, every meal is ceremonial. As it should be!

6 ounces (170 g) pork, duck, rabbit,
   or chicken liver
1½ cups (355 ml) whole milk
2 dried Brown Turkey
   (or Calimyrna) figs
¼ cup (60 ml) brandy
1 Spanish onion, peeled and julienned
1 shallot, peeled and julienned
2 cloves garlic, minced
1 cup (80 g) mushrooms,
   rough-chopped
4 duck gizzards (if available)

The order of things is important in pâté-making procedure, as it is in most culinary feats. The *farce*, which is the French word for the raw meat paste that is baked into a pâté or sausage, should be cold when it goes into the oven.

MAKE THE FARCE: Soak the livers in the milk, preferably overnight, but for at least 4 hours.

Remove any stems from the figs, quarter them, set them in a small container, and cover them with brandy for at least an hour.

In a large sauté pan with a bit of oil, sweat the onion and shallot over low heat for 5 minutes. Add the garlic, mushrooms, and

1 tablespoon plus 1 teaspoon
  kosher salt
½ teaspoon pink salt
1 teaspoon mustard powder
Pinch mace
½ teaspoon fennel seed
1 teaspoon dried marjoram
1 teaspoon chopped fresh rosemary
1 teaspoon chopped fresh
  thyme leaves
1½ pounds (680 g) ground pork
¼ cup (30 g) pistachio meats
2 eggs (100 g liquid egg)

gizzards, and sweat for 2 more minutes. Drain the livers and discard the milk. Add the livers to the pan, increase the heat to a medium flame, and stir. In a minute, add half the salts, along with the spices, herbs, figs, and the brandy the figs are soaking in. If you're cooking over an open flame, this may cause a flare. Be sure your stovetop has sufficient ventilation, or your eyebrows may be compromised. Once the brandy has flamed out of the pan, turn off the heat and let the pan cool to room temperature.

Add half the ground pork and all the pistachios to a large mixing bowl. Cover and keep refrigerated.

Meanwhile, in a food processor, pulse the contents of the pan until well chopped. Add the other half of the ground pork to the processor and process into a relatively smooth paste. Add one egg to the paste while the processor is running, and, once it is incorporated, add the other.

BAKE THE PÂTÉ: Preheat the oven to 350°F (175°C).

Transfer the meat *farce* from the processor to the chilled mixing bowl with the pork and nuts. Sprinkle on the remaining salts and work the paste with a rubber spatula or clean hands until the ground meat is incorporated. Refrigerate for at least an hour, transfer the *farce* to a pâté terrine mold (Le Creuset is my brand of choice) sprayed with oil, place the terrine mold in a roasting pan, and pour enough cold water into the pan to come halfway up the sides of the terrine. Cover the terrine with a lid and place in the middle of the oven for 60 to 70 minutes. When the internal temperature (ideally measured using a digital thermometer with a meat probe) reaches 125°F (52°C), remove the pan to the stovetop, leaving the terrine mold in the hot water. Allow the pâté to cool for an hour in the water bath. Wrap a brick or other weight in plastic and press onto the top of the pâté, tilting to allow any fat and liquid out of the mold. Carefully place the terrine on a sheet pan in the refrigerator, with the wrapped brick on top of it, for at least 4 hours and preferably overnight.

CB and FJ Finger Sandwiches

MAKES 12 LITTLE SANDWICHES

One of our first menus featured this cute little dish—a spin on PB&J, but using the soul-warming, seasonal flavors of chestnuts and figs. I highly recommend serving these sandwiches with a small snifter of warm brandied rosemary milk.

For the Chestnut Butter

1 pound (455 g) whole chestnuts

½ teaspoon plus pinch salt

1 tablespoon honey (use Italian chestnut honey if you are lucky enough to find some)

⅛ teaspoon rose water

½ cup (120 ml) olive oil

For the Fig Jam

4 ounces (115 g) dried figs, stems removed, figs cut in half

12 ounces (340 g) (approximately 12 each) fresh Black Mission or Brown Turkey figs, stemmed and quartered

½ cup (115 g) sugar

½ cup (120 ml) red wine

1 small stick cinnamon

2 tablespoons maple syrup

Zest and juice of 1 orange

PREPARE THE CHESTNUTS: Preheat the oven to 400°F (200°C).

Stab each chestnut with a fork to create an outlet for air so they don't explode all over your oven. Place the chestnuts on a baking sheet and roast on the top rack of the oven for 20 minutes. Remove from the oven and let cool to room temperature. Peel, removing all of the hard outer shell. The flesh should be tan colored. If it's black or mottled with discoloration, discard.

MAKE THE CHESTNUT BUTTER: Combine the roasted and peeled chestnuts in the bowl of a food processor with the salt, honey, and rose water. With the motor running, add the olive oil in a slow trickle, stopping often to scrape down the bottom and sides of the bowl so the other ingredients incorporate evenly with the chestnuts.

MAKE THE FIG JAM: Put all ingredients in a medium saucepan. Stir and cover the pot, simmering over a low flame until the ingredients are soft and mushy, about 15 minutes. Remove the lid and continue to cook over a low flame for an additional 10 minutes.

Remove the cinnamon stick and puree the jam in a food processor, scraping down the sides several times and spinning until the jam is one smooth consistency.

BUILD THE SANDWICHES: I think it's safe to say everyone has built a peanut butter and jelly sandwich at some point, so assembling this should be a piece of cake. Rustic white or wheat bread makes the best bookends for the CB and FJ. Remove the crusts and cut rectangles from each slice if so desired.

Maine Mussels Steamed in Porter with Leeks and Chorizo

SERVES 4

Maine mussels are the best in the world, in my opinion. Having never eaten the New Zealand green-lipped variety at the source, I recognize that my opinion may be naive. But I have eaten blue mussels in at least four European countries, and I maintain that the briny, almost oyster-like flavor of wild Maine mussels has no peer. Even rope-grown varieties, with their slick and streamlined shells, thrive in the Gulf of Maine's aqueous admixture, meaning anyone looking for a great mussel-eating experience need look no further.

One of Black Trumpet's most popular dishes, Moules & Frites, was also one of the simplest dishes to create. It's a no-brainer: french fries heaped on mussels cooked with shallots and white wine and drizzled with aioli. The recipe, technique, and presentation we used for that dish were direct thefts from my friend Gary at Central Kitchen. They are so good, I firmly believe they can't be improved on. But if you want the recipe, you won't find it here. You'll have to wait for Gary to write the Central Kitchen book.

Instead, I offer you mussels steeped in this wintry beer lover's broth. Dark, brooding, and rich, this may be the perfect bistro dish to share while plotting a Good Food Revolution.

8 ounces (225 g) chorizo, diced
2 tablespoons clarified butter/olive oil blend (page 13)
2 leeks, quartered, sliced ¼ inch (0.5 cm) thick, and soaked in cold water
1 clove garlic, minced
1 ounce (30 ml) porter
¼ cup (60 ml) tomato puree
1 pound (455 g) mussels
1 tablespoon unsalted butter
2 tablespoons chopped herbs (any combination of oregano, rosemary, thyme, and Italian parsley will work here)
½ teaspoon smoked paprika

In a large high-sided sauté pan, render the chorizo in the clarified butter over low heat. Cook, stirring occasionally, until the fat is rendered out and the chorizo begins to get crispy. Add the leeks and cook over low heat, 4 minutes, until they begin to soften. Add the garlic and cook 2 minutes. Add the porter and tomato puree and stir to combine. Add the mussels, cover, and steam over high heat for about 5 minutes, or until all the shells have opened. Strain all the liquid into another 1- to 2-quart (1 to 2 L) pan and add the butter, herbs, and smoked paprika.

Arrange the mussels in a large serving bowl and pour the liquid over the top. Serve with bread—ideally pumpernickel (recipe on page 38) or, if you feel extra ambitious, Pumpernickel Pudding (page 39).

The Beer & Game Dinner

I never could have predicted that, of all the events we have put on over the years, the most coveted ticket would be a seat to the Beer & Game Dinner. Over the course of a year, our sales of wine and seasonal specialty cocktails completely dwarf our beer sales. And as with everything we do at Black Trumpet, there was never much promotion for the Beer & Game Dinner—no snazzy ad copy in the early years, no e-vites or social media boosts in the later years. Just good old-fashioned word of mouth from one year to the next about what a fun adventure the dinner is.

This extraordinarily popular night of the year marks the only exception to the sacred food-sourcing philosophy upon which Black Trumpet was founded. We have sourced and served at this amazing event: insects, blood, tongues and feet, heads and tails, deadly creatures, invasive species, and animals ranging from alpaca to yak. The disconnect between building a sustainable local food system and sourcing, say, the hand-harvested, defecated coffee beans from a tree-dwelling Indonesian rodent has not escaped me. I am well aware that the dichotomy sends a conflicting, confusing message. But I also feel compelled to make each Beer & Game Dinner weirder than the one before, because the intrepid guests demand that we push the envelope. And at least I can say that the oddball, creative beers we serve at the dinner are local!

So if you want to sample the likes of python, llama, reindeer, geoduck, blood clams, duck tongues, or camel milk, get ready to book online on the day we announce that tickets are on sale. Oh, did I forget the fermented shark? That was an unforgettable gustatory marvel.

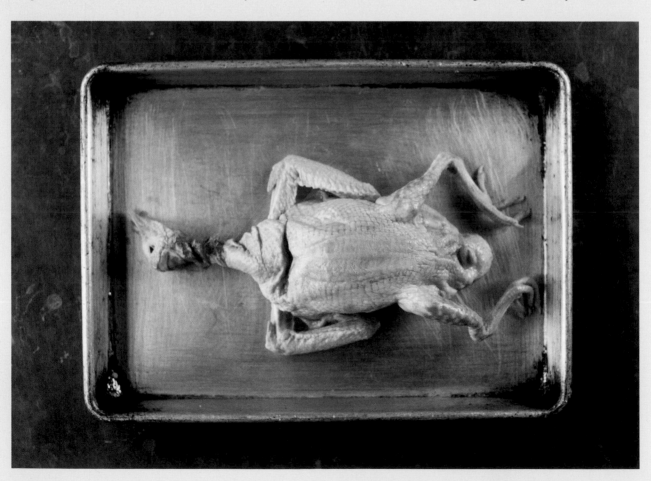

Pumpernickel Bread

MAKES 4 LOAVES

This recipe divides nicely, though you might be surprised at how quickly a household moves through this bread, even after a day or two. It makes great toast! But also consider making a full batch and turning half of it into the rich and savory pudding that follows.

For the sponge

2 teaspoons active dry yeast

2 cups (475 ml) warm water

2 cups (210 g) dark rye flour

½ cup (60 g) all-purpose flour

¼ cup (35 g) caraway seed

2 tablespoons packed brown sugar

2 tablespoons cocoa powder

For the bread

6 cups (725 g) all-purpose flour

1 cup plus 1 teaspoon (240 ml) warm
   water, divided

½ cup (120 ml) molasses

¼ cup (55 g) packed brown sugar

2 tablespoons salt

1 egg white (30 g)

MAKE THE SPONGE: Combine the yeast and water and let bloom 5 minutes. Add the remaining sponge ingredients and mix to combine. Cover tightly and let sit 1 hour.

MAKE THE BREAD: Stir down the sponge and top with the flour, 1 cup (235 ml) of the warm water, the molasses, brown sugar, and salt. Mix well with your hands and knead until the dough is combined, about 2 minutes. (This dough is pretty sticky, so I recommend using gloves.) Rub a large, clean bowl with oil or spray with pan spray. Add the dough, cover tightly, and let rise until doubled in size, about 1 hour.

Turn the dough out onto a clean work surface and divide into four equal pieces. Roll into loaves and place into sprayed or oiled loaf pans, spraying the tops of the loaves or rubbing them lightly with oil so they don't dry out. Let rise until doubled in size, about 1 hour.

Preheat the oven to 375°F (190°C).

Fork-whisk the egg white with the remaining teaspoon of water in a small bowl. Brush the tops of the loaves with the egg wash and bake, rotating every 10 minutes for 20 minutes, then every 5 minutes for about 35 minutes total, or until the bread is dark brown and firm to the touch. Let cool to room temperature in the loaf pans, remove, and serve or let cool and wrap tightly until ready to serve.

Pumpernickel Pudding

MAKES ONE 13 × 9 INCH (33 × 23 CM) PAN

1 large Spanish onion, julienned
2 tablespoons olive oil
1½ teaspoons salt, divided
2 loaves pumpernickel bread
    (preceding recipe), diced into ¾-inch
    (2 cm) cubes
1 quart (945 ml) heavy cream
10 eggs (500 g liquid egg),
    beaten lightly
2 tablespoons herb mix (page 22)
¼ teaspoon black pepper

Preheat the oven to 350°F (190°C).

Combine the onion with the olive oil and ½ teaspoon of the salt in a medium frying pan over low heat. Caramelize slowly, stirring occasionally, until the onion is soft and evenly browned, about 40 minutes. In a large bowl, soak the bread in the cream for 15 minutes, tossing gently to combine. Add the eggs, the herbs, the remaining teaspoon of the salt, the black pepper, and the caramelized onions, and toss gently to combine. Pour the mixture into a sprayed 13 × 9 inch (33 × 23 cm) pan and bake on the middle shelf, covered, for 1 hour. Uncover and bake an additional 10 minutes, or until the middle is set and the edges are golden brown and beginning to pull away from the sides of the pan. Let cool to room temperature, reheat as needed, slice, and serve with or without Maine Mussels Steamed in Porter with Leeks and Chorizo (page 35).

Spinach Freekeh

SERVES 6

We served this unusual unripe green wheat, more common in the cuisines of Eastern Europe and Asia Minor (although I first discovered it in New Orleans), with Nantucket bay scallops, a luxury that must be enjoyed in moderation and with utmost reverence. Freekeh, also marketed as greenwheat freekeh, may be found in some health food stores or online at inharvest.com.

¼ cup (60 ml) olive oil
½ Spanish onion, minced
1½ cups (225 g) freekeh
2 tablespoons white wine
2 cups (475 ml) vegetable stock
Parmesan rind (optional)
1 packed pint (3 ounces [85 g])
    winter spinach
½ cup (50 g) grated Parmesan cheese
1 tablespoon butter
1 teaspoon salt
½ teaspoon black pepper

Combine the oil, onion, and freekeh in a large pan over medium heat, stirring for 2 minutes to toast the grains. Deglaze with the wine. Add the stock, increase the heat to high, and bring to a boil. Reduce to a simmer (add the Parmesan rind here if you have one) and cook 10 minutes. Remove the rind and increase the heat to medium. There should be a little liquid left in the pan at this point. Add the spinach, folding with a spatula so it begins to wilt, about 40 seconds. Remove the pan from the heat and stir in the Parmesan, butter, salt, and pepper with a wooden spoon. Serve immediately or spread out onto a baking sheet to cool, then refrigerate until you're ready to serve.

Marfax Beans

SERVES 8

Marfax beans are historically significant, commercially near extinction, and considered by many Maine home cooks to be the perfect baked-bean choice. They are dense and flavorful, are more or less indestructible, and can withstand 24-hour cooking times if necessary. This recipe does not call for that kind of patience, but some classic Maine baked-bean recipes do.

½ pound (225 g) dried Marfax beans (substitute Jacob's Cattle or other dry Maine baking bean)

1 tablespoon olive oil

2 ounces (55 g) slab bacon, medium dice

2 ounces (55 g) cured fatback, medium dice

1 red onion, julienned

½ cup (120 g) tomato paste

½ cup (120 g) molasses

¼ cup (60 ml) balsamic vinegar

¾ teaspoon cayenne pepper

1½ teaspoons smoked paprika

1½ teaspoons dark chili powder (or substitute ancho chile powder)

1 cup (235 ml) beef or chicken stock

2 cups (475 ml) reserved bean liquid

2 teaspoons salt

PREPARE THE BEANS: Soak the beans in water overnight, using about two times the volume of water as the volume of beans. The next day, strain the beans, rinse, and pour into a large stockpot. Cover the beans with 2 quarts (1.9 L) water and bring to a boil over high heat, uncovered. Boil for 10 to 15 minutes, depending on the freshness of your beans, until al dente. Turn off the pot and let the beans cool in the cooking water.

COMPLETE THE RECIPE: Meanwhile, place a large pot on the stove over medium heat. Add the olive oil, bacon, and fatback. Render the meat until it is reduced to half its size, stirring occasionally, about 5 minutes. Add the onion and sweat over medium heat, stirring occasionally, about 3 minutes. Add the tomato paste and stir to combine. Cook until the mixture is sticky, 3 to 4 minutes. Strain the beans from their cooking water, reserving 2 cups (475 ml) liquid. Add the molasses, vinegar, spices, stock, beans, and reserved cooking water, and stir to combine. Bring the mixture to a boil over high heat, then reduce the heat to low and simmer. Cook for 2½ hours, until the beans are tender. Taste for seasoning, adding salt if necessary.

TO SERVE: Serve right away or keep on hand for a few days. Heat them up when the midwinter blues take hold, and enjoy with a nice rich, strong ale or stout and a hunk of pumpernickel.

Scallops with Couscous and Cider Cream Sauce

SERVES 4 FOR DINNER OR 8 AS AN APPETIZER

Our love affair with Cider Cream Sauce found many outlets on the menu. This one may have been the most popular. This recipe calls for sea scallops, because they are easier to come by, but feel free to up the scallop count and use bay scallops in season, if you are lucky enough to get your hands on them.

For the Cider Cream Sauce
1 tablespoon butter
1 medium red onion, in ½-inch (1 cm) dice
1 clove garlic, minced
1 tablespoon olive oil
¼ teaspoon salt
2 tablespoons white verjus (see the glossary, page 368) or cider vinegar
¾ cup (180 ml) boiled cider (available online, or page 17)
½ cup (120 ml) heavy cream

For the couscous
2 cups (475 ml) water
¾ teaspoon kosher salt
1 teaspoon olive oil
1 cup (225 g) Israeli couscous (the large, pearl-like type)

For the scallops
16 sea scallops (about 1 pound [455 g]), rinsed, "foot" removed, and patted dry
1 teaspoon salt
1 teaspoon ground grains of paradise or freshly ground black pepper
2 teaspoons olive oil

MAKE THE CIDER CREAM SAUCE: Place a 3-quart (3 L) saucepan over medium heat. Add the butter and let it melt, foam, and begin to brown, about 3 minutes. Add the onion and cook 2 minutes, stirring. Add the garlic, olive oil, and salt and stir. Cook for about 5 minutes, until the mixture becomes slightly sticky. Add the verjus or cider vinegar and deglaze the pan by removing the browned bits from the bottom with a wooden spoon.

Add the boiled cider to the pan and bring the mixture back up to a boil over medium heat, stirring occasionally, about 2 minutes. Add the heavy cream and return to a boil. Reduce the heat to low and simmer 5 minutes, reducing slowly. Remove from the heat and cool while you make the couscous.

When the couscous is done, put the cooled sauce in the carafe of a blender and blend on the highest setting, until completely smooth (about 30 seconds). Strain and season to taste with additional salt.

MAKE THE COUSCOUS: In a 1- to 2-quart (1 to 2 L) saucepan, add the water, salt, and olive oil and bring to a boil over medium-high heat. Add the couscous and bring back to a boil, uncovered. Cook until al dente, 7 to 8 minutes. Strain the water and put the couscous back in the pot, fluffing immediately with a spoon. Fluff again 5 to 10 minutes later.

MAKE THE SCALLOPS: Season the scallops on one side with salt and several grinds of, ideally, grains of paradise or black pepper.

Heat a seasoned 8-inch (20 cm) cast-iron skillet over high heat until it begins to smoke. Add the olive oil and the scallops. Sear without disturbing them until the scallops are the consistent color of a brown paper bag, about 3 minutes. Flip the scallops and remove the pan from the heat. Let them sit in the pan an additional 3 minutes.

Pour 1 cup (235 ml) of the Cider Cream Sauce over the bottom of a medium-sized serving platter. Mound the couscous over the sauce and place the scallops on top. Serve with sautéed cauliflower, bok choy, kohlrabi, or brussels sprouts.

Sour Cream Mashed Sweet Potatoes

SERVES 8

This basic side dish has accompanied scallops and pork on a few Black Trumpet menus. Although rich and filling, it will lend bright flavor to just about any winter supper.

10 small sweet potatoes, skins scrubbed clean
3 tablespoons olive oil
1 tablespoon plus 1 teaspoon kosher salt, divided
1 cup (235 ml) sour cream
½ cup (120 ml) brown butter (page 18)
¼ cup (55 g) brown sugar
½ cup (120 ml) heavy cream

Preheat the oven to 350°F (175°C). In a large mixing bowl, combine the sweet potatoes with the olive oil and 1 tablespoon of the salt. Toss to coat the potatoes evenly. Spread out on a baking sheet and roast on the upper shelf of the oven for about 40 minutes, or until soft.

Combine the sour cream, brown butter, brown sugar, and heavy cream in the same mixing bowl and stir to combine. When the sweet potatoes are cool enough to handle, break them up, skins included, into a food processor. Add the sour cream mixture and whiz until the mixture is smooth and all the ingredients are fully incorporated. Add remaining salt if needed.

Serve immediately or cool to room temperature and refrigerate. Reheat slowly over a low flame with a touch of vegetable stock.

Chowdered Potatoes

SERVES 6

These creamy potatoes, paired on our menu with Braised Pork Belly and Clams (recipe follows), are easy-to-make comfort food at its best.

2 tablespoons clarified butter/olive oil blend (page 13)
3 Red Bliss potatoes, skin on, large dice
3 blue potatoes, skin on, large dice
¾ teaspoon salt
¼ teaspoon black pepper
1 leek, quartered and chopped ¼ inch (0.5 cm) thick
1 cup (235 ml) heavy cream
3 bay leaves
1 tablespoon Black Trumpet herb mix

In a 12-inch (30 cm) high-sided pan over medium heat, add the butter/oil blend, potatoes, salt, and pepper; cook, stirring occasionally, until the potatoes begin to brown slightly, about 6 minutes. Add the leek and cook, stirring, until it softens and begins to turn translucent, about 5 minutes. Reduce the heat to low, add the cream and bay leaves, and simmer, uncovered, until the mixture thickens and the potatoes are fork-tender, about 10 minutes. Remove from the heat and let cool in the pan. Divide among six plates and serve with Braised Pork Belly and Clams, garnishing with freshly chopped herbs.

Braised Pork Belly and Clams

SERVES 8

This pork belly recipe, although intended to be served with clams, also tastes pretty darn good with Chowdered Potatoes (preceding recipe). You can even serve them all together for a "deconstructed" clam chowder.

For the braise

1½ pounds (680 g) pork belly, skin on, cut into 3-ounce (85 g) portions (about 1 × 3 inches [2.5 × 7.5 cm] each)

1 tablespoon salt

1 teaspoon ground black pepper

2 carrots, peeled, medium dice

3 stalks celery, medium dice

1 small white onion, medium dice

1 Thai bird chile, seeded and chopped

1 head garlic, peeled

1 cup (235 ml) tomato puree

2 pints (945 ml) good brown ale (half for belly and half for clams)

1 quart (945 ml) pork stock (or other meat stock)

½ stick cinnamon

2 whole star anise

2 Balinese long peppers

2 bay leaves

2 tablespoons maple syrup

For the finished dish

24 littleneck clams (Manila or mahogany clams may be substituted), scrubbed with a sponge to remove all grit from the outside of the shells

1 clove garlic, minced

BRAISE THE BELLY: Season the belly pieces generously with salt and pepper. In a heavy-bottomed or cast-iron pan over medium heat, render the belly pieces until well browned on all sides, about 15 minutes. Dump out most of the fat and add the vegetables, including the chile and head of garlic, to the pan. Sweat the vegetables for 2 minutes, then add the tomato puree. Simmer over low heat, stirring occasionally, for about 5 minutes, or until the tomato puree has formed a dark paste. Deglaze the pan, leaving everything in it, with 1 pint of the beer. Bring back to medium heat and cook the beer down for about 8 minutes. Add the pork stock and the next seven ingredients; bring to a boil. Transfer everything to a casserole dish or braising pan and place, covered, in a 275°F (135°C) oven for 2½ hours. Remove from the oven and let the belly cool to room temperature in the braising liquid. If you're preparing the dish in advance, store the belly and the strained braising liquid separately in the refrigerator. When congealed, remove the layer of fat that forms on the top of the braising liquid.

TO SERVE: When you're ready to serve, crisp up the belly pieces in a skillet, adding a little oil if necessary. When the belly is crispy, remove it to a towel and add the clams and garlic clove to the pan. When the garlic starts to smell aromatic and toasty, add the remaining pint of beer. Cover the pan and turn the heat to high. In 5 minutes or so, the clams will open. When they do, remove the lid and add the braising liquid to the pan. Arrange the belly pieces and clams in the pan and present to the table on a trivet for self-serve, or—as we do at the restaurant—plate in individual bowls with the belly in the middle and three clams per person around the belly, with a broken fried egg on top, and perhaps a few blistered cherry tomatoes as a garnish.

Telling Goat Stories

I have often referred to goat as "the other red meat." In most other countries, goats can be found grazing on some pretty diverse forage, from montane desert scrub to tropical island rain forest understory. These are places the cumbersome cow and obese domestic hog dare not tread, so human survival in rough terrain and adverse climate has to some extent required the adaptable goat, whose milk, hide, and meat provide a nomadic tribe or remote village with needed protein and dairy.

In America—where we tend to cultivate the landscape to accommodate livestock farming, rather than herding animals on existing natural forage—goat has yet to enter the mainstream carnivorous diet, ranking well below beef, pork, and sheep. Yet recent statistics show that "the goat meat industry is the fastest-growing segment of the livestock industry." This very encouraging news for the globetrotting goat comes from the International Kiko Goat Association's website, the same place I came across the assertion that "goat meat is the most widely consumed meat in the world." Indeed, pound for pound, the scrumptiously fatty global yield of pork outweighs the world's goat meat payload, but goat is more widely distributed and found in abundance in more countries than the less adaptable hog.

My first two run-ins with goats did not go well. The first was at a petting zoo in Florida. I was, I would say, about four years old. The sole memory I have retained from that period of my childhood was of me eating an ice cream cone and wearing a gaudy pair of 1970s polyester slacks, walking away from a goat ram I had been cautiously petting, far enough away from my parent that I felt self-conscious and maybe a little on edge. Before my young neuroreceptors could respond to an abrupt blow to my behind, I found myself flipped up in the air, ice cream cone in a separate orbit, eventually landing, keister first, on pavement, to the amusement of dozens of children and parent bystanders. The lesson? I'm not sure. But I know that goats scared me for a long while after that.

The second goat story involves castration, a medical procedure not often delegated to twelve-year-old boys.

But sure enough, when my childhood best friend's dad, who owned a gentleman's farm down the road from my house, asked me if I wanted to castrate one of his goats, I mustered the courage to oblige. The man was a respected vascular surgeon, and his son was very good at applying peer pressure. In fact, he would later persuade me to canoe with him out to an island in a bay on the Massachusetts South Shore . . . in February! We capsized and were rescued from drowning and freezing by an old man in a rowboat. But that's another tale for another tome. . . .

Back to the goats. I remember the instructions clearly, delivered with a lilting bedside monotone that only a surgeon can muster, to take a rubber band and carefully (I love that modifier!) wrap it around the base of the goat's scrotum as many times as the goat would allow, ensuring that it was very tight. "Oh, and watch out for kicking," the doctor said, as an afterthought. Of course, that afterthought summoned the childhood butting memory, which made for a very nervous castrator. My friend, the doc's son, had provided this service before, so was quick to delegate the "banding" process to me. Days later, he explained, he would have to go out and flick the scrota from the goats I was banding until they fell off, which was a far worse job than the actual banding. I believed him. If I had known that there were such things as vegetarians, I think I would have gone that route then and there, at around the same age my son later did.

I banded those rams, just as instructed. In the end, I guess it wasn't as bad as I had feared. Maybe a seed in my brain was planted that day that would enable me to perform the processing and butchery tasks I now use as a chef.

A few years into Black Trumpet, after sourcing goat very sporadically from a nearby farm with mixed results (attributable to differences in season, climate, breed, and diet), I learned about Shirley Richardson. Shirley is one of those outside-the-box thinkers who can change the course of an entire food system. We may never know that something as fundamental as the way we eat has been steered in a different direction until enough time has passed to give the pivotal moment historical perspective. Shirley Richardson witnessed a break in the American food supply chain that could actually be fixed, and she did something about it.

When goats are raised for dairy production (primarily cheesemaking), they must be either an alpha Romeo or a fertile lactofactor. In other words, it takes one goat stud and a lot of milking does to keep a vibrant and productive dairy herd. Given the odds associated with breeding pretty much anything, the ratio of male to female offspring is guaranteed to be pretty much even. So, Shirley wanted to know, where were all the male goats going from the generational broods at the goat dairies of New England? The unspeakably shocking answer she uncovered: They were going to their graves.

In a mammalian twist on parthenogenetic theory, the male goats in New England were without value. It was costly and pointless to raise and feed them, because they would never produce milk. And they can get into trouble with the rest of the herd if they go around trying to breed billy-nilly. At the time, only a fraction of a fraction of Americans consumed goat meat, but what they did consume was all coming from overseas. Seeing domestic dairy farmers with no place to pass the buck, as it were, and numbers that showed an uptick in domestic consumption of imported goat meat, Shirley took a huge risk and started a goat meat business. Vermont Chevon goats soon became the top choice of chefs in the Northeast and beyond.

Goat meat sales continue to rise as Americans learn that their preconceived notions about the flavor of goat meat have been flawed from the get-go. Side by side with lamb, goat often possesses a cleaner, more neutral flavor that lends itself to cooking a number of ways. I love the other red meat, and I am ecstatic to see that American consumers are finally catching on.

Gruit-Braised Goat

SERVES 12

After all that talk about goat being the other red meat, keep in mind that any goat recipe works just as well with lamb. The flavors are quite different: Both of them are more flavorful than commodity beef, yet the dishes that work for one tend to work for the other. So for the purposes of this book, let's consider goat and lamb meat interchangeable, with the caveat that the flavors are distinct.

Years ago, when I first bought goat meat for the restaurant, inspired by dishes I had eaten in Jamaican restaurants in Washington, DC; Toronto; and—of all places—York, Maine, the meat was imported from the exact opposite side of the world, freezer-burned in broken cryo bags and chopped into pieces with no regard for cut of meat, or bone for that matter. I realized then that it would be a long time before Americans treated goat the same way we treat beef or lamb.

Even today, if I want goat meat that is not imported, ground, or frozen in bony chunks, I have two choices: schlep out to Riverslea Farm in Epping where Liz and Jeff Conrad always have choice goat cuts in their freezer; or buy a whole fresh goat from Vermont Chevon. For meatballs, we grind the leaner, inside cuts; for sausages like merguez, we grind belly and flap muscles with a little leaf lard (the dense and flavorful fat that surrounds the kidneys of most animals); and we braise the rest of the animal for stews. This dish can be served as a stew right off the stove, but at the restaurant we shredded the meat, rolled it in plastic, and chilled it to form large logs that we then cut into disks to sear and serve with a reduction of the braising liquid.

8–9 pounds (3.6–4 kg) goat braising meat (legs, neck, shank, and rib all work well)

2 tablespoons plus 2 teaspoons kosher salt

1 tablespoon plus 1 teaspoon ground pepper

¼ cup (60 ml) olive oil

2 carrots, medium dice

2 stalks celery, medium dice

½ Spanish onion, medium dice

3 tablespoons minced garlic

¼ cup (60 g) minced fresh gingerroot

2 tablespoons ground fenugreek seed

1 tablespoon mustard powder

BRAISING THE GOAT: Preheat the oven to 300°F (150°C).

Preheat a wide, heavy-bottomed 8- to 10-quart (8 to 10 L) pan over high heat.

Coarsely chop the meat into large, same-sized chunks so it will cook evenly. Don't bother trimming the fat; it adds flavor to the braising liquid and can be skimmed off at the end. Sprinkle the meat with the salt and pepper.

Add the olive oil to the hot pan and carefully add the meat in a single layer (you will have to do this in two or three batches). Sear it to a golden brown without disturbing it, about 5 minutes. This brown sear is due to the Maillard reaction, or caramelization of sugars on the meat's surface. This searing step is key to a flavorful braise. If liquid starts to seep out of the meat, it will prevent the surface from searing and will begin to stew the meat. If this happens, it means the pan isn't

1 tablespoon ras el hanout (available at
  stockandspice.com)
2 cups (475 ml) tomato puree
1 pint (475 ml) gruit (or any rich and
  sweet ale that's not too hoppy)
2½ quarts (2.4 L) goat/lamb stock

hot enough or is too crowded, so either turn up the heat or remove some of the meat from the pan and sear it in the next batch.

Turn the meat and sear for 5 minutes on the other side. Transfer the meat to a bowl and repeat with the remaining meat until all of it is browned and moved to the bowl.

Add the carrots, celery, and onion to the pot and sweat in the goat fat for 2 minutes. Add the garlic and stir, cooking for 2 minutes more. Add the ginger, fenugreek, mustard powder, and ras el hanout and stir to combine with the vegetables. Add the tomato puree and cook down to a concentrate, stirring occasionally, about 4 minutes. Add the gruit or ale and boil down until the alcohol smell burns off, about 2 minutes. Add the goat or lamb stock, stir to combine, and bring back up to a boil.

Carefully transfer the goat meat back to the pot, cover, and reduce to a low simmer. The meat should be just barely submerged in the liquid. Check every half hour to ensure that the meat isn't sticking to the bottom of the pot. In 3 hours, the meat should fall apart at the pull of a fork.

SHAPING THE LOGS: Let the meat cool in the braising liquid until it's still warm but no longer too hot to touch. Strain out the liquid from the pan and transfer the meat to a clean bowl. Wearing rubber gloves, knead and shred the meat, adding salt and pepper if necessary. Shape the shredded meat into a log on an unrolled section of plastic wrap and roll the meat up like a burrito in logs about 3 inches (7.5 cm) thick, twisting the ends of the plastic wrap. Refrigerate for 3 hours or for up to 3 days.

TO SERVE: When you're ready to serve, remove the plastic and cut the log into equal slices that will each serve as one portion. In a nonstick or carbon steel pan with a couple of tablespoons of clarified butter/olive oil blend (see "Building Blocks," page 13), sear the disks of goat meat until crispy, flip over in the pan, and add braising liquid to reduce.

Moorish Meatballs

MAKES 32 ONE-OUNCE (28 G) MEATBALLS

I owe much of my passion for North African cuisine to Tom and Scott, my bosses at Lindbergh's Crossing. Tom's family had roots in France and North Africa, and the eye-opening flavors of the Maghreb definitely came to me first via Tom's family recipes. These meatballs represent one of my initial forays into this food culture.

One of the key ingredients here is the Fish pepper, a beautiful striated pepper that grows to about the size of an index finger and boasts a complex flavor as well as a healthy punch of heat. Brought to the States originally by Africans living in the mid-Atlantic region, this dynamic chile has been a staple in our heirloom garden for many years. To prepare Fish peppers in a winter dish such as this one, it is handy to have a few frozen vacuum-sealed bags of the peppers from the previous summer.

3 tablespoons olive oil, divided

2 medium shallots, minced

1 tablespoon minced garlic

3 Fish peppers (or 2 serrano), minced

1 teaspoon plus pinch salt, divided

1 teaspoon ras el hanout

1 teaspoon ground cumin

¼ cup (55 g) harissa (page 16)

1 teaspoon smoked paprika

½ teaspoon sumac

Pinch cayenne pepper

Pinch Urfa chile flakes (or substitute chili powder)

1 pound (455 g) ground beef

1 pound (455 g) ground lamb or goat

2 eggs (100 g liquid egg)

¼ cup (45 g) firmly packed mint, chopped

1 cup (115 g) fine bread crumbs (not panko)

Preheat the oven to 350°F (175°C).

Pour 1 tablespoon of the olive oil into a small 8-inch (20 cm) pan over high heat. Sauté the shallots, garlic, Fish peppers, and a pinch of salt over high heat for 2 minutes, until they begin to turn translucent. Remove the pan from the heat and add the ras el hanout and cumin while the pan is still hot. Let the mixture cool, and then add the harissa, smoked paprika, sumac, cayenne, and Urfa, stirring to combine.

Add the mixture to a large bowl with the ground meats, eggs, remaining teaspoon of salt, the mint, and the bread crumbs. Knead the mixture by hand for about a minute, until the ingredients are just incorporated.

Roll into 1-inch (2.5 cm) balls (approximately 2 tablespoons per ball). Heat a large sauté pan over medium heat. Add the remaining 2 tablespoons of oil and the meatballs in an even layer (you may need to do this in batches). Gently roll the meatballs around in the pan, browning all sides (about 2 minutes per side), then pop the pan in the oven and bake for 10 minutes, or until cooked through.

On our winter menu, these meatballs have served as the base for Market Kefta (page 55), in which they are stewed with a spicy tomato sauce, and then baked with an egg on top. The same meatballs can also be baked and served with Poblano Goat Yogurt (page 288) in the fall or Tzatziki (page 243) in the summer.

Mexiterranean Meatballs

MAKES 36 ONE-OUNCE (28 G) MEATBALLS

I originally coined the jocular term *Mexiterranean* when asked for the umpteen thousandth time what kind of food we serve at Black Trumpet. When received by a blank stare, I elaborated, "I am inspired by the food of the Mediterranean, but I lived in Mexico and love Latin American cuisine a lot. So . . ."

I like using these meatballs to make comforting, spicy soups. Any variation on poblano-spiked broth acts as a vehicle for the complex layers of flavors in these meatballs.

½ pound (225 g) 70% lean pork (up to 85% lean will work)
1½ pounds (680 g) ground beef
2 tablespoons minced garlic
2 tablespoons finely chopped fresh parsley
1 tablespoon finely chopped fresh mint
1 tablespoon finely chopped fresh cilantro
2 pinches dried Mexican oregano (or dried Italian oregano)
½ Spanish onion, very finely chopped
½ tablespoon chili powder
1 teaspoon cumin seed, toasted and ground in a spice grinder (see "Toasting Seeds" sidebar)
1 tablespoon kosher salt
½ teaspoon ground black pepper
2 large eggs (100 g liquid egg)
1 cup (115 g) bread crumbs

Place all the ingredients in a large bowl and, using your hands, knead the mixture to fully incorporate the eggs and bread crumbs and to emulsify the fat. Refrigerate the mixture.

When you're ready to make the meatballs, remove the mixture from the refrigerator and mold into 1-ounce (28 g) balls. Return to the refrigerator to chill for about 30 minutes before cooking. The formed meatballs can remain refrigerated in this state for a day or two if necessary.

To cook the meatballs, place a small frying pan over medium heat. When the pan starts smoking, brown the meatballs in batches, rolling them around so they don't stick to the pan. If you're serving the meatballs on their own with Poblano Goat Yogurt (page 288), transfer them to a roasting pan and bake at 400°F (200°C) for 6 minutes, or until they are just cooked through. Pour off the fat, leaving the meatballs in the pan, and add poblano sauce to the hot pan. Stir with the meatballs and serve right away.

Chorizo Meatballs

MAKES 36 ONE-OUNCE (28 G) MEATBALLS

These meatballs are great in paella, but we originally served them with a pan-fried Chicken Paillard and Black Olive Salpicon (pages 296 and 298 respectively).

2 pounds (910 g) lean ground pork
4 ounces (115 g) fatback, ground
1 egg (50 g liquid egg)
2 tablespoons plus 1 teaspoon
   minced garlic
1½ teaspoons dried Mexican oregano
1½ teaspoons Spanish smoked paprika
1¼ teaspoons salt
1 teaspoon chili powder
1 teaspoon cumin seed, toasted
   and ground
1 teaspoon fennel seed, toasted
   and ground
½ teaspoon black pepper
½ teaspoon cayenne pepper
½ teaspoon ground coriander
⅛ teaspoon ground cinnamon
1 teaspoon olive oil

In a large bowl, knead together all the ingredients except the olive oil until fully combined. Store the meatball dough or roll into thirty-six 1-ounce (28 g) meatballs and refrigerate for half an hour.

Preheat the oven to 400°F (200°C).

Bring a 10- or 12-inch (25 or 30 cm) high-sided cast-iron skillet up to the smoke point over high heat. Add the olive oil and enough meatballs so they fit in the pan in a single layer (you may need to repeat this step once or twice). Roll the balls around for a few minutes, until they begin to brown on all sides, and finish cooking them in the oven, 5 to 7 minutes. Serve.

Toasting Seeds

For dishes that require spices, it is a good idea to gently toast the spice seeds first in a dry pan to bring out their essential oils. Add seeds in a single layer to a dry 6- to 8-inch (15 to 20 cm) frying pan. Toast on medium-high heat, tossing constantly, until the seeds are aromatic and faint traces of their oil start leaching into the bottom of the pan, about 30 seconds for most spices. Remove to a spice grinder and grind to a powder.

Market Kefta

SERVES 8; MAKES 1 QUART (945 ML) SAUCE

Any of the meatball recipes in this book can be used for this recipe, but I'd suggest starting with the one we used for many menus, Moorish Meatballs (page 50).

Only the most unusual household would have eight individual cast-iron skillets, but small casserole dishes and pretty much any heat-safe crocks will also work. Even mix and match, as long as you account for variable cooking times dependent on the depth of your vessels. If you want to go family-style, on the other hand, you might consider putting meatballs in the Shakshuka recipe (which follows) and merging two outstanding dishes into one.

For the Kefta Sauce

1 tablespoon clarified butter/olive oil blend (page 13)

¼ red bell pepper, small dice

¼ poblano pepper, small dice

½ jalapeño pepper, small dice

¼ Spanish onion, small dice

⅛ bulb fennel, small dice

½ preserved lemon (page 16), pulp removed and discarded, rind in small dice

Juice of ½ orange

1½ teaspoons minced garlic

3 cups (710 ml) fire-roasted tomato puree

½ teaspoon salt

To serve (per person)

3 meatballs

½ cup (120 ml) Kefta Sauce

¼ cup (60 ml) meat stock

1 egg (50 g liquid egg)

MAKE THE KEFTA SAUCE: In a nonreactive saucepan, combine the clarified butter/olive oil blend with the next five ingredients and cook over medium-low heat until soft, about 10 minutes. Add the remaining ingredients and simmer until the flavors marry, about 10 minutes. The sauce should be fairly spicy and not too salty.

TO SERVE: Preheat the oven to 425°F (220°C).

Brown three meatballs in a 6-inch (15 cm) cast-iron skillet or other individual oven-safe pan. Add the Kefta Sauce and meat stock and bring to a simmer over medium-low heat. When bubbling throughout, crack an egg on top and simmer for about 1½ minutes on the stovetop. Slide into the oven and bake 5 minutes, or until the white is set.

Shakshuka with Duck Eggs and Herbed Semolina Dumplings

SERVES 5

I made this dish at a rare Black Trumpet brunch for the regional governors of Slow Food. I had made it before and not called it Shakshuka, but someone who apparently knew better pointed out that it was the best Shakshuka they'd had, so I determined I would call it that from then on. Essentially, it is a scaled-up version of our Market Kefta (preceding recipe), especially if Moorish Meatballs (page 50) are added. No worries if you can't find duck eggs; large local chicken eggs are also delicious in this recipe.

¼ cup (60 ml) olive oil
1 red onion, medium dice
2 red bell peppers, medium dice
2 green bell peppers, medium dice
4 serrano peppers, small dice
8 cloves garlic, minced
½ cup (120 ml) red wine
Juice of 1 orange
½ cup (115 g) harissa (page 16)
2 tablespoons brown sugar
1½ quarts (1.4 L) tomato puree
1 cup (235 ml) vegetable stock
10 Herbed Semolina Dumplings
   (recipe follows)
5 duck eggs (can substitute any other
   type of egg)

Preheat the oven to 400°F (200°C).

Heat the olive oil in a wide, high-sided pan over medium heat. Add the onion and peppers and cook, stirring, until slightly softened, about 3 minutes. Add the garlic and cook, stirring, 1 minute more. Add the wine and boil 2 to 3 minutes, until the alcohol scent wears off. Add the orange juice, harissa, and brown sugar; stir to combine. Add the tomato puree and stock, stir, and simmer 5 minutes.

Transfer the simmering liquid to a terra-cotta baking dish (at home, I use a 16-inch [40 cm] round Spanish cazuela, but any large casserole dish will do nicely). Add the dumplings carefully, making sure they don't sink down into the tomato liquid but also leaving room for the eggs (you want them to cook in the liquid, not on the dumplings). Crack the duck eggs into the open spaces between dumplings, nestling them on top of the tomato liquid.

Slide the pan into the oven and bake for 15 to 20 minutes, or until the egg whites are set. Serve immediately with Sesame Lavash (page 321), Pita Bread (page 244), or Ksra (page 129).

Herbed Semolina Dumplings

MAKES 20 DUMPLINGS

1 large russet potato
4 cups (945 ml) water, plus more for
   cooking dumplings
2 teaspoons salt
1¾ cups (285 g) semolina flour
1 teaspoon black pepper
¼ cup (25 g) grated Parmesan cheese
2 egg yolks (36 g)
2 whole eggs (100 g liquid egg)
2 tablespoons chopped Italian parsley
2 tablespoons chopped fresh tarragon
5 chopped chives

Preheat the oven to 400°F (200°C). Pierce the potato with a fork over its surface, place on a baking sheet, and bake 1 hour. Let the potato cool slightly, cut in half, and squeeze through a ricer into a large mixing bowl.

Bring the water and salt to a boil in a 3- to 4-quart (3 to 4 L) pot over high heat. Pour the semolina into the pot slowly and steadily, whisking constantly. Reduce the heat to low and continue whisking for 2 minutes. Off the flame, using a rubber spatula, add the black pepper, cheese, and mashed potato, folding to combine. Add the yolks and whole eggs one at a time, combining each addition until fully incorporated before adding the next. Fold in the herbs.

Bring a large pot of lightly salted water to a boil over high heat. In batches, drop tablespoon-sized balls of the dough (shaped into quenelles, if desired) into the boiling water, being careful not to crowd the pot. Cook for 3 minutes, remove with a slotted spoon, and repeat with the remaining dough.

These dumplings may be made in advance and held in the refrigerator for up to a day.

Baked Chestnut Gnocchi

SERVES 8 AS A MAIN COURSE

Black Trumpet menus have always offered at least one vegetarian item in each menu category. We quickly found that this effort appealed to a wide audience willing to travel a few hours for dinner, a vegetarian audience that demanded something more than the obligatory pasta dishes and salads.

This was one of our first popular vegetarian menu items at Black Trumpet, and we served these nutty, toasty gems with brussels sprouts and a Blue Hubbard and apple bisque sauce. Folks who like their gnocchi lighter than air may not see the merit in these hefty, hearty nuggets. Chestnut flour and ground chestnuts give these gnocchi a deep flavor and somewhat dense texture that puffs a bit in the oven. The tiny kernels of chestnut that stud each gnoccho are a welcome surprise.

If you have reservations about living out the Rockwellian dream of roasting chestnuts by an open fire, may I suggest the alternative technique of seeking out roasted and peeled chestnut meats? These can be stored indefinitely in a freezer.

2 medium Yukon Gold potatoes

3 tablespoons plus ½ teaspoon kosher salt, divided

6 ounces chestnut meats (the yield from ½ pound [225 g] roasted whole chestnuts), picked through for shells

½ cup (43 g) chestnut flour

½ cup (55 g) all-purpose flour

3 eggs (150 g liquid egg)

3 tablespoons olive oil

1 pat unsalted butter

Sprinkle the potatoes with 2 tablespoons of the kosher salt and bake them whole in a 400°F (200°C) oven for about 45 minutes, or until they're completely soft. Let cool for 10 minutes, and then rub the warm potatoes through a tamis or squeeze them through a ricer into a medium mixing bowl.

Meanwhile, in a food processor, spin the chestnuts until they are reduced to a fine rubble. Add the chestnut and all-purpose flours and the remaining salt; continue to process until combined. Transfer to a board or a large, wide bowl and make a well in the middle of the flour mixture.

Set a gallon (3.8 L) of salted water on the stove and bring it to a boil.

Break the eggs into the medium bowl and beat into the potato mixture with a fork until just barely combined. Transfer this potato mixture to the middle of the well in the flour. Using the fork, gradually incorporate the flour into the edges of the potato mixture. When a solid, sticky dough is formed, sprinkle some flour on the board and gently fold the dough over itself and knead a few times to incorporate all the ingredients. Be careful not to overwork the dough, as this can make for tough gnocchi. Cut the dough into three sections and roll out each section into a 1-inch-thick (2.5 cm) "snake," adding a touch more flour if necessary to prevent sticking.

Reduce the water to a simmer. Cut the "snakes" into 1-inch-long (2.5 cm) logs and roll them one at a time off the back of a fork (or, better yet, a gnocchi roller) into the hot water. The gnocchi will sink to the bottom and, a few minutes later, rise to the surface. You should periodically scrape any gnocchi off the bottom of the pot with a wooden spoon. When they rise to the surface, transfer them with a slotted spoon to an oiled surface like a sheet pan.

The gnocchi can be prepared in advance and refrigerated or frozen at this point.

TO SERVE: When you're ready to serve, heat the oven to 450°F (230°C). In a cast-iron skillet or other oven-safe pan, heat the olive oil with a pat of whole butter. When the butter is just melted, place the gnocchi in the pan and brown over a medium flame for 1 minute, then transfer to the oven for about 3 minutes, or until the gnocchi have puffed slightly. Serve immediately with roasted brussels sprouts and Levant-Spiced Pumpkin Soup (page 324), reduced in a pan to make a thick sauce.

Pretzel- and Chestnut-Crusted Meat Tarts

MAKES 10 TO 12 TARTS

I married into a family with roots in Montreal, an old-world city in the midst of the New World. For my in-laws, *tourtiere* is a family tradition, prepared on Christmas Eve, and it inspired this meat tart. One notable addition is the ricotta cheese, which makes the meat filling less dense and a little easier on the wallet when sourcing local meat, which can be quite expensive.

This recipe requires an 11-cup (2.6 L) food processor. If yours is smaller, be sure to divide both recipes into two parts and spin the ingredients in two batches.

For the chestnut-pretzel crust

12 frozen, peeled chestnuts

2 cups (300 g) pretzel crumbs (large pretzel sticks pulsed in a food processor until broken up)

½ cup (55 g) fresh bread crumbs

1 teaspoon cornstarch

1 teaspoon salt

1½ cups (340 g) unsalted butter, chopped into ½-inch (1 cm) cubes

½ cup (115 g) bone marrow (if available; if not, add more whole butter)

MAKE THE CHESTNUT-PRETZEL CRUST: Pulse the frozen chestnuts in a food processor until just smaller than pea-sized. Add the pretzel crumbs and spin just enough to incorporate. Add the bread crumbs, cornstarch, and salt, and spin just until combined. Add the butter and marrow (or just butter if marrow can't be found) and cut into the crumbs by pulsing several times in the food processor. Remove to a bowl and refrigerate until firm, about 30 minutes to 1 hour.

MAKE THE MEAT FILLING: In a food processor, spin the livers until smooth. Add the ground meats and blend until just combined. Add the ricotta and pulse to combine. With the motor running, add the

For the meat filling

12 ounces (340 g) beef livers
12 ounces (340 g) ground beef
6 ounces (170 g) ground pork
2 cups (455 g) whole-milk
  ricotta cheese
4 eggs (200 g liquid egg)
¾ teaspoon salt

For garnish

36 pearl onions
Olive oil
Salt

eggs and salt and whiz just until combined. Remove to a large mixing bowl and finish mixing with a spatula, to ensure there are no remaining chunks or streaks of ricotta or egg. Cover and refrigerate the filling.

MAKE THE GARNISH: Sauté the pearl onions in a hot pan with olive oil and salt for 4 minutes, then roast them in a 450°F (230°C) oven for 10 minutes.

MAKE THE MEAT TARTS: Spray twelve 4-inch (10 cm) cast-iron skillets, deep ramekins, or similarly sized bowls with pan spray. Place about ⅓ cup (70 g) crust into each vessel, pressing it firmly into the bottom and evenly up the sides. Place the pans on a baking sheet and refrigerate until the crust is firm, about 30 minutes.

Preheat the oven to 375°F (190°C).

Remove the baking sheet from the refrigerator and fill each shell with 5 ounces (142 g) of meat filling, spreading the meat to the edges with a rubber spatula or spoon. Bake 16 minutes, rotating the pan a half turn after 8 minutes, until the filling is set and the crust is golden brown and bubbling.

Let the tarts cool to room temperature, and then store in a refrigerator for at least an hour. When you're ready to serve, put the molds in a hot oven for 3 minutes, then invert the tarts twice to unmold them—once to free them from the molds and the second time to flip them over onto a baking pan. Arrange the roasted pearl onions on the top of the unmolded tarts and put them in a 400°F (200°C) oven for 5 minutes. The buttery crust will crumble somewhat, but don't be alarmed. The texture of the crust is meant to be crumbly, and there will be an inevitable loss of crumb in the process of reheating the tarts. Transfer to plates and serve immediately.

Cooking with Kids

When my youngest child was still eating pureed food, I began cooking with other people's children. The first program I worked with was Operation Frontline, which has since morphed into Cooking Matters, an initiative of Share Our Strength, a nationwide organization whose commitment to conquering hunger and malnutrition in our country continues to impress and inspire me. In the 1990s, Portsmouth began hosting its own version of Share Our Strength's Taste of the Nation dinners, now an annual event that draws hundreds of people, features dozens of restaurants and caterers, and most important— raises a ton of money for Share Our Strength.

In 2012, I organized an event at my children's elementary school called Farm Day, in which buses took 120 kids to nearby Riverside Farm, where they met Farmer Dave Tuttle and toured the greenhouses, each child transplanting a bean seedling from the greenhouse into the field, where an entire tilled row had been earmarked for the school project. Later in the day, when the buses returned, a diligent team of helpers and I made tacos for lunch from mostly locally farmed ingredients. The kids got to press their own tortillas from masa dough,

and they ate some pretty tasty local beef and beans shortly thereafter.

Having cooked in the classroom at my children's schools, and seeing the potential to affect the diets of young people, I teamed up with esteemed author and radio personality Kathy Gunst at a nearby elementary school, where we enjoined the students to roll out three delicious and colorful pastas—including a jet-black squid ink one the kids loved!—that we cooked up for a healthy snack. Kathy has since completed a project at that school that enables students to plant seeds every year in a greenhouse and nurture the plants until they can be offered in the cafeteria for lunch. Working with children is boundlessly rewarding, albeit exhausting. Sort of like farming. I propose that, in rethinking our connection to food, we reconsider the income imbalance that rewards doctors, lawyers, and bankers but marginalizes teachers and farmers.

This chapter contains a recipe for the Beet Pasta I served at the elementary school event with Kathy Gunst—the same one that makes the beautiful Beet Tortellini seen in the photo on page 64.

Jacketed Sweet Potato with Lentil Dal, Feta, and Blood Oranges

SERVES 8

Here's another very popular dish that was enjoyed by vegetarians and omnivores alike. The term *jacketed* is borrowed from the American South, where baked or deep-fried sweet potatoes served in their blistered skin (usually with cinnamon butter) is an iconic regional delicacy. We bake the halved sweet potatoes first, then deep-fry them to order, which gives the succulent skin great texture.

4 large sweet potatoes

Olive oil, for roasting

¼ teaspoon salt

Pinch black pepper

Lentil Dal filling (recipe follows)

2 quarts (1.9 L) canola oil, for deep-frying

½ pint (200 g) crumbled feta cheese, to garnish

2 blood oranges, to garnish

Preheat the oven to 400°F (200°C).

Cut four 5- to 6-inch-long (13 to 15 cm) sweet potatoes in half lengthwise and drizzle the cut sides with the olive oil, salt, and black pepper. Place the potatoes cut side down on an oiled sheet tray. Roast until soft, about 35 minutes. Allow the potatoes to cool slightly, and then carefully scoop out the interior. Combine the fluffy sweet potato interior with the Lentil Dal and set aside. Meanwhile, deep-fry the eight sweet potato shells at 325°F (165°C) for 4 minutes, until crispy and golden brown. Transfer them cut side down to towels to dry, then flip over onto plates so they resemble boats. Scoop an eighth of the dal into each shell/barquette and serve immediately.

For bonus points, you can spread and bake strained Greek yogurt in a 400°F (200°C) oven for about an hour, or until it dries out and browns around the edges, and crumble the resulting cheese over the top of the dal. Or take the easier path and just crumble feta. We also garnished this dish with blood oranges, which made damn fine companions to the other flavors on the plate.

Lentil Dal

2 tablespoons olive oil
1 red onion, small dice
1 tablespoon minced garlic
1 tablespoon minced fresh gingerroot
1 teaspoon whole cumin seed, toasted
1 teaspoon ground coriander
1½ teaspoons salt
½ teaspoon freshly ground black pepper
One 13.5-ounce (400 ml) can
  coconut milk
1½ cups (355 ml) vegetable stock
1½ cups (275 g) black lentils
1 teaspoon lime juice, from ½ lime

Add the oil and onion to a medium-sized pot over low heat. Sweat until the onion is soft, about 5 minutes. Add the garlic, ginger, cumin, coriander, salt, and pepper. Stir and sweat an additional 2 to 3 minutes.

Add the can of coconut milk, vegetable stock, and black lentils to the pot and stir to combine. Bring to a boil, then reduce the heat to low. Cover and simmer 20 minutes. Add the lime juice, stir to combine, and spread out on a sheet pan to cool to room temperature.

Beet Pasta

MAKES ABOUT 1 POUND (455 G)

For the beet puree
2 medium beets, scrubbed
   and unpeeled, cut into 1-inch
   (2.5 cm) cubes
1 quart (945 ml) water
1 teaspoon salt

For the pasta
1 cup plus 2 tablespoons (125 g)
   "00" pasta flour
1 cup (120 g) all-purpose flour
1 whole egg (50 g liquid egg)
2 egg yolks (36 g)
½ cup (120 ml) beet puree
¼ teaspoon salt

MAKE THE BEET PUREE: Bring the beets and water to a boil over high heat in a 2- to 3-quart (2 to 3 L) pot. Reduce the heat to low and simmer for about 1½ hours, until soft. Drain the water and pour the beets and salt into the bowl of a blender. Puree until smooth. Let cool to room temperature and refrigerate until you're ready to use it.

MAKE THE PASTA: Mix the flours and mound onto a clean work surface. In a bowl, whisk together the egg and egg yolks, beet puree, and salt. Make a well in the flour and add the beet mixture. Combine with a fork, pulling from the inside of the dry mixture to incorporate into the wet ingredients. Mix until the wet and dry ingredients are just combined. Lightly flour the work surface and knead for 5 to 6 minutes, until the dough is smooth and springs back three-quarters of the way when poked with a finger. Wrap tightly in plastic and flatten into a disk shape. Refrigerate at least an hour before rolling.

Beet Tortellini with Raisin Pine Nut Salad

MAKES ABOUT 24 TORTELLINI,
1 POUND (455 G) PASTA, ½ CUP (115 G) FILLING

After teaching children how to make colorful pasta, I put the beet version to work on our menu. We served three tortellini as a small dish, but this recipe can certainly be scaled up to make a pasta party. In fact, here's an idea: Invite your dinner guests to form, fill, and shape pasta with you, perhaps while enjoying an aperitif or a bottle of wine, then cook it up and sit down to dinner. It's an inclusive technique that gets people talking about their food and having a good time while learning a fun craft in the process. One tip, though: Be sure to plan ahead by having the pasta and filling made earlier in the day, or even the day before.

For the tortellini filling

½ cup (115 g) feta, not crumbled
1 teaspoon minced garlic
Pinch herbs (any combination of sage, rosemary, thyme, chives, oregano)
½ teaspoon dried red pepper flakes
½ cup plus 2 tablespoons (150 ml) good olive oil
2 tablespoons pine nuts
2 teaspoons honey

For the pasta

1 recipe Beet Pasta (preceding recipe)
¼ cup (40 g) semolina flour

For the egg wash

1 egg (50 g liquid egg), fork-beaten with 1 teaspoon cold water

MAKE THE TORTELLINI FILLING: In a small container, combine the feta, garlic, herbs, and red pepper flakes in ½ cup (120 ml) of the olive oil. Marinate the feta at least 4 hours, or overnight. Keep the leftover marinating liquid for dressings.

Combine the remaining 2 tablespoons of olive oil and the pine nuts in a medium pan over medium heat, tossing often, until the nuts turn an even golden brown. Remove to the bowl of a food processor and pulse until the nuts form a chunky paste. Add the feta and honey and 1 tablespoon of the feta marinating liquid and spin, stopping often to scrape down the bottom and sides of the bowl. Stop when the mixture is fairly smooth and the ingredients are thoroughly combined.

ROLL THE PASTA DOUGH: Remove the Beet Pasta dough from the refrigerator 15 minutes before rolling. Cut into three pieces and flatten the first with the palm of your hand. Pass through the widest setting on a pasta sheeter. Make a gate fold by folding one side of the sheeted dough to the center, repeat on the other side, and then fold in half so you have a long rectangle. Flatten with the palm of your hand, sprinkle with flour, and pass through the widest setting one more time. Sprinkle with flour, move the sheeter down two notches, and pass through the machine. Repeat one more time, or until you have passed the dough through the second-lowest setting on the sheeter. Spread the dough out on a clean, floured work surface. Repeat with the remaining two pieces of dough.

SHAPE THE TORTELLINI: Cut rounds in the dough using a 3-inch (7.5 cm) biscuit cutter or similarly sized jar or glass. You should have about twenty-four rounds. Place 1 teaspoon filling onto the middle of each round and, using a brush or your finger, egg wash half of the round. Fold the top half of the circle over the bottom and press lightly to adhere, forming a ¼-inch (0.5 cm) edge. Hold the half-moon with the straight side facing up and the fatter side of the filling (the side that wasn't flat against the counter) facing toward you. Egg wash the left corner of the half-moon and simultaneously indent the middle of the packet with an index finger. Fold the tortellini away from you, bringing the right side over to meet the left side, overlapping the two sides by about ½ inch (1 cm) and pressing gently to secure. Place the formed tortellini on a baking sheet sprinkled with the semolina flour and repeat with the remaining rounds, working quickly so they don't dry out.

TO SERVE: Bring a large pot of heavily salted water to a boil and boil the tortellini, in batches, for 3 to 4 minutes. Remove to a baking sheet coated with olive oil to prevent sticking. Repeat with the remaining batches.

You can serve these plump pink pillows with a sauce or on their own tossed in olive oil, or do as we did and serve them as a salad on a bed of lightly dressed, thinly sliced kale sprinkled with pine nuts and raisins to garnish.

The Holiday Goose Tradition

Every Christmas Eve, Black Trumpet offers a special menu in addition to our regular holiday season menu. There is usually a soul-warming soup and some variation on plum pudding for dessert, but the one constant is the goose main course. For the first few years, I sourced goose from New York State, because I had yet to make any local goose connections. The purveyor I was working with at the time had promised that I would be getting six fresh geese, so I requested delivery two days before Christmas Eve to ensure that I had enough time to cure and confit the legs (a two-day process).

As luck would have it, there was a storm somewhere along the 200-mile (322 km) route that the geese had to travel via FedEx, and the delivery was postponed a day. That in itself would have been sufficiently stressful, but the following day, when the box finally arrived, I frantically opened it to find that the six large geese were frozen solid. If I needed another reason to work with local farmers instead of purveyors I had never met in person, this was it. I called and yelled into the phone in front of my kitchen crew, who cowered in the far end of

the kitchen. I never wanted to be the stereotypical hot-headed, histrionic chef. I hung up the phone with the realization that my protests were futile. I had no choice but to shortcut the confit process. The birds went into a bus tub under running water for about six hours. I remember prying the still-frozen legs from the bodies of the birds and cursing the purveyor, the season, the weather gods, and even the innocent courier.

Despite that nearly violent holiday ordeal, word spread quickly about our annual goose dish, and by the third winter at Black Trumpet I had goose farmers in our area coming to me with a variety of anserine options. After a few more years, I met a farmer who—in addition to raising heritage-breed Chocolate turkeys and various breeds of duck—offered me Embden geese he had raised for the holiday season. I went to his farm, met the geese, beheld the perfect family farm scenario only a few miles from the restaurant, and committed to buying those geese from him. Their appeal is beyond compare, offering the texture of roast beef with a deeper-than-duck flavor.

Pheasant Two Ways:
Roulade and Leg Stewed with Prunes

SERVES 8

This is a great dish that can dress even a chicken in its fanciest garb, but there is something special about the richer taste of pheasant that works best, especially in the stewed leg portion of this recipe.

For our menu, we bought pheasant roosters, which are significantly larger than hens. If you are only able to source hens, keep in mind that this recipe will yield a little more than half of the roosters' yield, so plan on serving half as many people.

For the roulade

4 pheasant breasts (from 2 roosters), tenders removed
Salt
Black pepper
2 packed cups (100 g) fresh spinach
1 cup (115 g) grated cheddar cheese
10–12 thin slices Bavarian ham
¼ cup (60 ml) clarified butter/olive oil blend (page 13), divided

For the stewed pheasant legs

4 legs (from 2 roosters)
Salt
Black pepper
2 tablespoons clarified butter/olive oil blend (page 13)
8 prunes (pitted dates may be substituted)
1 small onion, rough-chopped
1 tablespoon honey
½ cup (120 ml) port
1½ quarts (1.4 L) stock (from pheasant, duck, or other poultry)

MAKE THE ROULADE: Preheat the oven to 400°F (200°C).

Blanch the spinach in salted boiling water for 30 seconds and remove to cool.

Pound the breasts under plastic with a meat mallet to ½ inch (1 cm) thick and sprinkle with salt and pepper. Spread each breast, skin side down, evenly with spinach, sprinkle with cheese, and layer the ham on top, covering the entire surface area of the pheasant breast.

Roll the breast into logs and tie with kitchen twine. Sprinkle the outside with salt and pepper. Add 2 tablespoons of the butter/oil blend to two different 10- to 12-inch (25 or 30 cm) pans over medium-high heat. Add the roulades, two to a pan, and brown on all sides for about 4 minutes total. Place the pans in the oven and roast 12 minutes.

Remove the roulades to a cutting board and rest 5 to 10 minutes. Remove the twine, and slice each breast crosswise into four ½-inch-thick (1 cm) slices (two per person). Reheat the slices briefly if necessary while preparing the rest of the dish components.

MAKE THE STEWED PHEASANT LEGS: Preheat the oven to 300°F (150°C).

Sprinkle the legs generously with salt and pepper. Heat a large pan over medium-high heat. Add the butter/oil blend and sear, skin side down, until golden brown, 4 to 5 minutes. Flip and transfer to a roasting pan with the remaining ingredients. Bring to a boil, reduce to a simmer, cover, and slide into the oven. Braise for 1¼ hours. Remove and let cool slightly. Separate the thighs from the drumsticks (eight pieces total) and serve one piece per person with two slices each of roulade.

Quail Adobado with Quince Hash

SERVES 6

For me, this is a desert-island dish, but not in the traditional sense. Yes, I suppose I might include quail on my list of things to bring to a desert island, but I mean to say that this is how I would prepare a small bird if I found myself already on a desert island, preferably in the Caribbean, and preferably one with lots of quail running around.

I highly recommend serving these birds atop Quince Hash (recipe follows), or something just like it.

1 tablespoon cumin seed

2 tablespoons annatto seed

½ teaspoon fennel seed

2 whole cloves

1 teaspoon dried red pepper flakes

1 teaspoon dried Aleppo chile flakes

½ teaspoon ground cinnamon

1 teaspoon salt

½ teaspoon brown sugar

6 quail, spatchcocked (rib cage removed) and butterflied

¼ cup (60 ml) clarified butter/olive oil blend (page 13)

1 teaspoon minced garlic

1 tablespoon Hot Sauce (page 21)

1 cup (235 ml) tomato puree

1 pint (475 ml) poultry stock

Preheat the oven to 400°F (200°C).

Toast the cumin, annatto, and fennel seeds and grind with the cloves. Blend the ground spices with the next five ingredients. Rub both sides of each quail liberally with the spice rub.

Add the butter/oil blend to a large, wide pan over medium heat and brown the quail, skin side down, for 1 to 1½ minutes, until golden brown. Flip the quail and add the garlic, Hot Sauce, tomato puree, and poultry stock to the pan. Bring the liquid to a simmer and cook 1 minute. Place in the oven and cook 6 to 8 minutes. Remove to a cutting board and let rest about 3 minutes. Halve each quail lengthwise and serve the halves over Quince Hash, one whole quail per person. Spoon some of the adobo sauce over the top and serve.

Quince Hash

SERVES 12

In this recipe, it is important that all vegetables are diced the same size for even cooking. If quince can't be found, add pear or apple later, toward the end of the cooking process.

¼ cup (60 ml) clarified butter/olive oil blend (page 13)

2 cups (450 g) quince, cored, medium dice (about 2 quinces)

2 cups (450 g) Long Pie pumpkin, peeled, medium dice (or substitute butternut squash)

2 cups (450 g) zucchini, medium dice

1½ cups (335 g) red onion, medium dice (about 1 large)

1 cup (225 g) Red Bliss potato, medium dice

1½ teaspoons salt

1 teaspoon black pepper

1 teaspoon minced garlic

¼ cup (60 ml) sherry vinegar

2 tablespoons maple syrup

½ teaspoon smoked paprika

Preheat the oven to 425°F (220°C).

Add the butter/oil blend to a large, heavy-bottomed sauteuse or other high-sided oven-safe sauté pan over high heat. When hot, add the next seven ingredients and cook 5 minutes, stirring frequently. Add the garlic and cook 2 minutes more. Deglaze the pan with the sherry vinegar, scraping up any browned bits, and add the maple syrup and smoked paprika, stirring to combine.

Place the pan in the oven and bake for 10 minutes until the vegetables begin to brown slightly. Remove from the oven, stir, and serve immediately.

Rabbit Butchery

Butchery of anything can be intimidating, even to professional cooks. Guys and gals in my kitchen still rely on me for the majority of butchery. And it makes sense. Meat is expensive and precious, and I would question the moral fabric of anyone who took to butchering without inhibition.

One of our country's most important butcher/educators is an author named Adam Danforth. His published works have illuminated the minds of many cooks, young and old alike, by demonstrating technique that can be applied to almost any animal to maximize yield and efficiency in the butchering process. Also an advocate for humane on-farm slaughter, Danforth continues to travel the continent with an important message about how we view meat, and how we treat it before and after it becomes food. The best chefs I know respect Danforth's viewpoint.

Adam and I sat on the board of Chefs Collaborative together for a couple of years, and—in the summer of 2015—he accepted my invitation on relatively short notice to conduct a butchery demonstration at Black Trumpet for chefs and other stakeholders in our local food movement.

The thing he said that resonated with just about everyone in the room was, "Once you know how to butcher one animal, you can butcher all animals."

To Prepare a Rabbit

Make sure the rabbit has been well skinned and cleaned. Rinse thoroughly if there is any uncertainty.

Cut along the edge of the spine where the legs meet the tailbone, until the legs can be pried from the body. Cut where you see the joint protruding and the legs will pop out.

Prop the carcass up on the forelegs so the spine is facing up and the tail end is closest to you. Draw a line, with the tip of your knife, down the middle of the spine. Gently pull the loin meat away from the spine as you carefully cut the two loins away from the ribs and spine.

Tracing along the rib cage with the tip of your knife, remove the flap (or flank) meat that is connected to the loin. The flap can be removed from the loin with one long cut. Set the flap meat aside with the legs to be braised.

John Flintosh—who has served two long terms at Black Trumpet—once noticed after braising rabbit forelegs that there's a tiny, sharp pin bone in the "elbow" that could cause choking. Before we braise, we take needlenose pliers and remove these pin bones.

On the underside of the carcass, mirroring the loin above, you can find the soft meat of the tenderloin, which can be harvested to make meatballs or sausage, or can be breaded or fried for rabbit nuggets.

If you like, you can remove the hip bone and femur from the rabbit leg to make it semiboneless, but this is somewhat time consuming.

Once the meat has been removed, set the carcass aside to make stock (see "Building Blocks," page 14).

Rabbit Fricassee

SERVES 12

---

3 rabbits, about 4 pounds (1.8 kg) each

1 cup (225 g) all-purpose flour

1 cup (225 g) chickpea flour

1 tablespoon plus ½ teaspoon salt, divided

1 teaspoon black pepper

¼ teaspoon ground nutmeg

Pinch cayenne pepper

¾ cup (180 ml) clarified butter/olive oil blend (page 13)

⅔ cup (150 g) medium-diced Spanish onion

⅔ cup (150 g) medium-diced celery

⅔ cup (150 g) medium-diced peeled carrot

¼ cup (55 g) minced garlic

3 cups (300 g) assorted mushrooms

1 teaspoon dried (or 1 tablespoon chopped fresh) tarragon

2 bay leaves

2 cups (475 ml) white wine

¼ cup (40 g) salt-cured capers, soaked in 1 cup (235 ml) water for 15 minutes

2 quarts (1.9 L) rabbit (or poultry) stock

½ cup (120 ml) heavy cream

Preheat the oven to 350°F (175°C).

Butcher the rabbits (see "Rabbit Butchery"). Set the loins aside (for a Fried Rabbit Loin recipe, page 172) and bone out the thighs (optional). Combine the flours, 1 tablespoon of the salt, the black pepper, nutmeg, and cayenne in a medium bowl. Starting with the hind legs, dredge in the flour mixture, tapping off the excess. Heat two large frying pans over medium-high heat. Pour 3 ounces (90 ml) butter/oil blend in each pan. Sear the hind legs for 2 to 4 minutes, until they're golden brown. Flip and repeat on the other side. Remove the browned meat to a large roasting pan. Next, dredge the forelegs, sear in the frying pans for 1½ to 2 minutes per side, and remove to the roasting pan. Finish with the flap meat, dredging, then searing for 1 to 2 minutes per side. If it looks like the flour in the bottom of the pan is beginning to burn, reduce the pan heat. Divide the onion, celery, carrot, garlic, mushrooms, tarragon, bay leaves, and remaining ½ teaspoon of salt evenly between the two pans and sauté, stirring to combine, about 1 minute. Deglaze with the wine, add the capers, and stir to combine, cooking 4 minutes. Add the stock, bring to a boil, and pour over the crispy meat in the roasting pan, making sure you don't completely cover the rabbit legs.

Cover the roasting pan with foil and braise for about 1½ hours, checking for doneness after an hour. Remove from the oven and let cool in the braising liquid. When cool, strain the liquid and discard the solids (these can also be kept if desired).

To finish the dish, combine the braising liquid and cream and reduce. Add the rabbit and heat through. Serve with pappardelle or other noodles.

Winter Root Veggie Potpie

MAKES 10 EIGHT-OUNCE (225 G) INDIVIDUAL PIES

When I was born, my mother was told by her appropriately named pediatrician, Dr. Kinder, that she should feed me a different color Gerber vegetable for every meal. Taking his word as gospel, she lived by this doctrine, and later swore to me that my love of vegetables and curiosity about food began then. I guess we could all adopt Dr. Kinder's words in our diet, making ours a Kinder, gentler, healthier nation.

This recipe uses many of the rainbow's colors. Dr. Kinder and my mother would certainly approve.

Note that this recipe calls for up to ten individual tart pans. Many cooks will prefer to make one large pot pie with this recipe and serve sloppy slices instead of individual pies. That is absolutely okay, just a bit messier.

For the brisée dough

12 ounces (340 g) all-purpose flour

1 teaspoon salt

1 cup (225 g) cold, unsalted butter, cut into 12 pieces

½ cup (120 ml) ice water

For the potpie

1 cup (225 g) dried chickpeas, soaked overnight in double the volume of water

¾ cup (170 g) unsalted butter, divided

1 medium-sized celery root (about 1 pound [455 g]), peeled and diced into 1-inch (2.5 cm) pieces

4 Red Bliss potatoes, scrubbed and cut into eighths (1-inch [2.5 cm] pieces)

1 cup (200 g) pearl onions, peeled

3 medium carrots, cut into obliques (quarter turns on the bias, ½ inch [1 cm] thick)

3 baby white turnips, quartered

1 pound parsnips, cut into obliques (quarter turns on the bias, ½ inch [1 cm] thick)

1 bulb fennel, halved, cores removed from each half, sliced ½ inch (1 cm) thick

MAKE THE BRISÉE DOUGH: In a food processor, pulse the flour and salt three to four times. Add the butter and pulse ten times, counting 1 to 2 seconds per pulse. With the motor running, add the ice water in a slow drizzle. Turn the dough out onto a clean work surface and, handling it as little as possible, mound into a disk, cover tightly with plastic wrap, and refrigerate for at least 30 minutes and up to a few days.

MAKE THE POTPIE: In a large pot, add the chickpeas and four times the volume of cold water. Bring to a boil over high heat and cook until al dente.

Melt ¼ cup (55 g) of the butter in a medium round high-sided sauté pan over medium-high heat. Add the next eight ingredients including the optional parsley root, if you like, and cook, stirring occasionally, until the veggies begin to turn golden brown, about 10 minutes. Remove the veggies, melt the remaining ½ cup (115 g) butter in the pan, and whisk in the flour, creating a roux. Cook, stirring occasionally, for 2 minutes. Add the stock and the next six ingredients, stirring occasionally, until the mixture thickens slightly, about 7 minutes. Add the browned vegetables, sweet potato, and black trumpets, and simmer until fork-tender, about 25 minutes. Add the chickpeas and raisins and simmer 10 minutes to allow the flavors to develop.

Preheat the oven to 375°F (190°C) and allow the dough to sit at room temperature for 10 to 15 minutes. Place 1 cup (235 ml) filling in ten 8- to 10-ounce (225 to 280 g) individual baking dishes or ramekins. Divide the dough into ten 1½-ounce (42 g) balls. Roll out each dough ball to ¼ inch (0.5 cm) thick and cut with a 4-inch (10 cm) biscuit

8 ounces (225 g) parsley root
   (optional)
1 cup (120 g) all-purpose flour
1½ quarts (1.4 L) vegetable stock
1 tablespoon chopped fresh
   winter savory
1½ teaspoons ground coriander
½ teaspoon cayenne pepper
½ teaspoon ground nutmeg
1 tablespoon salt
¼ teaspoon black pepper
1 sweet potato (about 1 pound [455 g]),
   peeled, quartered lengthwise, and
   chopped into 1-inch (2.5 cm) pieces
8 ounces fresh black trumpet
   mushrooms
⅓ cup (85 g) raisins, soaked in ½ cup
   (120 ml) orange juice for 30 minutes

For the final baking step
1 egg (50 g liquid egg)
2 tablespoons milk

cutter. Lay the pastry rounds over the top of the filling, tucking the ends into the baking dish. Whisk the egg and milk together in a small bowl and brush the top of the dough with the mixture. Score the crust with three slashes and place the baking dishes on a baking sheet. Slide into the oven and bake until the top is golden brown and the filling is bubbly, about 20 minutes. Let cool for about 10 minutes and serve.

The Incomparable Joys of Braised Meat

Downtown Portsmouth in winter boasts a certain snowbound charm. If the Public Works Department is on its game, the labyrinthine network of plowed snow walls makes being a pedestrian a kind of winter sport. As does surmounting the icy inclines of Portsmouth streets in cars with bad tires. If you enjoy shoveling out your snowbound car or drifting off the side of the road from time to time, you deserve to be in New England. These hearty souls constitute Black Trumpet's regular clientele in the winter. I love that people are willing to brave storms to dine in our cozy restaurant, and I especially appreciate those who have snowshoed or skied to our front door before the town plows have had a chance to clear the streets. As I may have mentioned, Black Trumpet boasts a soulful vibe and exudes a warmth that

our guests associate with comfort. It is my duty, then, to ensure that our menu follows through with this expectation. One way to guarantee that people will not be disappointed when they sit down to a Black Trumpet dinner in January is to fill the restaurant with the rich aroma of braising meat. All-day cooking is a hallmark of our kitchen in winter, and the caramelization of seared meat intermingling with the sweet reduction of booze and roots has been known to waft out our vents, carving an olfactory path through falling snow, and luring innocent victims into our upstairs wine bar. I have heard tell of urban chain restaurants pouring "flavor packets" of powder in their hood system to draw people off the street. Our marketing technique may be more wholesome and authentic, but the result is the same!

Braised Beef Short Rib

SERVES 10

Short ribs have appeared on half a dozen or so Black Trumpet menus. The marbled succulence of this cut can be prepared a few different ways—even as a seared steak—but I go back to braising it every time. Like shank, short rib melts in the mouth when braised, the caramelly reduction of its braising liquid clinging to the toasted crust of the reheated portion. Meatwise, this is the ultimate midwinter comfort food.

5 pounds (2.3 kg) beef short rib, bone-in
1 tablespoon salt
2 teaspoons black pepper
2 tablespoons olive oil
⅔ cup (150 g) medium-diced onion
⅔ cup (150 g), medium-diced peeled carrot
⅔ cup (150 g) medium-diced celery
8 cloves garlic
1 orange, halved and juiced, halves reserved
1 tablespoon chili powder
½ teaspoon cayenne pepper
½ cup (120 ml) dark beer
1 cup (235 ml) molasses
½ cup (120 ml) balsamic vinegar
4 cups (945 ml) veal stock (you can substitute beef stock or any other stock if necessary)
4 cups (945 ml) water
2 tablespoons butter, for finishing (optional)

Preheat the oven to 300°F (150°C).

Season the short rib meat generously on both sides with salt and pepper. Place a large, deep, heavy-bottomed pan over high heat. Add the olive oil and, when it begins to smoke, place the short rib in the pan in a single layer. Sear, undisturbed, for 1½ to 2 minutes, until golden brown and crusty. Flip and repeat on the other side. Remove the short rib to a large roasting pan and place the pan back on the stove, over medium heat. Add the next twelve ingredients to the pot, including the juiced orange halves, stirring to combine. Bring the liquid to a boil and pour over the short rib. Cover the roasting pan with foil and braise in the oven for 3 to 3½ hours, checking the progress after 2¼ hours. The ribs should be fork-tender. Remove from the oven and let cool slightly in the roasting pan. When it's cool enough to handle, transfer the meat to a cutting board and carefully remove the bones, cartilage, and fat membrane. Portion into ten pieces.

Meanwhile, strain the braising liquid into a saucepan, let it settle for a few minutes, skim the fat from the top with a ladle, and reduce over medium-high heat until the liquid coats the back of a spoon. Add the butter (if desired), stir to combine, and spoon over the short rib before serving.

Watermelon Radish
and Preserved Lemon Gremolata

At the risk of offending home cooks, most folks don't have in their possession sharp enough knives or the requisite skills to make beautiful gremolata (see the "Brunoise" sidebar), but I believe everyone can, and should, learn the basic culinary knife skills if he or she wants to execute food like a chef.

Gremolata, traditionally served with veal chops or other grilled meats, also tastes great on plump fish like halibut or grouper. On our menu, this particular gremolata garnished a braised beef short rib like the one in our recipe on page 77.

For preserved lemons, see page 16 in the "Building Blocks" section. If you don't have time to make them, preserved lemons are increasingly common, available in most specialty food stores, especially those with Middle Eastern products.

1 large watermelon radish, brunoised

1 medium shallot, brunoised

1 large clove garlic, minced

2 tablespoons finely chopped flat-leaf fresh parsley

2 tablespoons finely chopped fresh chervil

½ preserved Meyer lemon, the rind separated from the interior of the lemon, and brunoised (throw away the interior or save for a salad dressing or brine)

2 tablespoons plus 1 teaspoon olive oil

¾ teaspoon salt

Combine all the ingredients in a large bowl. Serve immediately, or refrigerate for up to 2 days.

Brunoise:
The Circle Gets the Square

The French have given the world some sadistic things (not the least of them being the marquis who invented sadism), but for inexperienced cooks the invention of the brunoise is right up at the top of the list.

For making gremolatas and mignonettes, this cut is important. The uniformity of cuts gives all the proverbial players on the field equal playing time on the palate, and the diminutive size of the cut maximizes flavor in a short period of time. And, a well-cut brunoise gives its creator bragging rights. When you serve a mignonette or gremolata at a party, you want to be able to boast, "Have you seen my brunoise?"

To execute this cut, and not your fingertips, follow these simple instructions.

For a shallot, top and tail the shallot, then cut it in half in the direction of the fiber. Peel the skin off both halves and place flat-side down. Parallel to the cutting surface, slide the sharp knife almost through the shallot four or five times in increments of ⅟₁₆ inch (0.2 cm). Now cut in the same direction straight up and down, at the same increment, again not quite all the way through the shallot. Finally, perpendicular to the first two sets of cuts, keeping your fingertips away from the blade, cut straight up and down to form tiny shallot cubes.

For almost all other vegetables, begin by "squaring off" what nature gives us in a spherical or cylindrical form, snacking on the scraps, saving them for dipping in hummus or other dips, or adding them to a vegetable stock. The resulting rectangular cube can then be easily cut in minuscule, even intervals to resemble the shallot brunoise in size and shape.

For the lemon rind in the gremolata recipe, remove the rind, lay it flat on the board, and cut into thin strips and then crosswise into tiny cubes.

Once you have conquered this cut, it's time to move on to the brunoisette, the only cut smaller in the Marquis de Sade's repertoire.

Beef and Beet Borscht with Nigella and Preserved Lemon Crème Fraîche

MAKES 16 ONE-CUP (235 ML) PORTIONS

For the borscht

2 tablespoons olive oil
1½ pounds (680 g) red beets (about
   3 large), scrubbed and quartered
½ pound (225 g) celery root, peeled,
   rough-chopped
3 carrots, rough-chopped
¼ red cabbage, rough-chopped
2 red onions, rough-chopped
12 cloves garlic, peeled
1 tablespoon plus 1 teaspoon salt
½ teaspoon black pepper
1 cup (235 ml) tomato puree
1 cup (235 ml) red wine
¼ cup (60 ml) red wine vinegar
1 tablespoon cumin seed, toasted
1 teaspoon nigella seed, toasted
1 teaspoon fennel seed, toasted
½ teaspoon ground cinnamon
Pinch cayenne pepper
½ gallon (1.9 L) beef stock,
   plus more for thinning
2 cups (475 ml) water
¼ cup (55 g) brown sugar

To garnish, per bowl

Leftover Braised Beef Short Rib
   (page 77), shredded and crisped
   in a pan with a pat of butter
1 tablespoon Preserved Lemon Crème
   Fraîche (recipe follows)
Pinch nigella seed
1 sprig dill

In a large heavy-bottomed pot, combine the olive oil with the next eight ingredients. Cook 5 minutes, stirring occasionally. Add the tomato puree and simmer 2 minutes. Add the red wine, vinegar, and spices; stir to combine. Add the stock, water, and sugar and bring to a boil. Reduce the heat to a simmer, cover, and cook for about 1¼ hours, or until the beets are fork-tender. Let the soup cool slightly, then puree it in batches in a blender until smooth, adding more stock as necessary to reach your desired thickness. Serve immediately with crispy short rib, crème fraîche, dill, and nigella seed, or let it cool to room temperature, refrigerate, and reheat over very low heat before serving.

Preserved Lemon Crème Fraîche

1 cup (235 ml) crème fraîche
1 preserved lemon (page 16),
   finely minced
Pinch salt

Fold everything together in a small bowl.

Valencian Orange Curd with Thyme Shortbread and Toasted Meringue

MAKES 1 SCANT CUP (220 ML) CURD, 3 CUPS (710 ML)
WHIPPED MERINGUE, 12 SHORTBREADS

Whipping things generally adds volume to them. This meringue is no exception. It is very hard to make a small amount of whipped things for this reason. I apologize if your household cannot go through the excess of meringue this recipe will make. Our staff has no issue whatsoever.

For the Orange Curd
1 tablespoon cold water
¼ teaspoon gelatin powder
2 eggs (100 g liquid egg)
2 egg yolks (36 g)
¼ cup (55 g) sugar
Juice of 1 lemon
Juice and zest of 1 orange, zest divided

For the Thyme Shortbread
2 cups (240 g) flour
½ cup (28 g) powdered sugar
½ teaspoon salt
1 cup (225 g) cold unsalted butter, cut
  into 10–12 pieces
¼ cup (15 g) chopped fresh thyme
Zest of 3 oranges, cut into long strips
  and chopped finely
Milk, for brushing the tops of
  the cookies

For the Toasted Meringue
4 egg whites (120 g)
1 cup (225 g) sugar
¼ teaspoon cream of tartar
Tiny pinch salt

MAKE THE ORANGE CURD: Bloom the gelatin by placing the water in a small bowl and sprinkling the gelatin evenly over the top. Let it sit for 5 minutes. Whisk the eggs, yolks, sugar, citrus juices, and half the zest in a medium bowl. Set up a water bath by placing 2 inches (5 cm) water in a high-sided pot over medium-low heat and bringing it up to a simmer. Set the mixing bowl on top of the simmering water and continuously move the liquid with a spatula until it thickens enough to coat the back of a spoon, about 10 minutes over low heat/lightly simmering water bath. If it gets too hot (if the liquid begins to bubble), remove from the heat for a minute, stirring continuously, then place the bowl back over the water bath and continue stirring. Add the reserved gelatin, stirring to dissolve, then remove from the heat and add the reserved zest. Cool to room temperature and refrigerate in a tightly lidded container.

MAKE THE THYME SHORTBREAD: Preheat the oven to 375°F (190°C). Grease a baking sheet. Add the flour, sugar, and salt to the bowl of a food processor and pulse to combine. Add the butter, thyme, and zest and pulse until the dough just comes together (about 15 seconds of pulsing). Scoop the dough out onto a clean work surface, mound, and press into a disk (being careful not to handle it too much). Wrap tightly in plastic and refrigerate until cold, at least 30 minutes or up to a day.

Remove the dough from the refrigerator and let it warm up slightly. Roll it out to ¼ inch (0.5 cm) thick and cut it into 1 × 6 inch (2.5 × 15 cm) rectangles. Halve the rectangles to get 1 × 3 inch (2.5 × 7.5 cm) shapes: dipping-cookie size. Place on the greased baking sheet and dock each rectangle with a fork, about five pokes per cookie. Brush with milk and slide into the oven. Check and rotate after 6 minutes. Bake 4 minutes more and remove when the cookies begin to turn

golden brown on the edges and bottoms. Let cool to room temperature in the pan and serve or store in a tightly lidded container for a few days.

MAKE THE TOASTED MERINGUE: Fill a 4-quart (4 L) pot with 2 inches (5 cm) water and bring to a simmer over medium heat.

Add all four ingredients to the detached bowl of a stand mixer and place over the simmering pot of water. Gently whisk the sugar/egg mixture until the sugar dissolves. Return the bowl to the stand mixer and, using the whisk attachment, whip on high speed for 4 to 5 minutes, until the mixture reaches stiff peaks.

TO ASSEMBLE: Place a small amount of the curd in a bowl. Top with a dollop of meringue. Torch the tip of the meringue (optional) and serve with two Thyme Shortbread cookies.

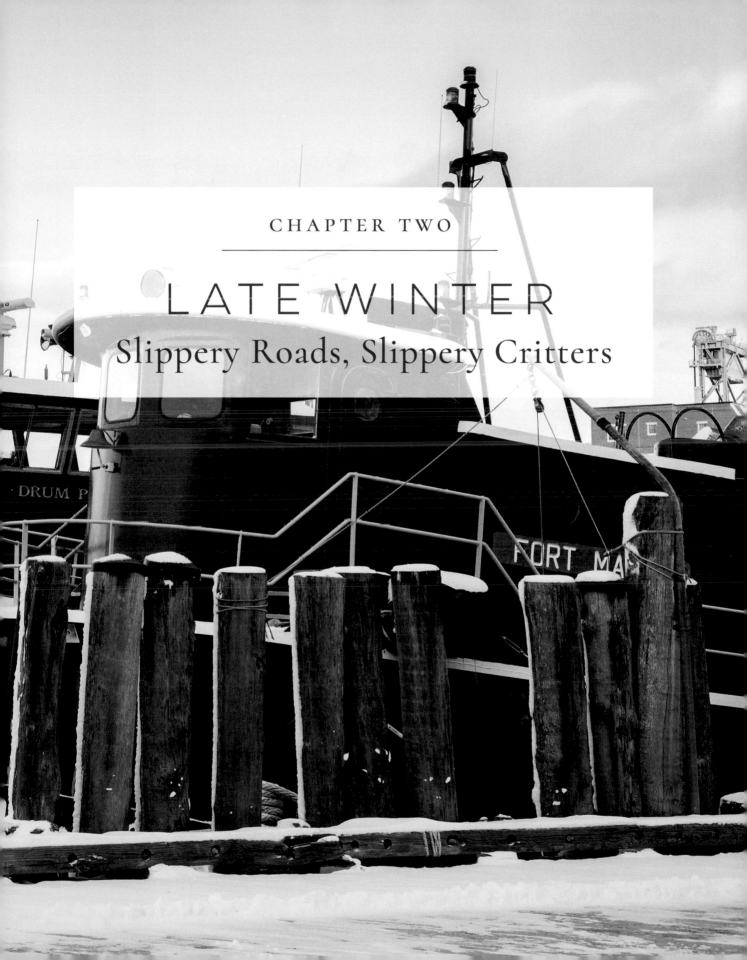

CHAPTER TWO

LATE WINTER
Slippery Roads, Slippery Critters

LATE WINTER RECIPES

As I've mentioned, we Yankees have been known to embrace each season with the knowledge that we are lucky to have four of them. We say it doesn't do any good to complain, and that's true, but we complain anyway. We cite the old saw, "If you don't like the weather, wait a minute." Also true. The result is a Yankee personality that can adapt to most any conditions. And that, I believe, constitutes the most desirable trait in a cook: *to adapt to most any conditions.*

As winter's major festivities overcome its minor brutalities, we find our larders at once nostalgic and expectant. Farmers and foragers hibernate. Fresh green food runs scarce. The pickles and preserves of summer fruits and the basement chest freezer's dwindling inventory conspire to remind us of the hardships our forebears faced. By comparison, our supermarket-centric food supply chain now boasts a luxury of plenty. From really far away. And that's not good. But it beats starvation.

To whoever stakes a claim that the local food movement is a trend, I defy you with all my heart, citing the sage admonition of Wendell Berry, that *culture* and *agriculture* are inextricably connected, and further pointing out that we are in the process of regaining awareness of our place in food, and its place in us, and must therefore through this awakening shed decades of prioritizing convenience over genuine quality of life. When we as a culture are able to fully recognize the value of food, we will have won a war against ourselves. This will be a landmark moment in history, and I hope to see it in my lifetime, but there is much to do!

This chapter highlights the few-and-far-between bonuses of New England in late winter. I have to say (and most Portsmouth diehards would agree) that, even as my longing for spring flavors surges with every passing day, those dark, cold winter evenings—with the smell of braising meat and stewed roots pervading the old brick walls—represent the most sacred, soul-warming season to enjoy Black Trumpet.

Black Beluga Lentil Soup

MAKES 6 CUPS (1.4 L)

This is an easy soup to make, and it serves as a great example of how vegan food doesn't have to be light or bland. Try this hearty spiced potage on a cold winter night.

1 tablespoon clarified butter/olive oil blend (page 13)
1 medium Spanish onion, small dice
1 stalk celery, medium dice
2 teaspoons salt, plus more to taste
¼ teaspoon black pepper, plus more to taste
½ teaspoon minced garlic
1 teaspoon minced peeled gingerroot
½ teaspoon ground cumin
⅛ teaspoon ground bay leaf
⅛ teaspoon ground caraway seed
1 quart plus 2 cups (1.4 L) vegetable stock, divided
1 Yukon Gold potato, peeled and medium dice
½ cup plus 2 tablespoons (150 ml) tomato puree
1½ cups (275 g) black beluga lentils

In a 4-quart (4 L) heavy-bottomed pot, combine the butter/oil blend, onion, celery, salt, and pepper, stirring to combine. Cook until the vegetables begin to soften, about 5 minutes. Add the garlic and ginger and cook, stirring, 1 minute more. Add the spices, stir to combine, then add 5 cups (1.2 L) of the stock, the diced potato, and the tomato puree. Bring up to a simmer and add the lentils. Cover and simmer, stirring occasionally, until the lentils are quite tender, about 35 minutes.

Remove 3 cups (710 ml) of the soup to the bowl of a blender and puree with the remaining 1 cup (235 ml) stock. Return the puree to the pot and stir to combine, adding salt and pepper to taste. Serve immediately or cool to room temperature, refrigerate, and slowly reheat over a low flame. Garnish with sour cream or yogurt, and thinly sliced hot chile peppers, if the mood strikes.

Pan-Fried Veal Sweetbreads with Lemon Caper Velouté

SERVES 12

Sweetbreads, a quaint term for the thymus gland of an immature animal, have had me in their thrall since my first taste of them. I am convinced that I will never again eat sweetbreads as good as the ones I ate at Susan Spicer's Bayona way back in the early 1990s, but that won't ever stop me from trying. This dish mixes sweet and tart flavors that buoy the otherwise rich and creamy sweetbreads.

We now live in a world where the home cook can buy sweetbreads online, and I believe everyone should have the pleasure of eating sweetbreads at home.

For the sweetbreads
2 pounds (910 g) veal sweetbreads
4 cups (945 ml) milk
3 quarts (2.8 L) poultry stock

For dredging and frying
¼ teaspoon salt, plus more for sprinkling
Black pepper, for sprinkling
1 cup (120 g) all-purpose flour
½ cup clarified butter/olive oil blend (page 13)

For the Lemon Caper Velouté
1 quart (945 ml) chicken stock (or substitute any poultry stock)
½ cup (115 g) unsalted butter
1½ preserved lemons (page 16), quartered, pulp removed, rind julienned
¼ cup (40 g) salt-cured capers, soaked 30 minutes in ½ cup (120 ml) water, drained
½ cup (60 g) flour
1 teaspoon chopped fresh thyme
½ teaspoon salt
¼ teaspoon black pepper

MAKE THE SWEETBREADS: Soak the sweetbreads in the milk for 24 hours. Remove to a medium pot with the cold poultry stock. Bring to a boil, reduce to a simmer, and poach for 3½ minutes. Remove the sweetbreads from the poaching liquid and drain in a colander covered with a clean cloth, weighing the sweetbreads down with a heavy can or brick to drain the excess liquid. When they're cooled to room temperature, peel the membranes and veins from the sweetbreads.

Preheat the oven to 400°F (200°C).

DREDGE AND FRY: Sprinkle the sweetbreads liberally with salt and black pepper. Place 1 cup (120 g) flour and salt in a large mixing bowl and dredge the sweetbreads, knocking off any excess flour.

Add 1 ounce (30 ml) of butter/oil blend to a 12-inch (30 cm) sauté pan over high heat. When it just begins to smoke, add some of the sweetbreads to the pan in a single layer (you should be able to do this in four batches). Sear about 1½ minutes, until golden brown and crispy. Flip, pour off the excess fat, and slide into the oven for 2 minutes. Remove from the oven, sprinkle lightly with salt, and repeat this process with the remaining sweetbreads. Serve immediately with velouté.

MAKE THE LEMON CAPER VELOUTÉ: Heat the stock in a small pot over medium heat and hold at a simmer.

Melt the butter in a medium high-sided saucepan over medium heat. Add the lemon rind and capers and stir to combine. Whisk in the flour until you get a wet, sandy consistency. Whisking constantly, slowly ladle the stock into the saucepan. Bring the mixture back up to a simmer, stirring often, until it thickens and coats the back of a spoon, about 20 minutes. Stir in the thyme, salt, and black pepper, and serve.

English Muffins

This recipe was a happy accident. In testing a burger bun recipe, we ended up with the perfect English muffin! When I was a kid, my mother would often make big fat burgers and serve them on little English muffins, so, according to my mom, this could be a burger bun recipe. You can follow my mother's lead here, or you can prepare the best from-scratch eggs Benedict ever. Your call.

2 cups (475 ml) warm water
  (about 105°F [40°C])
2 teaspoons active dry yeast
3 cups (360 g) all-purpose flour
2 tablespoons sugar
2 teaspoons salt
2 tablespoons melted unsalted butter
¼ cup (40 g) semolina flour

Pour the water into a small bowl. Sprinkle the yeast over the top and whisk to combine. Let sit 5 minutes. Pour the flour and sugar on top of the water/yeast mixture and pour the salt on the flour so it's not directly touching the yeast. Whisk the ingredients together until just combined. Add the melted butter and whisk until incorporated. The dough should be sticky and fairly runny. Place a sheet of plastic wrap directly on top of the dough so it doesn't dry out and let sit at room temperature for 1 hour.

Meanwhile, preheat the oven to 450°F (230°C). Add a baking sheet or pizza stone and heat for 10 minutes. Remove the baking sheet or stone from the oven, sprinkle the semolina flour on it, and, using a ladle, pour ½ cup (120 ml) of dough at a time, evenly spaced. Bake 5 minutes, flip, and bake 3 minutes more. Serve immediately or let cool and reheat. But enjoying them fresh out of the oven is best.

Pan-Fried Smelts with Meyer Lemon and Caper Aioli

SERVES 6

Like its distant cousins cusk, scup, cunner, and shad, the smelt bears an unfortunate name that I'm quite certain deters many would-be consumers. However, because it resides fairly far down on the food chain, it shares positive associations with herrings, anchovies, and sardines: Smelts are high in omega-3 fatty acids and—in many areas of the world—are relatively abundant.

Most smelts are packaged frozen and taste pretty good when thawed, but anyone who has eaten fresh smelts will tell you they are superior. Surprisingly mild, smelts can be substituted in most recipes for any faraway forage fish such as anchovies. I love anchovies in most any form, but smelts make a better introduction to small fish dishes, and they come from right nearby.

We served these fried fish headless and butterflied on a bed of lightly dressed shredded radicchio, but they would be just as delicious with any bitter or spicy salad mix.

For the Aioli

2 tablespoons salt-cured Moroccan capers, soaked in ¼ cup (60 ml) water for 30 minutes, drained and chopped
2 tablespoons (about 4 cloves) roasted garlic, chilled to room temperature
1 tablespoon Dijon mustard
2 teaspoons garum (see "Legal Fermentation Practices" on page 316)
2 egg yolks (36 g)
Juice of 1 Meyer lemon
½ teaspoon salt
¾ cup (180 ml) pure olive oil

For the smelts

1 cup (120 g) all-purpose flour
2 tablespoons cornstarch
1 teaspoon granulated garlic
1 teaspoon salt
¼ teaspoon pepper
1 large egg (50 g liquid egg)
1 tablespoon heavy cream
18 smelts, backbone removed (you can substitute sardines or anchovies)
2 tablespoons vegetable oil

MAKE THE AIOLI: Add the capers, garlic, mustard, and garum to the bowl of a food processor and spin until the ingredients form a paste. Add the egg yolks, lemon juice, and salt, and spin until combined. With the machine running, add the oil in a slow trickle to emulsify (it should take about a minute to pour). Adjust the salt to taste.

MAKE THE SMELTS: Preheat the oven to 450°F (230°C).

In a medium bowl, combine the flour, cornstarch, granulated garlic, salt, and pepper; whisk to combine. In a small bowl, whisk together the egg and cream.

Place a 12-inch (30 cm) frying pan on the stove over medium-high heat. Dredge the smelts in the flour mixture, coat with egg, and dredge again in the flour mixture. When the pan begins to smoke, add the oil and, working in batches, pan-fry the smelts in a single layer for about 20 seconds, until golden brown. Flip and repeat for 20 seconds on the other side. Slide the pan into the hot oven for 1 minute, until the batter puffs slightly, then remove and transfer to a paper-towel-lined plate. Repeat with remaining smelts and serve immediately over shredded radicchio or other roughage.

Yankee Collard Greens

SERVES 8

I went to college in the South and have since had the pleasure of working with a number of talented Southern chefs. I also harbor fond memories of childhood visits to my Carolina cousins. I established early on (and still maintain) that I could live on my cousins' biscuits, grits, and greens for three meals a day.

This recipe is about a 2 or a 3 out of 10 on the heat scale. Dial back the cayenne if you want less heat. We use an heirloom variety called Alabama Blue collards that, despite the name and Deep South provenance, has done very well in our garden.

1½ tablespoons olive oil
½ cup (85 g) bacon, diced into ½-inch (1 cm) pieces (about 3 ounces)
2 Spanish onions, medium dice (about 3 cups)
1½ teaspoons salt
½ teaspoon brown sugar
1 teaspoon cayenne pepper
2 bunches collard greens, washed and chopped into ribbons
2 tablespoons malt vinegar
½ teaspoon baking soda
1 cup (235 ml) stock (chicken, pork, and rabbit all work well here)

In a large, nonreactive pot, combine the olive oil with the bacon over low heat, and render the fat slowly, about 15 minutes. Add the onions and salt, stir to combine, and sweat for 10 minutes. Add the sugar and cayenne and stir to combine, cooking 5 more minutes. Add the collards, vinegar, baking soda, and stock, cover, and simmer 60 to 75 minutes, stirring occasionally, until the collards are tender and flavorful. Taste for seasoning and sweetness.

Borracho Beans

SERVES 10 TO 12

Of all the regional Mexican bean dishes, this one is my hands-down favorite. It is easy to make, especially if you are lucky enough to find fresh shelling beans. Two very similar New England heirloom beans, True Red and Vermont Red Cranberry, can be used fresh to expedite the cooking time of this dish.

Epazote, an herb that grows as a "weed" in Mexico and Central America, may be viewed as one of the great examples of dietary symbiosis in the world of food plants. It has been observed that beans and epazote grow well in each other's company because the chemical composition of one helps break down the digestive challenges that the other presents. In other words, if beans are the musical fruit, epazote is the mute button.

6 ounces (170 g) pork fatback, small dice (lightly smoked bacon may be substituted)
1 large red onion, diced
3 fresh serrano chiles, minced
1 tablespoon cumin seed
1 teaspoon dried Mexican oregano
1 teaspoon dried epazote
1 cup (235 ml) tomato puree
1 pint (475 ml) pale beer (not a hoppy one)
1 ounce (30 ml) mezcal
1 pound (455 g) dried yellow eye beans, soaked overnight (or substitute fresh shelling beans)
1 quart (945 ml) poultry or pork stock
1 teaspoon salt

In a heavy-bottomed pot, render the fatback for 5 minutes over low heat, then add the onion and chiles, increase heat to medium, and cook 3 more minutes. Add the spices and then the tomato puree. Deglaze with the beer and mezcal, scraping up any browned bits. Add the beans and stock, bring to a boil over high heat, reduce to a very low flame, and simmer for 1½ hours, or until the beans are soft. Stir in salt and adjust seasoning to taste.

Crispy Pig's Head Rillettes Cake

MAKES 16 CAKES

Pig heads are usually halved when we work with them, with brains and tongues removed. If you are able to find pig's heads, which I sincerely hope you are, you will find the meat from the cheek and jowl to be as delicious as any other part of the animal. Having said that, feel free to substitute a nice fatty pork shoulder.

1 pig's head, split, brains and tongue removed
1 pint (475 ml) ale
10 cloves garlic, peeled and bruised
5 bay leaves
2 tablespoons black peppercorns
1 tablespoon green peppercorns
2 stalks rosemary
4 ancho chiles, seeds removed
2 tablespoons salt, plus more for sprinkling the cakes
2 tablespoons brown sugar
1 small red onion, julienned
Pinch ground black pepper

Thoroughly rinse the head. Place it in a large pot with enough water to cover the head plus 2 inches (5 cm). Add the next nine ingredients and simmer overnight, for a minimum of 14 hours, over very low heat. At this point, there will be no meat left on the head and the jawbone will likely be floating on top.

Prepare an ice bath. Strain and reserve the liquid from the meat, spread the meat and bones out on a roasting pan, and let the liquid cool in the ice bath. When it's completely cold, the fat will have risen to the top and completely coagulated. Reserve ¼ cup (60 ml) of the fat and discard the rest. Reserve the remaining pig's head stock.

Shred the meat from the head, including all the jowl fat, and set aside in a bowl.

In a small pan, combine 3 tablespoons of the fat reserved from the stock with the onion over medium-low heat. Sauté until the onion is tender, sticking a bit to the pan, and just beginning to color. Add the shredded meat to the pan and deglaze with a splash of the pork stock.

Remove the pan from the heat and, when it's cool enough to handle, knead the pork-and-onion mixture, then form the meat into disks 2 inches (5 cm) in diameter and ½ inch (1 cm) thick, evenly dividing the fat in the pan among the meat patties. Refrigerate at least 1 hour.

TO SERVE: Place a 6- or 8-inch (15 or 20 cm) cast-iron or other heavy-bottomed skillet over high heat. Sprinkle the cakes evenly with salt and pepper and, when the pan is hot, place 1 teaspoon of the reserved fat and one cake in the pan. Cook 1 minute, flip the cake, and cook 30 seconds on the other side. Remove the pan from the heat, flip again, and let the cake cool slightly in the hot pan, about 2 minutes. Repeat this as many times as necessary, holding any finished cakes in a warm oven until they are all finished. Serve, either with a slaw and a pickle, or—for a heart-stopping soul food symphony—with Yankee Collard Greens and Borracho Beans (pages 92 and 93 respectively).

Head Foots
and Stomach Foots

I get asked quite a bit if I have a favorite food to eat. The answer changes, of course, as I continue to expose my taste buds to new flavors. But I can say with certainty that cephalopods—mainly squid, octopus, and cuttlefish—have propelled themselves to the top of my list of perennial favorites.

Cephalopods—whose family name translates as "head foots"—have meat-like qualities, take well to slow cooking, and lend their deep flavor to soups and sauces they encounter in the process. A richly braised octopus or cuttlefish knows no peer in all the ocean's realm, but squid is the tentacular delight Americans know best. In my childhood years living on Cape Cod, squid was used mainly for bait. My mother's boyfriend, an avid sport-fisherman, would use squid to catch dinner but would have never even imagined that squid could *be* dinner. Nearby households with Italian or Portuguese backgrounds knew a secret that he did not: Squid is abundant (read inexpensive) and, when properly cooked, can be as delicious as anything in the sea.

Naturally, I was chagrined to learn, in the early years of Black Trumpet, that most of the squid I was buying was coming from China. So I looked into it. And what I found was a shocking and seemingly wanton compound fracture in our food supply chain.

Going back to the Cape Cod chapter of my childhood for a moment, my first-ever outrage of this kind came when, in fourth or fifth grade, I toured an Ocean Spray cranberry bog on a school field trip. The Cape, being one of the country's largest natural cranberry habitats, takes great pride in its sovereignty over the quirkily astringent little berry that most Americans associate with Thanksgiving dinner. Cranberry bogs dot the coastal landscape and attract wildlife, which further enrich an ecosystem that is, in geological terms, essentially a glorified sandbar. The Cape attracts millions of people to its beautiful sand beaches and quaint towns, but let's face it, in a warming world with rising oceans, isn't the fate of the strip of land where these United States were born a little tenuous?

I digress. When I asked the tour guide on the fifth-grade trip where the cranberries were turned into juice, he explained that the fruit was shipped to Wisconsin, where the Ocean Spray facility processed and bottled the juice. "So," I pressed, "when my mom makes me drink cranberry juice, it's made of cranberries from here, but they have to go all the way to Wisconsin and back?" I remember dismissive laughter, a response to my questions I was all too familiar with. But the incongruity of the shipping equation really stuck with me.

So back to the early days of Black Trumpet, when I learned that one of the world's largest squid fisheries was just down the coast in Point Judith, Rhode Island—but then I noticed the diminutive font on the back of the 2.5-pound (1.1 kg) Rhode Island squid package that read PROCESSED IN CHINA—my childhood cranberry conundrum came flooding back to my brain. My consternation was heightened by the intervening adult years that had taught me much about the seemingly ridiculous modern food distribution system. Further inquiry revealed that I was buying squid from relatively nearby. Fishermen hauled squid in by the ton to the Point Judith docks, then packed it in all its inkjet glory in cubes that were then frozen and shipped to mainland China, where workers making unthinkable wages cleaned the squid and repacked them on an assembly line that added chemicals for preservation. Then, frozen again, the cleaned squid were ready for worldwide distribution, including back to New England, where they had begun their long journey to our plates.

At a fisheries workshop I attended in Woods Hole, Massachusetts, years later, I met a Rhode Island squid distributor who explained that the squid was once processed right by the pier where it was unloaded from the boats, but that the viscid ink effluent had clogged the town's septic system so badly that the residents voted to ban the processing of squid. The deal was made with a Chinese processor, and now Rhode Island ships almost all of its squid catch to China. Point Judith probably smells better and looks cleaner, but our inexpensive, well-traveled calamari is a lot worse for the wear.

In my years of trying to figure out why our food supply chain is the way it is, I have learned that deeper investigation can obfuscate the focus of one's outrage. This must happen to activists all the time. It's much easier to know a little and possess a lot of outrage than know a lot and be confused.

So there, I have confessed my feelings about cephalopods. I favor them over most other living food things. I respect the intelligence of the octopus, to be sure. We have a friend who worked as a diver at the New England Aquarium and retells the riveting mystery of a rogue octopus that was eventually caught slipping out of its tank to hunt and devour a preferred species of prey . . . in another tank! And I remember with both fondness and horror the dive instructor in the Bahía de Banderas off the coast of Puerto Vallarta who demonstrated the tenacity of the octopus when he surfaced from the depths wearing one, its body covering his mask, and the tentacles wrapped in an iron grip around his head. My children were slightly horrified by this odd prank. The instructor removed the octopus, laughed, and swam back to the boat, leaving us with a scarring image that belonged in a sci-fi horror film, but decidedly *not* on our family vacation.

While the "head foot" industry may have its issues, the "stomach foot" industry teeters on a sort of paradox; namely, that one European culture has taken the slimy bane of every gardener and farmer and turned it into a delicacy. Farmers hate slugs, yet—during one particular Farmer Appreciation Dinner (a semiannual celebration we host that offers half off our menu prices to all area farmers)—a dozen or so slug haters ordered Braised Snails with Mushrooms and Miso. Maybe eating the slippery sots was a sort of revenge for them.

Despite many efforts over the years, I have yet to find a garden snail producer in this country that puts out any kind of consistent product. In Burgundy, snails are so ubiquitous that one may romantically wonder—as I have—if the world's entire population of edible, farmed snails resides in the garish, fabled gardens depicted by the French impressionists. It seems unfair to me that France and Belgium should have cornered the market on the succulent, earthy, helical delights they call escargots

In wet years, a few of my farmer friends jest that they have enough slugs to start a snail farm, but otherwise only my pal Josh Jennings has looked into snail farming. Bewitched by photos from snaileries in Belgium, Josh briefly pondered touring the Belgian countryside in search of ideas (and, presumably, beer), but he snapped out of it when he awoke from a daymare (that's a daydreaming nightmare) with the image of thousands of voracious mucosal escapees devouring all the plants on the rest of his farm.

Because there are responsibly raised snails that taste pretty good after being canned, I continue to make an exception to our local sourcing philosophy every winter, when the requests for snails start trickling in from guests who count on Black Trumpet for their escargot fix. There is no better time than early February to make an exception to our "no cans" rule.

Periwinkles, an invasive species that may have come over to our shores on the wooden hulls of ancient Viking triremes, make a fine substitute, although they are considerably smaller. Whelks, the often overlooked scourges of lobster traps in the Gulf of Maine, may also be substituted for garden snails, but the briny flavor of whelk is quite a bit stronger, and the cooking time longer, so be forewarned.

Braised Burgundy Snails in Mushroom Madeira Cream Sauce

SERVES 6

1 small can snail meats, about 24

2 cups (475 ml) vegetable or chicken stock

½ ounce (14 g) dried black trumpet mushrooms

2 tablespoons olive oil

6 ounces (170 g) assorted fresh mushrooms (equal parts oyster, shiitake, and maitake), coarsely chopped

¼ teaspoon salt

¼ teaspoon freshly ground black pepper

1 carrot, peeled and medium dice

1 stalk celery, medium dice

¼ Spanish onion, medium dice

2 tablespoons minced garlic

½ cup (120 ml) Madeira wine

2 tablespoons chopped fresh herbs (1½ teaspoons each rosemary, sage, thyme, and oregano)

Splash heavy cream

1 tablespoon unsalted butter

Salt to taste

Open the can of snails and pour into a mesh strainer or colander under a stream of cold water. Rinse and strain thoroughly.

Bring the stock to a boil and pour it over the dried mushrooms. Let the mushrooms steep in the hot liquid for 5 minutes.

Heat a 12-inch (30 cm) high-sided pan over medium-high heat with the olive oil. Add the fresh mushrooms and cook for 2 minutes. Add the snails, salt, and pepper; stir to combine. Add the mirepoix (carrot, celery, onion), garlic, and Madeira, and deglaze the pan, scraping up the browned bits, about 2 minutes (until the alcohol scent wears off). Add the herbs and stir to combine. Add the reconstituted mushrooms and their liquid; bring to a boil. Reduce the heat to a simmer and cover, cooking 40 minutes. At the end of the cooking time, remove the cover and add the cream, butter, and salt to taste, stirring to combine. Serve immediately. Or if you're cooking in advance, remove the snails from the heat after simmering, allow them to cool to room temperature, and refrigerate. They can be held in the refrigerator for up to 5 days. When you're ready to serve, reheat the snails slowly in their liquid over low heat. When the liquid is hot and the snails are heated through, add the cream, butter, and salt to taste and serve immediately.

Sautéed Calamari with Harissa, Celery, and Preserved Lemon

SERVES 6

This elemental dish graced the first few Black Trumpet menus. It is one of the only menu items to make a comeback verbatim, as well as in a couple of related incarnations, because it is at once unusual and familiar, healthful yet indulgent, and always spot-on delicious.

12 squid tentacles
12 squid bodies, sliced ¼ inch (0.5 cm)
  thick into rings
Pinch salt
Pinch black pepper
2 tablespoons clarified butter/olive oil
  blend (page 13)
1½ preserved lemons (page 16),
  pulp removed and discarded,
  rind thinly julienned on the bias
2 stalks celery, sliced thinly on the bias
2 tablespoons harissa (page 16)
1 cup (25 g) loosely packed
  arugula, divided
1 cup (25 g) loosely packed celery leaves

On a plate, sprinkle the squid tentacles and sliced rings with salt and pepper. Heat a thin carbon-steel pan or wok (the point here is that it heats up quickly) over high heat. Add the butter/oil blend and, when the pan just begins to smoke, add the tentacles, tossing for 10 seconds. Add the rings and toss for 10 seconds. Add the preserved lemon and celery and cook, tossing to combine, for 30 seconds. Add the harissa, stir well, and cook 20 seconds. Remove the pan from the heat, add half of the arugula, and toss briefly to wilt. Divide the remaining arugula and the celery leaves evenly among six plates and divide the calamari mixture evenly on top. Serve immediately.

Mimolette Mornay

SERVES 8

Mimolette, a French cheese about the size and shape of a cannonball, uses annatto seed as a natural coloring, so has a bright-orange paste that, when aged and crystalline, takes on a buttery flavor akin to both Gouda and Parmesan. Nowadays, most of the Mimolette on the American market hails from Quebec, our neighbor to the north. You can substitute any aged orange cheddar for Mimolette in this recipe.

This sauce can be poured over pearl onions and baked in a casserole with bread crumbs during the holiday season, or it can be prepared as a sort of rarebit-meets-escargots, as we did on our menu one very cold winter.

1½ ounces (42 g) butter
1½ ounces (42 g) flour
½ onion, medium dice
½ teaspoon minced garlic
1 teaspoon salt
1½ cups (355 ml) whole milk
2 cups (230 g) grated
 Mimolette cheese
¼ teaspoon ground nutmeg
¼ teaspoon white pepper
¼ teaspoon paprika
Tiny pinch cayenne pepper

Melt the butter in a medium pot over low heat. Add the flour and whisk until the consistency is smooth and a nutty aroma appears, about 1½ minutes. Add the onion to the flour mixture and stir for 30 seconds. Add the garlic and stir, about 30 seconds more. Add the salt and stir to combine. Add the milk a little bit at a time, over medium heat, stirring constantly. As long as you add it slowly, the milk can be cold and it won't make the mixture clumpy. Continue stirring constantly until the mixture is smooth and begins to thicken, about 2 minutes. Add the cheese slowly, stirring constantly, until it has melted and is fully incorporated, about 2 minutes. You're looking for the color of the cheese to overtake the white béchamel and turn the sauce a beautiful shade of orange. Add the nutmeg, white pepper, paprika, and cayenne and stir to combine.

Pour the hot cheese mixture into the bowl of a food processor and pulse for 10 to 15 seconds. Scrape down the sides of the bowl and pulse for 10 to 15 seconds more. Strain the mixture into a bowl through a mesh strainer, using a ladle to push down the solid bits of onion and cheese. Serve immediately with braised snails and crusty French bread, or cool to room temperature and refrigerate for up to 5 days. The sauce can be reheated, slowly, in a double boiler over very low heat, stirring often with a spatula, until heated through.

Stuffed Squid with Sulfar Beans

SERVES 6

Home cooks, in my opinion, don't work with squid enough. Europeans—particularly in fishing communities—have developed techniques for working with squid that we see in American restaurants but rarely in home kitchens. Stuffing the squid bodies is one technique that appeared on an early Black Trumpet menu at around the time I came across Patti Qua's beans. Patti Qua founded The Beanery in Exeter, Maine, many years ago and has been growing and selling her organic New England heirloom beans ever since. The thin skins and big flavor of Patti's Sulfar beans make them the perfect paste bean for this application.

1 cup (225 g) dried Sulfar beans
  (substitute dried cannellini beans),
  soaked overnight in 3 cups
  (710 ml) water
1 quart (945 ml) cold water
1 cup (225 g) small-diced bacon
¼ cup (55 g) minced shallots
Tentacles from 6 squid, finely chopped
1 cup (150 g) small-diced stale bread,
  crusts removed
¼ cup (60 ml) harissa (page 16)
1 tablespoon dried oregano
¼ teaspoon dried red pepper flakes
Zest of ½ orange
6 squid bodies

In a medium heavy-bottomed pot over high heat, add the beans and water and bring them up to a boil. Boil, checking the beans for doneness after about 15 minutes. They may take anywhere from 30 to 40 minutes to cook, depending on freshness. The beans are done when they are mostly soft and barely al dente.

When they have finished cooking, remove the beans from the heat and drain. Set aside to cool slightly.

Meanwhile, over very low heat in a 10- or 12-inch (25 or 30 cm) pan, combine the bacon and shallots. Render the bacon until the meat browns and the shallots soften, about 20 minutes. Increase the heat to high and add the tentacles, sautéing quickly until they're just barely cooked through, about 1 minute. Return the heat to low, add 2 cups of the reserved beans and the rest of the ingredients except the squid bodies to the pan, and stir to combine, allowing the bread to soak up the liquid. Remove the pan from the heat and set aside to cool. When the stuffing is cool enough to handle, divide it among the six squid bodies and stuff them three-quarters full, so there's about 1 inch (2.5 cm) of unstuffed squid body remaining, as it will shrink considerably when cooked.

Place the stuffed squid bodies on a hot grill over medium-high heat, about 400°F (200°C). Close the grill and cook for 5 minutes. Remove the squid from the grill, let the stuffing cool and set up slightly.

Alternatively, preheat the oven to 400°F (200°C). Pan-sear the squid with a tablespoon of olive oil in a large pan over high heat, about 2 minutes. Roll the squid onto the other side, remove from the heat, and place on the middle rack of the oven. Cook 8 minutes, remove from the oven, and let cool slightly.

Slice the squid into thick rounds and serve immediately with any aioli.

Vuelve a la Vida with Totopos

SERVES 8

As a winter warmer, this dish—with its bright colors and flavors—may not make sense in theory, but its name, which refers to a hangover treatment, translates from Spanish as "back to life," so I have served it occasionally at Black Trumpet's pajama-friendly New Year's Day Hangover Supper. In the warmer climes of Mexico, beachside restaurants offer this dish with a mélange of seafood, and instead of tortilla chips for dipping, most places offer cellophane packages of *galletas saladas*, the equivalent of saltines. I have to admit, this pairing really works, but we at Black Trumpet are sticklers for making stuff from scratch, and masa harina (corn flour) is usually kicking around, so it's easy to make and fry tortillas. At home, you may want to consider the saltine route. Your guests may scoff at first, but only until they try the combination. You will certainly have the last scoff.

One last note: If you can only source baby octopus, keep in mind that they take less time to braise and make a stunning presentation, but they also tend to be farmed unsustainably in places where consideration of fair treatment and wages is virtually nonexistent, so I try to refrain from sourcing baby octopus for our menu. For this recipe, if you get a 4- to 6-count octopus, and choose to follow the recipe verbatim, you will have half an octopus left over. I recommend using the other half in the Octopus Strata with Chorizo Puree, the recipe for which follows on page 105.

For the sangrita
2 dried chipotles, seeded and stemmed
10 ounces (285 ml) tomato juice
5 ounces (150 ml) pineapple juice
Zest and juice of 2 limes
Juice of 2 oranges
2 tablespoons tamari
6 dashes Worcestershire sauce
¼ teaspoon Maggi (a popular condiment in Latin America)
¼ cup (55 g) sugar
¼ teaspoon salt
Pinch cayenne pepper

For the Totopos
2 cups (225 g) masa harina
½ cup (80 g) local heirloom flint corn meal (Cherokee White works well)
½ teaspoon salt

MAKE THE SANGRITA: Place the chipotles in a medium bowl. Add the remaining ingredients and stir to combine. Refrigerate overnight; remove the chiles before serving.

MAKE THE TOTOPOS: In a mixing bowl, mix the masa harina, corn meal, and salt thoroughly. Dollop the fat in the middle of the bowl and pour the hot water over the fat while working the dough with the opposite hand. Knead the dough until it yields a slightly crumbly ball. Masa is forgiving, but you have to know what to look for. If it is sticky when pressed into tortillas, the dough needs more flour. If it is dry and cracked, the dough needs more water. Even while working with batches of tortillas, the dough may require remoistening with wet hands. In the absence of a tortilla press (highly recommended), a cast iron pan, plastic wrap sprayed with oil, and a counter can produce the same result.

Divide the masa dough into balls, 1 inch (2.5 cm) in diameter. Roll the balls out to 5 inches (13 cm) in diameter, or flatten with a 6-inch (15 cm) tortilla press. Place an 8-inch (20 cm) cast-iron or other heavy

1 tablespoon pork lard or shortening

1¾ cups (415 ml) hot water

Vegetable oil for frying

For the Vuelve a la Vida

1 half of a 4- to 6-pound (1.8–2.7 kg)
    octopus

2 cups (455 g) Ceviche (page 205),
    made with about 1 pound fluke or
    other white fish

16 medium shrimp, peeled and
    deveined, boiled in salted water for
    2 minutes, then shocked in ice water

24 shucked oysters in their brine

4 ounces (115 g) Maine crabmeat or
    Chesapeake lump crab

2 cups Pico de Gallo (page 205)

2 canned chipotles, chopped

2 ripe avocados, halved lengthwise,
    pitted, and sliced ¼ inch (0.5 cm)
    thick, to garnish

Cilantro leaves, to garnish

frying pan over medium-high heat. Add the tortilla to the dry pan and cook 2 minutes. Flip and cook 1 minute longer. You're looking for the tortilla to puff slightly. If it hasn't yet, flip again and cook 30 seconds more. Remove to a plate and repeat with the remaining tortillas, stacking them to store.

Heat 2 inches of vegetable oil to 350°F (175°C) in a small, high-sided pot. Slice each tortilla into six wedges and drop these into the hot oil in a single layer (you'll need to do this in batches). Fry for 1½ minutes, until golden brown. Remove to a paper-towel-lined plate and sprinkle with additional salt. Repeat with remaining tortilla wedges. Serve alongside Vuelve a la Vida.

FINAL ASSEMBLY: In a large bowl, gently toss together all the Vuelve a la Vida ingredients except the avocados and cilantro leaves. Ladle the liquid and fish evenly into eight bowls, aiming to get roughly 2 ounces (55 g) ceviche, 1 to 2 ounces (28 to 55 g) octopus, two shrimp, three oysters, and 2 tablespoons of crabmeat in each bowl with about ½ cup (120 ml) sangrita and ½ cup (120 ml) Pico de Gallo. Garnish each bowl with a few slices of avocado, a handful of totopos, and several cilantro leaves; serve alongside the sangrita.

Braised Octopus

SERVES 8

This recipe calls for one mature octopus, 4 to 6 pounds (1.8 to 2.7 g). Look for Portuguese or Mediterranean octopus.

There are a couple of old wives' tales surrounding cooking octopus, which should be dispelled once and for all.

- "Add a cork to the braising liquid to tenderize the meat." (Having done it both ways, I can assure you it makes no difference.)
- "If you gradually drop the octopus into the boiling braising liquid, tentacles first, they will curl better," which makes them fit better in the pot than if you drop the whole thing in all at once. (In fact, if you drop the whole thing in at once, the tentacles curl anyway and you end up with the same product.)

There are several ways to tenderize octopus before it cooks. In Galicia and Sicily, I have been told, octopus fishermen beat the poor cephalopods against rocks before packing them for sale. However, in my opinion, octopus is best (and most humanely) tenderized by slow cooking.

1 mature octopus, about 4–6 pounds (1.8–2.7 g)
10 cups (2.4 L) water
3 cups (710 ml) dry white wine
⅔ cup (150 g) medium-diced onion
⅔ cup (150 g) medium-diced celery
⅔ cup (150 g) medium-diced carrot
2 bay leaves
2 sprigs thyme
2 sprigs oregano
Pinch dried red pepper flakes
1 tablespoon whole peppercorns
1 lemon, coarsely sliced
1 teaspoon kosher salt
6 whole cloves garlic, peeled
½ cup (115 g) tomato puree

Remove the octopus from the freezer and thaw in its package at room temperature for about 6 hours.

Bring all the ingredients except the octopus to a boil in a large stockpot over high heat. Carefully drop the octopus into the pot and bring the braising liquid back up to a boil. This should take about 5 minutes.

Turn the heat down as low as possible, ensuring that the octopus is completely submerged in the braising liquid, and cover the pot.

Simmer the octopus, covered, for 1½ hours. You can tell when the octopus is done because a tentacle that you tug will start to tear away from the body. If you choose to, for aesthetic reasons, you can peel off the outer pink skin of each tentacle, including the suction cups. This step isn't necessary; the head (minus the "beak") and the suction cups are all edible. It just looks a little better when it has been stripped of its outerwear.

From this point on, you can grill the octopus and toss it in a bowl with olives, cherry tomatoes, grilled bread, and arugula, or you can sauté the chopped tentacles with olives, artichoke hearts, and garlic, and serve with a teaspoon of lemon aioli. The braising liquid is also valuable, and some of it may be added back to the octopus when it is sautéed before serving.

Octopus Strata with Chorizo Puree

SERVES 16

After coming up with this dish on very short notice and baking a small demo batch, I insecurely offered a bite to Monica, our longtime general manager, and asked her if it was okay. She loved it, so I put it on the menu. Two days later, a restaurant critic ate this dish—one that almost didn't happen—on its first night on the menu, and gushed about it, so I include it here with the fervent hope that you, too, will find joy in it, as he and Monica did.

8 ounces (225 g) chorizo, sliced thinly on the bias

1 Spanish onion, julienned

1 Yukon Gold potato, sliced by hand or on a mandoline into rounds ⅛ inch (0.3 cm) thick

1 tablespoon butter (if necessary)

2 cups (400 g) ½-inch-diced (1 cm) stale bread cubes

1½ teaspoons fresh mixed herbs (sage, rosemary, thyme, chives)

1½ teaspoons smoked paprika

½ small octopus (9–10 ounces [255–285 g]), braised (see the Braised Octopus) and sliced thinly on the diagonal

10 eggs (500 g liquid egg)

1 cup (235 ml) heavy cream

2 teaspoons salt

½ teaspoon black pepper

In a medium-sized pan over low heat, render the chorizo until it is lightly browned, tossing often to color evenly, about 5 minutes. Remove to a large mixing bowl with a slotted spoon, leaving the fat in the pan. Add the onion to the pan and cook it in the chorizo fat, stirring occasionally, until translucent, about 5 minutes. Remove the onion to the bowl. Add the potato slices to the pan with the butter, if necessary, and cook until they soften and begin to turn a light golden brown, 2 to 3 minutes per side. You may want to cook these in two batches to ensure even cooking. Add the potatoes to the bowl along with the bread cubes, mixed herbs, paprika, and octopus; toss gently to coat. Transfer the mixture to a deep 13 × 9 inch (33 × 23 cm) pan, lined with parchment paper and coated with pan spray.

In a medium bowl, whisk the eggs with the cream, salt, and pepper. Pour the egg mixture over the ingredients in the pan and toss gently to combine. The liquid should come just to the top of the bread/octopus/chorizo mixture. If it comes up short, beat more eggs and cream and add until all the ingredients in the pan are just submerged. Cover the pan tightly with foil. Refrigerate 4 hours.

Preheat the oven to 375°F (190°C). Bake the strata, covered, for 30 minutes. Uncover and bake an additional 10 minutes, until the egg mixture is set in the middle. Let cool to room temperature, slice into sixteen pieces, and store in the refrigerator for up to 3 days. To reheat: Slice each portion into thirds. Reheat on a baking sheet for 10 minutes at 375°F (190°C). We served this dish with Chorizo Puree (recipe follows) and Black Olive Salpicon (page 298), which are like icing and sprinkles on this proverbial cake.

Chorizo Puree

MAKES 1 CUP (235 ML)

1 tablespoon clarified butter/olive oil blend (page 13)

4 ounces (115 g) chorizo, sliced into thin round disks

½ Spanish onion, julienned

½ cup plus 3 tablespoons (165 ml) stock (poultry, meat, pork, or vegetable stock all work)

Heat a 10-inch (25 cm) sauté pan over medium-low heat. Add the butter/oil blend and the chorizo slices in a single layer. Scatter the onion on top and reduce the heat to low. Begin rendering the chorizo, tossing occasionally to coat the onion in the rendered fat. Cook until the chorizo is fully rendered and beginning to brown, and the onions are soft, 15 to 20 minutes. While still warm, transfer the chorizo, onions, and fat to the bowl of a blender with the stock and puree until smooth, stopping occasionally to scrape down the bottom and sides of the bowl. The mixture should be smooth and spreadable. Serve immediately. Or refrigerate and bring back up to room temperature before serving.

The Duck Crusades

I think about duck a lot, particularly in the fall and winter. I love eating it, sure, but I think more and more about why it has become anathema in the American food system. Some people eat duck in restaurants, but very few cook it at home. I am told that cooking duck is daunting, and because it is expensive (relative to supermarket chicken), no one wants to experiment with it. I get that and am willing to excuse a certain amount of trepidation, but the truth is that duck is no more difficult to work with than any other poultry, so I strongly encourage home cooks to get their feet wet and dive into duck!

Perhaps because of my fondness for duck, I have a few experiences I'd like to humbly share:

Before I was a chef, when I was a tempestuous home cook with a passion for oddball ingredients but little knowledge of how to properly work with them, I made a trip to Boston's Chinatown to pick out a nice, fresh duck to whip up for a small dinner party. My friend Charlie rode shotgun. I mention Charlie because, were it not for a living witness, I would probably not admit that this story ever happened.

After spending a deliriously happy investigative hour or so scoping out Chinatown, I settled on a particularly attractive, freshly plucked bird hanging by the feet in a store window. It looked plump and perfect, but I wanted to be sure I had the best possible duck, so I asked the shop owner what kind of duck it was and where it came from. Charlie stood by, bemused no doubt, as the man vigorously nodded and smiled, saying nothing in response. There was to be a language barrier in our communication, it seemed, but I was determined to get the answer I was looking for. "What kind of duck is this?" I pressed. Nothing but gestures, a big smile, and more nodding—very agreeable, but not very helpful. After several more attempts, I had said the word *duck* enough times that the man had started saying it with me. Both of us were now smiling and nodding, I pointing at the bird the man was starting to wrap up in a bag, while he continued his mantra, "Duck duck duck," as though circling lotus-positioned kids in the popular childhood game. In the end, he showed me a number

handwritten on a scrap of paper, and I handed him cash in the amount written. It seemed like a good deal for duck. If it turned out well, I told myself, I would have to remember this place for future duck purchases.

When I returned home with Charlie to begin the process of cooking the fowl in some twist on the elaborate "Peking" tradition, I removed the duck from the bag and began to feel as though something was wrong. I looked at the bird lying supine on my cutting board and finally let my gaze fall on its feet. Charlie, standing next to me, was apparently engaged in a similar survey. "Hey," he blurted, as the very words were forming in my brain, "that duck doesn't have webbed feet."

"Yeah. Weird," I naively replied, slitting a piece of skin on the leg to reveal a pale buff flesh, not the rich mahogany hue I had expected. In life's most idiotic moments, when things don't go as expected, there is a stubborn refusal to accept error. In dire situations, this sluggish response time can lead to injury or even death. While Charlie let out a slow crescendo of rolling laughter, I stubbornly held on to the idea that this was a rare breed of pale-fleshed duck . . . with nonwebbed feet.

"It's a chicken!" he eventually managed to bellow between guffaws. Some friend, I think now. But we were cruel to each other, and that was part of our symbiosis that can only be found in twenty-something males of our species.

Indeed, language barrier excuse notwithstanding, I had driven forty-five minutes each way and spent an hour window-shopping for a duck, only to return home from Chinatown with an expensive chicken. Lesson learned. But my dancing days with duck were hardly over.

Early one spring nearly two decades hence, on a lightly researched whim, I bought a hundred fluffy, yellow ducklings.

Months earlier, while lamenting and pondering the lack of farmed waterfowl in our area of the country, I had tracked down the one guy in the United States who breeds a variety of rare duck called Duclair. He had recently moved his farm from New York State to Napa Valley when über-famous chefs—well, one chef at least—tasted his Duclair ducks and declared Duclair the finest of waterfowl menu fare. When I spoke to the elusive duck farmer, he shared with me that the breed was once the preferred duck in France, but for a number of reasons (none of them very good from my viewpoint), the bird was now essentially commercially extinct in its native country. So that meant that the farmer who had moved his flock out west was raising the most delicious duck on the market, but nobody—other than a handful of über-chefs—had access to these birds.

In a brochure the farmer sent me, the debonair Duclair, regal of stature and plumed in a slick brown coat with a silken emerald hood and a white tuxedo shirt, summoned me to buy a hundred duck chicks right then and there. I promptly phoned in my order.

When the duck chicks arrived, I divvied up and distributed the ducklings to two farms. The remaining twenty-five or so ended up at my house, where our chickens would later be not-so-psyched to share their already cramped coop. So with help from my dad, I annexed a duck coop that in turn featured an adjunct smokehouse. Friends and family soon tired of my joke about slowly smoking the ducks while they were still alive. The smokehouse was tightly sealed, I reassured their humorless faces, so there was no real threat of live-smoking our birds. *Hahaha*, I laughed alone.

After the ducks were full grown, and after their number had suffered a Darwinian loss due to infirmity, predation, and other sad facts of duck life, it became clear that the birds in no way resembled the royal Duclair in the catalog.

I went online. Duclairs in all photos looked the same: green head, white breast, brown back. Pretty straightforward—except for one photo that displayed a "Duclair" that was white from bill to tail, which was precisely what all our birds looked like. I clicked on the photo only to learn that the white Duclair was from the same farm I had bought my chicks from.

A series of phone calls ensued, and eventually I got an answer to why my Duclairs were white. It wasn't the answer I was hoping for.

According to the farmer, after teaming up with experts at the University of California–Davis, he was able to crossbreed his Duclair ducks with Pekins, the preferred breed of duck on American menus, which did away with the one factor that had most likely led to the downfall of the Duclair's popularity: dark feathers.

It seems that dark feathers on a duck leave the skin—even after assiduous plucking—flecked with unsightly dark spots. The fact that a distinct and delicious heritage breed may well not survive because consumers balk at the idea that their food once had feathers is absurd to me, and I will probably spend the remainder of my life trying to get this point through to people:

If you don't like thinking about what your food was when it was living, you should avoid that food. If that means avoiding rabbit because of a childhood pet memory, that's fine. If it means eschewing beef because of one eyelashed Bessie in a petting zoo, that is even better; we Americans eat way too much meat anyway, and we would do the world a big favor if we decreased our meat consumption even by a percentage point. Most Americans currently purchase food with a built-in mental wall that separates the ingredient from the source. We have become desensitized to the value that an animal's life has before it makes the ultimate sacrifice . . . for our nourishment. In my mind, we have to be okay with the idea of an animal being killed if we are going to eat meat. Period. Scratch that. Exclamation point.

How this pertains to Duclair ducks is simple. If people can't get past the dark spots on the skin where the feathers were plucked, or even some stray stubble where the feathers were not thoroughly plucked, we are ignoring the fact that we have taken that animal's life to make food.

Butchering Whole Ducks

Remove the two outside joints of the wing and reserve for soup stock. Unless you plan to roast the duck whole, remove the neck flap and reserve with the fat. Remove the legs by cutting into the space between the breast and the leg, using the tip of the knife to cut through the skin and joint. Be sure to include the sacred "oysters," located on the underside of the duck, leaving them intact on the leg. To remove the breast, slide your knife down the spine and cut carefully around the wishbone. Some people pull the wishbone out, but this can rip off some of the meat, so I take a little extra time to cut around the wishbone. Remove the tenders from the

breasts, saving them for other treats, and trim the breasts, reserving fat. Remove any silver skin from the flesh side and carefully "crosshatch" the skin side diagonally across the breast and then intersect those lines to create a checkerboard appearance. Be careful not to score so deep as to penetrate the flesh. Remove the base joint of the wing and set aside for a delicious snack, and put the cleaned carcass with the wings on a roasting pan in an oven to make a roasted duck stock.

A properly made duck stock will make any home cook swear off chicken stock for life. Duck stock boasts a richer, fuller flavor that can be used as a flavorful base for soups or as a reduction that will stand up to the boldest of red meats.

Over the span of Black Trumpet's existence, local duck farmers have become more plentiful and therefore more accessible. But we restaurant chefs have had to adapt our duck thinking somewhat to accommodate the differences between commodity ducks and local ones. On a local duck, the fat layer is much thinner than the very thick layer found on the majority of ducks sold in the United States, which means you need to treat it differently. Typically, we chefs like to score the skin on duck breasts to facilitate an even rendering in the pan. On a local bird, if the fat layer is thin enough, you may not even need to score the skin at all. The fat layer varies seasonally, breed to breed, and by how much exercise the animal had.

Seared Duck Breast

FOR 10 SERVINGS

Whether the duck breasts are local or commodity, and regardless of whether they are scored or not, it helps to lay them out in a refrigerator with the fat side facing up. In this recipe, we rub the flesh side generously with spices and refrigerate overnight, uncovered, to dry the skin.

For the rub
1 tablespoon ground mace
2 tablespoons ground star anise
2 tablespoons ground grains of paradise
1 tablespoon granulated garlic
¼ cup (40 g) ground coriander
Zest of 2 oranges

For the duck
10 5- to 6-ounce (140–170 g) pieces
  duck breast, boned and skin on
Pinch salt
Pinch black pepper
1 teaspoon clarified butter/olive oil
  blend (page 13) (if duck fat is
  available, use it!)

MAKE THE RUB: In a bowl, whisk the rub ingredients together until thoroughly combined.

PREPARE THE DUCK: Preheat the oven to 350°F (175°C).

Sprinkle the duck breast liberally on the non skin side with the spice rub. Let the breasts dry out, skin side up, in the refrigerator for at least 4 hours, preferably overnight. Add the salt and pepper to the spice-rubbed flesh side of the breasts. Heat a medium cast-iron or carbon-steel skillet, or other heavy-bottomed pan, over high heat. Add the fat and when it just begins to smoke, add the duck to the pan, skin side down. Turn down the flame and render, undisturbed, for 9 minutes. Again, this time will vary depending on the leanness of the duck and the amount of fat. You are looking for the skin to turn a deep golden brown and become fairly thin and crispy, which means that most of the fat has rendered into the pan.

Carefully remove most of the fat in the pan (and reserve it for confit), flip the breast, flesh side down, and place it in the oven for 2 minutes. Remove and let rest on a board for a few minutes before slicing thinly on the bias across the grain and serving.

Duck Confit

SERVES 10

A classic presentation of duck leg confit props an entire duck leg, crisped up after long, slow cooking, on top of a stew like the Provençal classic cassoulet. If I'm preparing the leg whole, I prefer to balance the heavy flavor of confit duck with something bright and tangy, like Bistro Bean Salad (page 256). However, the intensely flavorful, tender meat of confit duck can also be shredded and used more conservatively, as in the recipe for Duck Confit Phyllo Cigars (page 112).

For the cure
Zest of 1 orange
½ cup (75 g) kosher salt
1 tablespoon ground allspice
1 tablespoon chopped fresh thyme
2 teaspoons brown sugar
1 teaspoon ground black pepper
1 teaspoon ground cinnamon
½ teaspoon cayenne pepper
½ teaspoon granulated garlic
½ teaspoon ground mace
8 cloves, ground
2 star anise, ground

For the confit
1 quart (945 ml) cold duck fat
10 duck legs, cured in the rub
   (above) overnight

MAKE THE CURE: Toast the orange zest in a dry pan for 30 seconds. Remove it to a medium bowl, add the remaining ingredients, and mix well. Coat the duck legs evenly with the mixture and refrigerate overnight.

MAKE THE CONFIT: Preheat the oven to 450°F (230°C).
   Combine the duck fat and the legs, skin side up, in a large roasting pan. Roast, uncovered, on the top rack of the oven for 15 minutes, until the skins begin to blister and the fat is melted. Reduce the heat to 275°F (135°C) and bake for about 2 hours (checking after 75 minutes), until the meat is fork-tender.

Duck Confit Phyllo Cigars

MAKES 10 CIGARS

We have fought more than one battle with food vocabulary at Black Trumpet. Sometimes a hard-to-pronounce, inspirational (to me) ingredient or dish has such a mellifluous ring to it, I can't bear to dilute it for public consumption. Rachel Forrest, a local food writer, has made this her Black Trumpet mantra: "Every time I eat at Black Trumpet, I encounter a word I have never seen before." So when I originally put this dish on our menu, I called it by its Moroccan name—*briouat*—which refers to any phyllo or *ouarka* dough rolled into a "cigar" and baked. Knowing this was a very delicious dish that should be popular, and also knowing that our wait staff would have to answer yet another question about a confounding food word, I only let the sales suffer for a few weeks before changing the phrasing on the menu to Duck Confit Phyllo Cigar.

When we serve the cigars, we slice them on the bias and prop one half on top of the other. The first week after changing the phrasing, the dish's popularity doubled, and on the first night of the change, one customer complained rather loudly that the two bias-cut halves did not actually resemble a cigar in any way, shape, or form. I'm not sure if there was a lesson to be had there, but I know that people would rather take their chances on a food named after a tobacco product than they would a food with a foreign name.

Phyllo dough is readily available in the frozen-food section of most supermarkets. You can try to make it yourself, as we have, or you can surrender in advance to the idea that some things are best left to experts in their respective ethnic bailiwicks. After rolling out a mess of phyllo on a countertop, you might have trimmings, scraps, and a stuck-together amalgam of sheets you failed to get to in time. Don't throw these away; you can crumple them up on a well-oiled sheet pan, sprinkle cinnamon and sugar on top, and turn waste into taste!

For the duck filling

6 Duck Confit legs (preceding recipe), with reserved rendered duck fat from cooking
2 tablespoons clarified butter
2 red onions, julienned
1 tablespoon ras el hanout
1 teaspoon salt
½ cup (120 ml) red wine
¼ cup (60 ml) port wine
½ cup (75 g) raisins

PREPARE THE DUCK FILLING: Preheat the oven to 400°F (200°C).

When the duck legs are cool, shred the meat from the bone and reserve it in a medium bowl.

In a 10-inch (25 cm) sauté pan, add the butter, onions, ras el hanout, and salt over medium heat. Stir to combine. Cook for 4 minutes, until the onions have a bit of color but aren't burnt.

Reduce the heat to low, cover, and simmer for about 10 minutes, until the onions are soft. Deglaze the pan with the wine and port, scraping up the browned bits. Add the raisins, apricots, orange zest, and cilantro and simmer 5 minutes. Remove from the heat and let

10 dried apricots
Zest of 1 orange
¼ cup (15 g) chopped cilantro

For the phyllo wrapper
20 sheets phyllo dough
Rendered duck fat, for phyllo squares

cool slightly. Fold the onion mixture into the shredded duck, mixing to combine thoroughly.

PREPARE THE PHYLLO WRAPPERS: Meanwhile, working quickly and using a pastry brush, brush one sheet of phyllo with ¼ teaspoon rendered duck fat. Cover with another layer of phyllo and brush with another ¼ teaspoon duck fat. Repeat two more times, so you have a total of four layers of phyllo and the top layer is brushed with duck fat. Repeat this four more times, for a total of five rectangular piles, each with four sheets of phyllo. Always make sure to work as quickly and carefully as possible when you're handling phyllo, and cover the phyllo you're not using with a damp towel so it doesn't dry out and crack.

FORM AND BAKE THE CIGARS: Add ½ cup (115 g) of the meat-and-onion mixture horizontally across the (shorter) top and bottom sections of each phyllo rectangle, so there are ten piles of meat total. Using a sharp knife, cut each of the five sections of phyllo in half horizontally so there are ten separate pieces. Roll each piece tightly, allowing the contents to spread out slightly but still leaving about ½ inch (1 cm) of space on both ends. Brush a sheet tray with additional duck fat and place the cigars, seam side down, evenly spaced in two lines on the sheet tray. Brush the tops of each cigar with duck fat and place on the middle rack of the oven. Bake for 4 minutes, rotate the sheet tray 180 degrees, and bake another 2 to 3 minutes, until the cigars are golden brown and heated through.

Allow the cigars to cool slightly, trim off the frayed ends, and serve immediately.

Ryeberry Risotto

SERVES 12

This *ryerisotto* *tastes* like it was made in a traditional risotto manner, but wheat and rye berries don't contain the same starches as rice, so we puree the cooked berries to thicken the finished product, simulating risotto enough that we can get away with calling it that. Try this recipe with Seared Duck Breast (page 110), Cider-Glazed Carrots (page 283), and Date Orange Molasses (page 351).

¼ cup (60 ml) clarified butter/olive oil
   blend (page 13)
2 cups (370 g) rye berries
1 Spanish onion
1 teaspoon minced garlic
1 cup (80 g) chopped mushrooms
   (any kind)
1 quart (945 ml) boom stock (page 13)
2 cups (475 ml) water
1½ teaspoons salt
¼ cup (25 g) grated Parmesan cheese
¼ cup (55 g) butter

Pour the butter/oil blend into a large high-sided sauté pan over medium heat. Add the rye berries and onion and toast 1 minute, stirring. Add the garlic and stir, 1 minute. Add the mushrooms and cook 1 minute. Add the boom stock, water, and salt; stir to combine. Cover the pot and bring it to a boil. Reduce to a simmer for 30 minutes, or until the grains are springy but tender.

Ladle half of the rye berries with some of the liquid into a food processor. Spin for 30 seconds.

Return the pureed mixture to the pan and stir to combine. Simmer, uncovered, over low heat for 15 minutes. Add the Parmesan and butter, stirring briskly to combine. Serve.

Moroccan Chicken

SERVES 6

In the event that you return from a shopping trip to Chinatown with a duck that is really a chicken, here's one fun way to serve the bird. I will say that my insistence on using every part of every whole animal we buy has made exclusively sourcing local meat a reality for Black Trumpet, so I urge you to do the same. Chicken is expensive when it is raised by a local farmer, but when it comes to flavor there's no comparison: The local chicken will always defeat the pudgy, diluted, yellow-tinted bird from afar, talons down.

1 cup (120 g) all-purpose flour
2 teaspoons salt
1 teaspoon freshly ground black pepper
¼ cup (60 ml) grapeseed or peanut oil
One 4-pound (1.8 kg) chicken, cut into
   6 pieces (2 breasts, deboned; 2
   thighs, deboned; 2 drumsticks), all
   remaining bones made into a stock
⅔ cup (150 g) mirepoix (equal parts
   onion, celery, and carrot, medium dice)
2 teaspoons minced garlic
1 teaspoon minced peeled gingerroot
1 teaspoon ras el hanout
¼ teaspoon ground cinnamon
20 saffron threads
¼ cup (60 ml) sherry
2 tablespoons honey
Juice of 1 orange
Rind of ½ preserved lemon (page 16),
   coarsely chopped
2–3 dried apricots, chopped
2 cups (475 ml) chicken stock

Preheat the oven to 325°F (165°C).

Combine the flour, salt, and pepper in a medium bowl. Heat a large frying pan over medium-high heat, adding the oil. Generously dredge the breast, thigh, and drumstick pieces on all sides in the flour mixture, tapping off the excess. When the pan begins to smoke, add the pieces, skin side down, being careful not to crowd the pan (the pieces shouldn't be touching). Pan-fry for 2 minutes, undisturbed, until the chicken skin turns a deep golden brown. Flip the chicken pieces and cook for 1 minute on the other side. Remove the thighs and drumsticks, skin side up, to a small roasting pan and put the breasts aside, away from the heat. Add the mirepoix, garlic, ginger, ras el hanout, cinnamon, and saffron to the pan. Deglaze with the sherry, simmering for 1 minute and scraping loose the browned bits. Add the honey, orange juice, preserved lemon rind, apricots, and stock, stir to combine, and bring up to a boil. Pour the liquid down the side of the roasting pan, being careful not to cover the chicken pieces with the liquid. Keeping the skin relatively dry ensures that the skin will recrisp after braising.

Wrap the roasting pan with foil and poke a hole in the top to simulate a tagine. Place on the middle rack of the oven and cook for 25 minutes. Add the breasts, skin side up, and return to the oven, without the foil this time, for 20 minutes more. Serve immediately on a bed of couscous or steamed rice, or let the chicken cool to room temperature in the liquid and refrigerate for up to 5 days. To reheat, place the chicken and the liquid in a pan over very low heat and reheat slowly until the liquid is hot and the chicken is heated through.

Winter Flounder Roulades
Stuffed with Rouille

SERVES 8

Rouille is a semiancient Provençal bread, pepper, and garlic paste I first made with my friend Gary Strack when I helped him open his now revered Cambridge, Massachusetts, restaurant, Central Kitchen, in the last months of the last millennium. I have since played with a few takes on rouille, a recipe that is most commonly found as an accompaniment to Marseilles's greatest contribution to regional French gastronomy: the peerless fish stew known as bouillabaisse.

As Gary taught me, the key to a jaw-dropping rouille is finessing the puree so that the glutinous fried bread does not overpuree into glue itself. This can be avoided with simple restraint. Like an overworked bread dough, a rouille that spends too much time in the food processor will yield a gummy facsimile of the ethereal stuff the working ports of the Riviera gave the world.

The idea of rolling up thin and fragile flounder fillets with rouille as the binder can be attributed to then sous chef Carrie Dahlgren, one of the greatest workhorses to have graced my (or any!) kitchen.

For the rouille
6 cloves garlic
½ cup (120 ml) olive oil
10 ounces (285 g) day-old baked bread, or soft Pretzel Rolls (page 322), cut into large cubes
3 red bell peppers, roasted, peeled, and seeded
1 teaspoon salt
¼ teaspoon garum (see "Legal Fermentation Practices," page 316), if available (substitute one salt-cured anchovy if not)

For the roulades
16 flounder fillets, about 2 ounces (55 g) each
Salt
Pepper
Clarified butter/olive oil blend (page 13)

MAKE THE ROUILLE: In a large frying pan over low heat, slowly brown the garlic cloves in the olive oil for about 3 minutes. Add the cubes of bread (stale Pretzel Rolls add a lovely twist), and turn the bread over until browned on all sides, about 3 minutes more. Turn off the heat and let the bread and garlic cool in the pan.

In a food processor, spin the peppers until they are pureed. Add the bread, garlic, salt, garum, and any unabsorbed oil. Pulse, scraping down the sides, until the ingredients are incorporated but not yet gummy.

MAKE THE ROULADES: Lay the flounder fillets out on a large plastic cutting board, making sure the darker sides of the fillets are face up. Sprinkle each fillet lightly with salt and pepper, then spread rouille thickly on each fillet. Roll the fillets up tightly without letting the rouille ooze out. Store with the seam side down, covered, in a refrigerator until you're ready to cook.

Heat the oven to 400°F (200°C). In a nonstick pan, melt the butter/oil blend until it's just starting to smoke. Sprinkle the roulades with a little more salt and sear with the seam side down. Carefully transfer the roulades to a sheet of parchment paper sprayed with oil on a cookie sheet, keeping the roulades seam side down, and place in the oven for 5 minutes. Serve with shrimp and grits, or with the Chile Butter Sauce in the recipe that follows. Or with your doctor's permission, try it with both!

Chile Butter Sauce

MAKES ABOUT 1 CUP (235 ML)

I hesitated to put classic French butter sauces in this cookbook, knowing the amount of butter in the finished product would surely cause anxiety at best, coronary failure at worst. But the fact is that, like all fats, butter is delicious and satisfies one of our bodies' most elemental cravings. Taken in moderation, I would even argue that butter is good medicine for the ills of late winter.

1 dried brown meco chipotle chile, seeds removed, torn into little pieces
1 large shallot
1 teaspoon salt
1 teaspoon sweet smoked paprika
Pinch cayenne pepper
1 teaspoon dried Aleppo chile flakes
1 cup (235 ml) decent, dry white wine
Juice of 1 lime
1 cup (235 ml) heavy cream
¾ cup (170 g) whole, unsalted butter, cut into ½-inch (1 cm) cubes and refrigerated

Heat a nonreactive saucepan with the torn chipotle chile until the chile becomes aromatic. (Be sure to have good ventilation whenever you're toasting chiles!) Add the shallot, salt, paprika, cayenne, and chile flakes, and stir. Pour in the wine and lime juice, stir again, and let the liquid cook down until the pan is almost dry. Add the cream and repeat the process of reduction until the cream has thickened and turned a deep rose color. Turn off the heat and whisk in pats of butter one a time. The butter sauce should be thick enough to coat a spoon. Strain it into a container, pressing all the juices out of the shallot. The sauce can be kept in a warm place until ready to serve.

Loaf Kneaders
and Lumpy Ladies

One chef acquaintance of mine, before marrying long-time Black Trumpet pastry chef and baker Lauren Crosby, used to say that the biggest draw for him about noshing at Black Trumpet was knowing the breads he would be served with his meal were made in-house from scratch that day. He obviously had a romantic bias, but he also had a good point.

Seven days a week, we have always baked two breads for service, using conventional gas ovens with conventional hot spots. This is no small undertaking, and it is one I have never stopped appreciating.

When I first starting working in the kitchen at 29 Ceres Street, Lindbergh's Crossing's Chef Jeff didn't know exactly what to do with me, so he plugged me into the bread department, thinking he could teach me how to mix, proof, shape, and bake bread with proficiency. One could argue that, even today, eighteen years later, I have yet to acquire the level of proficiency that Jeff had hoped for, or that I require of my aspiring young bakers for that matter.

When I first started making baguettes at Lindbergh's, I would return home, utterly dejected, to my new bride, to whom I would bemoan my daily baking foibles. "Denise," I would report, "my baguettes looked like lumpy ladies lying down." Needless to say, Denise's support during this period of dismal self-doubt is the reason I stuck with cooking instead of throwing in the side towel.

It was around this time that I forged a connection (more like a marginally abusive relationship) with Paula, the Lindbergh's sous chef at the time. Paula has an honest, likable filterlessness about her, and two of my favorite insults she has lobbed at me over the years are, "You are a bad person who does good things," and "You should probably not be baking bread," I think I finally crossed over to Paula's good side when I made a mixtape for her (something friends used to do for friends in the halcyon days before playlists and Pandora) titled "Loaf Kneaders." The tape comprised songs written and performed by women. The "Lilith" movement was going strong at the time, and I knew Paula enjoyed listening to Joni Mitchell and Emmylou Harris. I also knew that the word *lady* evolved from the Old English expression for "loaf kneader." Hence, the title of the mixtape. Paula really liked it, and the etymology lesson. She herself went on to pursue a writing career. Since then, Paula has returned to Black Trumpet, as well as our heirloom garden and our spice shop, as an employee, and—like so many others on our staff—has performed just about every role in the back and front of the house that you could imagine.

The principal problem with baking for me is that it requires two traits I lack: patience and precision. I have always cooked by feel, adjusting as I go, and when I have to stop and measure, or wait for something to rise, or try to calculate the inevitable variants of humidity, altitude, and temperature (baking at 6,000 feet [1,829 m] in Mexico was a bit of a disaster), I go to my dark place, and no one likes a dark baker. Thankfully, I have been lucky to have always found youngsters who step up to the challenges of baking. Without them, Black Trumpet's bread service would be like that of most other restaurants, provided by an industrial outside bakery. Or perhaps worse, folks would be spreading butter on Chef Evan's "lumpy ladies."

Banana Cake

Better than any banana bread, and addictive beyond belief, this cake wants to be eaten with chocolate or pastry cream, or dare I say both?

1½ cups (180 g) flour
1 teaspoon baking soda
¼ teaspoon ground cinnamon
⅓ teaspoon salt
2 eggs (100 g liquid egg)
1 cup (225 g) sugar
½ cup (120 ml) vegetable or canola oil
3 bananas, peeled
¼ cup (60 ml) crème fraîche
  (or substitute sour cream)
1 teaspoon vanilla extract

Preheat the oven to 325°F (165°C).

Sift the flour, baking soda, cinnamon, and salt into a small bowl.

In the bowl of a stand mixer, combine the eggs and sugar and mix on medium speed with the whisk attachment until light and thick, about 5 minutes. With the motor running, add the oil in a slow and steady drizzle, to form an emulsion and keep the batter light and airy (this should take 1 to 2 minutes total).

In another small bowl, mash the bananas with a fork and fold in the crème fraîche (or sour cream) and the vanilla extract. Add to the mixer and blend on medium-low speed just until combined. Add the dry ingredients to the mixing bowl and fold in with a spatula until fully incorporated, being careful not to overmix.

Spray a 13 × 9 inch (33 × 23 cm) pan with pan spray, line with parchment paper, and spray the paper with pan spray. Pour the batter evenly into the parchment and bake for 35 to 40 minutes, until the cake has turned a deep golden brown and a cake tester inserted into the center comes out clean. Let cool to room temperature, cut into squares, and serve.

CHAPTER THREE

EARLY SPRING
Turning the Soil and All That Crap

EARLY SPRING RECIPES

The beginning of 2015 marked the snowiest winter on record for most of New England. On the home front, after climbing a ladder and shoveling off the 4-plus feet (1.2 m) of snow from our roof, my son and I jumped repeatedly into the drifted pile of snow below. We may never have a series of snowstorms like that again in my lifetime. The last time we did, Denise and I had just met. It was 1993. We both lived in Boston at the time, and the cars on her street in Back Bay were so deeply plowed in that the meter maids had to dig tunnels to give parking tickets to cars that had no hope of escaping their live burial. In Boston, meter maids and compassion have always been, and will always be, antithetical.

We occasionally have to deal with being snowbound, and winters like that one often bring about a less-than-rational euphoria when the first green things poke through the last vestiges of old, gray snow. A humbling reminder that we cannot and must not mess with nature, the record snows of 2015 stuck around well into April, causing especially loud rejoicing among the songbirds as they began their boisterous spring courtship.

Because of such absurd adversity, there is a sense among us Four Seasoners that spring is earned and deserved. Ironically or not, farmers and gardeners are so hell-bent on seeing the ground again, they trade in snow shovels for manure shovels before their back muscles have had a chance to weaken.

One of the most important rites of spring for me, my annual manure run goes something like this: I borrow or rent a dump truck. I drive to a horse farm in nearby Rye that features a miniature mountain range of well-cured horse poop of various vintages. If I am lucky enough to have, as I did one year, several volunteer trucks and shovelers, we can load several yards of manure for the garden in an hour or so. I drive the truck about 10 miles (16 km) to the garden, maxing out at 40 mph (64 kph), and dump the manure. Then I head to the sheep farm, where the not-quite-cured sheep dung is smoking hot in the cool morning air. At this point, I am lucky if I have any helpers remaining. (The novelty of poop scooping for a good cause usually wears off after the first round of shoveling.) So if I have to, I go it alone. Farmer Josh usually takes pity on me, and we will shovel away the next hour or so chatting about the travails of farming and cheffing, the crops about to be planted, and other symbioses between our two professions. I can't think of a better way to ring in the spring.

After enduring a long hard winter and a sometimes insulting early spring, we are greeted by the lusty chirring of mate-seeking amphibians, most notably peepers and wood frogs, their two-tone a cappella strains rising above all other sounds in a crepuscular crescendo. This is mating season for all things, sprouting season for perennial plants, and planting season for agriculturally minded folk like me. It is also this season that exposes one of the great Yankee challenges: mud.

By the time the ground is soft enough to turn, it is also soft enough to suck your boots off and digest unattended small children. More commonly, tractor and truck tires spin themselves into a deep quagmire from which only steel cables can rescue them. On the roadsides of northern New England, the "mud season" is literally marked by POSTED signs on temporary wooden poles that warn heavy vehicles to pass at their own risk. Our version of sinkholes, frost heaves thaw and leave craters about the size of a car wheel turned on its side. Navigating frost heaves like the ones commonly found in our neighborhood can be viewed as a sport worthy of its own video game, the prize for making it through being a pair of intact axles. My great-uncle Jack, after leaving the Northeast behind in favor of the milder San Francisco Bay Area, used to wistfully ask me if there were still signs for "frost heaves." For whatever reason, the things he missed most about New England were frost heaves and black ice, two of the things most of us would rather do without. Uncle Jack was a great man, but undeniably also an odd duck.

Fried Almonds, Olives, and Garlic

SERVES 6

Perhaps the simplest dish we ever created, this longtime favorite might merit its own chapter, replete with anecdotes of how it came to define the Black Trumpet experience for a whole lot of people. But instead of a chapter, I offer you a quick history of the beloved small dish and what you, the reader, really want: the recipe.

When I was a food writer in Boston in the early 1990s, I ate a meal at a minuscule restaurant in the famed North End that advanced my understanding of food considerably. The place was called Alloro then, and it had no more than five or six tables. The chef, a shy and strikingly beautiful woman named Suzanne Salter, had sent me out three dishes that night. One of them was the best spring pea soup I have ever had, and the others were soulful but refined takes on meat and fish that sent me reeling. Pure, clean simplicity seemed to be the secret ingredient in Suzanne's food, and to my palate the contrast with the cluttered and overwrought presentations that were then trending was a very welcome change.

Sadly for Boston, Salter left to pursue other dreams, and when she eventually touched down in Los Angeles, she laid the foundation for what would become a small empire of good food. Her first restaurant in LA, Lucques, became an instant hit, garnering praise from fickle Hollywood insiders, hipsters, and critics alike. I had the pleasure of finally dining at Lucques in the spring of 2006, as a biblical weather event was flooding our home and most of New England. Salter had married and changed her name to Goin, and she had just published her first book, *Sunday Suppers at Lucques*, the frontispiece of which depicts Goin holding a bowl of the restaurant's eponymous olives in one hand and a bowl of oily Marcona almonds in the other. Our meal began with an amuse-bouche of those luscious Lucques olives and almonds. The pairing of olives and almonds may have Spanish roots that predate recorded history, but nowhere had I encountered the pairing so soulfully executed as in that little dish at Lucques. Goin's ability to summon flavor from wholesome ingredients without ornament or excess has inspired me to think about cooking the way I do.

As I sat with good friends in a plush banquette at Lucques waiting to order food, noshing on the addictive olives and almonds, I pondered the notion of heating the olives and almonds in garlic and oil until the nuts and garlic had a perfect toastiness. In that instant, the soon-to-be-signature Fried Almonds, Olives, and Garlic dish was born.

When I returned to the postdiluvian state of emergency that was New England after Mother's Day, I began toying with the right combination of olives and nuts until I arrived at the following recipe.

2 cups (320 g) Castelvetrano olives (a bright-green, firm, buttery, brined Sicilian olive unlike any other)

6 cloves garlic, peeled and thinly sliced

¼ cup (60 ml) olive oil

2 tablespoons clarified butter/olive oil blend (page 13)

1 cup (140 g) raw, unblanched almonds

2 pinches kosher salt

½–¾ teaspoon coarse sea salt

Place the olives in a medium bowl with the garlic and olive oil, stirring to combine. Marinate at least 6 hours and up to 24 in the refrigerator.

Heat clarified butter/oil blend in an 8-inch (20 cm) cast-iron pan over medium-high heat. Add the almonds and salt and cook, shaking the pan occasionally, until the nuts begin to crack, 2 to 3 minutes.

Add the olives and the oil marinade to the pan. Make sure there's enough oil so the garlic and nuts are submerged while cooking. Cook for another 2 minutes, shaking the pan occasionally, until the garlic just begins to color but doesn't brown completely.

Remove the olives and nuts to a medium bowl and sprinkle with the sea salt. Serve immediately.

Saffron Pickled Quail Egg with Serrano Ham and Aioli in a Phyllo Nest

SERVES 6

This capricious spring dish was on the first menu at Black Trumpet, which opened in harmony with nature's rebirth, at least in theory (reality gave us a blizzard that nearly made the grand opening a worrisome whitewash). The effect of the small tapas-style dish is stunning—a tiny bright-yellow egg perched in an edible nest contrasted with the shaved ham. I imagine home cooks having fun with this one! Finding a source for kata'ifi and quail eggs is the biggest challenge. The rest is simple assembly.

6 quail eggs
¼ teaspoon saffron threads
   (about 20 threads)
3 whole cloves
¼ teaspoon grains of paradise
   (substitute black peppercorns)
¼ teaspoon dried Aleppo chile flakes
1 clove garlic, sliced thinly crosswise
¼ cup (60 ml) white wine vinegar
   (can substitute cider vinegar)
¼ cup (60 ml) water
2 teaspoons sugar
1¼ teaspoons salt
1-pound (455 g) package kata'ifi
   (found in the freezers of some
   Middle Eastern markets)
Olive oil and/or clarified butter
Thinly shaved ham
½ cup (120 ml) aioli (page 17)

Prepare an ice bath by combining equal parts cold water and ice in a medium bowl. Set aside.

Cover the quail eggs with cold water in a medium pot over high heat. Bring to a boil and set a timer for 3½ minutes from when the water first comes to a boil. When the eggs are done, shock them in the ice bath to arrest cooking. Peel the eggs and set aside.

Meanwhile, in a small, nonreactive saucepan, combine the saffron, cloves, grains of paradise, Aleppo pepper, and garlic. Dry-toast the spices over medium heat for 1 minute, shaking the pan occasionally. Toasting brings out the oils in the seeds and blooms the saffron. Add the vinegar and water and whisk to combine. Add the sugar and salt, whisking to dissolve. Bring the mixture just to a boil, then remove it from the heat and let it cool.

Once it's cool, pour the pickling liquid into a container (a pint mason jar or a recycled supermarket pickle jar works great). Add the peeled eggs, cover tightly, and refrigerate overnight. The pickled eggs are best consumed within 24 hours and will become tough after a few days in the liquid.

To make the phyllo nests, pull out a quarter of the kata'ifi from a 1-pound (455 g) box and unravel it enough to separate the filaments of phyllo. Arrange the kata'ifi into six "nests" on a sheet pan. Brush the nests with olive oil or clarified butter, or both, and bake at 400°F (200°C) for 4 minutes, or until the phyllo strands are golden brown and crispy. Remove from the oven and set aside.

Spread thinly shaved ham on plates. Place the phyllo nests on the ham. Spoon aioli onto the nests and level it out. Finally, put a quail egg on top of the aioli. Serve immediately.

Sweet Petite Frites with Sumac Aioli and Ghost Salt

MAKES ENOUGH FOR 8 TO 10 PEOPLE

These "Sweet Little Fries" are thinly cut sweet potatoes, almost julienned, deep-fried until starting to brown, seasoned with Ghost Salt, and served with a healthy dollop of Sumac Aioli.

Only in recent years have home cooks begun to realize the potential of sumac in their spice rack. Local staghorn and common sumacs make for wonderful forageable foods, but because they prefer highway-side drainage ditches and other highly trafficked areas, finding pristine sumac can be a chore, and picking through the seedheads and drying them for culinary use is no walk in the park, either. When we opened Stock + Spice, our retail shop adjacent to the restaurant, in 2014, we were surprised to find that sumac had a fervent following of home cooks who had previously only been able to find the spice online. Sumac is used a lot in Mediterranean cuisine and therefore has always had a place on Black Trumpet menus.

For the Frites
3 large sweet potatoes, hand cut into
⅛-inch-thick (1 cm) wands
Canola oil for frying
1 cup (235 ml) Sumac Aioli
½ teaspoon Ghost Salt

For the Sumac Aioli
1 cup (235 ml) Meyer Lemon and
Caper Aioli (page 91)
1 teaspoon sumac
Juice of ½ lemon

For the Ghost Salt
4 dried ghost chiles
2 cups (300 g) kosher salt

MAKE THE FRITES: In a fryer or stovetop pot, heat canola oil to 325°F (165°C). In batches, fry the sweet frites without overcrowding the oil for 5 minutes, or until completely tender and starting to brown. Transfer to a towel and sprinkle with ghost salt. Serve right away with Sumac Aioli or refrigerate and reheat later in a hot oven until crispy.

MAKE THE SUMAC AIOLI: Follow the directions for assembling the Meyer Lemon and Caper Aioli. Fold in the sumac and lemon juice. Serve immediately or refrigerate until chilled. This can be made up to 5 days in advance.

MAKE THE GHOST SALT: I firmly remember thinking we invented this product, until a few years later when one of my kitchen crew saw it for sale in a nearby downtown shop, thereby reinforcing my cynical belief that—at least with regard to cooking—anything worth doing has probably already been done.

In a mortar, muddle the dried chiles. Mix the chiles and salt in a bowl before transferring them to a sealable container. Seal the container for 3 weeks, stir, remove the smashed chiles, and store the salt. Throughout this process, and anytime ghost chiles are called for, work with gloves in a well-ventilated area and wash your hands and cutting boards thoroughly when you're finished. I definitely learned this the hard way.

Ksra (Moroccan Flat Bread)

MAKES 12 BURGER BUNS OR 4 FLATTISH BOULES

This bread requires a starter (see "Building Blocks," page 25). You can make an overnight starter if you don't already have one on hand.

If you leave the starter out at room temperature, it should be fed every day. When the water begins to separate out from the starter and turns grayish in color, this means the starter is dying and needs to be fed.

If you keep the starter in the refrigerator, it can be fed once a week (if using less often). It will keep indefinitely if you watch it closely and feed it when necessary.

For the overnight starter

¾ cup plus 1 tablespoon (200 g) warm, nonchlorinated water

1 teaspoon active dry yeast

2 cups plus 2 tablespoons (250 g) all-purpose flour

For the ksra

2 cups (475 ml) warm water

2¼ teaspoons (7 g) active dry yeast

2½ cups (300 g) all-purpose flour

½ cup (115 g) sourdough starter or overnight starter

1½ cups (170 g) wheat flour

½ cup (70 g) cornmeal, plus more for dusting the pan

1½ tablespoons salt

1½ tablespoons ground anise seed

1½ tablespoons harissa (page 16)

1 tablespoon Hungarian paprika

MAKE THE OVERNIGHT STARTER, IF NEEDED: Mix the water and dry yeast and let sit 5 minutes. Add the flour and mix until combined. Let the starter sit, wrapped, overnight.

MAKE THE KSRA: In the bowl of a stand mixer, pour the water over the yeast to dissolve. Add the flour and sourdough starter and mix with the dough hook on medium-low speed for 2 minutes, until fully combined. Cover the bowl with a damp towel and let rise 30 minutes.

Add the remaining ingredients and mix 5 minutes on medium-low speed. Cover with a damp towel and let rise 1 hour.

Preheat the oven to 400°F (200°C).

Turn the dough out onto a well-floured work surface. To make burger buns, portion the dough into 4-ounce (115 g) pieces and form into balls. Or make four large rounds. Dust a cookie sheet lightly with cornmeal and place the dough rounds on the sheet. Let rise 30 minutes.

Bake the bread on the center rack of the oven, for 15 to 25 minutes, depending on size, rotating halfway through. The bread should spring back when pressed and the bottoms should be lightly browned, with little color on top. Let cool to room temperature and serve.

Pine Nut Tarator

MAKES 1½ CUPS (355 ML)

Tarator is a sauce with origins in Egypt and Palestine, according to no less of an authority than Mediterranean cuisine expert and author Clifford Wright. Our version of his recipe is pine-nut heavy, which can be costly, so feel free to skimp on the pine nuts or substitute another favorite nut. Serve this spread with deep-fried broccoli or brussels sprouts, steamed green beans or asparagus, roasted carrots or cauliflower, or just dip ksra in it for a snack.

1 cup (140 g) pine nuts
1 tablespoon pure olive oil
½ Spanish onion, diced
¼ teaspoon salt, plus additional to taste
4 cloves garlic, chopped (about 2 tablespoons)
Juice of 1 lemon
Zest of ½ lemon
Juice of ½ orange
2 tablespoons tahini
1 tablespoon extra-virgin olive oil

Toast the pine nuts in a dry pan over low heat, tossing often, until they begin to turn golden brown. Set aside.

Add the pure olive oil, onion, and salt to a small frying pan over medium-low heat and cook until the onion begins to soften, about 5 minutes. Add the garlic and cook 1 minute more. Set aside.

Add the toasted pine nuts to the bowl of a food processor and pulse for about 10 seconds, until they're a crumb consistency. Add the onion, garlic, lemon juice and zest, orange juice, and tahini and pulse several times to combine. Scrape down the sides and bottom of the bowl and, with the motor running, add the extra-virgin olive oil in a slow and steady stream until the mixture forms an emulsion. Season to taste with additional salt.

Small Plates and the Chef's Meze

The restaurant opened in 2007 with a menu that was broken down into six sections: SMALL, MEDIUM, SOUPS, SALADS, MAIN COURSES, and CHEESES AND CHARCUTERIE. We quickly learned that our most devout fans would only select from what they referred to as the "top half of the menu," avoiding the MAIN COURSE section entirely so that they could enjoy a more diverse array of smaller plates.

Since the closing of Ciento in 2001, my thoughts about Portsmouth's readiness for the tapas concept had changed somewhat, and I believed enough people wanted grazing menus to merit the format described above.

To further encourage this menu-grazing mentality, I made "Chef's Meze Plate" the last item under the SMALL category on the menu. This dish, I explained to our staff, would change daily, featuring three little bites the chef had designed to coexist on the same plate. Little did I know that this would become our most popular dish right out of the gate, with the exception of Fried Almonds, Olives, and Garlic. People love to start their Black Trumpet experience with meze, which means "table" in Arabic and refers to the custom of presenting a platter of shared dips, spreads, salads, and finger foods, similar to Italian antipasti. Regardless of what is on the Chef's Meze Plate on any given night, guests still seem to enjoy the opportunity to explore our menu through the lens of a single small dish.

Homemade Ricotta

MAKES 1 PINT (425 G)

For a long time, I had trouble writing a recipe for ricotta that could be made by anyone in my kitchen. My technique, it turns out, was dependent on an acute eye for variable conditions that can't be documented. In other words, my ricotta recipe was no good unless I was the one following it. This is a phenomenon that occurs all too often in my kitchen, and one I'm sure other chefs can commiserate with. For this recipe, I couldn't settle for something unreliable, so—as has been the case on a number of occasions—I consulted Chef Mary Reilly.

Mary is a longtime Trumpet patron, good friend, and fellow chef whose restaurant, Enzo, down the coast apiece in Newburyport, was a treasure in its day. In a fortuitous chain of events, when Mary was losing a young cook, she called me up to find him a good home. Shortly after that, I hired Tim Cronin, who became the fourth Black Trumpet baker and pastry chef. Like so many other Black Trumpet veterans, Tim eagerly and capably filled positions in both front and back of the house.

Mary Reilly's intellect and passion for Italian cuisine continue to provide answers when I seek guidance with techniques, hard-to-find ingredients, and this, the perfect ricotta recipe.

4 cups (945 ml) whole milk
2 cups (475 ml) heavy cream
2¼ cups (535 ml) buttermilk, divided
Juice of 1 lemon
½ teaspoon sea salt

Combine all the ingredients except ¼ cup (60 ml) of the buttermilk and the sea salt in a large, nonreactive, high-sided pot over medium heat, stirring once to combine. Bring the temperature up to 190°F (88°C) (use a candy or digital food thermometer).

When the temperature of the liquid reaches 190°F (88°C) (the liquid around the edges of the pan should be beginning to foam), adjust the heat and hold the liquid at this temperature as best you can for 6 minutes. Turn off the heat and let the liquid sit in the pan for 10 minutes, undisturbed.

Meanwhile, fold a 12 × 24 inch (30 × 60 cm) piece of cheesecloth in half. Drape over a medium bowl and pour the remaining ¼ cup (60 ml) buttermilk in the bottom of the bowl. Soak the cheesecloth in the buttermilk for 2 minutes. This prevents the smaller curds from falling through the cheesecloth when it comes time to strain the ricotta, so you get a better yield.

Remove the cheesecloth to an 8-inch (20 cm) footed mesh strainer or colander and place the colander/strainer in the same bowl you used to soak the cheesecloth.

When the 10 minutes are up, gently pull the curds away from the sides of the pan with a wooden spoon, to make sure the whey is relatively translucent.

Using a ladle, carefully transfer the curds into the soaked cheesecloth, trying not to break up the curds any more than you have to (this is also why you leave the liquid undisturbed while bringing it up to temperature). Let the curds sit in the cheesecloth for 10 minutes. Lift the cheesecloth containing the curds out of the colander-lined bowl, tie together into a bag with kitchen string, and hang over the colander/bowl for 1¼ hours, to drain excess liquid from the curds.

Transfer the ricotta from the cheesecloth to a mixing bowl and, using a rubber spatula, gently fold in the sea salt just until incorporated. Refrigerate until you're ready to use it.

Ricotta Puffs

MAKES 18 PUFFS

We have served incarnations of this cheese puff on both our menu and our Chef's Meze Plate. When we make ricotta in-house, this "aftermarket" technique makes delectable morsels that pair well with just about anything. One of my favorite presentations included mango vinegar and roasted baby beets.

Unsalted butter, at room temperature, for molds
Flour, for dusting
1 whole egg (50 g liquid egg)
2 egg yolks (36 g)
2 cups (425 g) Homemade Ricotta (preceding recipe)
Pinch salt

Preheat the oven to 425°F (220°C).

Rub eighteen 1½-inch (4 cm) molds (1 ounce [30 ml] each) with butter and dust with flour, tapping out the excess. Place the molds on a baking sheet.

In a large mixing bowl, beat the egg and yolks with a whisk until pale and foamy, about 1 minute. Add the ricotta and salt and whisk to combine (about 30 seconds).

Fill each mold three-quarters full and slide the baking sheet into the oven. Bake, undisturbed, for about 10 minutes, until the ricotta mixture has puffed up like a soufflé and begins to turn golden brown on top. Serve immediately, as they will fall quickly.

Or let the puffs cool completely in their molds and, when you're ready to serve, reheat in a 425°F (220°C) oven for a few minutes until they're warm and slightly crispy.

Celery Buttermilk Dressing

MAKES ALMOST 1 QUART (945 ML)

This dressing keeps well in the refrigerator. I like to have it on hand in the spring and summer when garden vegetables are in need of a dip. This creamy dressing can also cool down a spicy baby mustard or mesclun mix topped with late-spring radishes. Or best of all, drizzle this dressing over whole fried fish with purslane, bacon, and a light pickle, as Enna captured in the stunning photo of fried herring.

2 egg yolks (36 g)
2 tablespoons Dijon mustard
½ cup (12 g) celery leaves
1 shallot, chopped
1 scallion, dark-green portion only
1 pint (475 ml) buttermilk
½ cup (120 ml) olive oil
¾ teaspoon salt
Pinch black pepper

Combine the yolks and Dijon in a blender. Add the celery leaves, shallot, and scallion tops. With the cover on and the motor running, add the buttermilk in a steady stream. Slowly add the olive oil until the vortex in the blender just begins to close. If you go too far, the dressing can be thinned with more buttermilk or a splash of water. Season with salt and pepper and serve or refrigerate.

How Does Our Garden Grow?

Strawbery Banke was the name given to Portsmouth by the first English settlers. The namesake plants that littered the wild riverbanks back then still poke through sidewalk cracks and bear their carnelian fruit every June. Many of the grounds and even a few of the houses from the colonial days stand as sentries of the old port, known then as Puddle Dock, where our scant remaining small fishing boats still unload their catch by Four Tree Island. On the modern site of Puddle Dock, the well-preserved plot of houses, walkways, and gardens bears the name of Strawbery Banke Museum, and it remains one of our country's most distinguished "living museums," replete with actors in period costumes churning butter, making barrels, and—of course—gardening.

For most of Black Trumpet's life, Strawbery Banke could not be spoken of without a mention of John Forti. John is a well-spoken, avuncular, joy-spreading minstrel with a love of old-time music, old-time farming practices, and good food. He was the horticultural director of Strawbery Banke from 2004 to 2014. As one of the founding leaders of our Slow Food Seacoast chapter, and as the outspoken voice of seed saving in our region, John did for heirloom seeds what John Chapman did for apples.

John was also one of the early local food activists who helped identify and promote the tenets of Black Trumpet. Needless to say, John was quite receptive when I approached him about maintaining a raised bed for the restaurant in his hallowed community garden on Strawbery Banke grounds. Restaurant staff and I maintained that bed for two seasons before Josh Jennings and I met to discuss a growth plan for our little Black Trumpet garden.

Josh, along with Jean Pauly, John Forti, Denise, and me, cofounded the Heirloom Harvest Project in 2011 in an effort to turn the proceeds of our annual Barn Dinner into something educational and self-feeding. The project thrived under the efforts of many volunteers and, ultimately, even created a paid position for a gardener who would document the growth of heirlooms each season.

These days, most chefs I know have some sort of garden. For that matter, with the recent DIY

(continued on page 138)

renaissance, most people I know are raising vegetables, fruit, and even poultry on their property, whether they rent or own. On the home front, since we first moved to southern Maine in 2003, my family has nurtured six raised beds, erected a hoop house (promptly perforated by an errant lacrosse ball weeks after its construction), built a smokehouse and a henhouse, and raised several generations of laying hens.

The growth of our Black Trumpet garden from a 4 × 8 foot (1.2 × 2.4 m) raised bed at Strawbery Banke to a ¾-acre (0.3 ha) organic plot on a real farm marks an evolution in our own awareness of ingredients and the stories behind them; but it also represents a paradigm shift in the consciousness of the average consumer. Our garden never would have grown if it didn't have the support of community leaders, volunteer staff, *and* consumers.

Chuck Cox—
The Quintessential New England Farmer

Veteran organic farmer Chuck Cox has raised more than a bounty of organic produce on his expansive property in Lee, New Hampshire. He and his wife, Laurel, have also raised a family of farmers and a community of supporters. At our first Heirloom Harvest Barn Dinner, to which we invited all the farmers who had grown out heirloom vegetables for the project, Chuck stood out in his sophisticated gentleman tweed, showing up with baskets of vegetables included in the growout.

Perhaps more than any other farmer, Chuck embodies the goals of Heirloom Harvest Project, his own legacy proving to be an heirloom unto itself. One of his children actively farms in Maine now, while another advocates for organic growing and small family farms all around the country. The entirety of the Cox family represents something you see a lot in our region: smart people with good ideas farming the land in responsible ways. Very few other areas of our country can boast such a high percentage of intellectual growers committed to both sustainability and community. As much as I take great pride in that distinction, I hope it changes soon, becoming more of the norm in the national farmscape.

The Miracle of Maple

What gives us gold in the spring and jewels in the fall? This is my feeble attempt at a riddle. The answer is, of course, the mighty sugar maple, whose sap reduces to the liquid treat we know and love as maple syrup, and whose leaves turn the deepest primary shades of yellow and red in the fall. These trees, although common throughout the Northeast, occur in the most dense profusion from southern Vermont through to the Canadian Maritimes. Their rambling bulwark of beauty draws endless tourists every year, hell-bent on catching the best array of color from a favorite overlook in the Green or White Mountains.

The thawing of these trees, and the sap that they ooze during a short window thereafter, mimics the thawing of our hardened resistance to winter. When the trees relax, we relax. Things start breeding again. Life begins again. The sugar maple tree, using this poetic license, therefore represents the true vanguard of spring. The flowing of its sap is our cue to let our guard down, if only for a minute, before mud season wells up below our feet.

Ryan Joyce, who is well known far beyond our local food community, grew up farming with his mom, Susan, and stepfather, Jim, at White Gate Farm in nearby Epping. R. J., as he prefers to be called, logged many years at Black Trumpet and remains one of the greatest legacies on our staff. Today he and his business partner, James—another Black Trumpet veteran—own and operate Louie's across town. They belong to a generation that has come through restaurants like ours and hung their own shingle, whether locally or outside our area. Knowing that these young entrepreneurs honed their skills at our place, and then followed their own dreams, provides one of the greatest satisfactions in running a restaurant, even if we create our own competition in the process. No one deserves success more than R. J. and his hardworking family.

My hardworking family and I captured the heart of spring in our hands one year when R. J. invited us to pull the buckets from dozens of maple trees on the farm and lug them through the mud to the sugar shack, where we watched our labor boil down to sweet gold bouillon before our eyes. One of my children lost a boot to New Hampshire quickmud that day, but we all gained a wealth of appreciation for the process that sap goes through to become the stuff of dreams.

Poultry Anthology

Any self-respecting New Englander of my vintage has been exposed at some point to the signature Yankee drawl of Marshall Dodge, the humorist who cocreated the "Bert & I" franchise. Bert & I were fictional Maine characters whose Down East yarns were immortalized in a collection of albums that anthologize lifetimes of Maine storytelling. The timeless anecdotes narrated by Dodge recall early radio entertainment and also pay tribute to the wit and wisdom that has marked the hardy, inscrutable Mainer since time immemorial.

One of my favorite Bert & I bits is "The Pet Turkey," and I can remember—in the mid-1970s of my early childhood—my grandmother playing the skit on her Radio Shack turntable. The tale follows a boy who inherits from his father the family tradition of killing the Thanksgiving turkey. The narrative is peppered with the refrain, "I looked at the bird, and bird looked at me . . ." In the end, after several attempts by the boy to perform the bloody deed, the father allows the boy to keep the would-be dinner as a pet.

Albeit couched in hilarity, the boy's conundrum is exactly what vexes anyone who has looked dinner in the eye and struggled with turning a beast into food. This is the very ethos that turned my son into a fully committed vegetarian at the ripe age of eleven. After years of raising laying hens for egg production, the creature that eventually turned my son into a committed vegetarian was, um, a lobster.

Our first two chickens were delivered to our house, either by the higher hand of Fate or by some nearby chicken farmer who had grown tired of the two birds, or perhaps it was an anonymous gift from a neighbor who foresaw us playing a foster family role to every stray chicken in our area. Our flock came with all the usual trials and tribulations.

Like the beleaguered boy in the Bert & I skit, we gave up early on raising meat birds. Our young children and my elderly father insisted on naming the birds, and we cared for them by building elaborate structures, and heating, lighting, and watering systems. This meant that we could not possibly behead and pluck the creatures we had come to distinguish for their personalities.

When a heavy iron gate loosely propped at the entrance to our home garden came off its hinges and fell on the leg of one bird, my father named it Spavy (an antiquated term, he explained, for a "club-footed gimp"). When I joked at the dinner table about euthanizing Spavy for our next meal, no one laughed. In fact, my children refused to speak to me for the remainder of the meal.

Since then, we have raised and buried many poults—chickens and ducks—who have given us sacred eggs in the most unexpected gestational rhythms. When our friend Garen (the same Garen who gifted the wooden crate at the front of the book) invited my kids and me to round up a few of the layers he was retiring, it made for a frenzied hunt, the four of us trying to outsmart captive birds with minuscule brains by cornering and barehanding them into a large dog crate. This exercise took hours and lingered into dusk. But eventually, we brought Garen's birds home, and although they did not lay with any regularity or profusion, they proved to be fighters, and they defied the odds by sticking around through a few predator attacks and more than a few weather assaults. These tough birds ended up being our last flock of layers.

Herbs, Calluses, and Creatures of the Night

In the mid-1990s, living in the cradle of transcendentalism known as Concord, Massachusetts, I had delusions of writing the definitive modern Herbal, an update on the colonial works of Gerard and Culpeper. So I ordered a bunch of weird herbs and planted the seeds at the end of my driveway in an amateurish eyesore of questionable soil. Instead of parsley, sage, rosemary, and thyme, I grew papalo, nepitella, shiso, Peruvian mint, rau om, and sweet cicely, among others. The origins of each herb, if connected as dots on a globe, might have made a fascinating map of world conquest. To my surprise, most of the herbs did exceedingly well, attributable perhaps to the fact that my friend Murph had built (and lived in) an igloo on that very spot the winter before, leaving remnants of campfire snacks to compost

in the soil. I never did write the modern American Herbal. It's a good thing, too, because I had a lot yet to learn about herbs. In fact, I still do.

Fast-forward to 1998, the year Denise and I married, and the year we decided to move to Portsmouth. As I've mentioned, a single meal in one of the window seats on the second floor of Lindbergh's Crossing tipped the balance for us. We had considered the move to Portsmouth and wanted to be closer to my ailing grandfather. We ate rabbit, drank French wine, and then we relocated to Portsmouth. It was almost that simple. I think back on the ease with which Denise and I made life-changing decisions in those years, and I feel drawn

to the idea that—in the postrestaurant, postparenting years—we might again enjoy a little caprice from time to time.

The first time I prepped in the kitchen at 29 Ceres Street, I was given a short handwritten list that included the words *chop herbs*. This made me happy, even confident, because I had developed a fondness for herbs that by then had run deep in my blood. Or so I thought.

Having been on a seven-year sabbatical from professional kitchens, I took on this simple prep task first, knowing that any dummy could make quick work of chopping herbs. I was determined to plot my course for attacking the remaining prep list while performing the mind-numbing labor of removing and chopping the tiny, individual leaves of thyme, rosemary, and oregano.

Whether I became entranced by the Zen nature of this task, or whether I was just plain slow, an hour of my shift passed by before I completed my first prep task. The eyes of young Chef Jeff beheld my pint or so of chopped herbs, and he flashed a big, nervous smile, which I misread to mean he was pleased with my work. The reality was, Jeff was wondering what kind of incapable moron he had hired.

Worse yet, my single hour-long task had produced a blister at the base of my left index finger. Among veteran cooks, this location on the chopping hand ultimately becomes a badge of honor we refer to as our knife callus. When cooks become chefs and gradually move away from the hands-on duties of cooking in favor of board-based office work (a term I use to describe the career phase that includes clipboards, keyboards, sounding boards, and advisory boards, but decidedly *not* cutting boards), they invariably watch in horror as their hard-earned knife callus begins to soften and, eventually, vanish entirely.

So with blistered hand shaking somewhat at this point, I moved on to find that all my other prep tasks involved some kind of repetitive chopping—julienned vegetables, mirepoix, brunoised shallots. . . . By the end of my shift, not only had I failed to complete my prep list—this is a serious taboo that can put any kitchen in a bad place!—but I was internally whining about the now bleeding blister the haft of my knife had carved in my soft, rookie hand.

There is no moral to this story, although I suppose it does have a happy ending if you consider the eventual ascent through the kitchen ranks that ensued, but I have to credit Chef Jeff and his patience with my domestic knife skills and rusty kitchen habits. I have often said that any other chef would have fired me at the end of that first shift, but Jeff saw something in me that I myself still look for in the eyes of young, aspiring cooks. I guess it is heart that I had, and that I seek, like a tin chef, in today's young cooks. It is a desire to learn, and to grow, and to improve every day, coupled with a humble awareness that there is always room for improvement.

After a few months of chopping herbs, vegetables, and lots of other ingredients, I developed a pretty rugged knife callus, and a sense of humility to match. I had worked my way up through the ranks; been named sous chef of short-lived but brilliant Ciento; moved with wife and daughter to Mexico, and landed what appeared to be a pretty sweet gig as executive chef of a Cajun-themed restaurant in San Miguel de Allende, a surreally picturesque colonial mountain town in the center of Mexico.

My wife, Denise, and I—always sensitive to the signposts on the sinuous path of our life together—had packed up our one-year-old daughter and moved to Mexico with relatively little forethought. After Ciento closed and Denise was laid off from a job she had no fondness for, change was imminent, nothing in particular was keeping us rooted to where we lived, and there was an opportunity to consult on a restaurant opening in a quaint, historic Mexican village. San Miguel, like Portsmouth, boasts a staggering array of restaurants that cater to visitors, English-speaking expatriates, and natives alike. The one I ended up in, called Harry Bissett's at the time, was definitely geared toward gringos.

In my interview, I convinced the two American owners that I was somehow going to learn Spanish and be a trusted leader in a kitchen with a staff of twelve diligent Mexican women and one shady American youth who was kept on staff because he was from Louisiana and had a few authentic Cajun recipes up his sleeve. One of the owners, lighting a cigarette and assuming a Bogartesque pose, asked me if I had ever eaten civet, a classic French dish of wild hare braised in its own blood. I demurred. We would laugh together months later when one of the many women on my kitchen staff would show up for work one morning holding a freshly killed jackrabbit by the ears. The women on my staff had ways of making my job difficult but always educational.

I became the rooster of the henhouse, learned to speak Spanish more or less fluently in six months, fired the Cajun kid after his drug problems led to theft, introduced a few dishes to the already massive menu, worked pretty much all the time, helped the owners open a retail gourmet store next door that would eventually be managed by Denise, and made friends with many of the people on staff. I attended *quinceañeras* (celebratory rites of passage for Latinas on their fifteenth birthdays), cooked for parties, and was even a groomsman at the wedding of the other owner, a gringo who was marrying a gorgeous Mexican woman. After the first year, I had fully immersed myself in the idiosyncratic cultural whirlpool that can only be found in expat enclaves like San Miguel de Allende.

Native populations throughout the Americas have for millennia incorporated into their rites some form of sweat lodge. In certain cultures, this looks like a large-scale, crude steam room under a tent. In central Mexico, the venue for a sweat lodge, referred to as a *temazcal*, is traditionally more intimate. Picture something like an adobe igloo. When Angel, the affable captain of the restaurant's front of the house, invited me to attend a ceremony at the local *temazcal*, I accepted without reservation. I wanted exposure to every aspect of Mexican life, which meant defaulting to yes when asked to participate in pretty much any activity my schedule would allow.

So when the day came to rendezvous with Angel in a protected park near a desert canyon a few miles outside of town, I had been prepping and working in the kitchen all morning, and I had not had a chance to shower before going to the *temazcal*. I would later regret this. Just before sunset, a group of about twelve of us converged outside the igloo, where a table had been set up with piles of herb branches—*tomillo, romero, salvia, lavandera*—all aromatic culinary herbs, most of which were on my cutting board that first shift in the Lindbergh's kitchen. The high priestess of the ceremony was a woman named Tati, and she spoke English with a pacifying cadence that immediately put the few gringos in the group at ease.

Our first assignment, Tati explained, was to pick the herb leaves from their stems. Everyone was handed a sheaf of herbs, and we sat cross-legged around the table picking the leaves while Tati and a beefy Mexican man began loading a pile of hot stones into the igloo. Before long, I had completed my sheaf, with a neat stack of stems laid alongside the pile of leaves. I looked up for the first time, breaking the Buddhist bubble only

tedious repetition can create, to find that everyone else had just tiny piles of herb leaves. Maybe five minutes had gone by, and the other participants had almost nothing to show for their efforts. They were like I was that first day in the Lindbergh's kitchen. Now, as my gaze rose past the participants to Tati, I noticed that she was looking at me in awe. "You did that so fast," she said. "But this is supposed to be relaxing!" Now incapable of doing this kind of prep work slowly, I explained to her that I was a chef, and everyone in the herb-picking klatch nodded in unison. Without further words, Tati delivered a huge pile of unpicked herbs to the space on the table directly in front of me. "It is not a race," she scolded, and then laughed a beautiful, pattering laugh that sounded like desert rain.

Relieved that she wasn't upset with me, I went back to work, and this time I was acutely aware that the others in the group were looking on in disbelief as my hands stripped the leaves from the stems in a flurry. Soon, we all had piles in front of us, mine significantly larger than the others. Tati instructed us to rise, which we did, and then she doled out the herb branches we had denuded, which she explained would begin the process of cleansing our bodies and spirits of toxins. After a demonstration from Tati and the large man, we stripped down to our bathing suits and began to brush one another from head to toe with the stems. We were invited to brush ourselves in places we did not want to be brushed by others. The leaves we had picked from the stems, according to Tati, were going to be thrown on the hot stones throughout the ceremony.

Once the sun had set and the internal temperature of the *temazcal* hut had reached supersauna proportions, we ducked one by one through the doorway and found seats side by side in a semicircle around the central fire pit. Minutes passed, and then more minutes, as we silently meditated, and as the temperature climbed to the limits of human tolerance. This was when the aromas of not only what I had recently eaten, but also all the food I hade chopped, peeled, butchered, and portioned earlier that day, began to emanate from my pores like a glowing toxic plasma. I was certain that my body's contribution to the olfactory miasma that had developed in the igloo was unmistakably attributable to me and therefore indelibly linked to my identity for the rest of my life. I wanted to stop the ceremony and scream, *I have never smelled like this in my life!* But Tati (was it me, or was she throwing extra handfuls of herbs on my side of the fire pit?) broke up my self-conscious anxiety by commencing an extemporaneous chant. A low moan, a haunting spiritual dirge, a rhythmic pulse so primal and guttural as to fit right in to the scene. Someone to my right chimed in with a higher-pitched whine, neither shrill nor offensive. Then another voice. And soon, without any rehearsals, we had a full-on a capella hoedown going on.

It was in the dizzying denouement of this moment that I sensed something scratching at my lower back. It felt like a short thorny shrub was brushing up against my sweat-drenched skin. I tried to ignore it at first. But it proceeded to move up my back, extending the area of contact to most of my back and shoulder blades. I dismissed the idea that it might be an herb stem from our earlier cleansing ritual; it was too big and decidedly lacking in herbal aromatics. Soon I further dismissed the idea that it was a plant of any kind.

Significantly regretful of every bad choice I had made in my life to date, and whispering undeliverable promises to the tribal deities who were listening to our chant, I opted to tap my friend Angel on the leg. He was sitting cross-legged to my immediate left, enjoying the interconnected spirituality of the moment. I had startled him, but I could see his somewhat demonic silhouette in the dark. I leaned slightly in his direction and, despite the darkness in the igloo, asked him if I had

something on my back or if I was hallucinating from heatstroke and lack of oxygen.

Angel later explained to me what transpired in the next few seconds, because to me it was essentially a clip from a foreign art-house film. Angel stood up quickly, hitting his head on the inside of the igloo. He called a halt to the chanting and the peaceful proceedings, alerted Tati that I had something on my back. Tati and the large guy next to her tottered over to me, flicking an enormous horned lizard, perched like a pirate's parrot, off my left shoulder. Evidently, it was perched there, basking no doubt in my primordial scent, puffed up in a defensive posture that defied any human to knock it off. By the time the lizard hit the sand floor, an exodus from the igloo was well under way. We regrouped outside, Tati having recovered her composure but still wielding a flashlight like a handgun. When I located Angel in the dark, he was laughing hysterically. He patted me on the back, right where the lizard had been, and assured me that he would never in his life forget those few seconds. I assured him that I felt the same way.

Once the reptile was removed from the hut, we reentered and finished the ritual. Afterward, Tati pulled me aside to say that it was a sign. Thinking she meant a sign of the devil, I asked her defensively, "A sign of what?"

"A sign that you have a deep communion with nature. You are very lucky."

I like this quote I found when I located a field guide with a description of the reptile that climbed my back: "To the uninitiated, their dragon-like appearance is quite formidable." Yes, it certainly is. And yes, I am lucky.

Tea-Smoked Young Chicken

MAKES 3 BIRDS FOR 6 PEOPLE

The French call spring chickens *poussins*. Both the English and French terms simply refer to young birds that weigh about half of their fully mature potential. The meat on these young chickens is sweet and tender, perfect for serving half a bird per person. If you can't find *poussins*, most markets offer Rock Cornish game hens. They will do nicely.

This particular brine should be used only if you're smoking the birds per this recipe. If you want to roast the birds instead, use Bird Brine (page 295).

For the brine
1 quart (945 ml) water
½ cup (75 g) salt
2 tablespoons sugar
5 sprigs thyme
2 bay leaves
2 tablespoons loose dried Lapsang souchong tea leaves
2 cups (475 ml) ice cubes
3 *poussins* or Rock Cornish game hens

For smoking
1 cup (170 g) applewood chips
¼ cup (12 g) loose dried black tea leaves

This technique for brining is what I call a quick brine, and it allows the process of brining, smoking, and roasting a bird to happen all in one day.

MAKE THE BRINE: In a saucepan, bring the first six brine ingredients to a boil. Turn off the burner, whisk well until the sugar and salt are dissolved. Add the ice to the pan and let the mixture cool completely. Put the hens in a deep casserole dish and cover with brine. Refrigerate for 3 hours.

SMOKE THE BIRDS: If you don't have a dedicated smoker, you can use a Weber-style grill or even a gas stove, as long as you have sufficient ventilation. If you're using a stove, as we do in the restaurant, line a roasting pan with aluminum foil and place the wood chips and black tea leaves on the foil where they will be directly over the burner. Then place a perforated insert pan, broiling pan, or grill grate on top of the chips.

Again ensuring proper ventilation, put the birds breast side up on the rack, wrap the pan tightly with foil, poking a few small holes in the foil with the tip of a knife, and place the pan over a high flame for 5 minutes. Lower the flame and keep the pan covered for another 5 minutes. Turn off the flame and continue to keep covered 5 more minutes.

At this point, you can either stuff the birds or leave them as is, but they need to be seasoned lightly on the skin and seared in a hot pan with oil, then finished in a 450°F (230°C) oven for about 10 minutes.

On our menu, we made a sausage forcemeat and mixed it with 'nduja, an Italian salumi spread that we had on hand. The stuffing was unexpectedly scrumptious. For a sweet-and-savory main course, serve the birds family style with Peach Brioche Bread Pudding (page 272) or with sunchoke red rice (as it was on our menu).

Pork Schnitzel with Pretzel Spätzle

SERVES 8

When conjuring this medium-sized dish, I couldn't resist the Teutonic tongue twister that proceeded to plague our servers during its popular run on the menu. The portions here are small because we served this as a "medium dish." By all means, feel free to scale up and serve this as a main course.

For the schnitzel

1 pound (455 g) pork loin,
   sliced horizontally into ½-inch pieces
1 teaspoon salt, plus more for sprinkling
½ teaspoon black pepper, plus more
   for sprinkling
½ cup (120 ml) canola oil
1 cup (120 g) flour
1 teaspoon chopped fresh sage
1 teaspoon chopped fresh rosemary

For the Pretzel Spätzle

2 cups (240 g) all-purpose flour
¼ teaspoon kosher salt
¼ teaspoon baking powder
3 eggs (150 g liquid egg)
¾ cup (180 ml) milk
½ gallon (1.9 L) water
1 teaspoon salt
1 tablespoon baking soda
1 tablespoon olive oil
2 tablespoons clarified butter/olive oil
   blend (page 13)

MAKE THE SCHNITZEL: Place the pork slices on a cutting board between two pieces of plastic wrap. Pound out to ¼ inch (0.5 cm) thick and sprinkle both sides very lightly with salt and pepper.

Pour the oil into a large frying pan over a medium flame. Heat about 3 minutes, until the oil is shimmering.

Combine the flour, salt, pepper, and fresh herbs in a medium bowl. Dredge the pork slices in the flour, tapping off the excess, and place in a single layer in the frying pan (you will need to do this in batches). Pan-fry 1 minute on the first side, until golden brown. Flip and fry for 1½ minutes more. Remove to a plate and let rest 5 minutes before serving. Repeat with remaining pork slices. Serve with Pretzel Spätzle.

MAKE THE PRETZEL SPÄTZLE: Preheat the oven to 400°F (200°C).

Sift the flour into a medium-sized bowl. Add the salt and baking powder and whisk to combine. In a separate bowl, combine the eggs and the milk, whisking by hand until the mixture is well aerated and you start to see bubbles. Continue whisking until the mixture starts to foam on top (about 2 minutes of vigorous whisking). Using a spatula, fold the wet ingredients into the dry, mixing just until the ingredients are combined and form a craggy ball. Cover the dough directly with plastic wrap and let it sit at room temperature for 1 hour. At this point, you can also refrigerate the dough overnight. Remove the dough from the refrigerator and bring up to room temperature for about an hour before proceeding with the recipe.

Heat the water, salt, and baking soda in a large pot over medium heat until the liquid comes to a boil. Keep a close eye on the pot as the water will want to foam over the sides.

While you're waiting for the water to boil, rub a sheet pan with the olive oil (or olive oil spray—I love Spectrum brand) and set it aside. Once the water comes to a boil, reduce the temperature to medium and place a colander over the pan of boiling water. Using a plastic bowl scraper or rubber spatula, force about a quarter of the dough through the holes of the colander and into the boiling water.

Allow the spätzle to cook for about 45 seconds and remove to the baking sheet, using a spider or slotted spoon. Toss to coat with the oil. Repeat with the rest of the dough, until all of the spätzle dough has been cooked.

Heat an 8- to 10-inch (20 to 25 cm) frying pan over medium heat. Add a quarter of the clarified butter/oil blend and sauté about one-quarter of the spätzle (it should fit in the pan in a single layer) until golden brown. Slide the pan into the oven for about 90 seconds to puff up the spätzle slightly. Repeat with the other three batches, and serve immediately. If you're cooking to order, the spätzle can be made up to a day in advance, refrigerated, and pan-fried in one-dish portions just before serving.

Goat's Milk Caramel

MAKES A LITTLE OVER 1 QUART (945 ML)

This recipe hails from the region in Mexico where I used to live, where it is known as *cajeta*. Flavored variations include vanilla, red wine, peanut butter, and chocolate. Heavy cream is added because you need more fat than the goat's milk can muster to achieve the perfect texture.

We have served this in the company of cakes, puddings, and flans over the years, but it might be best enjoyed poured over vanilla ice cream.

1 quart (945 ml) pasteurized
  goat's milk
3 cups (680 g) sugar
1 teaspoon baking soda
¼ teaspoon salt
½ cup (120 ml) heavy cream
1 vanilla bean, split lengthwise
1-inch (2.5 cm) piece of bark of canela
  (also known as Ceylon cinnamon)

Pour all the ingredients into an 8- to 10-quart (8 to 10 L) high-rimmed, heavy-bottomed pot or Dutch oven over medium heat, whisking thoroughly to combine. Whisk occasionally over the next 30 to 35 minutes, monitoring the pot so the mixture doesn't foam over. Remove from the heat when it turns the color of a brown paper bag. Strain the mixture through a fine-mesh strainer, cool to room temperature gradually (not in an ice bath, or it may crystallize). Store covered, at room temperature, for up to 5 days.

Olive Oil Cake with Prune Jam and Whipped Ricotta

MAKES ONE 8-INCH (20 CM) CAKE; SERVES 12

This simple cake, created by Lauren Crosby, is one of my favorites from the Black Trumpet archives. And it is by far the best olive oil cake I have tried. I like to tell our guests that the use of olive oil in place of animal fat somehow makes this recipe healthier (ha!). I also love that this dessert can be enjoyed at any time of day, especially for breakfast, and always in the company of a shot of good espresso.

½ cup (120 ml) freshly squeezed orange juice (from 3 or 4 oranges)
2½ cups (570 g) sugar, divided
2 cups (240 g) flour
½ teaspoon baking powder
½ teaspoon baking soda
3 eggs (150 g liquid egg)
1¼ cups (295 ml) whole milk
¼ cup (60 ml) brandy
1½ cups (355 ml) olive oil
Zest of 1 lemon
2 teaspoons ground anise seed
1 teaspoon salt

Preheat the oven to 325°F (165°C).

Spray the bottom and sides of an 8-inch (20 cm) springform pan.

Combine the orange juice and ½ cup (115 g) of the sugar in a small pan over medium heat and simmer until the sugar dissolves. Remove from the heat and set aside to cool.

Sift the flour, baking powder, and baking soda into a medium bowl and set aside.

Whip the eggs in a stand mixer (using the whisk attachment) on medium speed for 1 minute. Slowly add the remaining 2 cups (455 g) sugar and whip on medium speed until dissolved, about 3 minutes.

Pour ¼ cup (60 ml) of the cooled orange syrup, along with the milk, brandy, and olive oil, into the egg-and-sugar mixture; whip on low speed until incorporated. Add the zest, anise seed, and salt, and mix just until combined. Using a spatula, fold the dry ingredients into the batter, mixing just until combined.

Pour the batter into the prepared springform pan and bake on the middle shelf for about 1¼ hours, until the cake is dark golden brown, it's set in the middle, and a cake tester inserted in the middle comes out clean.

Let the cake cool to room temperature and brush with the remaining orange syrup before slicing into twelve pieces. Serve with Prune Jam and Whipped Ricotta (both recipes follow).

TO SERVE THE CAKE: Place a slice of cake on a dessert plate. Dollop some Whipped Ricotta on top, sprinkle with chocolate shavings, and serve with a spoonful of Prune Jam. Repeat with the remaining slices.

Prune Jam

MAKES 12 PORTIONS

We tested this recipe with plums dehydrated in-house, but you can use any prune or dried black plum.

8 prunes
4 dates, pitted
½ cup (115 g) sugar
¼ cup (60 ml) red wine
2 tablespoons apple brandy
2 tablespoons honey
Zest of ¼ orange

Combine all the ingredients in a small, heavy-bottomed pan. Bring to a boil over medium-high heat, reduce the heat to low, and simmer 3 minutes. Remove from the heat and let the mixture cool in the pan. Transfer to the bowl of a food processor and pulse several times, stopping often to scrape down the bottom and sides. Continue pulsing until the ingredients are fully incorporated and smooth.

Whipped Ricotta

MAKES A LITTLE MORE THAN 1 PINT (475 ML)

2 cups (455 g) whole-milk ricotta (see
  Homemade Ricotta, page 131)
1 cup (115 g) powdered sugar
1 teaspoon vanilla extract

Whip the cheese on low speed in the bowl of a stand mixer fitted with the paddle attachment, about 2 minutes. Add the sugar and vanilla and continue whipping until combined.

CHAPTER FOUR

LATE SPRING

The First Blush

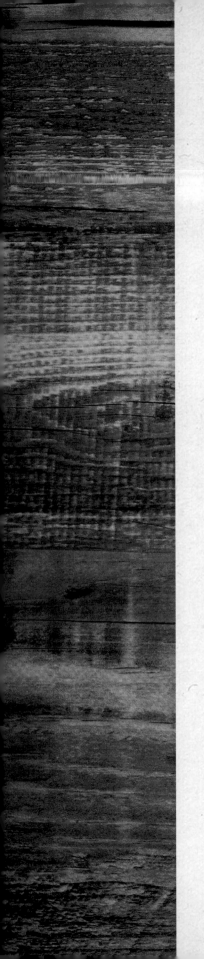

LATE SPRING RECIPES

In the Black Trumpet kitchen, late spring is the season that we welcome sprouts and baby vegetables from our local farmers, and if we're lucky, overwintered roots also make an appearance. If winter weather cooperates by laying an early blanket of snow that acts as a thermal buffer for the soil's crust, spring is sure to yield the sweetest parsnips and turnips of the year, rendered as such by the magic of energy storage, all of which adds up to an off-the-chart Brix count, which is the measure of stored sugars, nutrient density, and, usually, flavor.

But most of all, I like to rhapsodize over rhubarb. In this chapter, you will see that I have a very special place in my heart for rhubarb. Available from late spring through August, she has always found a home on my menu. I love her. She loves Black Trumpet. And when other natural vagaries plague the larder, rhubarb is there for me.

Crunchy Garden Radishes with Malt Aioli, Tamari, and Micro Herbs

SERVES 6

This radish "salad" is versatile and tastes great served with a smear of Malt Aioli and some chopped mint. Serve it alongside Fava Bean Hummus or Potted Fava Bean Pâté (pages 162 and 164 respectively) and Vinegar Chickpea Crackers (recipe follows) for a snack, light lunch, or dinner appetizer.

For the radish salad

12 radishes of assorted shapes, colors, sizes
1 jalapeño, ribs and seeds removed, quartered lengthwise and sliced thinly crosswise
1½ tablespoons coarsely torn Italian parsley
Juice of 1 orange
Juice and zest of 1 lime
¼ teaspoon salt
Pinch black pepper

For the Malt Aioli

1 cup (235 ml) malt vinegar
1 clove garlic, coarsely chopped
1 tablespoon Dijon mustard
2 egg yolks (36 g)
1 cup (235 ml) olive oil
½ teaspoon salt

MAKE THE RADISH SALAD: Combine all the ingredients in a medium bowl and stir to combine. Refrigerate for 1 hour to let the flavors develop, and serve.

MAKE THE MALT AIOLI: In a small, nonreactive pot over medium heat, reduce the malt vinegar to ¼ cup (60 ml). Set it aside and let it cool to room temperature. In the bowl of a food processor, add the garlic and mustard; pulse to combine. Add the cooled malt vinegar and the egg yolks and pulse until the mixture forms a thick paste. With the motor running, add the olive oil in a very slow, steady stream, so it creates a thick and creamy emulsion. This should take about a minute total. Add the salt and pulse briefly until incorporated. Remove to a container and refrigerate until cold. The aioli will hold for up to 3 days in the refrigerator.

Vinegar Chickpea Crackers

MAKES 30 TO 40 CRACKERS

This is a very simple cracker that people love. It pairs well with hummus and other oily Mediterranean spreads and dips.

For ease of production and consistency, we use a pasta sheeter to roll out the dough. If you don't have a pasta sheeter, you can hand-roll the dough, but it won't come out quite as crisp and even.

These crackers can be made vegan by substituting olive oil for the clarified butter.

1½ cups (130 g) chickpea flour
½ cup (60 g) all-purpose flour
½ teaspoon salt
¼ cup (60 ml) tepid water
¼ cup (60 ml) malt vinegar
¼ cup (60 ml) clarified butter/olive oil blend (page 13)
1 egg (50 g liquid egg)
1 teaspoon water
2 teaspoons coarse sea salt

Preheat the oven to 375°F (190°C).

Combine the first six ingredients in a medium bowl, making sure the water isn't cold or it will ruin the texture of the butter. Stir to combine, then scrape out onto a lightly floured work surface and knead for a minute or two. Cut the dough in half and press both halves flat with the palm of your hand.

Assemble a pasta sheeter on the widest setting. Roll out both pieces of dough and place on the counter. Using a pizza wheel or scalloped crimper, taper off all four edges of the dough and cut each sheet horizontally in half to make four long sheets, then cut vertically into 1½-inch (4 cm) squares. You should get approximately forty squares total.

Spray a baking sheet with nonstick cooking spray and arrange the dough squares in a single layer. Combine the egg and water in a small bowl, beating with a fork. Brush the egg wash on each cracker and sprinkle each one with a tiny pinch of coarse sea salt. Bake for 6 minutes. Rotate the pan 180 degrees and set the timer for 6 more minutes. When done, the edges of the crackers should be golden brown, 12 to 13 minutes total. Allow the crackers to cool, dry out, and crisp up in the pan before serving. They will store for a few days in an airtight container, and if they do get a little stale, they can be refreshed in a low oven for a few minutes.

Coban Salad

SERVES 8

This salad gets its name from a Turkish "shepherd's salad," which contains chopped seasonal vegetables, a light dressing, and crumbled feta or farmer's cheese. Our version gets a little extra boost from the Harissa Vinaigrette, but otherwise offers the same satisfying, healthful crunch one might expect from the Turkish standard.

Like its much more common relative, Greek salad, the Coban (pronounced *cho-BAN*) should always be made with the freshest possible ingredients.

2 garden cucumbers, peeled, seeded, and cut into ½-inch (1 cm) cubes
1 red bell pepper, seeded and cut into ½-inch (1 cm) cubes
1 green bell pepper, seeded and cut into ½-inch (1 cm) cubes
6 radishes, washed, medium dice
6 young spring carrots, washed, cut crosswise into ½-inch (1 cm) pieces
4 ramp bulbs (or scallion bulbs), sliced thin
1 cup (225 g) goat's milk feta cheese
2 lemons
1 teaspoon salt
Freshly ground black pepper to taste
1½ cups (355 ml) Harissa Vinaigrette (recipe follows)

When you're ready to serve the salads, toss all the ingredients except the vinaigrette in a large mixing bowl. On each plate, pour 1½ ounces (45 ml) of the vinaigrette (go lighter for anyone who objects to the heat in the dressing) and spread it out. Divide the salad ingredients evenly among the plates and serve right away.

Harissa Vinaigrette

MAKES ABOUT 1½ CUPS (355 ML)

½ cup (115 g) harissa (page 16)
½ preserved lemon (page 16), halved, pulp removed, and rind finely chopped
2 tablespoons finely chopped shallots
¼ cup (60 ml) malt vinegar
½ teaspoon salt, plus more to taste
¼ cup (60 ml) walnut oil
½ cup (120 ml) grapeseed oil

Combine the first five ingredients in the bowl of a blender. Puree until smooth. Add the walnut oil all at once and puree until combined. With the motor running, add the grapeseed oil in a slow and steady stream until the mixture thickens and becomes smooth. Season to taste and serve with Coban Salad.

Fresh Maine Crabmeat on a Polenta Cake with Pea Shoots, Morels, and Tomato Vinegar

SERVES 6

Here we have an überpopular dish that captures the heart of the season. The presentation is both beautiful and simple, and the flavors of late spring coalesce in the most harmonious way. Whether from the Chesapeake Bay or the Gulf of Maine, picked crabmeat can range from awful to awesome, but regardless of origin, it is necessary to pick through the already-picked-through meat to ensure that no remaining shell is mixed in with the glorious succulence of good crab.

Morels are expensive and hard to come by. Other mushrooms can be substituted if necessary. And as this recipe indicates, if you can't find the world's best tomato vinegar, you can choose to omit it or try to make the second-best in your own kitchen. Lemon juice also works.

For the Polenta Cake
2 tablespoons butter
3 tablespoons olive oil, divided
1 Spanish onion, medium dice
2½ teaspoons salt
1 tablespoon minced garlic
2 cups (475 ml) milk
2 cups (475 ml) water
½ cup (120 ml) heavy cream
1½ cups (245 g) coarse-ground polenta
2 eggs (100 g liquid egg)

For the morels
6 medium morels, cleaned of sand
1 teaspoon olive oil
Pinch salt and ground black pepper

For the Tomato Vinegar
1 tablespoon A l'Olivier Tomate Basilic
  tomato vinegar
or your own version:
1 cup (235 ml) tomato puree
1 cup (235 ml) cider vinegar
½ teaspoon salt

MAKE THE POLENTA CAKE: Preheat the oven to 350°F (175°C).

In a heavy-bottomed pot over low heat, melt the butter and add 2 tablespoons of the olive oil. Add the onion and salt, and cook, stirring occasionally, about 4 minutes. Add the garlic and cook 3 minutes more, until it just begins to stick to the bottom of the pan. Add the milk, water, and heavy cream; stir to combine. Bring the liquid to just under a boil. You'll notice that the liquid around the perimeter of the pan will begin to quiver and foam. This should take about 5 minutes, so watch it carefully. Reduce the heat to low and, while stirring constantly, gradually pour in the polenta so it doesn't clump. This can be done with either a whisk or a wooden spoon. Stir until the mixture thickens considerably and the consistency of the polenta is no longer sandy or gritty. This should take about 5 minutes. At this point, turn off the stove and continue to stir the mixture with a whisk. Beat in the eggs until fully incorporated. The constant whisking will help the polenta cool down and will temper the eggs at the same time.

Rub the bottom and sides of an 8 × 10 inch (20 × 25 cm) baking pan with the remaining tablespoon of olive oil. Spoon the polenta into the pan, smoothing and spreading the top so it's even on all sides.

Bake, uncovered, on the middle shelf of the oven for about 25 minutes total, checking and rotating a quarter turn after 15 minutes,

To assemble

8 ounces (225 g) Maine or Chesapeake
   lump crabmeat

½ cup (28 g) pea shoots or tendrils

and every few minutes thereafter. The polenta should puff up slightly like a soufflé, and the edges should have begun to turn golden brown.

Remove from the oven and let cool to room temperature. Cover and refrigerate for several hours or overnight. When you're ready to serve, use a 2½-inch (6 cm) round biscuit cutter to cut circles out of the cold polenta.

MAKE THE MORELS: Preheat the oven to 400°F (200°C) and slide a sheet tray into the oven.

Slice the morels into rounds, about ¼ inch (0.5 cm) thick. Place the morels on the hot sheet tray, drizzled with the olive oil and sprinkled with salt and pepper.

Bake about 10 minutes, or until the mushrooms are crisp around the edges and golden brown.

MAKE THE TOMATO VINEGAR (IF A L'OLIVIER IS UNAVAILABLE): Combine the tomato puree, cider vinegar, and salt in a small bowl. Strain through a mesh strainer, pushing down to get out all the liquid. Set aside or refrigerate until you're ready to use it.

FOR THE FINISHED PLATING: Heat the polenta cakes in a 400°F (200°C) oven for 5 minutes. Add the morel slices for the last minute in the oven. Transfer the polenta to plates, scatter morels around the polenta cake, and place 1½ ounces (40 g) crabmeat on the hot polenta. Arrange the pea tendrils and drizzle the plate with the tomato vinegar.

A Note About Fava Beans

There is a long-standing tradition at Black Trumpet of subjecting young cooks to the most tedious tasks imaginable. It is a test, I suppose, of a cook's patience, humility, and ability to multitask, but such labors also provide cooks with a happy Zen cushion in the midst of the inevitable kitchen hubbub. There is nothing like double-shucking fresh fava beans to find that elusive happy place! Unlike peas and other shell beans, the insidious fava bean—one of my favorite flavors of late spring—requires that we remove two layers before we get to the creamy, bright-green inner bean.

For recipe consistency purposes, I have weighed out the beans themselves—*not* the pods with the beans in them—because the ratio of bean to shell can vary wildly from one pod to the next.

Frozen fava beans—sometimes easier to source—do just fine in both recipes below.

Fava Bean Hummus

MAKES 1½ CUPS (355 ML)

½ Spanish onion, small dice

2 whole cloves garlic

1–1½ tablespoons olive oil, plus more for sautéing

5 pounds (2.3 kg) fava bean pods, shucked and blanched (yield should be about 8 ounces [225 g] beans)

1 teaspoon salt, plus more to taste

¼ teaspoon whole cumin, toasted and ground to a powder

¼ teaspoon ground coriander

2 teaspoons tahini

Juice and zest of 1 lemon

2 tablespoons chopped fresh mint leaves

1½ teaspoons honey

Black pepper to taste

Sauté the onion and garlic with a little olive oil over low heat until the garlic is soft, about 10 minutes. Add the favas and cook another 5 minutes, until they are soft but not falling apart.

Add the salt and spices and sauté 1 minute more. Add the tahini and lemon juice and zest; stir to combine, letting the tahini soften and melt in the pan. Let the mixture cool and scrape into a food processor. Add the mint and honey to the processor and puree until chunky, scraping down the sides of the bowl. Add the favas and puree until smooth, drizzling in 1 to 1½ tablespoons olive oil, as needed, to loosen up the mixture. Season to taste with additional salt and black pepper and serve.

Potted Fava Bean Pâté
with Rhubarb Gelée

The way we incorporate fat in this recipe is of utmost importance. The favas need to be warm but not hot and the butter cold, or the emulsion will separate. If you're using a food processor rather than a blender, the favas need to be slightly softer to get the same smooth consistency. The order of operations is also key: The favas need to cool to the correct temperature in order to puree properly, and the gelatin needs to bloom for 5 minutes before stirring or it will become clumpy and won't set up properly.

Also, I am loath to throw any recipe by-product away. Waste is costly, not only to the narrow financial margins of a restaurant, but also to the greater ecology of the food system. So the dry, pink pulp that remains from the making of the rhubarb gelée is usually incorporated into a chutney or cheese condiment. Rhubarb catsup was a big hit for our 2014 spring BT burger.

Serve this verdant spring dip with focaccia toast or raw early-spring vegetables.

½ cup (115 g) sugar

½ cup (120 ml) water

½ pound (225 g) rhubarb, chopped into 1-inch (2.5 cm) chunks (about 5 small stalks)

½ cup (120 ml) olive oil

½ Spanish onion, medium dice

3 tablespoons minced garlic (about 8 cloves)

1½ cups (325 g) fresh fava beans, blanched, shocked, and peeled (see note on page 162)

½ cup (115 g) freshly shelled English peas, raw

1 teaspoon salt

2 tablespoons plus 2 teaspoons coarsely chopped fresh parsley

2 tablespoons plus 2 teaspoons coarsely chopped fresh mint

½ teaspoon ground cumin

½ teaspoon ground coriander

¼ cup (55 g) cold butter, chopped into 1-inch (2.5 cm) cubes

1 tablespoon gelatin powder

In a small pot, combine the sugar, water, and rhubarb over medium heat, stirring to combine. Bring to a high simmer, reduce the heat to medium-low to maintain the simmer, and cook, stirring occasionally, until the sugar has melted and the rhubarb is soft and barely falling apart, 30 to 35 minutes. Remove from the heat.

In the meantime, in a medium pot, add the olive oil, onion, and garlic and poach over low heat for 8 minutes, until the onion has softened. Add the blanched favas, raw peas, and salt; stir to combine, cover, and poach over low heat for an additional 8 minutes, until the peas and favas are soft. Add the herbs and spices to the pan, stir to combine, and remove from the heat.

While the fava mixture cools, strain the rhubarb through a china cap or mesh strainer into a medium bowl, lightly mashing the rhubarb to remove all the liquid. Reserve the rhubarb mash for another use.

Remove the fava mixture to the bowl of a blender, Robot Coupe, or food processor. Add the cold butter chunks and puree until smooth.

Sprinkle the gelatin evenly over the top of the rhubarb liquid and let it sit 5 minutes.

While the gelatin blooms, line up six 4-ounce (120 ml) mason jars or ramekins of the same size and, using a spoon and working quickly, carefully fill the jars, leaving a ½-inch (1 cm) gap at the top. Rap the

jars on the counter to even out the filling and remove air bubbles. Place them on the flattest tray you can find.

When the 5 minutes are up, gently whisk the gelatin into the rhubarb liquid, being careful not to create too many air bubbles. If there are some, remove them with a spoon before proceeding.

Spoon 2 teaspoons of the gelatin mixture on top of each ramekin and slide the tray into the refrigerator. Refrigerate at least 2 hours, or until the gelée is set. If you're not serving right away, cover the ramekins and hold in the refrigerator for up to 5 days.

Rhapsody in Rhubarb:
A Femme Fatale

It's fair to say that I have a complicated relationship with rhubarb—one that began with mutual distrust but resulted in an ongoing, passionate affair. Rhubarb is one of those foods that is not easy to get to know, and it does not always behave as we might want it to. With its beguiling, primitive appearance and sweet-meets-astringent flavor, *Rheum rhabarbarum* is surely the femme fatale of the culinary garden. And even if you are able to find pleasure in the stalks of raw rhubarb, may I remind you that its broad, Mesozoic-looking leaves contain oxalic acid, which is outright toxic to humans? My dear rhubarb, you continue to unveil mysteries after all these years. That's why we play so well together.

When we have attempted to grow rhubarb at home over the years, transplants have failed because the leaves that are so harmful to us are apparently delicacies for chickens. Although they are fond of other plants (especially the immature fruit of our two quince bushes), our hens seek out the rhubarb plants, devouring the broad, young leaves and leaving only stem stubble behind.

Most of us associate rhubarb with strawberries and have probably eaten that classic tandem in the form of pie or crisp at some point. My first exposure to rhubarb came as a child eating strawberry rhubarb pie and resenting the fact that rhubarb got in the way of enjoying the merits of the far superior strawberry. Of course, I can now appreciate that strawberries are both costly and supernaturally sweet when cooked, so it makes sense to partner them with the sour counterpoint rhubarb brings to the party. Maybe this is where the secondary, darker meaning of *rhubarb*—an altercation or donnybrook—comes from.

It was on a trip with my then girlfriend Denise to the Northwest Territories and the Arctic that I gained exposure to the idea of rhubarb as a healthy snack food. I should say up front that, perhaps because of their shared Canadian provenance, my wife and rhubarb go way back. She tells of eating rhubarb raw from a young age, sometimes dipping it in sugar to reduce the bracing astringency that bursts from the red stalk. But she and now our children have always been fine with straight rhubarb, munching it out of hand like celery, unflinchingly accepting the quirky vegetable's saliva-summoning juices.

In 1997, somewhere in northern Alberta, after the last outpost of culinary civilization, Denise and I delved deep into Wood Buffalo Provincial Park, the last vast and densely wooded dominion of wood buffalo. Although we traveled to the remote park to catch a glimpse of the even rarer whooping crane, it was the buffalo that took our breath away. A beast whose heft and mass are unrivaled even by the magnificent moose and the remote musk ox, the park's namesake mascot lumbers with a timeless and imperious majesty, yet can disappear among the shadows of the forest like a bulky sylph.

After traveling for two weeks in the remote boreal region, and after having eaten little more than camping food, fish we caught, and a lifesaving loaf of bannock bread cooked in seal fat, we craved vegetables so badly that—at the first sign of a farm stand—we pulled off the main road. The road sign was hand-painted and very small, but it suggested that there was farm-fresh food nearby, so we followed the dirt road until we arrived at a working farm. This was the end of June, just north of the sixtieth parallel. Back home in New England, we would have been harvesting the first summer crops—cucumbers, strawberries, peas and string beans, baby carrots and turnips, head lettuces—and already saying our seasonal good-bye to radishes, ramps, and fiddleheads. But that was way down at forty-three; at sixty-something, spring had just arrived, and when we got out of our banged-up, bug-splattered rental car, the farmer who greeted us informed us that all he had ready to eat at that point was rhubarb. My reaction was visible, I am sure. I think he found us—two dirty, mosquito-crazed travelers jonesing for produce—rather amusing. We bought a dozen or so stalks of rhubarb, and Denise—officially now my fiancée—proceeded to eat them with a relish that revealed volumes about her. We returned from that trip with a benthic appreciation for nature and conservation, and a respect for both indigenous peoples and scientists, but also a taste for rhubarb that has only expanded as our aging palates gravitate toward more complex flavors.

I now realize that rhubarb—the femme fatale—and my wife are inextricably linked in ways that transcend mere metaphor. After years of courtship and marriage, I continue to uncover new appreciation of both Denise *and* rhubarb. They are really very simple beings that seem complicated at first. Learning how to work with them is a rewarding challenge that yields a richer result. That's how I think of rhubarb, and marriage, and I guess what it means to discover happiness as we grow old together.

Rhubarb Pickled Onion

MAKES 2 CUPS (475 ML)

1 red onion, preferably Red Wethersfield, julienned thinly with a mandoline or sharp knife
8 ounces (225 g) rhubarb, ends removed, medium dice
1½ cups (355 ml) cider vinegar
½ cup (120 ml) water
1 tablespoon salt

Place the onion in a small bowl and set aside.

In a nonreactive pot, bring all the remaining ingredients up to a boil over high heat. Reduce the heat to low and simmer until the rhubarb is tender, 5 to 10 minutes. Carefully press the hot liquid and vegetables through a strainer, into the bowl with the onion. Let the liquid and onion cool to room temperature. Cover and refrigerate for at least a day before serving.

Rhubarb Chlodnik
with Spice-Roasted Strawberries,
Crème Fraîche, and Caviar

SERVES 6

I came across a reference to this soup in a book I was reading at the time. References to rhubarb pop up only so often, so I put on my culinary sleuth cap and pursued all things chlodnik until I had the answer I wanted. The word itself, pronounced *kwod-knee-YIK*, means "cold soup." Which is not very interesting, I admit. But references in Polish cookbooks to the rhubarb incarnation of this chilled national soup got my juices flowing. Immediately, I conjured Eastern European flavors of soured cream and pearlescent fish eggs. And the soup was born. When it appeared on our menu, at least three members of our staff could claim a Polish genotype in their immediate family. So I made sure to win their approval before the odd soup went on our menu. In early summer, it proved to be a hit, much to my surprise. At least, as much of a hit as a chilled rhubarb soup could be outside its native Poland.

3 tablespoons olive oil, divided
1 pound (455 g) rhubarb, cut into
  ½-inch (1 cm) sections
1 cup (225 g) strawberries, quartered,
  plus 6 more
½ cup (120 ml) tomato puree
1 teaspoon ground coriander
1 star anise
2 tablespoons harissa (page 16)
3 tablespoons honey
1 teaspoon salt
¼ cup (60 ml) red wine
2 cups (475 ml) vegetable stock
½ cup (120 ml) heavy cream
1 cup (235 ml) crème fraîche,
  plus more for serving
1 teaspoon sugar
¼ teaspoon Red House Pepper Blend
  (page 22)
Pinch salt
½ ounce (14 g) spoonbill or
  transmontanus caviar

Heat 2 tablespoons of the olive oil in a heavy-bottomed pot over medium-low heat. Add the rhubarb pieces and cook for 5 minutes, until they have softened but haven't colored. Add all but six of the strawberries along with the tomato puree, spices, and harissa; cook, stirring, for 3 minutes. Add the honey, salt, and red wine and simmer for 3 more minutes. Add the vegetable stock, bring to a boil, and turn off the pan. Let cool in the pot for 15 minutes. Add the cream, stirring to combine. Transfer to a mixing bowl and fold in the crème fraîche. Refrigerate until cold, and hold for up to 5 days before serving.

Preheat the oven to 400°F (200°C).

Halve the six remaining strawberries and coat with the remaining tablespoon of olive oil as well as the sugar, pepper mix, and salt in a small bowl. Pour the strawberry mixture into an 8-inch (20 cm) sauté pan and roast for 10 to 15 minutes, until the berries are soft and a syrup begins to form. Remove from the oven and serve on top of the chlodnik with a dollop of crème fraîche and a demitasse spoonful of caviar.

Rhubarb and Chicken Dumpling Soup with Crottin Brûlée and Shaved Artichokes

I have a reverse philosophy to most people's when it comes to dark and white chicken meat. I default to using the flavorful dark meat in a dish and always view the white meat as a by-product. This is one way I have found to utilize the white meat.

For the Chicken Dumplings

2 boneless, skinless chicken breasts, coarsely chopped

2 cups (240 g) cooked rice

2 spring onion (or ramp) tops

1 tablespoon minced garlic

2 tablespoons salt

2 teaspoons dried chervil

2 teaspoons dried dill

⅛ teaspoon mustard powder

⅛ teaspoon ground mace

For the soup

2 quarts (1.9 L) homemade or store-bought low-sodium chicken stock

1 red onion, julienned

4 stalks rhubarb, sliced ¼ inch (0.5 cm) thick on bias

4 stalks celery, sliced ¼ inch (0.5 cm) thick on bias

2 cups (475 ml) tomato puree

12 whole cloves garlic

1 tablespoon sugar

1½ teaspoons peppercorns

2 fresh or 4 dried bay leaves

Handful of dill stems

Pinch crushed dried red pepper flakes

Salt and pepper to taste

For the Crottin Brûlée

8 crottins goat cheese (Vermont Creamery makes a lovely crottin, or you can shape your own from an 8-ounce [225 g] log of chèvre)

2 teaspoons sugar

MAKE THE DUMPLINGS: Combine all the dumpling ingredients in the bowl of a food processor and pulse until fully incorporated, stopping a few times to scrape down the bottom and sides of the bowl. The raw mixture can be refrigerated for up to a day before you make the soup. Before cooking, shape the mixture into tablespoon-sized meatballs and refrigerate for 10 minutes before dropping them into the soup to cook, so they retain their shape.

MAKE THE SOUP: Bring the stock to a boil over high heat in a 4-quart (4 L) nonreactive pot. Add the onion, rhubarb, and celery to the pot, and reduce the heat to a simmer. Remove the vegetables after 1 minute and spread them out on a cookie sheet to cool. Add the remaining ingredients to the pot, bring up to a boil over medium-high heat, reduce the heat to low, and simmer 30 minutes. Strain the broth. At this point, you can refrigerate the vegetables and the broth separately if you are making it on another day. To continue with the recipe, return the broth to the pot and bring back up to a boil over high heat. Reduce the heat to a simmer and add the dumplings. Cook the dumplings until firm to the touch, about 5 to 6 minutes. Add the cooked vegetables and simmer 2 to 3 minutes. Adjust the seasoning with salt and pepper. Serve the soup with three to four dumplings per person, a crottin brûlée in the center, and scattered with a few slices of artichokes per bowl.

MAKE THE CROTTIN BRÛLÉE: Sprinkle a crottin with a pinch of sugar and torch until golden brown on top. Repeat with the remaining seven crottins. Alternatively, spoon 2 tablespoons soft goat cheese into a 1-inch (2.5 cm) ring mold. Pack it tight and remove the mold. Sprinkle with sugar and torch as instructed above. Repeat seven times.

For the Shaved Artichokes

2 quarts (1.9 L) water

1 cup (235 ml) white wine

¼ cup (60 ml) honey

8 whole cloves garlic

1 lemon, thinly sliced

3 tablespoons salt

1 tablespoon peppercorns

3 bay leaves

1 stick cinnamon

8 baby artichokes, rough outer leaves removed, ¾ inch (2 cm) of the tip and the bottom stem cut off

MAKE THE SHAVED ARTICHOKES: Combine all the ingredients except the artichokes in a 3-quart (3 L) pot over high heat. While you wait for the water to come to a boil, prepare an ice bath by combining ice and cold water in a medium bowl. When the water boils, add the artichokes and reduce the heat to a simmer. Cook 2 minutes, until soft. Remove the artichokes to the ice bath to stop the cooking. When the artichokes are cool and you are ready to serve the soup, remove them from the ice bath and slice thinly with a mandoline or a sharp knife. Garnish the soup with several slices per bowl.

Fried Rabbit Loin with Cheesy Polenta Pudding and Rhubarb Salsa

SERVES 8

For the fried rabbit

4 rabbit loins from 2 rabbits
2 cups (475 ml) buttermilk
1 cup (120 g) flour
1 teaspoon salt, plus more for sprinkling
½ teaspoon black pepper, plus more for sprinkling
2 eggs (100 g liquid egg)
1 cup (50 g) panko
Canola or vegetable oil, for frying

Place the loins in a medium bowl and cover with buttermilk. Refrigerate 1 to 3 hours. Remove the loins from the buttermilk and pat lightly with a towel so the flesh is still tacky and not completely dry.

Whisk the flour, 1 teaspoon salt, and ½ teaspoon black pepper in a medium bowl. In another bowl, whisk the eggs. In a third bowl, add the panko. Using the standard breading procedure, drop the loins, one at a time, in the flour, covering completely and tapping off the excess. Coat with the egg, and roll in the panko, pressing lightly to help it adhere. Set aside and repeat with the remaining loins.

Add oil 1½ inches (4 cm) up the sides of a medium high-sided pot. Place over medium-high heat, and when the temperature of the oil reaches 325°F (165°C), lower the breaded loins carefully into the oil. Deep-fry for 3 minutes, until the loins are golden brown on the outside and cooked through. Remove to a towel-lined plate and sprinkle lightly with salt and pepper. Let rest 2 minutes before slicing. Serve with Cheesy Polenta Pudding, Rhubarb Salsa (recipes follow), and—for a flavor-packed bonus—some Smoked Almond and Arugula Pesto (page 350).

Pickled Habanero

YIELDS ABOUT 16 RINGS

Use gloves when handling habaneros. Always. For your own good.

2 habanero peppers, seeded and sliced horizontally into thin rings
¼ cup (60 ml) cider vinegar
2 tablespoons water
Juice from ½ lime
1½ teaspoons salt
½ teaspoon sugar
½ teaspoon coriander seed

Place the sliced habanero in a small jar or bowl.

In a small, nonreactive pot, heat the remaining ingredients over medium heat, until the sugar and salt dissolve and the mixture just comes to a boil. Let the liquids cool to room temperature, then pour over the habanero slices. Cover and refrigerate for at least 3 days before using. The pickles can last, refrigerated, for up to a month.

Cheesy Polenta Pudding

SERVES 8

1 tablespoon butter
1 Spanish onion, diced
1 tablespoon salt
1 teaspoon black pepper
1 tablespoon plus 1 teaspoon
  minced garlic
3 cups (710 ml) whole milk
½ cup (120 ml) heavy cream
1 cup (165 g) white, coarse polenta
¼ cup (25 g) grated Parmigiano-
  Reggiano cheese

In a medium-sized pot over medium heat, melt the butter, add the onion, salt, and pepper, and stir occasionally until the onion begins to soften without coloring, about 4 minutes. Add the garlic and cook, stirring, for 2 more minutes. Add the whole milk and heavy cream and bring the mixture up to just under a boil, keeping a close eye on it because the liquids will want to foam over. Lower the heat to a simmer and gradually pour the polenta into the pot, whisking constantly. As you whisk, you'll notice that the polenta will gradually begin to stiffen. Gradually let it absorb the liquid while you continue to whisk evenly and constantly, never allowing it to set up. Continue whisking for 4 minutes, allowing the polenta to bubble and pop. Add the cheese and stir to combine. Serve immediately, or if you're planning to reconstitute the polenta, let it cool, refrigerate, and reheat by bringing up to a simmer slowly with additional milk and cream.

NOTE: Use a heavy-duty whisk for this recipe, not the frail piano-wire variety. Don't panic if the polenta is either too loose or too stiff. Polenta is forgiving. Just add more liquid if it's stiff, or cook it longer if it seems loose. You really can't mess it up.

Rhubarb Salsa

MAKES 1½ CUPS (355 ML)

2 large stalks rhubarb (about 6.5
  ounces [185 g]), brunoised
½ large leek (about 3.5 ounces
  [100 g]), brunoised
1 tablespoon chopped fresh chervil
½ teaspoon chopped Pickled Habanero
½ cup (120 ml) lemon juice
½ cup (120 ml) water
½ cup (115 g) sugar
½ teaspoon salt

Combine the rhubarb, leek, chervil, and habanero in a small bowl.

Combine the lemon juice and water in a small, nonreactive pan over high heat and reduce by about two-thirds. Remove from the heat and add the sugar and salt, stirring until they dissolve. Let the mixture cool to room temperature, then pour over the vegetables and stir to combine. Serve immediately or refrigerate for up to a day before using.

On Ramps

Helvetia, West Virginia, is the putative world headquarters of the ramp. Before Helvetia (a remote town named after the Swiss population that settled there), few Americans knew about the wild leeks that huddled against the elements in the damp soil of riverbanks in most every temperate growing zone in the country. After *Saveur* magazine blew the cover and attracted national attention to Helvetia's bounty in 1995, every chef in America worth his or her salt soon understood the need to ring in spring menus with a dish that utilized ramps in a very visible way. Since I have cooked professionally, I have cooked with ramps in their season. But as the fascination with ramps became a national craze, I—like many other foragers—began to worry about the sustainability of ramp harvesting.

The ramp teeters on the same gangplank as cod, both species that we once took for granted, both wild human foods that are notoriously difficult to farm. If we as a species gobble up all the ramps and all the cod, the trophic balance of the world shifts somewhat, and there is only so much shifting an ecosystem can handle. As much as it hurts to write, this is why fishermen and foragers must remain considerate of bird's-eye legislation and regulation that limit harvests, even if such limits threaten their livelihoods. The greater populations of wild food stocks have to drive policy governing regional legislation. In other words, anyone who takes up foraging should also take up the ethics and etiquette that ensure a sustainable harvest for future generations (see "Ethics, Etiquette, and Ecology" on page 316).

Ramp Pasta

MAKES 26 OUNCES (735 G)

I love this colorful and flavorful pasta, which can be rolled out to any desired noodle shape and cooked with bright spring vegetables (Italians refer to this simply as *primavera*, their word for "spring"). In this recipe, frying the ramps helps pull out their natural oils, flavoring the pasta and moistening the dough. You can also blanch the leaves in salted boiling water for 2 minutes if you prefer to cut down on the oil.

½ pound (225 g) ramp leaves, stems removed and reserved for another use
1½ cups (355 ml) pure olive oil
3 cups (320 g) "00" flour (all-purpose flour works, too)
5 whole eggs (250 g liquid egg), lightly beaten with a fork
1 tablespoon salt
1 teaspoon ground black pepper

Pan-fry the ramp leaves in ½ inch (1 cm) oil in a 12-inch (30 cm) skillet over medium-high heat for 20 to 30 seconds, or until they begin to wilt. You may need to do this in two or three batches. Remove to a cookie sheet lined with a clean kitchen towel or paper towels, separating the leaves as best you can. Blot the leaves with a cloth to remove the excess oil and let sit, uncovered, until the leaves dry out and crisp slightly, about 15 minutes.

In a food processor, spin the leaves with the flour until fully incorporated, about 3 minutes. Scoop the flour into a sifter or mesh strainer and sift into a medium bowl. Make a well in the flour and add the eggs, salt, and pepper. With a fork, gradually pull the dry ingredients into the wet. Using a bowl scraper, cut the wet ingredients into the dry. When all the ingredients have been incorporated and the dough looks craggy, scrape it out onto a floured work surface and knead until it is smooth and elastic and springs back three-quarters of the way when poked with a fingertip, about 10 minutes. The dough should be bright green and fragrant.

Flatten the ball of dough into a disk and wrap tightly with plastic wrap. Refrigerate for at least an hour or up to 2 days before rolling out with a pasta machine.

Spring Mushroom and Fiddlehead Paella with Saffron Rice, English Peas, Peppers, and Spring Garlic

SERVES 6

This bright spring paella can easily be made vegetarian by omitting the sausage. Or for a spicy twist, substitute Chorizo Meatballs (page 53) for the sausage. Vegetable stock can also be substituted for the nettle brodo, which is our regular vegetable stock pureed with equal parts blanched wild stinging nettles. Stinging nettles, found in backyards everywhere, have been the scourge of many childhood romps, but anyone can overcome the painful filaments on the uncooked plant by using heavy-duty gloves when harvesting and then boiling the plants. The nettle's flavor is distinctly earthy yet mellow, and the health benefits rival those of chaga, quinoa, and yoga.

1 tablespoon olive oil
1 pound (455 g) sweet Italian sausage, sliced into ½-inch (1 cm) chunks
1 red bell pepper, medium dice
½ Spanish onion, medium dice
1 tablespoon minced garlic
½ cup (40 g) assorted spring mushrooms (morels, chicken mushrooms, oyster mushrooms)
1 cup (225 g) Calasparra rice
1 teaspoon salt
2 cups (475 ml) nettle brodo (or vegetable stock)
½ cup (115 g) fresh English peas
Pinch saffron
½ cup (50 g) fiddlehead ferns
2 tablespoons chopped fresh chervil
4 leaves fresh sage, chopped
6 small cipollini onions or large ramp bulbs
½ teaspoon Red House Pepper Blend (page 22)
Chopped green garlic or crispy rings of fried morel mushrooms to garnish (optional)

In a 12-inch (30 cm) paella pan over a medium flame, heat the olive oil and add the sausage chunks, pepper, and onion, stirring for 90 seconds. Stir in the garlic and mushrooms and simmer for 1 more minute, then add the rice and salt, stirring to coat everything in the pan. Add the remaining ingredients except the garnish and simmer, covered, over low to medium heat for 10 minutes. Check the rice, and if it is still a bit al dente, add more brodo/stock and simmer for 5 more minutes. Finish over a high flame to crisp up the sides of the paella, and serve right away, garnishing with fried garlic or morels.

The Long and Winding Road: A Tragic Loss, a Pair of Bucks, Fermented Hay, a Wet Placenta, and a Prison Break-In

One man's quest for good food and drink plays a marginal role in this story, but it plays a far greater role in the story of Black Trumpet and our tight-knit restaurant community as a whole. It is not a story that has a happy ending, I suppose, but maybe it does, and maybe I came to arrive at that conclusion belatedly, having had to pass through a short period of bewilderment and a long spell of bereavement.

Lindsey Altshul was a beloved troubadour of fine food with a deep fondness for the Beatles and beer. He often celebrated his birthday by taking his friends out to Black Trumpet. There was usually a tequila toast (or two). But most of the time, Lindsey occupied a bar stool by himself, slowly partaking in Black Trumpet dishes the way a chef dreams about—a long, slow sojourn through the menu, ordering the most technically difficult charcuterie and braised meat dishes and enjoying them with relish. Whenever we had offal (sweetbreads, heart, and kidneys in particular) on the menu, I would contact him, and he would usually show up for dinner.

One year, when life was good, Lindsey decided to open his own place, and as luck had it, that place quickly became a delicious landmark less than 4 miles (6 km) from my rural Maine home. His Pepperland Café would become a mainstay in my family's life—a reliable outing every time, whether it was the renowned brunch that featured delicious and clever dishes like Erica's Strata and old Warner Bros. cartoons on a big screen, or a casual dinner paired with an excellent beer he was excited about from his cellar. When Lindsey opened Pepperland, the craft beer revolution was just getting under way, and there were few ambassadors in our country as devoted as Lindsey. He made pilgrimages to Belgium. He brought beer styles—gueuze, rauchbier, Kölsch, Berliner Weiss, lambic—into our midst and expounded on their merits like a benevolent Jesuit on a crusade.

Because of his passion for the gustatory good life, Lindsey made a lot of friends. He ate in all the restaurants that were doing anything above and beyond the commercially viable (but gastronomically uninteresting) profile that had in recent years pigeonholed the New Hampshire Seacoast as a tourist stopover without a culinary heart. Lindsey was, as the saying goes, all heart, and he gravitated to places that shared his passions.

When the newspaper report came out of a man found on the rocks of a beach I had frequented in my childhood summers, I felt this soul-sucking, gut-punching emotion, something akin to dread, fueled by the trickle of rumor that it was Lindsey's body.

This tale begins with an ending, the last time I laid eyes on Lindsey. He was busy and somewhat distracted that day and was going about his rounds at Pepperland when I walked in with a sample of a local rum I had infused with fermented hay that I had harvested on an odd road trip that took me and my friend, Rob Booz, a few hours north into the heart of Maine. Lindsey was unfazed by the odd concoction and, in his understated way, appeared to share my enthusiasm for the sweet-and-sour grassy flavor.

The premise of the road trip was to see the farm whence I had begun sourcing all the beef for Black Trumpet. Archer Angus was the name of the program, and owners Ray and Linda Buck had already made friends with our kitchen crew by delivering meat personally to our door.

I worked closely with the Bucks and brought their Archer Angus cuts to national events that showcased the best American grassfed beef. Their product impressed chefs from all over the country. As their brand expanded throughout New England, and as they began to bring other livestock farmers into their fold, ensuring that they all adhered to the same protocol of rejecting subtherapeutic antibiotics, I felt the need to set up a road trip to visit the farm and meet the people raising the cattle on their own turf.

Grassfed beef cattle live a pretty decent life—even those that graze on the rugged, seasonally volatile topography of central Maine. When winter rolls around, the bales of choice hay culled from the surrounding fields at Archer Angus's Chesterville, Maine, farm are set out for winter forage. When the snow is hip high, the cattle find themselves confined somewhat to large sheds and cleared paddocks where they can access water and hay. The hay that Ray Buck was toting around in his futuristic lunar-landing mini tractor the day we visited had undergone the early stages of fermentation. Rob and I felt compelled to smell and even taste the hay to better understand what our meat was eating. And to our shock, we gravitated to the intensely floral, yeasty aroma of, well, rotten grass. We shoved a few clumps of really juicy, stinky stuff in the back of my car to incorporate into various culinary experiments, including bread, beer, cheese, and cocktails. My daughter never forgave me for the stench this imbued, apparently permanently, in the sensitive microfibers of her nostril cilia.

Earlier in the day, when we had first arrived at the farm, a dusting of spring snow; a parade of handsome, healthy cattle; and Linda in her overalls and work gloves, painted the perfect picture of Maine farming in the colder seasons. Dozens of head of cattle were moving with a purpose toward Linda, who was distributing suppertime fare to the corral where they had congregated. As I approached Linda and her ruminant beasts, I nearly stepped on a bloody, bubbling substance I learned was the placenta of a calf born that morning. It was, as you might expect, as alien yet familiar a thing as our sheltered eyes can behold. When our son Cormac was born, we asked the midwife to pack up the placenta to go. That was the latter of two human placentas I am likely to see in this lifetime. Being a nutrient-rich power pack girded in a layer of mucilage, the placenta (a word that means "flat cake" in ancient Greek) is sometimes consumed by parents in a strange cannibalistic ritual. I am simultaneously intrigued and horrified by this idea, so when I saw the fairly sizable, recently plopped placenta lying by the

herd, I remembered that we had buried the placenta that had fed our son in utero by the sour cherry tree in our backyard. That tree never did particularly well, being somewhat prone to invaders like tent caterpillars and Japanese beetles, but on the summer after Cormac's twelfth birthday, as he publicly admitted the first pangs of attraction to a member of the opposite sex, the cherry tree burst with a profusion of stunning red fruit.

Rob and I had embarked on our road trip with a secondary agenda. A longtime baker and friend had once greatly influenced my understanding of bread and encouraged me during the graceless reentry phase of my culinary career at Lindbergh's Crossing (see "Loaf Kneaders and Lumpy Ladies" on page 118). Michael Scholz put love and care into bread baking like nobody else I had met. When he moved into the heart of Maine with his wife, I suspected I might never see him again. But years later, Michael and his business partner created two entities that would serve as a powerful magnet to anyone who loves the art of baking bread. The Kneading Conference he co-founded, coupled with Maine Grains, the wholesale bread business he started with fellow bread guru Amber Lambke, put the Skowhegan area on the nation's food map. Archer Angus was less than an hour away from Skowhegan, so I talked Rob into joining me on a detour through the beautiful area of Maine best known for its annual Common Ground Fair. When we arrived in Skowhegan, a still-ungentrified mill town, we had to scout around for a while before locating the building where Maine Grains was setting up its new production facility. To our surprise, the building turned out to be a prison. After trying several doors to get inside and see the work-in-progress that was Maine Grains, we found ourselves more or less breaking into a hatch by the prison yard's basketball court. Defenses against trespassers trying to *enter* the prison were insufficient, and we heroically stormed the ramparts until we found a breach in the fortifications. More accurately, we eventually found an open door. When we ascended dark stairs to the atrium above the makeshift kitchen, we cast our eyes on the proud centerpiece of the inchoate Maine Grains at Somerset Grist Mill facility—a gorgeous, handmade wooden-slat mill that would be used to process locally grown grains into sublime bread flour. After seeing the mill and amid pangs of guilt about breaking and entering, Rob and I fled, finally hunting down Michael at his home, which I identified by driving around a nearby Maine town looking for a house with a children's playset and a large stone bread-oven chimney. Shockingly, I found the house that fit this profile, knocked on the door, and congratulated Mike on his phenomenal accomplishments, including creating a bakers' mecca in the heart of Maine—no small feat!

When Rob and I returned from our outing, having seen local grain and beef, raised and processed by hard-working people we know and trust—we celebrated our education at Pepperland with a beer. With Lindsey. He was preoccupied but managed to eke out a smile when we sat down at a table in his bar. When he came to our table, we discussed fermented hay and its culinary/ brewing merits. We left him, just a few weeks before he left us for good, with a small token from our adventure. I will always treasure his wit and wisdom and will always wish he could have been with us just a little longer, to witness the Good Food (and Beer) Revolution taking off. Lindsey was a troubled man, as it turns out, but a good one. He helped people. Some of us never got to return the favor.

Tim's Sesame Burger Buns

MAKES 8 BUNS

For years our many "BT Burger" incarnations, for all their popularity, suffered somewhat from bun inconsistency. The recipes for buns drew from many cultural influences and tasted great when fresh out of the oven, but after a few hours, they became stale and chewy. Overnight storage wasn't even an option. Pan grilling in butter salvaged the buns but made them greasy. Then along came Tim Cronin, another longstanding employee with a hatrack full of Black Trumpet roles. Of Tim's many contributions, this burger bun recipe—simple, storable, and texturally perfect—was both a godsend and a hallmark for many BT Burgers to come.

1 tablespoon active dry yeast
¾ cup plus 2 tablespoons (200 g) warm water
¼ cup (55 g) sugar
2 tablespoons clarified butter
1 whole egg (50 g liquid egg)
1 egg yolk (18 g) (reserve white for egg wash)
4 cups (490 g) flour, plus more as needed
1 teaspoon salt
1 tablespoon plus 1 teaspoon white sesame seed

Combine the yeast, water, and sugar in a medium bowl and let bloom 5 minutes. Add the remaining ingredients except the reserved egg white and the sesame seeds; mix by hand until a ball of dough forms. Turn the mixture out onto a clean work surface and knead gently—the dough is quite soft. It should be tacky but not sticky. If it sticks to your fingers while you knead, add flour 1 tablespoon at a time until it becomes tacky. Spray a large mixing bowl with pan spray and add the dough. Cover with a damp, clean cloth and let rise until doubled in size, about 1 hour.

Preheat the oven to 375°F (190°C).

Turn the dough out onto a work surface and portion into eight 3½-ounce (100 g) balls. Round the balls and place them on a sprayed cookie sheet. Gently flatten the balls with the palm of your hand and spray the tops so they don't dry out. Let rise 45 minutes. Whisk the reserved egg white with a fork and brush over the top of each burger bun. Sprinkle each with ½ teaspoon sesame seeds and slide into the oven. Bake on the middle rack of the oven for 7 minutes, rotate the pan, and bake 5 more minutes, or up to 7. The buns should be golden brown and should spring back when gently prodded with a finger. Cool to room temperature on a cooling rack and serve immediately or store in a tightly lidded container for up to 2 days.

Masa:
The Gift of Chicomecoatl

During the heyday of the ancient Aztecs, Mesoamerican culture had created a calendar, pretty much invented team sports, built cities with ornate temples on sometimes remote and rough terrain, and—perhaps most important—developed ways to grow and process maize, a humble grassy grain, using techniques that we still use today. According to the USDA, corn is the second-largest cash crop in the United States, trailing marijuana by a fair margin. Corn has become a centerpiece on the table of our national food conversation, a staple in our diet (and our economy), and a source of controversy whose production, processing, and genetic modification have deep roots in the nutrient-poor soil of America's industrialized food system.

The Aztec goddess of corn, Chicomecoatl, not only brought corn to the people but also taught them how to nixtamalize it. Nixtamalization is a process—namely, boiling corn in a lime solution—that turns the tough outer shell of native corn kernels into something our digestive systems can process, releasing from inside the kernel the valuable proteins and nutrients our human bodies need.

The kernels of modern varieties of sweet corn (what most Americans think of when we think of corn as food) do not have as thick and tough an outer shell, but—without getting too graphic—most of us are aware that it is still a challenge for our bodies to process sweet corn eaten right off the cob.

Although few people think about it, we eat a lot of nixtamalized corn in this country. Every bag of tortilla chips is made from nixtamalized corn. In the South, hominy grits are made from corn that has been nixtamalized. At Black Trumpet, we have been using this ancient process with great success for a few years, making it possible to create our own masa from heirloom varieties of New England corn like the Stowell's Evergreen and Roy's Calais varieties that have been grown out over the years by the Coxes at Tuckaway Farm in nearby Lee, New Hampshire.

Masa Pasta

MAKES ABOUT 2 POUNDS (0.9 KG) DOUGH

This dough is different from masa dough. A soft, wet masa dough may be used to fill tamales (see Lobster and Kelp Tamales, page 254), and a drier version is used to make totopos (see page 102), whereas this recipe is a pasta dough through and through, versatile and perfect for either Mexican ravioli or noodles for a spicy soup broth.

⅔ cup (75 g) masa harina
⅔ cup (110 g) semolina flour
¼ cup (30 g) all-purpose flour
Pinch salt
2 eggs (100 g liquid egg),
  lightly beaten with a fork
1 teaspoon olive oil
¼ cup (60 ml) warm water

Combine the three flours and the salt in a medium bowl, whisking lightly to combine. Mound onto a clean work surface. Make a deep well in the center and add the eggs and olive oil. Pulling from the sides with a fork, bring the dry ingredients into the wet until everything is combined. Add 2 tablespoons of the warm water and knead the dough just until it comes together in a ball. If it's still dry, add more water 1 teaspoon at a time, until it comes together. Form into a disk, wrap tightly with plastic wrap, and refrigerate at least an hour.

Masa-Crusted Soft-Shell Crab
with Mole Verde

SERVES 8

I gained an appreciation for soft-shell crabs in Washington, DC, in my late teens. Even before my first exposure to truly great American and French chefs putting their spin on this delicacy, I ate cultural variations that included a simple Thai dish with basil and curry that I still think about.

If hard-pressed, one can find frozen, "dressed" crabs year-round, but I insist on working with only live crabs, because their flavor and texture are exponentially superior.

8 soft-shell crabs
3 eggs (150 g liquid egg)
2¼ cups (535 ml) buttermilk
2¼ cups (535 ml) heavy cream
1½ cups (168 g) masa harina
1 teaspoon salt, plus more
 for sprinkling
½ teaspoon black pepper
Canola oil, for pan-frying

To clean the crabs, use sharp scissors or a knife to cut the face off each crab just behind the eyes. (Be careful not to cut too far back, or you will accidentally cut off the claws—they connect to the body just below the eyes.) Remove the tips of the claws and the sharp points on either side of the body. Flip the body over and clip off the flap covering the belly (these are the sex organs). Flip the body back over and pull back the shell on both sides to reveal the gills. Carefully rip them out.

Preheat the oven to 450°F (230°C).

In a large bowl, whisk together the eggs, buttermilk, and heavy cream. Add the crabs to the mixture and soak overnight in the refrigerator.

Remove the crabs from the liquid, place them on a drying rack, and lightly pat with a clean towel to make them tacky but not dry. Combine the masa, salt, and pepper in a medium bowl. Dredge the crabs thoroughly in the mixture, tapping off the excess.

Heat ½ inch (1 cm) oil in a 12-inch (30 cm) pan over medium heat to 325°F (165°C). Add four dredged crabs to the pan, shell side down, and fry 2 minutes. Flip and fry 1 minute. If you have a splatter screen, place it over the pan when you flip the crabs. They've been known to explode at this point, threatening bystanders without discretion. Transfer the crabs to a baking sheet and sprinkle with salt. Repeat with the four remaining crabs. Transfer the baking sheet to the oven and bake 4 minutes. Serve immediately on a bed of wilted greens or grits with Mole Verde (recipe follows).

Mole Verde

MAKES 2 CUPS (475 ML)

Mole Verde is a wonderful sauce that can accompany a wide variety of dishes. One of my favorite taco shops back in San Miguel served a similar green mole with Chicken Thighs (page 199) and black beans. It was unforgettable!

Variations on this theme have graced a number of Black Trumpet menus. This particular recipe is accompanied by Masa-Crusted Soft Shell Crab (preceding recipe). If authentic pepitas are hard to come by, sunflower seeds may be substituted.

Also, the type of lettuce used in this recipe will have an impact on the flavor. Milder lettuces, like Bibb and romaine, work best. Fresh garden lettuce is often too bitter.

4 tomatillos, husked and quartered

4 jalapeños, ribs and seeds removed, minced

1 Spanish onion, small dice

2 tablespoons olive oil or sunflower oil

6 Boston (aka Bibb or butterhead) lettuce leaves

2 tablespoons pumpkin seeds (pepitas) or sunflower seeds

1 tablespoon dried epazote leaves (available at stockandspice.com)

1 tablespoon dried marjoram

1 teaspoon whole cumin seed

1 cup (235 ml) vegetable stock

¼ cup (55 g) masa dough for totopos (page 102)

¾ cup (45 g) packed fresh cilantro, stems and leaves

1½ teaspoons salt

Cook the tomatillos, jalapeños, and onion in the oil over low heat in a heavy-bottomed pot, stirring occasionally, until soft (12 to 15 minutes). Add the lettuce, seeds, epazote, marjoram, cumin, and stock; stir to combine. Bring up to a simmer and cook 5 minutes. Remove to the bowl of a blender, add the masa dough, cilantro, and salt, and puree until smooth. Serve immediately or let cool to room temperature and refrigerate for up to 5 days.

English Pea Panna Cotta

SERVES 8

This is a delightfully refreshing dessert that Lauren came up with to capitalize on a prolific late-spring pea crop. We grew Lincoln peas that year and have stuck with that heirloom variety ever since for their sweetness and long growing season.

2 cups (475 ml) whole milk
½ cup (115 g) sugar
¼ teaspoon salt
1 tablespoon coarsely torn mint leaves
1 cup English (shelling) peas
2 tablespoons cold water
1 tablespoon gelatin powder
1 cup (235 ml) heavy cream

Pour the milk, sugar, salt, and mint leaves into a medium-sized nonreactive pot over medium heat. Bring to just under a boil, looking for the milk around the perimeter of the pan to begin to foam. Add the peas and immediately remove the pot from the heat. Steep the peas in the hot milk for 2 minutes, until they are bright green and slightly soft.

Meanwhile, add the cold water to a small heat-safe bowl and sprinkle the gelatin evenly over the top. Without stirring, place the bowl over very low heat—either directly over a gas flame or in a simmering double boiler. Once the gelatin starts to dissolve, begin whisking. When the gelatin mixture begins to turn clear and syrupy and is completely smooth, remove it from the heat and add to the milk-and-pea mixture. Stir to combine and pour into the bowl of a blender. Blend on high speed until smooth, 10 to 20 seconds, and strain through a mesh strainer into a bowl. Cool to room temperature. While the mixture cools, whip the heavy cream to soft peaks using a whisk and a small bowl, about 3 minutes of vigorous whisking. Lightly whisk the cream into the pea mixture. Pour into molds or ramekins, cover, and refrigerate for at least 4 hours and up to overnight to let the panna cotta set up.

Serve the panna cotta in individual ramekins or run a knife around the outside of the mold and invert onto a dessert plate.

CHAPTER FIVE

EARLY SUMMER
The Deepest Blue and Green

EARLY SUMMER RECIPES

As the first rays of summer warm the topsoil and the briny main, industrious farmers and fishermen go full throttle, laboring to cram a year's worth of work into a few months of optimal harvest. Like farmers, fishermen have no choice but to harvest what the market will bear. Because technology that isolates certain fish has advanced quite a bit, boats can now target some species with reliable accuracy.

We consumers are faced with an imperative: We have to begin eating different species of seafood than we are accustomed to now. I know no one likes to be told what to eat, or what to do for that matter, but the greater fishing community, along with its catch, has gone from boom to bust in my lifetime, and it has also become increasingly apparent that policy will not reverse the downward-trending population of either fish or fishermen in my remaining lifetime.

Many fisheries advocates believe the end is nigh for fish and fishing as we know it, and that may be true. The demand has to change now in order for regulators, fishermen, and our entire marine ecosystem to have even a pirate's peg leg to stand on in the decades ahead.

Rhubarb Tomato Soup

MAKES 6 CUPS (1.4 L)

Unlike the two rhubarb-based soups in chapter 4, this one has to wait until tomato season and rhubarb season overlap, which doesn't last long. When those seasons do line up, this bowl of comfort will summon you on a cool summer night. Both tomato puree and rhubarb freeze well for the purposes of this soup, so it is possible to make this recipe when the chilled souls of late fall are screaming for it. At the restaurant we sometimes serve this with dill grilled cheese croutons, but it also tastes great with simple grilled cheese.

5 small or 2 large Roma, paste,
  or cherry tomatoes
1½ tablespoons olive oil,
  plus more for drizzling
1 teaspoon salt, plus more
  for sprinkling
1½ large red onions, julienned
1 carrot, peeled, medium dice
1 stalk celery, medium dice
4 rhubarb stalks (about 1 pound
  [455 g]), cut on the bias ½ inch
  (1 cm) thick
3 cloves garlic, minced
1½ cups (355 g) tomato puree
3 tablespoons peeled and minced
  fresh gingerroot
½ cup (120 ml) sherry
⅓ cup plus 2 teaspoons (85 g) sugar
2 cups (475 ml) chicken stock
Ground black pepper

ROAST THE TOMATOES: Set the oven at 450°F (230°C), halve the tomatoes, squeeze out the seeds, drizzle with olive oil and a sprinkle of salt, and roast on a cookie sheet for 15 to 20 minutes, until they're shriveled and starting to brown around the edges. Let cool slightly.

MAKE THE SOUP: In a medium pan over low heat, combine 1½ tablespoons olive oil with the onions, carrot, celery, rhubarb, and garlic. Cook, stirring occasionally, until the vegetables are tender (but without adding color to them)—about 15 minutes.

Increase the heat to medium-high and add the roasted tomatoes, tomato puree, and ginger, cooking at a high simmer. Reduce the mixture slightly, stirring occasionally, about 5 minutes. Add the sherry and deglaze the pan, scraping up any browned bits and cooking until the scent of alcohol wears off, about 3 minutes. Add the sugar, chicken stock, pepper, and 1 teaspoon salt; bring to a boil, then reduce the heat to low and simmer 5 minutes more, to allow the flavors to develop. Remove the pan from the heat, allow the mixture to cool slightly, then transfer it to a blender and puree until smooth. Serve immediately with grilled cheese, or let the soup cool and refrigerate it for up to 5 days.

Chilled Cucumber Soup

MAKES 8 CUPS (1.9 L)

4 medium pickling cucumbers
1 tablespoon olive oil
½ bulb fennel, rough-chopped
¼ Spanish onion, diced
3 garlic scapes, chopped (about
  3 tablespoons)
½ ripe avocado
1-inch (2.5 cm) section gingerroot,
  peeled, rough-chopped
1 cup (235 ml) whole-milk plain yogurt
¾ cup (180 ml) buttermilk
1 tablespoon honey
Juice of 1 lime
½ bunch fresh mint leaves
2 tablespoons packed fresh
  lemon balm leaves
2 fronds fresh dill
¾ teaspoon salt
⅛ teaspoon white pepper

Wash the cucumbers, cut off the ends, then quarter, seed, and chop them roughly.

Pour the olive oil into a 10- or 12-inch (25 or 30 cm) pan over medium heat. Add the fennel, onion, and garlic scapes and sweat for about 15 minutes, until the vegetables are soft. Transfer them to the bowl of a blender and puree until smooth. Add the cucumbers and the remaining ingredients and puree again until smooth. Strain through a fine-mesh strainer (optional) for a smooth texture, adjust for seasoning as necessary, and refrigerate. Serve chilled.

Scarlet Turnip Vichyssoise

SERVES 6 TO 8

The beauty of this delicious soup is that it can be served chilled in early summer using the spring planting of scarlet turnips, or it can be served hot in October, when the first autumn crop of scarlet turnips comes out of the ground. These are very special roots, almost gaudily colored in their hot-pink skin. We have grown varieties of pink-fleshed potatoes that further enhance the color of this soup if you can find them. If not, any red-skinned potato will do just fine.

1 tablespoon butter

¼ cup (60 ml) olive oil

1 pound (455 g) scarlet turnips, quartered

1 leek, quartered and chopped (white and light-green parts)

½ bulb fennel, coarsely chopped

1 tablespoon salt, plus additional to taste

½ teaspoon baharat spice blend (available at stockandspice.com)

Pinch cayenne pepper

½ cup (120 ml) white wine

3 medium red-fleshed potatoes, skin on, chopped into 8 pieces each

4–4½ cups (945 ml–1 L) vegetable stock

Heat the butter and oil in a 4-quart (4 L) pot over medium-low heat. Add all the vegetables except the potatoes and sprinkle with salt, stirring to combine. Simmer 10 minutes, stirring occasionally. Add the spices, deglaze with the wine, and simmer about 3 minutes, or until the alcohol scent wears off. Add the potatoes and vegetable stock, and bring the mixture just to a boil over high heat. Reduce to a simmer and cook 10 to 15 minutes, or until the potatoes are tender. Remove from the heat, let cool slightly, transfer to a blender, and puree until smooth. Adjust the seasoning to taste and serve.

Carrie's Biscuits

MAKES ABOUT 18

There are almost as many family recipes for buttermilk biscuits as there are families, but this one from longtime Black Trumpet sous chef Carrie is fool-proof, incredibly easy, and always delicious without being overly greasy. Our monthly kitchen meetings, which drag our staff into the building on the first Monday morning of every month, were made much more bearable by the presence of these hot, poppable treats, fresh out of the oven.

2 cups (240 g) all-purpose flour
1 teaspoon sugar
1 teaspoon salt
1 tablespoon baking powder
½ teaspoon baking soda
½ cup (115 g) cold butter,
  cut into 12 pieces
¾ cup (180 ml) cold buttermilk,
  plus more for brushing biscuits

Preheat the oven to 375°F (190°C).

Whisk the flour, sugar, salt, baking powder, and baking soda in a medium bowl. Add the butter, cutting in the pieces with knives or a pastry cutter until they are the size of large peas. Drizzle the buttermilk on top, distributing evenly over the dry ingredients, and mix gently until just barely combined. Turn the dough out onto a clean work surface and, handling as little as possible, mound it into a loose square. Roll out to ½ inch (1 cm) thick and cut rounds with a 2¼- to 2½-inch (5.5 to 6 cm) biscuit cutter. The scraps can be combined and rolled out again to make additional biscuits. Evenly space the rounds on a baking sheet, leaving some room for expansion. Brush the tops with buttermilk and bake for about 6 minutes, rotate the pan a half turn, and bake 6 minutes more, until the biscuits are puffed and golden brown. Let cool slightly on the pan and serve.

Chelo Rice

SERVES 6 TO 8

I went through a weird phase during which I became obsessed with the cuisine of Georgia and Azerbaijan. I don't know why this happened. I certainly didn't have any familial or social connection to this region. I don't even know anyone from there. I guess I have to blame the Internet. Anyway, aside from a number of glorious ferments and pickles I came across during this phase, this odd rice dish is the only fruit of my research to appear on a Black Trumpet menu. Think of it as a cross between Spanish paella rice and Japanese *okonomikayi*. Try it with spicy grilled vegetables or, as it was on our menu, with whole roasted fish.

1½ cups (330 g) basmati rice
2 tablespoons plus 4 cups (975 ml) water, plus more for rinsing rice
¼ teaspoon saffron threads
1 egg (50 g liquid egg)
1 tablespoon yogurt
1 tablespoon plus ½ teaspoon salt
6 tablespoons (85 g) melted butter

Rinse the rice five times in cold water and set aside. Crumble the saffron into a small bowl and whisk together with the egg, yogurt, and 2 tablespoons of the water; set aside. Meanwhile, bring the remaining 4 cups (945 ml) water and the salt to a boil over high heat and add the rice. Bring the water back up to a boil and cook 6 minutes. Drain the rice and rinse in lukewarm water.

In the same pot, combine 3 tablespoons of the melted butter with the saffron-and-yogurt mixture. Carefully spoon the rice on top, creating a pyramid in the center of the pot. Drizzle the rest of the melted butter over the rice. Drape a clean, damp dish towel over the top of the pot. Cover with the lid and turn the ends of the towel up over the top of the lid so the towel doesn't catch fire. Cook 10 minutes over medium heat, then reduce the heat to low and cook an additional 20 minutes. Remove the pot to a water bath and let cool 5 minutes, without removing the lid. Uncover, fluff the rice with a fork, and remove to a plate, being careful not to dig down and disturb the crust. Detach the crust, which should be golden brown and slightly burned in some places, and crack it over the rice.

Bacon-Strawberry Vinaigrette

MAKES 1 PINT (475 ML)

This dressing works well on any bitter mesclun mix or a salad of baby Asian mustard greens.

4 ounces (115 g) bacon, diced
3 shallots
1 pint (340 g) strawberries,
    hulled and quartered
¼ cup (60 ml) white verjus
¼ cup (60 ml) sherry vinegar
2 tablespoons Dijon mustard
2 tablespoons honey
2 tablespoons agave nectar
½ teaspoon salt
2 tablespoons olive oil

Preheat the oven to 350°F (175°C). Roast the bacon in a single layer on a cookie sheet, turning occasionally, until the pieces are golden brown and the fat is rendered out, about 15 minutes.

Peel the shallots and roast them whole on a cookie sheet, turning occasionally, until soft and beginning to brown, about 25 minutes.

In a medium pan over high heat, add the strawberries and sauté 30 seconds. Deglaze the pan with the verjus and cook until the liquid evaporates, about 1 minute.

Add the bacon, shallot, and strawberries, and the remaining ingredients except the olive oil, to the bowl of a blender and blend on high until smooth, about 10 to 20 seconds. Add the olive oil in a slow and steady stream to create an emulsification. Remove from the blender, cool to room temperature, and refrigerate.

Chicken Tinga

MAKES 8 SALADS OR 16 TACOS

Perhaps only Mexican culture could have turned boiled chicken into something this delicious. One of my favorite things to pack on a summer picnic (if I went on summer picnics) would be this zesty "chicken salad," which can be enjoyed hot or cold, as weather and mood dictate.

For the chicken
2 quarts (1.9 L) water
1 cup (225 g) mirepoix (page 13)
6 whole cloves garlic
3 dried avocado leaves (or substitute 2 bay leaves)
1 teaspoon coriander seed
½ teaspoon black peppercorns
4 chicken wings and 4 legs

For the salsa verde
6 poblano chiles
1 tablespoon cumin seed
1 teaspoon coriander seed
1 Spanish onion, medium dice
1 pound (455 g) tomatillos, husks removed
1 clove garlic
2 bunches cilantro, leaves washed and picked
Pinch dried Mexican oregano
Salt, to taste
Lime juice, to taste

COOK THE CHICKEN: In a medium pot, bring everything except the chicken to a boil. Reduce to a simmer and add the chicken. Cook at a simmer for 1 hour. Remove the chicken; strain, and set aside the resulting stock; then, when the chicken is cool enough to touch, shred it into a bowl, being careful to pick out any small bones.

MAKE THE SALSA VERDE: Preheat the oven to 400°F (200°C).

Fire-roast the poblanos by holding them over an open flame with a pair of tongs, allowing the skin to burn and blister on all sides. Remove from the flame and let sit in a wrapped bowl until cool enough to handle. Peel the peppers and butterfly them by running a knife down the length of one side. Remove the seeds and ribs and coarsely chop.

In a small dry pan over low heat, add the cumin and coriander and toast, shaking the pan occasionally, until the seeds begin to release their oils and you can smell a slight aroma, about 3 minutes. Remove to a small bowl and set aside. In the same dry pan, add the onion and whole tomatillos. Place the pan in the oven for 10 minutes, stirring every few minutes, or until the tomatillos have browned and softened considerably, releasing their juices into the pan. Remove the pan from the oven and let cool.

In a blender, puree the roasted chiles with the tomatillo mixture, garlic, spices, and herbs. If the mixture is too thick, add some of the stock left from boiling the chicken. Add salt and lime juice to taste. In a bowl, mix the shredded chicken with enough salsa verde to saturate it.

Serve chilled, over a summer salad, or reheat with the salsa verde and serve in tacos. Any leftover salsa verde can be used as a condiment on pretty much anything, but my personal favorite Mexican breakfast, chilaquiles, might be the best use of all: stale tortilla chips baked with salsa verde, chicken stock, and cheese, topped with a fried egg.

Duqqa-Battered
Fried Squash Blossoms

MAKES 8

Squash blossoms have a delicious, delicate, sweet, and earthy flavor. They can be battered and fried with a stuffing or on their own. Try stuffing the blossoms with goat cheese and following the rest of this recipe, serving the crisped flowers on Chilled Zucchini Soup (page 261).

Egyptian duqqa is just one of dozens of spice blends I have fallen in love with since opening a spice shop next door to the restaurant. Versatile and relatively subtle, duqqa lifts up scrambled eggs and also pairs well with the equally subdued flavor of squash blossoms. Although this was a summer dish at Black Trumpet, most winter squash plants continue to flower right into October, barring any early frosts. It is optimal to pick male flowers, best identified by the shape of the flower and the type of organs inside, so the females can remain on the plant to bear fruit.

¾ cup (90 g) all-purpose flour
½ cup (45 g) chickpea flour
1½ teaspoons baking powder
½ teaspoon cornstarch
½ teaspoon salt, plus more for sprinkling
1½ teaspoons Duqqa Spice Mix
   (recipe follows)
1 cup (235 ml) water
1 tablespoon clarified butter
Vegetable oil, for frying
8 large squash blossoms

Combine the flours, baking powder, cornstarch, ½ teaspoon salt, and Duqqa Spice Mix in a medium bowl. Add the water and whisk until combined. Add the clarified butter and whisk until combined.

Pour 2 inches (5 cm) oil into a small, high-sided pot. When the temperature reaches 350°F (175°C) on a thermometer, carefully dip a squash blossom into the batter and drop into the hot oil. Fry for about 1 minute, until crispy and golden brown on one side. Turn over and fry 1 minute on the second side. Remove to a paper-towel-lined plate and sprinkle lightly with salt. Repeat with remaining squash blossoms. Serve immediately.

Duqqa Spice Mix

YIELDS ABOUT 3½ CUPS (830 ML)

2 cups (450 g) dried chickpeas
    (almonds or any other nut can
    be substituted)
½ cup (70 g) sesame seed
¼ cup (15 g) coriander seed
2 tablespoons cumin seed
2 tablespoons black peppercorns
2 tablespoons grains of paradise
3 tablespoons dried mint
3 tablespoons fresh thyme

Soak the dried chickpeas overnight in twice the volume of water, and drain. (If you're substituting nuts, omit the soaking, cooking, and drying steps.)

Preheat the oven to 200°F (95°C).

Place the chickpeas in a large pot covered with 2 inches (5 cm) cold water. Bring to a boil over high heat, reduce to a simmer, and cook until soft, about 20 minutes. Remove to a baking sheet and bake for 4 hours, or until completely dried out.

Remove the dried chickpeas to a blender or spice grinder. Add the remaining ingredients and grind until smooth.

Le Fin (excerpts from my blog,
Grandpa, What's a Cod?, posted November 2013)

During the last three years of my career as a chef and restaurant owner, I have undertaken a Melvillian quest to find an answer to an unanswerable question. This blog tracks the pursuit of that question, which is: *Should I buy fish from our local boats, or should I buy fish that is most plentiful and sustainable?* The goal of this pursuit is that my children's children will never have to ask the question posed in this blog's title.

In May 2009, three fishing boats from Ogunquit and Wells, Maine, landed some beautiful bluefin tuna. That afternoon, the fishermen—none of whom had a license to sell tuna—brought their catch directly to several restaurants in town, whose chefs each purchased a portion of the fish to serve in their restaurants. Shortly thereafter, a local fisheries officer from NOAA (National Oceanic and Atmospheric Administration) slapped a fine on each fisherman and chef involved in the bootlegged tuna transaction. The fines levied on fishers and restaurants totaled over $100,000. Pretty much every chef I knew at that point, myself included, pooped his pants a little when word got out, not because any of us had done anything worthy of a fine, but just that it could happen at all.

A few months later, while I was away on a trip, my sous chef purchased locally landed bluefin tuna from a legitimate fishmonger and ran it as a special on a Saturday night. The special was posted on a then nascent Facebook, as we'd been doing since the marketing meteor of social media first crashed on our doorstep. Within twenty-four hours, one person's post on our Facebook page expressing outrage about our choice to offer "endangered" bluefin tuna led to a barrage of defensive responses from our loyal fan base. *Chef Evan and Black Trumpet are as conscientious as they come!* the defenders cried. But my heart was filled with doubt.

A week later, I found myself attending a Chefs Collaborative sustainable seafood initiative at a highly regarded restaurant in Cambridge, Massachusetts. I pleaded my case to a roomful of chefs about the conundrum we chefs face trying to do the right thing for our local economy but also for our greater ecology. My confession met with nods and grimaces from some of the most respected chefs in the Greater Boston area. Since then I have attended sustainable seafood symposia from Italy to Seattle. In Italy, at Slow Food's Terra Madre conference, I was particularly moved by a fisherman from a small island nation in Oceania who could not afford to eat the fish he caught, which fetched top dollar in Japan and Europe, so when he fed his family fish, it was usually inexpensive, cellophane-wrapped farmed salmon from Europe. More stark images of a fractured food supply chain to come. Stay tuned . . .

There is a statistic that gets bandied about whenever I find myself around sustainable seafood cognoscenti that at once depresses and motivates me. In New Hampshire, the state with by far the smallest shoreline, over 90 percent of all fish consumed comes from overseas. Meanwhile, the crews of our few New Hampshire fishing vessels, who are struggling to meet ever-changing regulations while facing severely depleted wild stocks, are shipping over 90 percent of their catch outside New Hampshire.

Once, on a trip to Greece, Denise and I ate in a charming taverna at the base of a dock where fishing boats came and went by the minute, or so it seemed. When we sat down at a table, a boat was unloading its bounty into the kitchen behind us. Fish were still wiggling. The restaurant enforced a strict policy that each patron should meet the fish they were going to enjoy before it was cooked for them. There was no menu—just the fish itself on parade. A direct connection from sea to consumer with no red tape? This doesn't have to be a faraway fantasy. It has been a way of life for most of the world for most of human history.

A direct connection between the source of the seafood and the place where it is served is an important step toward ensuring that our community eat its own catch instead of falling into the absurd status quo that punishes fishermen *and* chefs for working together, while ensuring that our already restricted ocean harvest be shipped to the ends of the Earth instead of to our own tables.

Keper Connell and the Bluefin Tuna

My friend Keper, whom I have known since his days as a Ciento busser, grew up in the restaurant industry and ended up in the fishing industry: out of the proverbial pan and into the fire! As a commercial fisherman running a charter fishing company on the side, he does what he can to make a buck, but it gets harder and harder every year, as the "days at sea" quotas changed to catch limits, which in turn shrank for our dwindling fleet to the point where fishing is no longer a viable livelihood for anyone. Keper bristles outwardly at the controversy that surrounds bluefin tuna, citing statistics that fly in the face of those published by seafood watchdog nonprofits and agencies. He makes the valid observation that the subspecies of bluefin found in the Gulf of Maine has a relatively robust population that is better regulated than any other bluefin tuna in the world. He adds that, because these sleek and speedy giants of the tuna family travel thousands of miles a year, it is next to impossible to make an accurate assessment of their number. The trouble with counting fish, which most everyone agrees is necessary, is that it is not an exact science.

Every so often, during the summer season, Keper will catch a bluefin tuna and bring it to a local fishmonger. Like other tuna fishermen, he rarely does this, because a good-quality bluefin tuna will fetch a much higher price on the international market, where Japanese sushi buyers have been known to pay over $1 million for a single fish. Although that price is extremely unusual, it is not uncommon to see a highly rated bluefin auctioned for over $10,000. That's a good day at sea for any fisherman, especially in desperate times such as these.

If I'm lucky, when his tuna ship does come in, Keper might bring me a piece of the toro (belly) from a prized bluefin as a gift. One year he did just that. I prepared a rice and bean salad at home, found a vinaigrette in the fridge concocted by one of my children, barely seared the outside of a cube of the fish, placed it on top of the salad, plopped down on a bar stool at my kitchen counter, and devoured the fish and the salad with exclamatory ardor. Again I was reminded that the simple and the unexpected make the most memorable tastes. And maybe I also put more weight on every bite of bluefin I eat, knowing that it may be the last time I get to taste it.

Ceviche with Pico de Gallo

SERVES 6 AS AN APPETIZER

By now, most people are familiar with ceviche, a technique that cures raw fish in citrus juice, yielding the perfect starter to any meal on a hot summer day. My first time eating ceviche in a true *cevicheria* was in 1993 with my friend and fellow chef Damon Bruner. We had driven across the border together from his home in San Diego, finally settling on a beachside shack outside Ensenada, where the simplest preparation of acid-cured fish arrived in a heaping plastic bowl with a side of totopos and nothing else. We devoured it along with a few short Coronas, joined a game of beach volleyball, and sat back down to eat more ceviche. If memory serves, we stopped again before the border, at Rosarito this time, and ate more ceviche at a roadside stand. As much as I love sitting down with my family to a model ship packed with sushi, ceviche is the raw fish preparation for me.

Halibut—with its thick, sweet ivory flesh—makes a fine ceviche fish, but it is very expensive, and it is not exactly the poster fish of sustainability. We ran this dish using halibut on our menu before I started my kayak trip on the proverbial turbulent sea of sustainable seafood. Now I know better, and I would urge you, the maker of this recipe, to seek out fluke from Rhode Island, or whatever buttery, white-fleshed fish is abundant in your nearest waters.

For the ceviche
Juice of 6 limes
1¼ teaspoons salt, plus more to taste
12 ounces (340 g) fish, diced in ¼-inch
   (0.5 cm) cubes

For the Pico de Gallo
1 jalapeño, ribs and seeds removed,
   brunoised
¼ medium red onion, small dice
2 Roma tomatoes, quartered lengthwise, seeds squeezed out, small dice
2 teaspoons finely chopped
   fresh cilantro

MAKE THE CEVICHE: Place the lime juice and salt in a tall, high-sided, nonreactive container and stir to dissolve the salt. Add the chopped fish, making sure it is covered completely in liquid. Marinate in the refrigerator for about 4 hours, stirring periodically. The fish is done curing when it is opaque in color and the flesh is firm. Once the fish is cured, it can be stored, with the citrus juice strained off, for up to 2 days.

MAKE THE PICO DE GALLO: In a medium nonreactive mixing bowl, combine the jalapeño, onion, tomatoes, and cilantro. Stir to combine.

TO SERVE: Drain the liquid from the fish and toss with the Pico de Gallo. Add salt to taste. Serve immediately.

Tuna Caesar with Parmesan Tuiles and Caesar Aioli

SERVES 6

Right off the bat, this dish became a Black Trumpet classic, garnering plaudits from a wide swath of our clientele. The recipe has a complex array of parts, but the extra effort pays off in the form of a stunning presentation and pleasing flavors to match.

For the Parmesan Tuiles

1½ cups (150 g) freshly grated Parmesan cheese (use the small holes of a box grater)

For the Caesar Aioli

2 salt-cured Italian anchovies
1 whole egg (50 g liquid egg), cold
2 egg yolks (36 g), cold
1 tablespoon Dijon mustard
3 cloves garlic
½ cup (120 ml) pure olive oil
Juice of 2 Meyer lemons
½ cup (120 ml) extra-virgin olive oil
2 teaspoons garum (see "Legal Fermentation Practices," page 316)

For the croutons

10-inch (25 cm) length of day-old baguette
¼ cup (60 ml) olive oil
2 cloves garlic, peeled, rough-chopped
Pinch salt

For the salad

18 Castelvetrano olives
1 small head romaine lettuce, chiffonade
1 pound (455 g) yellowfin tuna, diced into ½-inch (1 cm) cubes
Olive oil

MAKE THE PARMESAN TUILES: Preheat the oven to 450°F (230°C).

Spread a heaping ¼ cup (25 g) grated cheese on a Silpat-lined cookie sheet and, using your fingertips, spread it into a circle about 5½ inches (14 cm) in diameter. Repeat with the remaining five piles of cheese (you may need to do this in two batches). Place the pan on the top rack of the oven and bake 3 to 4 minutes, checking often and rotating the pan halfway through, until the cheese is golden brown and bubbly. Have ready some upturned bowls or containers (as many as you have cheese rounds), 2 to 3 inches (5 to 7.5 cm) in diameter. Remove the cheese circles from the oven, let cool for 20 seconds, then carefully flip the cheese rounds onto the upturned bowls using a wide spatula. Press very gently with your thumb and forefinger to mold the cheese to the bowl, being careful not to press or pull the hardening cheese too hard or it will crack or tear. Let the cheese bowl sit on the mold for 2 to 3 minutes, until completely hardened. Carefully remove the cheese bowls from the molds and set aside.

MAKE THE CAESAR AIOLI: Soak the anchovies in 1 cup (235 ml) water for 30 minutes and then drain.

Combine the eggs, mustard, and garlic in the bowl of a food processor and blend until smooth. Add the anchovies and blend until smooth. With the motor running, add the regular olive oil to the bowl of the processor in a very slow and steady stream, then slowly add the lemon juice, and finally add the extra-virgin olive oil (still very slowly), tasting for bitterness halfway through. If the aioli becomes bitter, substitute regular olive oil for the remaining extra-virgin olive oil. Finish with the garum oil. Remove the aioli to a container and refrigerate overnight to allow the flavors to develop.

MAKE THE CROUTONS: Preheat the oven to 300°F (150°C).

Remove the crust on all four sides of the bread with a serrated knife. Quarter the bread lengthwise, dice into ¾-inch (2 cm) cubes, and place in a small mixing bowl. Add the olive oil and garlic to a small frying pan and heat slowly over low heat until the garlic just begins to color, about 10 minutes. Strain the oil into the mixing bowl with the bread, sprinkle with salt, and toss until all the pieces are fully coated. Place the bread on a cookie sheet and bake for 10 to 12 minutes, until crispy throughout and beginning to turn golden brown. Set aside.

ASSEMBLE THE SALAD: Smash, pit, and roughly chop the olives. Divide the lettuce into six even piles and place in the bottom of the six Parmesan bowls. Sauté the tuna cubes in olive oil in a very hot pan for about 20 seconds on each side. Add the croutons to the pan and remove it from the heat. Place three olives and one-sixth of the tuna-and-crouton mixture on top of each bed of lettuce. Using a squeeze bottle, squirt some of the dressing over the ingredients in the bowls. Serve immediately.

Tuna Tartare with Coconut and Coriander

SERVES 12

Most of the ingredients this recipe calls for can be found in your average super-market these days. Fish sauce is one possible exception. I have developed a fondness for the Red Boat brand, which is organic and a bit less of a punch in the nose than other brands. If you substitute another brand of fish sauce, use half as much.

1 can (400 ml) coconut milk
¼ cup (60 ml) heavy cream
1 teaspoon sugar
1 tablespoon minced peeled gingerroot
1 stalk lemongrass, minced
½ teaspoon coriander seed, toasted and ground
1½ teaspoons Red Boat brand fish sauce
2 pounds (910 g) sushi-grade yellowtail tuna, diced into ½-inch (1 cm) cubes
2 jalapeños, small dice
2 shallots, minced
1 tablespoon finely chopped fresh cilantro
½ teaspoon salt
2 tablespoons olive oil

Bring the first six ingredients to a boil in a small pot over high heat, watching closely so the mixture doesn't boil over. Remove from the heat and let steep for an hour. Stir in the fish sauce and strain the mixture through a fine-mesh strainer. Let it cool to room temperature, then refrigerate until cold.

In a large mixing bowl, combine the tuna, jalapeños, shallots, cilantro, salt, and olive oil; fold gently with a spatula to combine. Fold in the coconut milk mixture until combined and taste for salt. Serve immediately.

On our menu, we served this early-summer delight in a radicchio leaf, but any crunchy lettuce leaf will also do. And blanched, mashed English peas make a lovely accompaniment for the tuna as well.

Nigella-Crusted Seared Tuna
with Martini Sabayon

SERVES 8

Nigella, a seed used in Indian cuisine, has had me in its thrall since we first met. Newcomers to nigella shouldn't need any further enticement to love the mellow, floral notes of this alluring spice, but if they do: The complex, beautiful blue flower from the same plant is known as love-in-a-mist. Conversely, some plant catalogs refer to nigella as devil in a bush, so I guess the beauty of the plant rests in the eye of the beholder. We have grown the flower in our garden and served it at the restaurant, and it makes for a stunning visual on the plate, but too many plants for our available space would be required to provide enough seeds for spice harvesting. This is another reminder that, sometimes, we have no choice but to source good things from far away.

Think of nigella as a softer, sweeter version of caraway seed, which—to me—can easily overwhelm a dish by making everything it touches turn into rye bread. Nigella also accents most vegetables, but especially carrots and beets, very nicely.

1 pound (450 g) sushi-grade
  yellowfin tuna
1 teaspoon salt
½ teaspoon black pepper
1 tablespoon whole nigella seed

Take 2-ounce (55 g) cubes of good-quality tuna, and roll each piece in a mixture of salt, pepper, and whole nigella seed. Sear the tuna on all sides in a very hot pan with olive oil/butter mix for 20 seconds on each side. Slice the tuna with a sharp knife and serve with a dollop of Martini Sabayon (recipe follows).

Martini Sabayon

MAKES ABOUT 2 CUPS (475 ML)

This is a strange twist on a classic French sauce, also called a foamy sauce. More often than not, it is served with fruit for a light dessert. For reasons I can't explain, I first came up with the idea of putting martini ingredients into a sauce when my friend Kevin Flannery in Concord, Massachusetts, asked me to be his barbecue competition partner.

When I met Kevin, I was making sandwiches, selling birdhouses, and writing for a living—in that order. The food writing gig was spotty, the birdhouse gig less so, and the sandwich-making job quite secure. I enjoyed the interaction with customers, and Kevin was a regular. I agreed to join Kevin's team, and the two of us entered our first competition shortly thereafter. It was a pretty small event, as I would later learn, with only a dozen or so teams competing in the chilly parking lot of a hunting club, where we staked out our smoker and camping tent for the overnight ritual.

The next day, we won first place for our smoked, grilled chicken, which was glazed in a sticky sauce made from gin, vermouth, lemon, and olive juice. As you can see, this recipe calls for no olive juice, but the tuna and the sauce both pair well with green olives, especially the buttery Castelvetrano variety used in our beloved Fried Almonds, Olives, and Garlic (page 124).

¼ preserved lemon (page 16), minced

1 thumb gingerroot, peeled and coarsely chopped

8 juniper berries, crushed with the blunt end of a knife

¾ cup (180 ml) sweet vermouth (we use Dolin Blanc, which is perfect if you can find it)

Zest and juice of 1 lemon

½ cup (115 g) sugar

½ teaspoon salt

4 egg yolks (72 g)

¾ cup (180 ml) heavy cream

Make a syrup by combining the first seven ingredients in a small saucepan over low heat. Simmer, stirring occasionally, for 8 minutes, until the flavors have developed. Strain through a mesh strainer into a medium bowl, pressing on the solids with a ladle to capture all the liquid. Set aside and let cool.

Add the yolks to the bowl with the syrup and whisk to combine.

Set up a double boiler by bringing 2 inches (5 cm) water to a simmer over medium-low heat in a high-sided pot. Fit the bowl into the pot, making sure the bottom of the bowl doesn't touch the water. Stir constantly but gently with a whisk, keeping the liquid moving so it doesn't cook on the side of the hot bowl. As it thickens, it will start to get paler and foamier; finally it will become somewhat shiny, about 5 to 6 minutes total. At this point, it should also be thick enough to coat the back of a spoon. Remove the bowl from the water bath and allow the mixture to cool to room temperature, stirring occasionally.

Meanwhile, in a large, cold mixing bowl, whip the cream to soft peaks. Fold gently into the syrup until the mixture turns a uniform pale-yellow color.

Serve immediately.

Baked Stuffed Quahog Chowder

SERVES 8

This early Black Trumpet dish developed an immediate following with its unique presentation—a fusion of the New England classic "baked stuffed clam" and clam chowder.

2 ears corn

2 tablespoons melted butter

½ teaspoon salt, plus more to taste

8 quahogs, each 3–4 inches (7.5–10 cm) in diameter

1 tablespoon whole butter

1 teaspoon minced garlic

1½ (355 ml) cups white wine

3 ounces (85 g) bacon, small dice

1 small yellow onion, small dice

3 stalks celery, small dice

2 medium carrots, small dice

¼ cup (30 g) flour

½ cup (120 ml) heavy cream

1 quart (945 ml) whole milk

½ pound (225 g) Red Bliss potatoes, skin on, small dice

2 bay leaves

½ teaspoon black pepper

¾ cup (40 g) panko

Preheat the oven to 400°F (200°C). Drizzle the corn with 2 tablespoons melted butter, sprinkle with ½ teaspoon salt, and place on a baking sheet. Roast the corn in the oven, turning once or twice, for 25 minutes, or until the corn is cooked through and the kernels are beginning to brown. When cool enough to handle, cut the corn from the cob and set aside.

Add the quahogs, 1 tablespoon butter, and the garlic to a 10- to 12-inch (25 to 30 cm) heavy-bottomed, high-sided pot over high heat. When you can smell the garlic and it begins to toast (about 30 seconds), add the wine, cover the pot, and cook until the wine comes to a boil. Reduce the heat to medium and continue cooking until the lid starts shaking and spewing foamy liquid, about 12 to 15 minutes. Check the clams to see if they have opened and are cooked through. If not, reduce the heat slightly, half cover the pan (to prevent it from boiling over), and continue cooking until the clams are fully open.

When the shells are cool enough to handle, remove them from the pot, strain the liquid through a fine-mesh strainer, and set it aside. You should have 3 to 4 cups (710 to 945 ml) liquid (this will be your clam broth for the chowder). Pick the clams from the shells, remove and discard the tough "foot," finely chop the clams, and set them aside in a medium bowl. Scrub the shells under hot water to remove any remaining sand and debris. Set aside.

Wipe out the pan and add the bacon over medium-low heat. Render the fat from the bacon, stirring occasionally, until the bacon is starting to brown but is still pliable and not too crispy, 10 to 12 minutes. Drain off all but 2 tablespoons of fat and add the onion, celery, and carrots to the pot. Cook, stirring occasionally, until the vegetables begin to soften, about 3 minutes. Add the flour and toast slightly, stirring to coat the vegetables, about 3 minutes. Pour the clam broth into the pot in a slow and steady stream, whisking constantly with a heavy-duty whisk. Bring the mixture to a boil, whisking often in a figure-eight pattern to make sure none of the flour is trapped in the bottom of the pot. Reduce the heat to low, add the cream, and bring to a simmer, whisking often. Simmer until the mixture is thick

enough to coat the back of a spoon, about 5 minutes. Add the milk, potatoes, roasted corn, bay leaves, and pepper; simmer over low heat for 20 to 25 minutes, until the potatoes are fork-tender. Make sure the mixture doesn't come up to a boil after you add the milk or the liquid will curdle and—worse yet—foam up over the edge of the pot and encrust your stovetop with a dairy mess. Taste for seasoning and add salt if necessary.

Remove the bay leaves, strain the solids, and reserve the broth. Transfer the solids to the bowl with the chopped clams and, when it's cool enough to handle, mash the mixture lightly with your fingers. Fold in the panko and stuff the clamshells with the mixture, about 3 ounces (85 g) per clam. Let cool to room temperature and refrigerate until you're ready to use it.

When you're ready to serve, place the stuffed clams with the open end facing up on a cookie sheet or roasting pan and bake at 450°F (230°C) for 10 minutes. Meanwhile, heat the chowder to just under a boil. Place one stuffed clam in a soup bowl and pour boiling broth over the top. Repeat with the remaining seven clams. Serve.

Risotto-Stuffed Tomato
with Summer Squash Bisque

SERVES 8 (BISQUE WILL SERVE MORE IF USED AS A SAUCE)

This dish—half main course and half soup—captures the heart of midsummer, a season when tomatoes, basil, and anise hyssop are prolific.

For the risotto

1 medium Spanish onion, small dice

2 tablespoons clarified
(or melted) butter

1 tablespoon minced garlic

4 cups (800 g) arborio rice

¼ teaspoon saffron threads

1 teaspoon salt

1¾ quarts (1.7 L) water, heated to
just below a boil

¼ cup (25 g) grated Parmesan cheese
(use the small holes of a box grater)

2 tablespoons whole butter

For the Summer Squash Bisque

2 ounces (55 g) clarified butter

1 stalk celery, small dice

1 small carrot, small dice

½ small Spanish onion, small dice

1 zucchini

1 summer squash or pattypan squash

1 cup (80 g) chanterelles

4 cloves garlic, minced

2 teaspoons salt

½ cup (120 ml) tomato puree

½ cup (120 ml) sherry

3 cups (710 ml) vegetable stock

1 cup (235 ml) heavy cream

¼ cup (15 g) loosely packed fresh basil
or anise hyssop leaves

To serve

8 medium round tomatoes

1 teaspoon salt

Calendula petals or squash blossoms,
to garnish

MAKE THE RISOTTO: Sweat the onion in the clarified butter in a large heavy-bottomed high-sided pan over medium heat for about 5 minutes. Add the garlic and stir, 30 seconds. Add the arborio rice and toast, stirring often, 3 to 4 minutes. Add the saffron and salt and stir to combine. Add water, 6 ounces (180 ml) at a time, stirring well, every 2 minutes or so. When the rice begins to look dry, add 6 more ounces (180 ml) water, repeating until the rice is al dente, about 20 minutes' total cooking time. The rice should be slightly soupy at this point, but not stiff, or it will become pasty when you add the cheese. Off the heat, gently fold in the cheese and whole butter with a spatula. At this point, it should ooze into a bowl, like a stiff porridge. Spread the risotto out on a cookie sheet to stop the cooking process and let it cool to room temperature.

MAKE THE SUMMER SQUASH BISQUE: Place the butter in a 4-quart stockpot over medium heat. Add the celery, carrot, onion, squashes, and chanterelles, and cook 2 minutes, stirring. Add the garlic and salt and cook, stirring occasionally, 15 to 18 minutes, or until the vegetables begin to stick to the bottom of the pan. Add the tomato puree, scraping up the browned bits, and cook 5 minutes. Add the sherry, cook 5 minutes more, and then add the stock. Simmer 10 to 12 minutes, add the cream, stir, and simmer 10 more minutes. Add the basil or anise hyssop and stir to combine. Transfer to a blender and puree until smooth. Serve immediately or cool, refrigerate, and reheat slowly over very low heat.

TO SERVE: Preheat the oven to 400°F (200°C).

Cut a shallow hole in each tomato that measures 1½ to 2 inches (4 to 5 cm) in diameter. Hollow out the tomatoes with a serrated tomato spoon or a melon baller, trying to remove all the seeds and most of the pulp, but leaving some of the juice (this will help steam the risotto while it bakes). Be careful not to poke a hole through the bottom of the tomato. Fill each tomato with about ⅓ cup (80 ml) risotto rice and sprinkle the top of each with a pinch of salt. Transfer

the tomatoes to a cookie sheet and bake 10 to 13 minutes, until the tomatoes begin to split and the rice begins to turn golden brown.

Spoon ¼ cup (60 ml) of hot soup into the bottom of each bowl, top with a risotto-stuffed tomato, garnish with calendula leaves or squash blossoms, and serve.

The Other Heirloom Tomato

When most people hear the word *heirloom* in the context of food, they conjure images of multicolored tomatoes in all shapes and sizes. The tomato has become a brilliant ambassador for the heirloom vegetable, yet it is only one handsome workhorse in the heirloom wagon train. In our heirloom garden, we grow potatoes, lettuces, corn, beans, eggplant, and carrots, among dozens of other vegetables.

We also grow very few slicer tomato plants, because—in our climate—tomatoes tend to produce a ridiculous abundance of fruit in a fairly short period of time. In the restaurant, we can't keep up with slicer tomato production, even if slicers are used in several late-summer menu items. But paste tomatoes are another story, because they make great soups and sauces; have a rich, deep flavor when cooked; lose little water weight, because they are way less juicy; and can be frozen, canned, smoked, and preserved with relative ease for later use.

Here are the varieties we have grown in our heirloom garden over the years:

- **PRINCIPE BORGHESE:** Small grape, intense flavor, making the best straight tomato sauce I have tasted to date.
- **COSTOLUTO GENOVESE:** Ribbed, flat, and meaty.
- **AMISH PASTE:** Long, Marzano-like, but drier and firmer, excellent for canning whole.
- **SAN MARZANO:** Bright red, long and conical, great for canning whole or as puree.
- **JERSEY DEVIL:** Challenging to grow the one year we tried, which may have had to do more with the drought our garden (and our community) endured.

Tomato Mustard Aioli

MAKES 2½ CUPS (590 ML)

This all-purpose condiment can be served on burgers hot off the midsummer grill, but it also makes a lovely dip for raw vegetables freshly harvested from the garden. Whatever its application, this is a wonderful accoutrement to have on hand.

1 pound (455 g) paste tomatoes (substitute Roma plum variety)
1 cup (235 ml) pure olive oil, divided
½ teaspoon salt, plus more for roasting tomatoes and to taste
2 tablespoons prepared horseradish
1 clove garlic
1 tablespoon nigella seed
1 teaspoon ground coriander
Pinch ground cardamom
Pinch ground mace
3 tablespoons Dijon mustard
3 egg yolks (54 g)
1 cup (235 ml) extra-virgin olive oil

Preheat the oven to 250°F (120°C).

Halve the tomatoes lengthwise, drizzle with ½ cup (120 ml) of the pure olive oil, and sprinkle with salt. Place the tomatoes, cut side up, on a baking sheet fitted with a cooling or drying rack. Roast for 2 hours and let cool.

In a food processor, pulse the horseradish, garlic, and spices until the mixture forms a paste. Add the mustard, egg yolks, and oven-dried tomatoes and process until smooth, scraping down the bottom and sides of the bowl. With the motor running, gradually add the remaining ½ cup (120 ml) of the pure olive oil in a slow and steady stream—this should take about 1 minute. Next, add the extra-virgin olive oil and check the consistency. The aioli should be thick, shiny, and smooth. Thin with ice water (add it by the teaspoon) if the aioli is too thick and season with additional salt if necessary.

Garden Tomato Soup
with Shellfish and Saffron Cream

SERVES 8

One of the most eye-popping dishes to come out of the Black Trumpet kitchen, this soup can easily be served as a meal in a large bowl with a side salad and a hunk of grilled rustic bread.

For the soup
4 pounds (1.8 kg) paste tomatoes, cored, rough-chopped
1 cup (60 g) packed fresh basil leaves
1 tablespoon sugar
2 tablespoons plus ½ teaspoon salt, divided
1 cup (225 g) medium-diced Spanish onion
1 cup (225 g) medium-diced celery
1 cup (225 g) medium-diced carrot
12 cloves garlic
2 tablespoons olive oil
1 cup (235 ml) vegetable stock
Pepper, to taste
16 cherrystone clams
¾ cup (180 ml) white wine
40 mussels
16 medium white shrimp, peeled and deveined

For the Saffron Cream
1 clove garlic
½ teaspoon saffron
½ cup (120 ml) cream
Pinch salt

In a nonreactive pot, combine the tomatoes, basil, sugar, and 2 tablespoons of the salt; simmer, covered, over low heat for 45 minutes. Strain the tomato mixture through a mesh strainer or china cap into a bowl, pressing on the solids with a ladle to capture all the liquid. Place the onion, celery, carrot, garlic, olive oil, and remaining ½ teaspoon salt in a heavy-bottomed nonreactive pot and cook for 15 minutes, until the vegetables have begun to soften. Add the strained soup and bring to a simmer over medium heat. Simmer until it thickens slightly, about 10 minutes. Transfer the soup to a blender and blend until smooth, adding up to a cup of vegetable stock to thin the liquid, if necessary. Season to taste with salt and pepper as needed.

Meanwhile, place the clams and the white wine in a separate pan with a lid and bring to a boil. Add the mussels and shrimp, cover again, and reduce the heat to medium. Simmer 3 minutes, or until all the clams and mussels are open.

MAKE THE SAFFRON CREAM: Slice the garlic lengthwise into seven or eight thin slices. In a hot, dry pan over a high flame, add the garlic slices and cook 1 minute. Add the saffron and toast 10 seconds. Add the cream and salt and reduce the heat to a simmer. Simmer 2 minutes and strain through a mesh strainer.

FINISH THE DISH: When you're ready to serve, heat up the tomato soup and the shellfish separately. When it's hot, pour the tomato soup into bowls, dollop the Saffron Cream in the middle, and arrange the seafood around the periphery of the bowl.

Seafood Paella

SERVES 8

Paella, in its many guises, has found its way onto over half of Black Trumpet's menus. I have cooked paella for parties of over a hundred people, and I still love the intensity a large-format paella requires of its maker.

I have learned over the years that paella poses risks to the home cook because certain elements of its construction require cat-like reflexes, a willingness to accept a few minor burns, and a good dose of muscle memory that can't be taught. Despite that, there is really no mystery to making a good paella. It's all about the timing. And the right pan. And maybe a little luck. Because the paellera, the pan after which the dish is named, is made of very thin metal, and because the pan should always be heated over a high open flame (gas or propane are fine), everything during assembly in the pan has to happen in rapid succession. The difference between the hard-earned golden-brown crust known as pega, which lines the bottom and edges of the rice in the final presentation, and a burned mess, should be fairly clear. Patience and speed come together to make the perfect paella. After making thousands of them at this point, I still taste every one to be sure the seasoning is spot on.

In order to keep this Seafood Paella on the menu throughout the summer, we rotate through seasonal ingredients. For example, when the first English peas come in, they perfectly punctuate the paella's piquancy, but later in the season, when the peas have dried up, we might add fresh fava beans, green chickpeas (if I am lucky enough to find them locally), or fresh shelling beans. Later in the year, Mountain Paella, which relies less on fresh produce and more on meat protein, comes into play. You can find that recipe on page 342.

If time is an issue, I suggest making the rice ahead of time so as to eliminate one of the bigger variables in the process.

For the rice

2 cups (475 ml) water

3 tablespoons olive oil

1 tablespoon unsalted butter

1 small sweet or Spanish onion, in ½-inch (1 cm) dice

1 clove garlic, minced

1 generous pinch saffron (about 20 threads)

1 cup (200 g) Calasparra rice (available in specialty markets, or—in a pinch—substitute arborio)

1 teaspoon salt

MAKE THE RICE: Bring the water to a boil in a 1- to 2-quart (1 to 2 L) pot over medium-high heat. Meanwhile, in a 2-quart (2 L) pot over medium-low heat, add the olive oil, butter, and onion; sweat until the onion begins to soften, about 4 minutes. Add the garlic and saffron and stir for 1 minute. Turn the heat to low and add the rice. Toast for 4 minutes, stirring occasionally, until the rice is lightly toasted.

Add the boiling water and salt to the rice, stir, cover, and simmer for 13 to 15 minutes, until the water is absorbed and the rice is al dente. Remove the pan from the heat and pour the rice onto a rimmed sheet pan to stop cooking and cool.

For the paella

2 tablespoons olive oil

6 ounces (170 g) fresh chorizo (not dry-cured), sliced into 1-ounce (28 g) pieces

8 clams, scrubbed and rinsed to remove sand and grit

8 scallops, washed, patted dry, and sprinkled with salt

8 ounces (225 g) flaky white fish (pollock or redfish are good options), cut into 1-ounce (28 g) pieces and sprinkled with salt

8 ounces (225 g) fishy fish (I like bluefish, but mackerel, herring, even salmon work well), cut into 1-ounce (28 g) pieces and sprinkled with salt

½ red bell pepper, cored, seeded, and in ½-inch (1 cm) dice

½ green bell pepper, cored, seeded, and in ½-inch (1 cm) dice

1 clove garlic, minced

½ teaspoon salt, plus a pinch for sprinkling

1 cup (215 g) fava beans, peas, or other fresh legume

½ cup (120 ml) homemade fish stock, low-sodium clam juice, or low/no-sodium chicken stock

16 mussels, rinsed

16 medium shrimp (16–20 per pound)

¼ teaspoon hot smoked paprika

2 tablespoons chopped fresh parsley

MAKE THE PAELLA: Preheat a grill or oven to 425°F (220°C).

Heat the olive oil in a 12-inch (30 cm) paellera, or a carbon-steel or cast-iron pan, over medium heat until it barely begins to smoke. Add the chorizo and render for 4 minutes, until it begins to brown. Push the chorizo to one side of the pan and add the clams, pushing them up against the chorizo.

Turn the heat to high and add the scallops and both fish, searing on one side without disturbing, for 3 minutes, until they begin to color.

Remove everything but the clams from the pan. Add the peppers, garlic, salt, and fava beans. Toss to coat in the chorizo pan oil. Cook 2 minutes, then add the reserved 3 cups of cooked rice. Fold the rice gently with a spatula to incorporate the vegetables. Place the clams on top of the rice. Add the fish stock and stand the mussels faceup along the outside perimeter of the pan. Add the raw shrimp just inside the mussels and carefully assemble the fish in the middle, drizzling any residual oils on top. Sprinkle a pinch of salt, the paprika, and the parsley over the top.

Remove the pan from the heat and place on the preheated grill or in the oven. Bake for 10 minutes, until the stock is absorbed and the outer edges of the rice are golden brown and crispy. Serve.

Pega

Our seasonal paellas are made with two goals in mind: The first is that our love of the sacred art of paella comes across in the form of deliciousness, regardless of whatever prior context a guest might have for paella; and the second, that the bottom and edges of every paella we sell must possess the magic crust known as pega to Spaniards. *Pega*, which means "glue," describes the crunchy rice crust that forms when a paella is finished over high heat. The reduction of stock, absorbed into the rice, eventually dries to the point of almost burning, creating what the French call a Maillard effect. Pega-less paella deserves scorn. *¡Viva la pega!*

Saffron Yogurt Panna Cotta

MAKES 6 PORTIONS

This is a recipe longtime pastry chef Lauren created, perhaps summoning the spirit of original Black Trumpet dessert maker Jasmine Inglesmith's saffron-poached pear that had once graced the cover of *Portsmouth Magazine*. If you don't have silicon molds, use small, 4-ounce (120 ml) mason jars—that way you don't have to bother unmolding before serving.

If you prefer a solid yellow color in the finished product, you can strain out the saffron. Otherwise, leave the saffron in the panna cotta for a pretty, streaky look.

2 cups (475 ml) full-fat plain Greek yogurt
1 cup (235 ml) heavy cream
½ cup (120 ml) milk
¾ cup (170 g) sugar
2 pinches saffron (about 1 teaspoon loosely packed)
1 tablespoon gelatin powder
½ cup (120 ml) cold water

Whisk the yogurt and cream together in a medium bowl. Warm the milk and sugar in a small pot over low heat until the milk just begins to foam around the edges and the sugar dissolves. Remove from the heat, add the saffron, and let it steep 10 minutes.

In a small bowl, sprinkle the gelatin evenly over the cold water and let it bloom 5 minutes. Rewarm the milk over low heat and whisk in the gelatin until it dissolves, making sure there are no clumps. Remove from the heat and let it cool slightly. Pour the milk through a mesh strainer into the yogurt and cream mixture and whisk until smooth. Spray six 4-ounce (120 ml) silicon molds or mason jars with pan spray (if you're planning to unmold) and pour the mixture evenly into each one, about three-quarters full. Refrigerate overnight to set. If you're unmolding, remove the panna cotta from the refrigerator about 5 minutes before serving. Loosen the sides carefully with an offset spatula and turn the mold over onto a plate, lifting and gently shaking so the panna cotta comes out.

We served this panna cotta with rosewater whipped cream, pistachios, and baked phyllo crisps. I like the phyllo texture with this dessert, but for a simple summer dessert, try serving it with fresh fruit and a drizzle of local honey.

Acting Globally

Sometimes I think we here in the liberal-leaning Northeast harbor a slightly skewed vision of the role of America's military overseas. We lament the hazards and atrocities of war and military occupation, but we seldom hear stories like this one, about good and earnest young soldiers who see outside of their place in their unit, wherever they may be stationed, and want to make the world a better place.

When we first opened a spice shop, a mutual acquaintance connected me to Kimberly Jung, a young Army platoon leader who had been stationed in Afghanistan and returned from a tour of duty with new business partners, an acceptance to Harvard Business School, and a bold idea. Kimberly and her partners had witnessed endless fields of opium poppies in the fecund Helmand province, burned to a crisp by the Marines. Afghan farmers had been given little choice by the Taliban regime but to raise these poppies for the drug trade and were assured a certain revenue for the lucrative cash crop.

Saffron, also harvested from a showy bloom, trades on the open market at prices that often exceed opium poppy prices. The difference is, of course, that saffron is legal. And it's delicious. Farmers switching their plantings from poppies to saffron crocuses may upset the Taliban, but they can do what everyone ultimately wants: make decent money while doing the right thing.

Jung and her start-up company, Rumi Spice, have brought this uplifting story to the American market. Sourcing spices from far away involves uncertainties that bother me, so this little saffron thread of hope makes me feel like we are not far from knowing more about all the spices we cook with and how they are farmed.

Red Quinoa Coconut Milk Pudding with Rhubarb Compote, Hibiscus Whip, and Kata'ifi

SERVES 6 TO 8

This standout of Lauren's achieved epic renown in short time. One guest, after eating this dessert, told Denise, "I don't understand what it is, but it's the best dessert I've ever had." This has become a sort of mantra that we apply to the overall Black Trumpet experience. This recipe, along with many others in this book, now enables you to make a few things you don't understand.

For the quinoa pudding
(makes about 6 cups [1.4 L])
2 cups (475 ml) water
1 cup (180 g) quinoa (preferably the
  red variety)
Two 13.5-ounce (400 ml) cans
  coconut milk
½ cup (115 g) sugar
3 tablespoons cornstarch, combined
  with 2 tablespoons cold water to
  make a slurry
1 tablespoon maple syrup
1 teaspoon vanilla extract
½ teaspoon salt
¼ teaspoon cinnamon

For the Rhubarb Compote
1 pound (455 g) rhubarb, medium dice
¾ cup (170 g) sugar
Juice of ½ lemon (about 1 tablespoon)

For the hibiscus syrup
1 cup (235 ml) water
1 cup (225 g) sugar
½ cup (15 g) dried hibiscus flowers

For the Hibiscus Whip
1 cup (235 ml) heavy cream
¼ cup (60 ml) hibiscus syrup
  (see above)

MAKE THE QUINOA PUDDING: In a 2-quart (2 L) pot, bring the water and quinoa to a boil. Cover, reduce the heat to a simmer, and cook 15 to 20 minutes, until the water is absorbed and the quinoa is fluffy. Remove the quinoa to a medium-sized bowl.

Meanwhile, in a separate pot over medium-low heat, whisk the rest of the ingredients together and bring to a simmer. Whisk until the mixture is smooth and thickened enough to coat the back of a spoon. This should take about 10 minutes.

Pour the thickened coconut milk pudding over the cooked quinoa and let it cool to room temperature. Cover the bowl tightly with plastic and refrigerate several hours or overnight, until the pudding is fully set. Remove from the refrigerator when it's cold and set, and serve or hold for up to 2 days.

MAKE THE RHUBARB COMPOTE: Combine all the ingredients in a small, nonreactive pot. Bring to a high simmer over medium heat and, stirring frequently, cook down until the mixture thickens slightly, about 5 minutes. Cool to room temperature and refrigerate for up to 5 days.

MAKE THE HIBISCUS SYRUP: Bring the ingredients to a boil in a small, heavy-bottomed pot over medium-high heat. Whisk until the sugar dissolves and cook down until the mixture is slightly syrupy, about 15 minutes. Strain the syrup into a container and cool to room temperature. Refrigerate until you're ready to use it, up to 5 days.

MAKE THE HIBISCUS WHIP: Whip the cream by hand until the mixture begins to stiffen. Drizzle in the hibiscus syrup, whisking to fully combine and bring the mixture to soft peaks.

For the Kata'ifi

¼ pound (115 g) thawed kata'ifi
  (shredded phyllo dough,
  found in specialty markets)
2 tablespoons clarified butter,
  for brushing

MAKE THE KATA'IFI: Preheat the oven to 400°F (200°C). Place eight nests of kata'ifi on a cookie sheet, evenly spaced. Brush with clarified butter and place on the center rack of the oven. Bake 3 minutes, rotate, and check after 2 minutes more. The kata'ifi should be golden brown around the edges and beginning to brown in the center. Remove from the oven, cool in the pan, and break into pieces.

ASSEMBLE THE DESSERT: Spoon the pudding into a bowl, dolloping jam on one side and whipped cream on the other. Top with kata'ifi and drizzle lightly with syrup.

Apricot Crepes with
Tahini Caramel, Lemon Balm Cream, and Sesame Crumb

SERVES 10

I have a confession to make: When it comes to desserts, I am not a fan of supersweet or chocolate-based offerings. I usually have a couple of those on the dessert menu to appeal to the masses, but my own taste leans in the direction of fruit-based desserts if it leans at all. When Lauren came up with this one, I nearly died and went to heaven.

For the crepes
1 cup (120 g) flour
1 cup (235 ml) milk
¼ cup (60 ml) carbonated soda water
1 egg (50 g liquid egg)
¼ cup (55 g) sugar
½ teaspoon vanilla extract

For the apricot filling
1 cup (125 g) dried apricots
1 cup (225 g) sugar
1 cup (235 ml) water
10 fresh apricots, peeled and pitted, medium dice

MAKE THE CREPES: Combine all the ingredients in the carafe of a blender and blend until smooth. Strain the lumps, if necessary. Store in the refrigerator for a few hours before using.

To serve, spray an 8-inch (20 cm) nonstick pan and preheat over a medium-low flame. Using a ladle or a cup with a spout, pour 3 ounces (85 ml) of the batter into the pan, swirling the pan as you pour so the batter evenly covers the bottom in a thin layer. Cook for 2 to 3 minutes, until the crepe browns slightly. Flip and cook 1½ to 2 minutes, until the edges begin to turn golden brown and crispy. Repeat with the rest of the batter.

MAKE THE APRICOT FILLING: Combine the dried apricots, sugar, and water in a small pot over medium-low heat. Simmer just until the liquid begins to turn syrupy and the apricots are soft, 8 to 10 minutes. Puree the mixture in a blender until smooth and cool to room temperature. In a Robot Coupe or food processor, combine the cooled puree with the fresh apricots and pulse several times until chunky. Use immediately or refrigerate for up to 5 days.

For the Sesame Crumb

1 cup (120 ml) flour
½ cup (50 g) rolled oats
1 cup (225 g) sugar
½ cup (115 g) packed brown sugar
½ cup (70 g) white sesame seed
1 teaspoon ground cinnamon
1 teaspoon salt
1 teaspoon light sesame oil
  (not the toasted Asian variety)
¾ cup (170 g) cold butter, cubed

For the Tahini Caramel

1½ cups (335 g) sugar
⅓ cup (80 ml) water
1 tablespoon honey
1 cup (235 ml) heavy cream
3 tablespoons tahini
¾ teaspoon salt

For the Lemon Balm Cream

1 cup (225 g) sugar
1 cup (235 ml) water
2 packed cups (120 g)
  lemon balm leaves
1 cup (235 ml) heavy cream

MAKE THE SESAME CRUMB: Preheat the oven to 400°F (200°C).

Combine the first seven ingredients in a medium bowl. Cut the sesame oil and butter into the dry ingredients with a pastry cutter or bench scraper. When the butter pieces are manageable, work them with your hands until the butter is evenly incorporated and is the size of peas. Divide the crumb dough evenly between two Silpat-lined baking sheets. Bake one at a time on the center rack of the oven for 15 to 20 minutes, rotating twice. The crumb should smell nutty and look golden brown throughout. Repeat with the second baking sheet.

Let the crumb cool in the pan to room temperature. Break it up and crumble with your hands or a mallet. Hold in an airtight container for up to 2 days before serving.

MAKE THE TAHINI CARAMEL: In a small, heavy-bottomed pot over medium heat, combine the sugar, water, and honey. Cook, swirling occasionally (but not stirring with a spoon), until the mixture just begins to turn amber and reaches 350°F (175°C) on a candy thermometer, 10 to 12 minutes. Remove the liquid from the heat, add the cream, and allow it to bubble. Whisk to combine. Stir in the tahini and salt and stir. Cool to room temperature and serve immediately or hold in the refrigerator for up to 5 days.

MAKE THE LEMON BALM CREAM: In a small pot over medium heat, combine the sugar, water, and lemon balm. Bring to a high simmer and cook until syrupy and thick, about 10 minutes from when it comes to a simmer. Strain out the lemon balm leaves and cool the liquid to room temperature. When it's cool, refrigerate or drizzle to taste into partially whipped cream, then finish whipping to soft peaks to make Lemon Balm Cream.

CHAPTER SIX

LATE SUMMER
Butter Dripping from My Chin

LATE SUMMER RECIPES

Summer is the time when tourists begin to flood the streets of Portsmouth. On a good beach day, thousands of people pour into downtown looking for dinner. Portsmouth has more seats in restaurants than residents for this very reason. This ratio presents great challenges in the off-season, but we welcome the bountiful summer business while it lasts. This chapter offers some beachy anecdotes and Black Trumpet recipes that can be prepared at home and served on the deck or packed for a picnic.

Celeriac Rémoulade

MAKES 2 CUPS (475 ML)

I like having rémoulade around. It's great on everything in the summer and could be considered the spicy Cajun stepchild of three puritanical Yankee condiments—mustard, catsup, and tartar sauce—the last two of which are served automatically with fried anything at any of the Portsmouth seafood restaurants that dot our short coastline. This recipe stores well and tastes even better on day 2. Note that having three different Black Trumpet Building Blocks on hand can make this preparation a snap.

½ cup (115 g) peeled and grated celeriac
1 tablespoon salt-cured capers, soaked
  30 minutes in ½ cup (120 ml) cold
  water, drained and chopped
1 red bell pepper, roasted and chopped
½ jalapeño, seeds and ribs
  removed, minced
1 shallot, minced (about 3 tablespoons)
1 cup (235 ml) basic aioli (page 17)
2 tablespoons house mustard
  (page 21)
1 tablespoon Dijon mustard
1 tablespoon harissa (page 16)
1 tablespoon chopped fresh tarragon
½ teaspoon salt
Pinch black pepper
Pinch smoked paprika
Tiny pinch ground cloves

In a small bowl, fold all ingredients with a spatula until combined. Refrigerate until ready to serve.

Chermoula

MAKES ABOUT 2½ CUPS (590 ML)

Versatile and packed with flavor, chermoula can act as a marinade, salad dressing, grilling "mop," sauce, or even a zingy base for tartar sauce. We have used it in many incarnations, but it seems to do best with fish, chicken, and grilled meats like lamb.

As always, when handling chile peppers, it is best to wear latex gloves. Also, try to remove skin and seeds without using too much water—the water will dilute some of the essential oils in the peppers. I suggest removing as much as possible on your own, then running the pepper briefly under cold water to get rid of what remains. They don't have to be perfect; a few lingering seeds or a strip of skin won't ruin the final product.

4 poblano peppers

2 tablespoons plus ¼ cup (90 ml) olive oil, divided

2 Fish peppers or jalapeños, ribs and seeds removed, rough-chopped

1 Spanish onion, julienned

6 cloves garlic, minced

1 cup (60 g) packed fresh mint leaves

½ cup (30 g) packed fresh cilantro (stems are okay to include)

½ cup (30 g) packed fresh parsley leaves

1 bunch scallions, green parts only, rough-chopped

Juice of 1 lime

Zest of 2 limes

½ cup (120 ml) vegetable stock—if needed

1 teaspoon salt

Over high heat, blister the poblanos directly over the flame, turning every few minutes until all four sides look fully charred. Remove to a bowl, wrap in plastic, and let the peppers steam for an hour. Remove the peppers from the bowl, peel them, remove the stems and seeds, and roughly chop.

Add 2 tablespoons (30 ml) of the olive oil to a small sauté pan over medium heat and sauté the jalapeños and onion for 3 minutes. Add the minced garlic and sweat 2 more minutes on a low flame, stirring occasionally. Remove from the heat and let the ingredients cool in the pan.

Add the remaining ingredients, except the salt and the last ¼ cup (60 ml) olive oil, to the carafe of a blender and puree until smooth. Scrape down the sides with a rubber spatula; with the motor running, add the oil gradually (count to 30). This will make the mixture creamy, smooth, and shiny. If it seems too thick, puree again, gradually adding vegetable stock until it reaches the desired consistency. Season with salt and whir to combine. Use immediately or refrigerate up to 5 days, until you're ready to use it.

Chermoula Tartar Sauce

MAKES APPROXIMATELY 2¼ CUPS (535 ML)

This book contains two tartar sauce recipes (the other, Green Tomato Tartar Sauce, can be found on page 287). This is the one to select when you want to up the spice quotient on your fried summer fare. Note that you will need a few recipes from elsewhere in this book to get started.

1 tablespoon salt-packed capers
2 cups (475 ml) garlic aioli (page 17)
1 tablespoon minced shallot
1 tablespoon minced pickled onion or shallot (see Rhubarb Pickled Onion, page 167)
1 preserved lemon (page 16), minced (about 1½ tablespoons)
3 tablespoons chermoula (preceding recipe)

Soak the capers in water for 30 minutes, drain, and chop finely.

Spoon the aioli into a large mixing bowl. Add the capers, shallot, pickled onion, preserved lemon, and chermoula; fold together. Refrigerate for several hours or up to 4 days. The mixture will stiffen and flavors will deepen over time.

Beer Batter for Fish Fry

MAKES 3½ CUPS (830 ML)

This recipe for a basic fried fish batter works with any mild, flaky white fish. I particularly like Acadian redfish dipped in this batter. As long as the oil is the right temperature and is not overcrowded with fish pieces, this recipe works like a charm every time.

2 cups (240 g) all-purpose flour
2 tablespoons cornstarch
1 tablespoon baking soda
1 tablespoon smoked paprika
1 tablespoon salt
1 pint (475 ml) British-style light ale (like Bass Ale)
1 egg (50 g liquid egg)
1 tablespoon clarified butter
1 tablespoon olive oil

Whisk the flour, cornstarch, baking soda, paprika, and salt in a medium bowl. Whisk the beer, egg, butter, and olive oil in a separate bowl. Pour the wet ingredients into the dry and fold with a spatula until smooth. Refrigerate 1 hour before using.

Frying time for the fish depends on the size of the pieces. When each piece is the color of a brown paper bag, remove to towels or a drying rack. Serve promptly when the last piece comes out of the fry oil, with either Celeriac Rémoulade (page 229) or Green Tomato Tartar Sauce (page 287).

Calamari Canasta

SERVES 8

In many regions of Mexico, street vendors offer up a perfect midday snack on hot days: long thin wedges of sweet and crunchy jicama, squirted with a healthy dose of lime juice and then sprinkled with Tajín or spicy red chili powder. This midsummer squid dish was influenced by that Mexican treat, developed in the Black Trumpet kitchen into a vehicle for one of my favorite foods, fried squid. At the time, sous chef Mike was brewing a spectacular hot sauce he had conjured, so we drizzled that over the squid and served it all on top of shaved jicama, which absorbed some of the fat from frying the squid and lots of flavor from the sauce. The Spanish word *canasta*, which means "basket," refers to the metal vessel we served the squid in, lined with parchment paper, like Belgian frites, but even better.

1 pound (455 g) whole squid, cleaned
1 cup (120 g) flour
1 teaspoon cornstarch
½ teaspoon salt, plus more to finish fried squid
½ teaspoon smoked paprika or pimiento
¼ teaspoon ground coriander
¼ teaspoon cayenne pepper
¼ teaspoon black pepper
1 jicama, peeled and julienned
Juice of 1 lime
Oil, for frying

Slice the squid body into thin rings and cut the tentacles away from the beak. In a mixing bowl, whisk the next 7 ingredients together to make the dredge. Toss the squid in the dredge and let it absorb for 2 minutes. When you're ready to fry, shake the pieces into a strainer or colander over the bowl to remove any excess flour.

Toss the jicama in the lime juice and season with a little salt. Set aside.

Set a wide pot of canola oil or a tabletop fryer to 350°F (175°C). Working in two or more batches, fry the squid for about 1 minute and remove to a towel. Sprinkle with salt and serve immediately over the jicama, soused with your favorite hot sauce. (May I suggest ours? See "Black Trumpet Building Blocks," page 21.)

Smoked Bluefish

SERVES 16 OR MORE PEOPLE (BUT HOLDS UP WELL IN THE FRIDGE)

Bluefish has played a weird role in my life. I equate it in many ways to brussels sprouts, having been introduced to both bluefish and brussels sprouts at the same time, when I was living with my mother on Cape Cod in the late 1970s. For whatever reason, my mother's boyfriend, a Christian icon of a man—mustachioed and handsome, a carpenter by trade and fisherman by hobby—managed to extend the season on both brussels sprouts and bluefish well beyond the few weeks each one should exist, and in my memory the two actually coincided in a state of horrific prandial planning for several months, although I'm sure the reality was different. As I remember it, bluefish caught on Saturday was Sunday dinner most weeks, and brussels sprouts, boiled to mushy, gray oblivion, inevitably found themselves on the plate with the oily, smelly fish. Of course, as I grew as a cook, I learned that—like just about every food ingredient in the world—brussels sprouts and bluefish are spectacular when properly prepared.

Whatever preconceptions you or I may have, bluefish (aka *Pomatomus saltatrix*) is an interesting migratory fish species that is the only remaining member of its taxonomic family. Although it is often associated with mackerel, the two represent entirely different niches in the evolutionary model. The many members of the mackerel family share the oily quality and strong flavor of bluefish, but bluefish boasts a heftier, meatier flesh that takes marinades and cures well, grills up beautifully, and smokes like no other fish.

Bluefish fillets, much like tuna loins, have a bloodline that should be removed. The bloodline can be identified as the dark grayish-brown part of the meat found in the middle of the fillet. Leaving a little is okay, but copious amounts will taste bitter.

One 8-pound (3.6 kg) bluefish
1 tablespoon black peppercorns
1 teaspoon mustard seed
1 teaspoon fennel seed
1 teaspoon cumin seed
1 teaspoon ground coriander
1 tablespoon chopped fresh chives
¼ cup (15 g) chopped fresh dill
½ cup (75 g) salt
¼ cup (55 g) brown sugar
Zest of 2 lemons
2 cups (340 g) applewood
  smoking chips

Preheat the oven to 400°F (200°C)

Scale, gut, and fillet the bluefish. Refridgerate the fillets until you are ready to cure them. Save the livers and cheeks from big fish for other treats. Salt the carcass and roast for 20 minutes. When it's cool enough to handle, pick the cooked meat from the bones and set aside for rillettes or pâté.

Combine all the cure ingredients (peppercorns through lemons) in a mixing bowl and toss until combined. Transfer in batches to a spice grinder and pulse until coarsely ground. Rub the flesh side of the bluefish fillets liberally with the cure and refrigerate in a tightly lidded container for 3 days.

Note: I highly recommend smoking anything outdoors. If you have no choice, make sure the kitchen is extremely well ventilated.

Line a 4-inch-deep (10 cm) hotel pan with foil and pile in two 1-cup (170 g) mounds of wood chips, one on each side, so they're lined up lengthwise over two stove burners. Fit a perforated pan inside the hotel pan and spray it with pan spray. Gently wipe away the bluefish rub so the excess is wiped off but there's still a little remaining. Place the fish on the perforated pan and cover tightly with foil. Poke two or three holes in the foil and turn the burners on high. Smoke 4 minutes on high heat, reduce the heat to low, and smoke an additional 8 minutes, without touching the foil lid. Turn off the heat, leaving the covered pan on the stove, undisturbed, and let sit an additional 10 minutes. Remove the fish from the smoking pan. It should be firm-fleshed with a distinct smoky flavor.

When the bluefish cools to room temperature, remove the skin, check for bones, and store up to a week in the refrigerator. Snack frequently, or serve in tea sandwiches as is or in a spreadable mousse.

Buttermilk Dill Rolls

MAKES 32 ROLLS

These late-summer treats make perfect picnic fare, or they can be filled with shredded barbecued meat or smoked fish and downed as sliders.

¾ cup (180 ml) warm water
1 teaspoon active dry yeast
1½ tablespoons sugar
1½ tablespoons vegetable oil, plus more for oiling the bowl
1½ cups (355 ml) buttermilk
4½ cups (540 g) flour
1½ tablespoons salt
1½ tablespoons dried dill leaves
Semolina flour, for dusting the pan
1 egg (50 g liquid egg), beaten lightly with a fork

Preheat the oven to 375°F (190°C).

Combine the water and yeast in a medium bowl. Bloom 5 minutes. Add the sugar, oil, and buttermilk; mix to combine. Add the dry ingredients and the dill and mix until combined. Knead the dough until smooth, about 2 minutes. Rub the bowl with oil and add the dough. Cover with a damp cloth or plastic wrap and let rise for 1 hour. Turn the dough out onto a floured work surface, weigh out into 1½-ounce (42 g) pieces, and roll into balls. Place the balls on a sprayed baking sheet dusted with semolina flour. Let rise for 20 minutes. Brush the tops of the rolls with the egg wash and bake for 20 minutes, or until golden brown, rotating halfway through. Let cool and serve.

Socca

SERVES 12

I have blathered over and over again about how much I respect and appreciate the women line cooks I have worked with, but I have not adequately credited the women chefs who have influenced my career. Julia Child came first, of course. Then Alice Waters. Then her protégée, Suzanne Goin. Then Ana Sortun. Barbara Lynch. Melissa Kelly. While I have never worked directly with any of them, these women have quietly impressed me and driven me to broaden the spectrum of my own culinary perspective.

Based on a dish I ate at Ana Sortun's Oleana in Cambridge, Massachusetts, I took a stab at making socca—a leavened chickpea crepe—from a recipe I found in a Mediterranean cookbook. We precooked the socca, reheated it, and served it with smoked fish. The result was a tasty but sometimes greasy and rubbery manifestation of Sortun's version. Somewhat dejected, unable to master the socca, I took it off the menu after a short run. A few years later, I had socca again at Melissa Kelly's Primo, a fabled institution in Rockland that has made that remote part of Maine a dining destination. Her socca was ethereal, reminding me of Sortun's, but with a distinct crispiness that countered the light texture of the crepe's interior. It was then that I realized there was only one way to prepare socca, and that was "to order," meaning we would whip up new batter every day and fire up a pancake every time an order came in. What a difference!

1¼ cups (295 ml) warm water
  (around 105°F [40°C])
1½ teaspoons active dry yeast
1 tablespoon sugar
1½ teaspoons tahini
1½ cups (130 g) chickpea flour
½ cup (60 g) all-purpose flour
1 teaspoon salt
Olive oil, for frying

Pour the water into a small bowl and sprinkle the yeast over the top. Bloom the yeast for 5 minutes. Add the sugar and tahini and stir to combine. Add the dry ingredients, salt last. Stir thoroughly to combine, and let the mixture sit for 30 minutes.

Pour 1 teaspoon olive oil into a seasoned 12-inch (30 cm) cast-iron pan over medium heat. Add 1 ounce (28 g) of the socca dough and spread out with a spoon so it's thin like a pancake and about 4 inches (10 cm) in diameter. Repeat three more times for four pancakes. When you see bubbles forming around the periphery of the pancake (about 45 seconds), flip and cook 45 seconds more on the other side. Remove the pancakes to a platter and repeat with the remaining dough. Serve immediately.

Chickpea-Dredged Eggplant Fries

SERVES 8

This gluten-free snack can be served with any number of dipping sauces and meze. Here, I suggest the Turkish salad Patlican Salatasi (recipe follows) and any savory yogurt sauce.

4 Japanese or Ping Tung Long eggplant, peeled
½ teaspoon salt, plus more for salting eggplant
3 cups (710 ml) sunflower oil, preferably from Coppal House Farm
2 cups (170 g) chickpea flour, divided
3 eggs (150 g liquid egg)
½ teaspoon dried Aleppo chile flakes

Cut the eggplant into ¼ × 3 inch (0.5 × 7.5 cm) pieces. Salt liberally and place on a parchment-covered baking sheet for half an hour. Gently press out the excess water from the eggplant.

In a high-sided sauté pan, heat the oil to 350°F (175°C) over medium-high heat.

While the oil heats, place 1 cup (85 g) of the chickpea flour in a medium bowl. In another bowl, whisk the eggs lightly with a fork. In a third bowl, combine the remaining cup (85 g) chickpea flour, ½ teaspoon salt, and the Aleppo pepper.

Using standard breading procedure, dip the fries first in the chickpea flour, then in the egg, and finally in the second bowl of chickpea flour combined with salt and Aleppo pepper. Repeat with the remaining eggplant. Fry in a single layer, so as not to crowd the pan, for 3 to 4 minutes, or until golden brown and crispy on the outside. Remove to a paper-towel-lined sheet pan and sprinkle with salt. Repeat with the remaining fries and serve immediately with Patlican Salatasi or yogurt sauce.

Patlican Salatasi

SERVES 8 AS A SIDE DISH

Although we could have called this preparation Turkish Eggplant Salad on our menu, I think you'll agree that this dish's native name flows beautifully off the tongue, giving everyone a chance to practice their Turkish in case they may someday be lucky enough to order this salad in its place of origin. That is certainly my goal.

3 red bell peppers

¾ pound (340 g) eggplant, skin removed, cut into ¾-inch (2 cm) cubes

½ cup plus 3 tablespoons (165 ml) olive oil, divided

¼ teaspoon plus pinch salt, or more to taste

Pinch black pepper

½ Spanish onion, medium dice

1 tablespoon minced garlic

½ cup (120 ml) tomato puree

2 tablespoons chopped fresh cilantro

2 tablespoons chopped fresh mint

1 teaspoon sumac

½ teaspoon dried Aleppo chile flakes

1 large heirloom tomato (we used an Oxheart variety), rough-chopped

1 cherry pepper, minced

Preheat the oven to 450°F (230°C).

Place the red bell peppers on a baking sheet and slide into the top rack of the oven. Roast, turning the peppers with tongs every 7 minutes, for 35 minutes, or until the flesh is soft and the skin has blistered and begun to blacken on all sides. Remove to a bowl, cover tightly with plastic wrap, and allow to steam for 30 minutes. Remove the skins, stems, and seeds and dice into ¾-inch (2 cm) pieces.

Reduce the oven heat to 425°F (220°C).

Toss the eggplant with 2 tablespoons (30 ml) of the olive oil, ¼ teaspoon of the salt, and the pepper; place on a baking sheet. Roast 15 minutes, until golden brown and fork-tender. Set aside.

Sauté the onion in a medium frying pan over medium-low heat with 1 tablespoon olive oil and a pinch of salt for 5 minutes, or until it begins to soften. Add the garlic and sauté 30 seconds more. Add the tomato puree and whisk in the remaining ½ cup (120 ml) olive oil. Stir in the herbs and spices and let cool.

When the mixture reaches room temperature, gently fold in the bell pepper, eggplant, heirloom tomato, and cherry pepper with a spatula. Adjust salt to taste. Serve.

Smoked Eggplant Salad

SERVES 6

This salad offers a secondary use for smoked eggplant. I love the intermingling of fresh late summer flavors, especially when served with fresh Pita Bread (page 244).

1 large eggplant, halved

Salt

1 cup (170 g) small applewood chips

2 red slicer tomatoes, medium dice

2 yellow slicer tomatoes, medium dice

½ red onion, medium dice

2 green peppers, roasted, peeled, and seeded, medium dice

1 bulb fennel, medium dice

1 tablespoon chopped fresh cilantro

8 cloves garlic, poached in olive oil and coarsely chopped (1 tablespoon oil retained)

2 tablespoons minced peeled gingerroot

Juice of 1 lemon

2 tablespoons sherry vinegar

1 tablespoon cumin seed, toasted and ground

¼ teaspoon black pepper

3 tablespoons olive oil

Generously salt the eggplant halves and let sit 1 hour. Pat dry.

If you don't have a smoker, fashion a small, shallow bowl from a 9-inch-square (23 cm) piece of foil. Place the wood chips in the bowl and place the bowl in a small, high-sided pot. Place a steamer insert on top of the foil bowl and place the eggplant halves on the steamer insert. Cover the pan tightly with foil and turn the burner on high for 1 minute. Reduce the heat to low and smoke for 20 to 25 minutes. Check to make sure the eggplant is soft all the way through.

Remove from the heat and wrap the smoked eggplant in plastic while it's still hot to continue cooking and to preserve the smoke flavor, about 2 hours.

Scoop the flesh from the eggplant, coarsely chop, and combine with the tomatoes, onion, peppers, and fennel in a large mixing bowl, folding gently to combine.

In a small bowl, whisk the cilantro, garlic, ginger, lemon juice, sherry vinegar, cumin seed, ¼ teaspoon salt, and black pepper. In a steady stream, whisk in the olive oil and 1 tablespoon reserved garlic oil, creating an emulsion.

Pour the dressing over the chopped vegetables, folding gently to combine. Season to taste and serve. This salad can be made ahead of time, but its brightness will be muted if it's stored overnight.

Smoked Eggplant Soup with Falafel and Tzatziki

SERVES 8 AS A MAIN COURSE

This soup is hearty, almost a stew, and it combines three staple dishes of the Middle East—baba ghanouj, falafel, and tzatziki—into one. Keep in mind that the falafel and tzatziki are wonderful on their own, as an appetizer, a snack, or even a main course. The soup, on the other hand, really benefits from the crunch of falafel and the tangy foil that tzatziki brings to the party.

2 medium eggplants, skin on, halved
1 cup (170 g) small applewood chips
⅔ cup (150 g) medium-diced
  Spanish onion
⅔ cup (150 g) medium-diced
  peeled carrot
⅔ cup (150 g) medium-diced celery
2 tablespoons olive oil
2 teaspoons minced garlic
2 tablespoons salt
2 tablespoons chopped fresh oregano
1 tablespoon cumin seed
1 tablespoon Urfa chile flakes
  (or substitute dark chili powder)
Pinch cayenne pepper
¼ cup (60 ml) white wine
½ cup (85 g) sun-dried
  tomatoes, julienned
¼ cup (45 g) sun-dried (or roasted)
  red peppers, julienned
1½ cups (355 ml) tomato puree
2 quarts (1.9 L) vegetable stock
½ cup (115 g) chickpeas,
  soaked overnight

Follow the smoking procedure for eggplant from the previous recipe, Smoked Eggplant Salad.

Chop the smoked eggplant into 1-inch (2.5 cm) cubes. Sweat the onion, carrot, and celery in olive oil over medium heat for 4 minutes. Add the minced garlic, eggplant, salt, and spices. Deglaze with white wine. Add the sun-dried tomatoes, sun-dried peppers, tomato puree, stock, and chickpeas; simmer until the chickpeas are soft, about 30 minutes. Adjust the seasoning and serve.

Falafel

MAKES 28 ONE-OUNCE (28 G) BALLS

2 cups (450 g) dried chickpeas
1 cup (225 g) fresh, raw chickpeas
  (substitute an extra cup of dried if
  fresh are unavailable)
2 teaspoons cumin seed, toasted
  and ground
6 cloves garlic, minced
1 teaspoon dried Maras or
  Aleppo chile flake
1 teaspoon ground coriander
½ teaspoon ground turmeric
1 teaspoon sugar
1 tablespoon baking powder
1½ cups (130 g) chickpea flour
½ Spanish onion, minced
1 tablespoon salt
¼ cup (60 ml) water
Vegetable oil, for frying

Soak the dried chickpeas in a large bowl filled with 4 cups (945 ml) water, overnight. Drain.

In a large pot over high heat, bring the soaked chickpeas to a boil in 8 cups (1.9 L) water. Reduce the heat to low and simmer until toothsome, but not completely soft, about 45 minutes (cooking time will vary from batch to batch).

Combine the cooked and raw (or dried) chickpeas, cumin, garlic, Maras/Aleppo pepper, coriander, and turmeric in the bowl of a food processor. Spin until the mixture becomes granular. Add the sugar and baking powder and pulse to combine. Add the chickpea flour, onion, salt, and water; pulse to combine. Working quickly so the mixture doesn't dry out, form the falafel mixture into 1-ounce (28 g) cakes. Keep a small bowl of water nearby to dampen your fingers while rolling.

While rolling, preheat a small 2-quart (2 L) pot or tabletop fryer filled with 2 inches (5 cm) vegetable oil over medium-high heat. When the temperature of the oil reaches 350°F (175°C), add several falafel cakes, so they fit in a single layer and don't crowd the pan. Fry 3 minutes, or until golden brown. Remove to a paper-towel-lined plate, sprinkle with salt, and repeat with the remaining falafel. Serve immediately with tzatziki, on their own, or in the Smoked Eggplant Soup.

Tzatziki

MAKES ABOUT 1½ CUPS (355 ML)

1 cup (235 ml) strained, full-fat
  Greek yogurt
1 pickling cucumber, skin on, quartered,
  and seeded, small dice
1 clove garlic, minced
2 tablespoons chopped fresh mint
1 tablespoon chopped fresh dill
Juice of 1 lemon
1 teaspoon honey
½ teaspoon salt
½ teaspoon sumac

Fold all the ingredients together and chill overnight, or at least several hours before serving.

Pita Bread

1½ cups (355 ml) warm water (about 105°F [40°C])

1 tablespoon plus ½ teaspoon active dry yeast

1 tablespoon honey

2 tablespoons olive oil

1 tablespoon sugar

1 cup (115 g) whole wheat flour

2 cups (240 g) all-purpose flour

1 teaspoon paprika

2 teaspoons salt

Pour the water into the bowl of a mixer fitted with the hook attachment and sprinkle the yeast on top, stirring lightly to combine. Let bloom for 5 minutes. Add the honey, oil, and sugar to the bowl. Layer the dry ingredients on top so the flours act as a barrier between the salt and the yeast. Mix with the dough hook for 10 minutes on medium speed. Remove the bowl from the mixer, cover, and let the dough rise for 90 minutes.

Punch down the dough and scrape it out onto a lightly floured work surface.

Place a large sheet pan in the oven and preheat the oven to 450°F (230°C). Gather the dough and cut it into eight equal pieces. Roll the pieces into balls and let them rest 10 minutes. Roll the balls out to ¼ inch (0.5 cm) thick and let rest 10 more minutes. Carefully remove the sheet tray from the oven and place four dough rounds on it. Bake for 6 minutes. The pita should have puffed considerably and should be golden brown on the underside. Bake for 2 minutes on the other side. Repeat the baking process with the other four dough rounds. Let cool slightly and serve, or hold for a few hours. These are best served the day they're baked.

Chanterelle Corn Bisque

My daughter, Eleanor, went through a long spell of preferring soup over all other foods. During this phase, when she came in to Black Trumpet to eat, she would often order both soups (we used to always have two on each menu) before delving into her main course. This is probably the reason she grew 6½ inches (16.5 cm) in one year. When I asked her what her all-time favorite soup was, this is the one she summoned.

2 tablespoons clarified butter/olive oil blend (page 13)
1 pound (455 g) chanterelles
3 ears corn, shucked, corn cut from cob
⅔ cup (150 g) medium-diced onion
⅔ cup (150 g) medium-diced carrot
⅔ cup (150 g) medium-diced celery
2 tablespoons minced garlic
Splash sherry
2 cups (475 ml) tomato puree
1 bay leaf
¼ cup (15 g) fresh thyme, chopped
1 teaspoon ground nutmeg
⅛ teaspoon ground cloves
1 teaspoon salt
Pinch black pepper
2 cups (475 ml) heavy cream
1 quart (945 ml) boom stock (page 13)

Pour the butter/oil blend into a medium stockpot over medium-low heat. Add the chanterelles, corn, onion, carrot, and celery; cook, stirring occasionally, until they begin to soften, about 10 minutes. Increase the heat to medium, add the garlic, and cook 1 minute. Deglaze the pan with the sherry, cooking until the alcohol scent wears off, 1 to 2 minutes. Add the tomato puree and next six ingredients, stirring to combine. Bring the mixture to a high simmer and reduce slightly, about 10 minutes. Add the cream and boom stock, bring to just under a boil, reduce the heat to low, and simmer 10 minutes, until the flavors have combined. Adjust the seasoning if necessary and serve.

The Lobster Bake:
An Ancient Ceremony
Wrought Three Ways

When July 4 rolls around, while the rest of the country is greasing up the grill and dreaming of hot dogs and fireworks, Maine vacationers and residents alike are building beachstone cairns—or, at least, readying their large pots—for the state mascot and planning the ceremony that will dress the mighty crustacean in its most regal attire, the unmistakable ruby robe that sheathes the succulent ivory flesh, flecked with red freckles and bursting with briny juice. The Atlantic lobster, *Homarus americanus*, is revered worldwide for its sweet, plump meat. Unlike its lesser-flavored cousins around the world, the North Atlantic lobster when properly prepared is surely one of life's simplest pleasures.

My grandfather, William Kenneth Fritz, grew up in Eliot, Maine, across the river from the front door of Black Trumpet, on a short dead-end street whose terminus plunges down the rocky bank of the Piscataqua River. Like most everyone in the neighborhood back in the day, my grandfather's family kept lobster traps. Unlike today, most of those traps were close enough to shore that one could pretty much live on lobster without owning a lobster boat or elaborate hauling gear. I can picture my grandfather as a young man in a rowboat pulling up half a dozen traps early every morning, but I have no evidence that he actually did that. I do have an oral history that suggests he and his mates would frequently jump off the Kittery bridge into frigid water and float to a peninsula now known as Pierce Island. And there is another apocryphal story about how he one day rowed a boat from Newcastle to the Isles of Shoals and back, a 14-mile (23 km) round-trip journey on open ocean swells. He, like me, was a mischievous, thrill-seeking lad; his foibles may have even surpassed my own in grandeur. But my favorite factoid about my grandfather, who spent the majority of his career working as an electrician at the Portsmouth Naval Shipyard, was that he absolutely detested lobster. A childhood overexposure to the "bugs" (as he sometimes referred to them) apparently turned him off lobster for the rest of his life.

Because lobster was so plentiful, most working-class Maine residents like my grandfather regarded the crustacean as a dietary staple, not the delicacy it is in today's global food market. For many tourists, lobster has become the coast of Maine's answer to caviar: easy to access, ceremonial to pick, and delectable to eat; an exemplar of its terroir and worth every penny, whatever the price. But for my grandfather, it was a reminder of a childhood surfeit that forever spoiled the glory of the lobster-eating experience for him. When we would go to the nearest local lobster pound for lunch or supper, he would order a tuna fish sandwich while the rest of the family tore into the Twin Lobster Special. This was affordable because I *was* the rest of the family. Not long after his departure from this world, I organized and executed my first-ever lobster bake. I'm sorry, Gramp, but it was really good.

The lobster bake, which involves no actual baking and may feature much more than lobster, can be approached from a number of different angles. Structurally primitive piles of rocks, seaweed, and fire are the only equipment required for a traditional bake, but there are plenty of shortcuts that make sense for anyone wishing to avoid windborne sand, temperature variances, and other unsavory complications.

One of my favorite clambake/lobster bake memories dates back to a few years before Black Trumpet was born and can be summed up in a simple piratic couplet: Happy young kids and balmy air / Sand in our mouths and we didn't care. I had been working at Ciento with Chef Jeff and was also helping my friend Gary with his restaurant start-up, Central Kitchen, in Cambridge, Massachusetts. Commuting between Portsmouth and Cambridge a few days a week, with a newborn at home, I spent just under a hundred hours a week in professional kitchens, so I don't remember how it came to be, but my two bosses, Gary and Jeff, each with partners and kids, converged with me and my family on a beautiful rocky beach at the end of our road one perfect summer evening, with very little notice. I brought clams, lobsters, and corn in a cooler. I secured a fire permit, built a fire pit, prepared a formidable rock pile, and harvested seaweed with help from the kids present. We had a growler of Ipswich Ale on hand, and a bottle of good French pink wine, as I recall. The fire-building and stone-lugging rituals created a male bonding ceremony, and the child herding and socializing fulfilled the most primordial needs of the womenfolk. We all ran around, feeling frolicsome and (to borrow a phrase from Updike) young at being old. When it came time to eat, as the sun fell below the dinnertime yardarm, we stacked the hot rocks on the fire pit, carefully layering nests of seaweed with clams, lobsters, and corn.

The next thing I recall we were gathered around the stones, butter dripping from our chins and elbows, immersed in the ritual, insouciant. I can't remember what else we brought to eat. I'm sure there were delicious side dishes, but I do remember thinking, as the sky grew the color of the Provençal rosé we were quaffing, that chef friends gathered on a beach with their loved ones at sunset, cooking and eating in the most primitive manner possible, etched one of the most vivid postcard memories I have of coastal New England life.

In the years that followed, my family was fortunate enough to be included in another family's great tradition. On a small island off a large island in Down East Maine, the Pierce family has celebrated lobster in a ceremony that dates back a couple of generations. We have enjoyed many ritual summer exploits on Sutton Island that have included great adventures (among them: young, rebellious adults nearly capsizing in a sailboat, my son rescuing a drowning dog from the frigid sea, and a group of us on a deep-sea fishing trip, adrift with a failed motor, getting towed back to port by the Coast Guard); milestone moments (a revered patriarch's final lobster bake before succumbing to illness, and my son's long walk with a foamy-mouthed lobster that triggered his decision to be a vegetarian). We have contributed our adjunct family to the already vast clan of Pierces who have inherited the sacred summer turf that may best exemplify what it means to summer on

the coast of Maine. Our family feels a tremendous sense of gratitude for having shared in this experience.

Most summers, our visits to the Pierces' vacationland include a lobster bake on a promontory of sea-polished stone that juts from their property on Sutton Island. This tradition represents the second approach to a lobster bake, and this is one I highly recommend for the first-timer, being ever so slightly less labor intensive. Here's how to do it:

Find a perfect spot on the beach, being sure to factor in the high-water mark, and build a fire made of driftwood and kindling from abandoned lobster traps. Always surround the fire pit with stones, as Smokey always implores of campers. Secure a really big pot, preferably one that holds more than 10 gallons (38 L) of liquid and has been passed down from generation to generation, and fill it two-thirds of the way with seawater. Schlep the splashing pot in a Sisyphean march—or better yet, assign the task to a pair of bravado-crazed teens—from the crashing waves to the fire pit. When the fire is raging, place the pot—covered loosely with tinfoil that will most likely be removed by the heat of the fire, or the wind, or both—on the fire, and bring to a boil. (This may happen excruciatingly slowly, so be sure to have as hot a fire as possible.) By this point, the lobsters should have been paraded from their nearby holding tank to the fireside "kitchen." Once the water is at a rapid boil, drop the lobsters into the pot and boil for 10 minutes, or until their carapaces have turned a uniform shade of fire-engine red. Corn still in the husk, soaked in salt water, can be placed strategically around the base of the pot, where each ear will smolder to perfection, blackened husks peeling away to reveal steamed, smoky, succulent kernels of pure joy. Meanwhile, the children present should have been tasked with skipping stones into the tide, posing for pictures, and hand-selecting the finest flat beachstones on the point to be used as personal plates for each lobster. Designate a master cracker who can make quick work of prepping each lobster before it is served. And of course, have plenty of butter on hand. And on chin. And on forearm.

Fifteen or so years after my primitive lobster bake on the beach in Rye, I got involved with the esteemed Shoals Marine Lab, a fantastic marine science research facility sponsored by Cornell University and the University of New Hampshire. Having worked with the University of New Hampshire's Sea Grant program to develop markets for the fruits of their aquaculture research, I was already acquainted with some of the personalities behind the SML. Furthermore, I had two connections from my past to the lab. One was my former roommate Sarah, who had put up with me during a regrettable phase of my early twenties when I struggled through a breakup and a belittling job in industrial advertising; and the other was a man whom I have always regarded as a culinary and personal mentor. Sam Hayward, the chef of Portland, Maine's vanguard restaurant, Fore Street, took his first job out of college with the then nascent Shoals Marine Lab. Without prior cooking knowledge, he assumed the helm of a kitchen that has since produced many generations of talented cooks committed to working magic from ingredients that have to be ferried out to Appledore Island, where the physical lab makes its home.

After sitting down with the busy and brilliant Jenn Seavey (whose family has deep roots in the Isles of Shoals) and several administrators and scientists, we forged a concept for a summer program and called it Take a Bite Out of Appledore. The idea was to create an educational environment that celebrated the fragile fisheries in the surrounding Gulf of Maine, while also casting a spotlight on the work of Shoals Marine Lab. My part, we concluded quickly, would be to create meals that paid tribute to the rich history of the islands and their resources while offering opportunities to forage and explore the environs both on land and in water.

Part of the programming for this magical August weekend ended up being a casual lobster bake, situated on the concrete slab of a landing that had served as a high-tide mooring in years past, that would be the first meal paying guests would be treated to after arriving on the island. Because a fire of unknown origin (arson has always been suspected) had burned the grand Appledore Hotel to the ground 101 years before our event, the organizers of the Take a Bite retreat took a cautious position when I brought up doing an authentic lobster bake on the rocks of a cove adjacent to the overgrown footprint of the hotel itself. "No open fires" was the mantra that would ultimately turn an old-fashioned clambake into a propane-fueled, pot-steamed adaptation of the tradition. In no way did the technical adjustment put a damper on the glorious scene of twenty people sitting down at an unforgettably dramatic sunset, serenaded by a sound track of seabirds, to a meal of seaweed-steamed lobster and clams, grilled mackerel, sea vegetable salad, corn pudding, and sundry other side dishes. For my part, I basked in the golden opportunity to cook alongside Sam Hayward, who had happily agreed to join our team, thereby giving the weekend retreat some celebrity star-power. For all his well-earned celebrity, Sam Hayward deserves more than anything to be known as a cheerful, caring, and deeply thoughtful person. Working with him will remain one of the most enjoyable and humbling moments of my career. Being perhaps the iconic Maine chef, Sam was also no slouch when it came to executing the modern lobster bake plan.

This third rendition of the lobster bake looks a lot like the second one, except that propane burners stand in for a fire pit, the pots are a little smaller (and less battered), and the rest of the meal tastes like really good restaurant food.

Sugar Kelp Slaw

SERVES 8

When Michael Chambers brought me my first bucket of sugar kelp he had
"farmed" through the UNH Sea Grant program, I took it upon myself to play
with it until I had explored all the possibilities my chef mind could muster.
This simple slaw, and the two recipes that follow it, represent the greatest hits
of that experimentation process.

1 cup (80 g) fresh sugar kelp,
   chiffonaded
½ head napa or green cabbage,
   chiffonaded
½ pound (225 g) celeriac, peeled
   and julienned
¼ cup (60 ml) Malt Aioli (page 154)
1 teaspoon Champagne vinegar
½ teaspoon salt
Pinch black pepper

Bring a quart of water to boil in a small pot over high heat. Prepare an
ice bath and, when the water boils, blanch the sugar kelp by dunking
it in the boiling water for 10 seconds, until it turns bright green, and
then plunging it into the ice water until cool. Remove the kelp from
the ice water and place in a large mixing bowl.

    Add the cabbage and celeriac to the bowl and toss the vegetables
to combine. In a small bowl, place the aioli, Champagne vinegar, salt,
and pepper; whisk to combine. Pour the mixture over the vegetables
and toss. Add salt to taste. The mixture can be held in the refrigerator
for up to 4 hours before serving.

Asian Seaweed Salad

SERVES 8 TO 10

I served this as part of a lobster bake at the first Take a Bite Out of Appledore event on the Isles of Shoals.

All these seaweeds thrive in coastal waters throughout the Gulf of Maine. If you don't want to take the time to snorkel for your dinner, these sea veggies can be bought dried, boiled until tender, and chopped into very thin strips. If you're working with fresh seaweed, be sure to rinse it well and pick through it for any unwanted visitors to your salad.

The fish sauce, rice vinegar, and togarashi can be sourced online (may I suggest stockandspice.com?) or at Asian markets. Togarashi is a flavor-packed (and relatively salubrious) Japanese seafood seasoning made from dried seaweed, sesame, and spices. Making the conversion from fresh to dried seaweed is not a perfect science, but in most cases a ratio of 10 to 1 applies.

2-foot length of sugar kelp
  (about 100 g), chiffonaded
1 cup (85 g) fresh alaria, chiffonaded
1 cup (85 g) fresh dulse
½ cup (40 g) fresh sea lettuce
  (*Ulva lactuca*)
2 large carrots
½ head napa cabbage
6 leaves lacinato kale, rolled
  and chiffonaded
1 red onion, julienned
2 jalapeños, ribs removed, julienned
2 scallions, sliced thinly on deep bias
1 thumb gingerroot, peeled and minced
3 tablespoons toasted sesame oil
½ cup (120 ml) rice vinegar
2 tablespoons agave nectar (or honey)
Juice of 1 lime
Juice of 1 orange
½ teaspoon fish sauce
Salt and pepper to taste
Togarashi

Chop the leaves of all the seaweeds except the sea lettuce into very thin strands. One at a time, dip each seaweed variety in boiling water for about 15 seconds. Remove to an ice bath and repeat until all the seaweed is blanched. Run the carrot and the cabbage through the finest blade on a Japanese mandoline, or—using a very sharp knife—slice into the thinnest possible ribbons. Combine all the vegetables in a large mixing bowl.

In another mixing bowl, whisk together the ginger, oil, vinegar, nectar, citrus juices, fish sauce, and salt and pepper. Pour the dressing over the vegetables and toss to combine. Portion the salad and serve with a sprinkle of togarashi on top.

Lobster and Kelp Tamales

SERVES 6

This wry twist on traditional tamales may take a bit of handwork, but it makes a stunning presentation and tastes great when served piping hot. Unlike most tamales that call for inedible wrappers like corn husk and banana leaf, this one is 100 percent edible.

The lobster-processing procedure used in many professional kitchens may not appeal to some home cooks. Killing a lobster by cutting through the center of its carapace, between the eyes, is the same thing to me as dropping it live into boiling water. The issue is that tail meat and claw meat require different cooking times, similar in some ways to a Thanksgiving turkey whose dark and white meats require (but don't often receive) different cooking times. So if anyone preparing lobster for this recipe doesn't mind the difference in texture (overcooked claw meat can be rubbery), the lobsters can be killed in boiling water and then dismantled.

For the filling

2 gallons (7.5 L) water
¼ cup plus ½ teaspoon (50 g) salt, divided
Two 1¼- to 1½-pound (570–680 g) lobsters
1 tablespoon olive oil
1 Spanish onion, julienned
1 poblano chile, stem and seed removed, julienned

For the Lobster Stock

2 lobster bodies, lightly pounded with a mallet
¼ cup (60 ml) tomato puree
2 tablespoons dry sherry
1 stalk celery, medium dice
1 small carrot, peeled, medium dice
½ small yellow onion, medium dice
4 cloves garlic, peeled
6 sprigs thyme
Small bunch chervil or tarragon
1 bay leaf
1½ teaspoons black peppercorns
2 Tepin chiles (optional)
Water to cover

MAKE THE FILLING: Fill a medium-sized stockpot with the water and ¼ cup (40 g) of the salt; bring to a boil. In the meantime, separate the tails, crusher claws, and pincher claws from the lobsters. Put the tails in one deep bowl, the crusher claws in a second bowl, and the pincher claws and knuckles in a third bowl. Pour the boiling water over the lobster parts until they're fully submerged, and cover each bowl with plastic wrap. Cook the tails 7 minutes, the pinchers and knuckles 10 minutes, and the crackers 13 minutes. Remove the parts carefully from the water and set aside in a large bowl until cool. When they're cool enough to handle, clean the meat out of the shells, chop coarsely, and set aside.

Combine the olive oil, onion, poblano pepper, and remaining ½ teaspoon salt in a 10-inch (25 cm) pan over medium-low heat. Sweat until soft, about 10 minutes, and set aside.

MAKE THE STOCK: Sear the two lobster bodies in a deep, dry, nonreactive pot over medium-high heat until you begin to smell toasting shells. Add the tomato puree and toast for about 3 minutes. Deglaze the pan with the sherry, scraping the browned bits with a wooden spoon. Add the next nine ingredients, ending with the chiles (if you're using them). Add enough water to almost fully submerge the bodies, bring to just under a boil, reduce the heat to low, and simmer 30 minutes. Strain into a container and allow the stock to cool slightly. This will be the stock used to make the tamales.

For the Masa Dough

2 cups (225 g) masa harina

1 cup (235 ml) lobster stock
  (preceding recipe)

¼ teaspoon salt

Six 8-inch (20 cm) squares sugar kelp

ASSEMBLE THE TAMALES: Combine the masa harina, lobster stock, and salt in a large mixing bowl and mix with your hands to combine.

Lay the squares of sea kelp out on a board or table and fill each with one-sixth of the masa mixture, shaping and flattening it into a rectangle, leaving ½ inch (1 cm) of space on the top and bottom and 2½ inches (6 cm) on each side. Fill each tamal with one-sixth of the onion mixture and one-sixth of the lobster mixture. Starting with one side, roll the kelp like a burrito, tucking in the top and bottom as you go. Repeat with the remaining five tamales.

Pour 2 inches (5 cm) water in the bottom of a large pot and fit it with a steamer basket. When the water comes to a boil, transfer the tamales, seam side down, to the steamer basket, stacked tightly so the steam will still get through but they won't unfurl. Cover and steam 10 minutes, until cooked through. Halve the tamales on the diagonal and serve in the kelp shell.

Duck Leg Confit on a Bistro Bean Salad Tossed in Apricot Sherry Vinaigrette

MAKES 12 SALADS

After the dog days of summer are over and lengthening nights start to chill the air, reach for this recipe, which makes good use of the last garden legumes of the season. For the Duck Confit recipe, see page 111.

For the Apricot Sherry Vinaigrette (makes about 3 cups [710 ml])
2 cups (260 g) dried apricots
2 cups (475 ml) sherry vinegar
1 cup (235 ml) sherry
¾ cup (180 ml) water
1 cup (225 g) sugar
2 tablespoons honey
2 medium shallots, minced
2 cloves garlic
1 teaspoon salt
½ teaspoon dried Aleppo chile flakes
¼ teaspoon black pepper
½ cup (120 ml) olive oil

For the Bistro Bean Salad (serves 8 by itself, or 12 if accompanying duck leg)
1 cup (225 g) dried yellow-eye beans
1 cup (225 g) dried black turtle beans
½ pound (225 g) fresh Romano beans
½ pound (225 g) Chinese long beans
4 bunches watercress
1 medium shallot, julienned
¾ cup (180 ml) Apricot Sherry Vinaigrette
Salt and pepper to taste

MAKE THE APRICOT SHERRY VINAIGRETTE: Place the apricots, sherry vinegar, sherry, water, sugar, and honey in a small, nonreactive pan over medium heat. Bring to a boil and cook down for about 25 minutes, until the mixture has reduced by half and the apricots are still, barely, covered with liquid. Let cool slightly off the heat.

Combine the apricot mixture with the shallots, garlic, salt, and Aleppo and black peppers in the bowl of a blender and puree, stopping once to scrape down the sides of the bowl. With the motor running, add the olive oil in a steady stream to emulsify. Thin slightly with water if necessary. Let cool to room temperature and serve (with Duck Confit and Bistro Bean Salad) or refrigerate.

MAKE THE BISTRO BEAN SALAD: Soak the yellow-eye beans and black turtle beans separately in four times their volume of water. Refrigerate overnight. Drain and rinse the beans and place in separate pans covered with twice as much water as beans, about 1½ quarts (1.4 L). Bring up to a boil, reduce to a simmer, and cook until the beans are fork-tender but not mushy (times can vary depending on how long the beans have been stored). Let cool to room temperature in the cooking liquid, drain, and set aside.

Meanwhile, bring a large pot of salted water to a boil. Have an ice bath ready. Blanch the Romano beans for 40 seconds and shock in the ice bath. Remove the stem end from the long beans, blanch 20 seconds, and shock in the ice bath. When cooled to room temperature, combine all the beans in a large bowl. Add the watercress, shallot, and vinaigrette; toss to combine. Add salt and pepper to taste and serve.

When serving with duck leg, spoon some vinaigrette on the plate, mound some salad on top, and perch the reheated duck leg on the salad.

Navajo Fry Bread

MAKES EIGHT 6-INCH (15 CM) ROUNDS

I have enjoyed most of my favorite flavors while traveling, but perhaps the most unexpected blissful bite came around the time I proposed to Denise. We were a few ticks north of the Arctic Circle, holed up in a 10 × 20 foot (3 × 6 m) wooden box a local woman had offered us after watching us try in vain to pitch a tent in fierce Arctic winds. After kindly settling us into her one-room "hunting shack," she returned with a huge arctic char, a close relative of salmon, she had just reeled in and a loaf of bannock bread she had baked that morning. They were both incredible and sustained us for a few days. When I asked what made the bread so damn delicious, the woman replied, "Seal fat." I immediately conjured images of bludgeoned baby harp seals, but then looked out on the expanse of tundra, beyond the trophy musk ox skull by the door of the shack, and thought, *What else are people going to eat around here?* The skull recalled the parliament of live musk ox, radiating outward from a shared butt huddle, that we beheld the previous day. Thusly justifying seal killing for food, we ended up devouring the bread with gusto.

Later, on a trip to the Southwest, I discovered Navajo bread in Santa Fe and quickly concluded that there must be an equivalent of bannock bread and Navajo bread in all indigenous cultures. At least I will say that this recipe for Navajo bread—adapted by longtime Black Trumpet baker Lauren Crosby—reminds me a lot of the Arctic bannock, and I highly recommend stuffing it like a pita or rolling it up with braised pork shoulder, as we did while recipe testing for this book!

4 cups (480 g) flour
2 tablespoons salt
2 tablespoons baking powder
2 cups (475 ml) warm water
Oil, for greasing the bowl
2 tablespoons plus 2 teaspoons lard
   (beef tallow or pork lard, preferably)

Combine the first three ingredients in a medium bowl and whisk to incorporate. Add the water in a slow stream, mixing with a fork to combine. Turn the mixture out onto a work surface, and with your hands, knead until it forms a dough and the liquid is fully incorporated, about 2 minutes. Rub the mixing bowl lightly with oil and add the dough ball. Cover with plastic or a damp cloth and let the dough sit for 15 to 30 minutes. Turn the dough out onto a lightly floured work surface and divide into eight even pieces. Pinch the pieces into balls, punch down, and roll into 7-inch (18 cm) rounds. If the dough contracts, stretch it gently like pizza dough. Let the dough rest 5 minutes.

Preheat the oven to 375°F (190°C).

Heat a 6-inch (15 cm) cast-iron or other heavy pan over medium heat until it begins to smoke. Add 1 teaspoon of the lard and a round of dough. Cook 40 seconds, flip, and cook 40 more seconds. Transfer to the oven and bake 4 minutes to finish cooking. The dough should be golden brown and crisp on the outside, soft and chewy on the inside. Repeat with the remaining seven dough rounds. Serve immediately or hold for up to a few hours before serving. These are best served the day they're baked.

Roasted Squash Salsa

SERVES 8 AS A SIDE DISH

This recipe calls for Castelas Spanish black olive oil. This product may be hard to find, but it is worth the search in my opinion, because there is nothing quite like it. A little goes a long way, so I urge everyone who loves olives the way I do to keep a bottle around at all times. It's great for finishing salads, for enriching tapenade, or as a garnish for chilled soups like the Chilled Zucchini Soup on page 261.

In this recipe, if you don't have Castelas, you may wish to find some black Spanish olives and chop them up into the salsa.

1 pound (455 g) summer squash
Olive oil, for roasting
1 teaspoon kosher salt
½ teaspoon freshly ground black pepper
½ red onion, small dice
1 red bell pepper, small dice
1 jalapeño, ribs and seeds removed,
  small dice
Juice of 2 lemons
1 tablespoon Castelas black olive oil

Preheat the oven to 425°F (220°C).

Rub the squash with olive oil, sprinkle with half the salt and pepper, and roast on a baking sheet until soft, about 40 minutes. Remove from the oven and let cool 30 minutes. Large-dice the squash and place in a medium-sized mixing bowl. Fold in the onion, peppers, lemon juice, and black olive oil gently with a spatula. Add remaining salt and pepper to taste and serve immediately or refrigerate for up to 3 days.

Summer Squash and Beet Hash

SERVES 8

1 red beet

2 tablespoons olive oil, plus more
    for roasting

1 pound (455 g) summer squash,
    zucchini, or a combination of the two

2 tablespoons butter

½ pound (225 g) Red Bliss potatoes,
    washed, skin on, medium dice

½ Spanish onion, medium dice

1 tablespoon minced garlic

1 teaspoon whole untoasted
    cumin seed

½ teaspoon chili powder

⅛ teaspoon cayenne pepper

½ teaspoon salt

½ teaspoon black pepper

2 tablespoons sherry vinegar

Preheat the oven to 350°F (175°C). Rub the beet in olive oil and slice in half. Place cut side down on a cookie sheet and roast 30 to 45 minutes (depending on size), until soft. When it's cool enough to handle, peel the beet and medium dice. Set aside.

Seed (if necessary) the squash and medium dice.

Place a broad, high-sided, heavy-bottomed pan (12-inch [30 cm] cast iron works well) over medium heat. Add the olive oil, butter, and potatoes and sauté for 2 to 3 minutes, until they just begin to turn opaque. Add the squash and onion and cook 3 more minutes, stirring occasionally. Add the garlic and spices and cook 3 more minutes. Add the salt and pepper and stir to combine. Deglaze the pan with the sherry vinegar, scraping up the browned bits. Cook 3 to 5 minutes, until the potatoes are soft and the liquid has evaporated. Top with the beets and serve immediately, or allow the mixture to cool and refrigerate. Reheat in a pan, adding the beets just before serving so the color doesn't bleed and turn everything pink.

Stone Fruit Salad

MAKES 4 CUPS (945 ML); SERVES 8

In the hottest weeks of summer, this deliciously refreshing salad can be served as a starter or—omitting the vinegar and shallot—as a light dessert.

3 peaches

2 nectarines

4 fresh apricots

4 red plums

1 medium shallot, peeled and julienned

2 tablespoons packed lemon balm leaves

2 tablespoons packed mint leaves

2 tablespoons packed Thai basil leaves

Juice of 1 orange (about ¼ cup [60 ml])

2 teaspoons rice wine vinegar

2 teaspoons honey

¼ vanilla bean, split and scraped

¼ teaspoon salt

Halve, pit, and slice the stone fruit into ¼-inch-thick (0.5 cm) wedges. There should be about 4 cups (945 ml) of sliced fruit total. Place in a medium bowl with the shallot and herbs.

Combine the orange juice, vinegar, honey, vanilla bean, and salt in a separate bowl, stirring to dissolve the honey and salt. Pour the mixture over the fruit and herbs and toss gently to combine. Taste for seasoning and serve immediately. Note that this salad does not store particularly well, so plan to serve all you have prepared.

Chilled Zucchini Soup

SERVES 6 TO 8

2 pounds (910 g) zucchini, ends removed, rough-chopped
2 onions, julienned
2 tablespoons olive oil
2 tablespoons salt
3 tablespoons minced garlic
1½ tablespoons cumin seed, toasted and ground
1 tablespoon ground coriander
1 teaspoon dried Mexican oregano
Pinch ground nutmeg
Pinch chile de árbol powder
1½ cups (355 ml) whole-milk yogurt
1 cup (235 ml) unsalted vegetable stock

In a large, high-sided sauté pan, combine the zucchini, onions, olive oil, and salt; cook over low heat, stirring occasionally, about 10 minutes, or until the vegetables are soft and their juices have evaporated in the pan. Add the garlic and spices and cook 2 minutes, stirring to combine. Remove from the heat and pour into the bowl of a blender. Add the yogurt and puree until smooth. Remove to a container, thin with vegetable stock, and refrigerate several hours, until cold. Stir before serving.

Pickled Stone Fruit

MAKES 3 CUPS (710 ML)

Only slightly more stable than the Stone Fruit Salad recipe on page 260, this quick pickle will hold for a maximum of 2 days in the refrigerator before the fruit oxidizes and turns brown, unless you want to preserve the pickle by canning it, which will eliminate oxygen and—a few months later—add a surprisingly tangy fruit lift to heavy midwinter meals.

2 plums
2 nectarines
2 fresh apricots
¼ cup (60 ml) white wine
2 cups (475 ml) water, divided
½ cup (120 ml) white wine vinegar
1 ancho chile, torn into large pieces
1 stick cinnamon
¼ cup (55 g) sugar
2 tablespoons salt
1 tablespoon honey

Halve and pit the fruit. Cut into ½-inch-thick (1 cm) slices and place in a bowl with the wine and 1 cup (235 ml) of the water. In a small, nonreactive pot, combine the remaining water, vinegar, chile, cinnamon stick, sugar, salt, and honey. Bring to a boil and simmer 30 minutes. Let cool, strain over the fruit, and stir to combine. Refrigerate for 4 hours and serve, or can.

Twice-Baked Eggplant Markeb

SERVES 12

6 eggplants, each 6–8 inches
   (15–20 cm) long
1 tablespoon salt, plus more to taste
3 red bell peppers
2 tablespoons plus 2 cups (505 ml)
   olive oil, divided
1 cup (140 g) pine nuts
1½ cups (85 g) shredded old
   bread cubes
2 Spanish onions, large dice
12 cloves garlic, minced
2 tablespoons minced peeled
   gingerroot
1½ cups (355 ml) tomato puree
1 tablespoon sumac
1 tablespoon harissa (page 16)
¼ cup (15 g) chopped fresh oregano
2 tablespoons honey
Black pepper to taste

Preheat the oven to 450°F (230°C).

Halve each eggplant lengthwise and scoop out the guts, leaving 1 inch (2.5 cm) of thickness throughout. Chop the guts into 1-inch (2.5 cm) cubes, sprinkle the guts and eggplant halves with 1 tablespoon salt, and rest, cut side down, on two parchment-lined sheet trays for 1 hour.

Place the bell peppers on a roasting pan and slide into the top rack of the oven. Roast, turning every 7 minutes, until they're soft and all four sides begin to blister and blacken, about 35 minutes total. Remove to a bowl, cover tightly with plastic, and allow the peppers to steam for 30 minutes. Remove the plastic and, when the peppers are cool enough to handle, remove the stems, seeds, and peels. Chop the peppers into a medium dice and set aside.

Reduce the oven temperature to 375°F (190°C). Remove the eggplant and parchment from the two sheet trays and rub each tray with 1 tablespoon of the olive oil. Return the eggplant halves, cut side down, to the trays and bake for 15 to 18 minutes, until soft.

Pour 2 cups (475 ml) olive oil into a large, high-sided sauté pan over medium-low heat. Add the pine nuts and toast, stirring, until they begin to brown, 2 to 3 minutes. Remove with a slotted spoon to a paper-towel-lined plate.

Add the chopped eggplant to the pan and sauté until soft. Remove to a large bowl, squeezing some of the oil from the eggplant back into the pan. Add the shredded bread cubes and the pine nuts to the bowl and stir to combine. Add the onions to the pan and sauté until soft, about 10 minutes. Add the garlic and ginger and sauté 1 minute. Add the tomato puree and roasted peppers and simmer 15 minutes. Add the sumac, harissa, oregano, and honey; stir to combine.

Bring the oven up to 400°F (200°C).

Pour the excess oil out of the pan and add the pan ingredients to the bowl with the eggplant, bread, and nuts. Stir vigorously, making a homogenized mush. Taste and adjust the seasoning with additional salt and pepper. Stuff the mixture evenly into the eggplant boats. At this point, the eggplant can be refrigerated for up to a few hours. Bake until the stuffing is bubbling around the edges, and serve.

Chile Pasta

This slightly spicy pasta, pink with flecks of red chile, rolls out to beautiful fettuccine noodles. These noodles turn the sockeye salmon dish (following recipe) into a filling summer dinner that will be sure to satisfy even finicky family palates.

1 pound (455 g) "00" flour
1 tablespoon paprika
½ teaspoon cayenne pepper
½ teaspoon dried Aleppo chile flakes
1 tablespoon chili powder
½ teaspoon salt
2 eggs (100 g liquid egg)
¾ cup (180 ml) water
1½ teaspoons olive oil

Add the flour, spices, and salt to a large bowl and whisk to combine. Combine the eggs, water, and oil in another small bowl, whisking to break up the eggs. Turn the dry mixture out onto a clean work surface, make a large, high-sided well in the middle, and pour the wet ingredients into the well. Using a fork, draw some of the flour into the egg mixture until the eggs are no longer runny. Using your hands, push a bit of flour aside and pull the rest into a mound. Using your fingers or a bowl scraper, cut the wet into the dry parts until fully incorporated into a craggy ball, working in more flour as necessary. The dough should be tacky but not adhesive. Knead the dough for about 10 minutes, until it is smooth and firm, and springs back to three-quarters of its original shape when poked with a finger. Mold into a disk and wrap tightly with plastic wrap. Refrigerate for at least an hour and up to 2 days before using.

Sockeye Salmon with Chile Fettuccine, Bacon, and Chanterelles in Gin Tomato Cream Sauce

SERVES 6

In the early years of Black Trumpet, I worked closely with a husband-and-wife team of Alaskan salmon fishermen. They would catch the sweetest kings, cohos, and sockeyes in their respective seasons and ship them to me via FedEx. For a while, I was their only customer in the Northeast. One year, FedEx raised their prices so significantly, it was no longer profitable for those beautiful salmon to make their beeline flight along the Canadian border to my door. Luckily, it was around this time that I became aware of the impending crisis in Bristol Bay, Alaska.

Bristol Bay, located in a remote corner of Alaska, had been selected by a few multinational corporations as an ideal site for a copper mine. When two nonprofit organizations, Chefs Collaborative and Trout Unlimited, jointly brought to my attention exactly what was at stake—no less than the last remaining wild population of sockeye salmon on Earth—I immediately plotted ways to get involved. I am pleased to report that, after a couple of years of lobbying efforts that included petitions signed by concerned chefs all over the country, the corporate mining interests backed away from the project that would have threatened a sacred fishery as well as an ancient indigenous culture that had thrived there for centuries.

If you are preparing this dish in an area where sockeye salmon is not available, you can easily substitute steelhead trout or any other salmon. When ordering salmon from your fishmonger or supermarket, be sure to ask whether it is wild or farm-raised (the price often tells you first), and if it is farm-raised, whether or not it is fed an organic diet. If enough people start asking for Bristol Bay salmon, fish markets will have no choice but to seek it out, thereby ensuring that a healthy market for sockeye will prevent any further exploration into mining Bristol Bay.

Although aesthetically monochromatic, this dish boasts a wild flavor complex that is guaranteed to win the favor of special someones everywhere. So don't be afraid to take this on, and feel free to sauté up some shrimp with the noodles to add another scrumptious component to an already flavorful dish.

Six 5-ounce (140 g) fillets sockeye salmon (or suitable substitution), skin side scored

Pinch salt, plus more for sprinkling

1 pound (455 g) Chile Pasta dough (page 264)

1 tablespoon olive oil, plus more for cooked pasta

1½ cups (355 ml) Gin Tomato Cream Sauce (recipe follows)

12 large or 24 small chanterelles

Black pepper

½ teaspoon minced garlic

1½ cups (300 g) Bacon Lardons (see Warm Kale Caesar Salad, page 281)

Liberally salt the skin side of all six fillets. Bring a large pot of heavily salted water to a boil over high heat.

Once the pasta dough has sat for 30 minutes at room temperature, place it on a clean, lightly floured work surface and cut into four pieces. Cover three with plastic or a clean cloth so they don't dry out, and flatten the other piece to about ½ inch (1 cm) thick with the palm of your hand. Using a pasta sheeter at the widest setting, roll the dough out. Make a gate fold by folding both sides of the dough into the middle and then folding the entire piece in half again. Flatten again with the palm of your hand and roll the shortest side through the widest setting once again. Move the setting down two notches and roll again. Move down two notches and roll. At this point, you want the machine to be on the third-narrowest setting. If not, move the setting down however many notches you need to to get to this setting, and roll again. Lightly flour both sides of the dough and pass it through the fettuccine cutter attachment on the pasta machine. When the first ball of dough is rolled out, twist the strands of fettuccine into single-serving nests and place on a baking sheet sprinkled with semolina flour. Repeat the rolling-and-cutting process with the three remaining pieces of dough.

When the pot of water reaches a boil, add the six piles of fettuccine one at a time, being careful not to overcrowd the pot, and cook for 2½ minutes, or until al dente. Remove to a baking sheet and toss with olive oil as the pasta cools so the pieces won't stick.

Once the pasta is completely cooled and lightly coated with olive oil, it can be refrigerated. Reheat by dropping the pasta in boiling water just to heat through, or by reheating in a pan with sauce.

When you're ready to serve, heat the Gin Tomato Cream Sauce in a small pot slowly, over low heat, stirring occasionally.

Meanwhile, heat a large cast-iron or carbon-steel pan over high heat until it just begins to smoke. Add the olive oil and enough fish so that it fits in the pan in a single layer, skin side down. Sear 3 minutes, until golden brown, pressing down gently on the flesh side with a spatula or another heavy frying pan to ensure that the skin is browning evenly. Flip the fish, reduce the heat to low, and cook 1 minute. Remove the fillets to a baking sheet and hold, skin side up, in a very low oven until the remaining pieces are cooked. Repeat with the remaining fillets. Heat the same pan over a high flame, adding oil if necessary, and add the chanterelles. Sear for 30 seconds undisturbed, flip, and add a pinch of salt and pepper, the minced garlic, bacon, and pasta. Cook 30 seconds, tossing a few times to combine the flavors.

To serve, ladle ¼ cup (60 ml) Gin Tomato Cream Sauce on the bottom of each plate. Mound about ⅓ cup (75 to 90 g) pasta, tossed well with bacon and mushrooms on each plate; top with the fish, skin side up. Serve immediately.

Gin Tomato Cream Sauce

MAKES ABOUT 1 QUART (945 ML)

I know guests enjoyed this sauce anytime it was on the menu, but I think its most ardent fan was sous chef Carrie. We found plenty of applications for this addictive sauce, but the one that endured the longest was in our sockeye salmon dish—a Black Trumpet Hall of Famer for sure.

1 tablespoon salt-cured capers
2 teaspoons olive oil
1 large shallot, finely chopped
1 tablespoon minced garlic
¼ cup (60 ml) Hendrick's gin
2 cups (475 ml) tomato puree
Juice of 1 orange
2 tablespoons finely chopped fresh dill
1 teaspoon salt
1½ cups (355 ml) heavy cream

Reconstitute the capers by soaking them in 1 cup (235 ml) water for 30 minutes. Drain, finely chop, and set aside.

Pour the olive oil into a medium, heavy-bottomed, nonreactive pot over medium heat. Add the shallot and garlic and cook, stirring occasionally, until softened, about 5 minutes. Carefully add the gin to the pan and back away, allowing it to flame up and burn off the alcohol, about 2 minutes. Add the capers, tomato puree, orange juice, dill, and salt; cook over a low flame, stirring occasionally, for 15 minutes. Add the cream and heat through, about 4 minutes. Remove the pot from the heat, let it cool slightly, and transfer the contents to the bowl of a blender. Puree until smooth and serve immediately, or cool to room temperature and refrigerate until you're ready to use it. Reheat over a very low flame, stirring occasionally, until heated through.

Fried Sour Cream Pound Cake with Whipped Mascarpone, Macerated Blueberries, and Lemon Curd

MAKES 1 LARGE LOAF; SERVES 12 TO 14

Any of these components can be made and served together, but for the gold star, try all of them in a dessert bonanza that immortalized Lauren Crosby forever in the eyes of many happy guests.

For the pound cake
½ pound (225 g) unsalted butter, at room temperature
3 cups (680 g) sugar
1 cup (235 ml) sour cream (we like Brookford Farm's)
3 cups (360 g) flour
½ teaspoon baking soda
6 large eggs (300 g liquid egg), at room temperature
1 teaspoon vanilla extract

For the Lemon Curd
4 whole eggs (200 g liquid egg)
9 egg yolks (160 g)
1 cup (225 g) sugar
1 cup (235 ml) freshly squeezed lemon juice (from 6 large lemons)
2 tablespoons lemon zest (from 3 lemons)

For the Macerated Blueberries
4 cups (680 g) fresh blueberries, divided
1 cup (225 g) sugar
½ cup (120 ml) water

For the Whipped Mascarpone
2 cups (455 g) mascarpone cheese
1 cup (115 g) powdered sugar

MAKE THE POUND CAKE: Preheat the oven to 350°F (175°C). Butter and flour a 9 × 5 × 3 inch (23 × 13 × 7.5 cm) loaf pan.

Cream the butter and sugar in a mixer on medium-high speed with the paddle attachment until it is light and fluffy, 5 to 6 minutes. Add the sour cream and mix until incorporated, scraping down the sides of the bowl.

Sift the flour and baking soda into a small bowl. Turn the mixer down to medium-low speed and add the dry ingredients to the bowl in three additions, alternating each with the addition of two eggs. Add the eggs one at a time, making sure each is fully incorporated before adding the next. Next, add the vanilla extract and mix until fully combined. Scrape the batter into the prepared loaf pan and bake on the center rack of the oven for about 90 minutes, rotating a half turn every 30 minutes. The cake is done when it is golden brown, the edges begin to pull away from the sides of the pan, and a cake tester comes out clean.

Allow the cake to cool in the pan for 10 minutes, then remove it to a cooling rack to finish cooling to room temperature. Wrapped tightly in plastic, the cake will keep up to 3 days.

MAKE THE LEMON CURD: Fill a wide, deep pot with 2 inches (5 cm) water and heat to a simmer. In a medium bowl, whisk the eggs and yolks. Add the sugar in a slow, steady stream, whisking constantly. Add the lemon juice in a slow, steady stream. Add the zest and stir to combine. Place the bowl over the simmering water and stir continuously, using a rubber spatula, until the mixture thickens, 5 to 6 minutes. Be sure to scrape the bottom and sides of the bowl often while stirring. Switch to a whisk and whisk the mixture constantly and vigorously until it is smooth and pudding-like, about 4 more minutes. Remove to another container and let cool to room temperature, whisking occasionally. Use immediately or refrigerate for up to 3 days.

MAKE THE MACERATED BLUEBERRIES: Combine 1 cup (170 g) of the blueberries with the sugar and water in a small nonreactive pot over medium-low heat. Bring to a simmer and cook until the mixture becomes syrupy, about 15 minutes. Puree the syrup in a blender until smooth, remove to a bowl, and fold in the remaining 3 cups (510 g) fresh blueberries. Serve immediately or refrigerate for up to 5 days.

MAKE THE WHIPPED MASCARPONE: In a large bowl, briefly whisk the mascarpone by hand until smooth and fluffy. Add the sugar and fold it into the cheese with a spatula, being careful not to overmix or the cheese will turn granular and yellow in color. Serve immediately or refrigerate for up to 5 days.

TO SERVE: Fry slices of the pound cake in whole butter until light golden brown, transfer to a towel or drying rack. Spread the curd liberally on the plates, bank the pound cake on the curd, top with whipped cream, and pour the blueberries and their syrup over the top.

Corn Mousse

SERES 10

This is a fairly quick and simple dessert that will blow dinner guests away. It can be made a day in advance and should be served with fresh summer fruit.

3 ears sweet corn, kernels removed, both cobs and kernels reserved

3½ cups (830 ml) heavy cream, divided

1½ cups (340 g) sugar

2 tablespoons (7 g) gelatin powder

¼ cup (60 ml) cold water

Place the corncobs and kernels in a medium pot over medium-low heat. Add 1½ cups (355 ml) of the cream and bring to a low boil. Boil until the cream has thickened and reduced by two-thirds, about 20 minutes. Add the sugar, stirring until dissolved. Remove from the heat and let the mixture cool to room temperature. Remove the cobs, "milk" them by running the blunt end of a knife firmly down each side, catching the liquid in the pot, and discard the cobs. Puree the corn, cream, and "milk" in a blender until smooth. Clean the pot and strain the corn mixture back into it. Combine the gelatin and water in a small bowl and let soften, 5 minutes. Squeeze out the extra water and combine the softened gelatin with the corn mixture over low heat, whisking just until the gelatin is dissolved. Let the mixture cool to room temperature.

Using a wire whisk and a large mixing bowl, whip the remaining 2 cups (475 ml) cream to soft peaks. Gently fold the whipped cream into the corn mixture and refrigerate for at least 3 hours, or until you're ready to serve.

Serve with fresh summer berries or sliced peaches, or both!

Itchy Ankle Farm

For the rest of my life, peaches will remind me of Itchy Ankle Farm.

Having lived in the South and eaten the plump, slobbery, sun-blushed nectar of Aphrodite right in the heart of its dominion, I maintained some skepticism when I received a call from a woman declaring open season on her peach trees. Maria Southworth and her family maintained a sizable plot of peach trees on their property in Madbury, New Hampshire, the fruits of which proliferated that year to the point where thousands of perfectly good peaches, now "grounded," had to be given to a black bear rehabilitation program at the nearby university. Those bears must have rehabilitated in a state of near ecstasy, I would later realize.

In short order, I visited the Southworths' then nameless farm and almost collapsed at the sight of four long rows of mature peach trees almost laughably bursting with golden fruit. Even after the first bear-food gleaning, the ground before me was carpeted with rotting fruit. I reached up to the first tree, plucked a warm peach, and tasted the magic—every bit as exquisite as the larger southern fruits, but maybe even more so for having survived numerous New England winters.

I returned many times, often with the rest of my family, to pick peaches, as well as blueberries and apples, from the Madbury property. Denise and I even fantasized about one day buying the property and keeping the fruitful farm going for future generations, but most of all, we watched our kids migrate from disbelief to discomfort as they beheld, and then picked, bottomless bushels of fruit, about half of which seemed to end up in their tummies.

One particularly hot summer afternoon, picking peaches in the tall grass, my daughter commented on how itchy her legs were. Not itchy enough to stop picking peaches, but itchy enough to distract her from the prize. Later, when the oils from hidden poison ivy had entered the scratches on both children's legs, the ankle itching began in earnest. By the next outing, my kids had dubbed the Madbury property "Itchy Ankle Farm." Maria liked the name so much, it stuck.

Peach Brioche Bread Pudding
with Ginger Bourbon Caramel Sauce

SERVES 9

This recipe, which I originally made for a dairy company looking for novel ways to promote their cream, far exceeded my expectations, so I put it on our dessert menu. I confess that the recipe presupposes that the home cook may have stale brioche on hand. In the likely event that this is not the case, I have included a good brioche recipe that also happens to make the best French toast and grilled cheese you and your family will ever sink your pearlies into.

For bonus points and an even richer final product, you may consider pairing Goat's Milk Caramel (page 147) with this in place of the Ginger Bourbon Caramel.

For the brioche
1⅓ cups (315 ml) whole milk
⅔ cup (150 g) unsalted butter, diced
1 teaspoon active dry yeast
3 eggs (150 ml liquid egg)
2 tablespoons plus 2 teaspoons sugar
5¼ cups (630 g) flour
2 teaspoons salt
1 egg (50 g liquid egg) plus 1 teaspoon
  water, fork-whisked

For the bread pudding
7 large eggs (350 g liquid egg)
1½ cups (340 g) sugar, divided
2½ cups (590 ml) heavy cream
1 cup (235 ml) whole milk
1-inch (2.5 cm) cubes cut from 1 loaf
  day-old brioche (or other egg bread)
4 large ripe peaches, halved, pitted,
  and diced into ½-inch (1 cm) pieces
2 tablespoons (28 g) fresh gingerroot,
  peeled and grated
1½ ounces (45 ml) bourbon
Juice of ½ lemon

MAKE THE BRIOCHE: Warm the milk in a pan over low heat. Add the butter and whisk until combined. Let cool slightly. Add the yeast to the bowl of a mixer and pour the milk mixture over the top (be careful that the milk isn't too hot or it will kill the yeast). Whisk lightly to combine and let the mixture bloom 5 minutes. Add the eggs and sugar, whisking to combine. Add the flour and top with the salt. Fit the mixer with the dough hook attachment and mix on medium-low speed for 5 minutes, or until the dough begins to look smooth and starts to slap the sides of the bowl. Remove the dough from the hook and cover the bowl with a clean, damp cloth. Let rise 1 hour.

Preheat the oven to 350°F (175°C).

Using a rubber spatula, remove the dough to a clean work surface and divide in half. Roll both halves tightly into balls, and then shape into loaves. Spray two loaf pans with cooking spray and place the loaves in the prepared pans. Cover and let rise 1 hour. Brush with the egg wash and bake on the middle shelf of the oven for about an hour, rotating a few times throughout. When cool enough to handle, remove the bread from the loaf pans and let it cool to room temperature on a cooling rack.

Reserve one loaf for another use. Remove the bottom and top crust in a very thin layer from the other brioche, discard, then cut it into 1-inch (2.5 cm) cubes, storing it in a tightly lidded container for 1 to 2 days.

For the Ginger Bourbon Caramel Sauce
¼ cup (60 ml) water
1 cup (225 g) sugar
1 cup (225 g) unsalted butter,
  cut into 16 pieces
½ cup (120 ml) heavy cream
½ teaspoon vanilla extract
Pinch salt
Reserved ginger bourbon peach syrup

MAKE THE BREAD PUDDING: In a large mixing bowl, whisk the eggs with ¾ cup (170 g) of the sugar until light and foamy. Add the cream and milk and whisk to combine. Add the brioche cubes, tossing gently with a spatula to combine. Cover and refrigerate 1½ to 2 hours.

Meanwhile, combine the peaches with the remaining ¾ cup (170 g) sugar along with the ginger, bourbon, and lemon juice in a small saucepan over low heat. Simmer 5 to 10 minutes (depending on ripeness), until the peaches have started to break down. Remove from the heat and let cool in the pan. When cool, strain the peaches and reserve the liquid.

Preheat the oven to 350°F (175°C).

Butter a 9-inch-square (23 cm) baking pan. Add half of the soaked brioche to the pan, scatter the peaches evenly over the brioche, and top with the remaining brioche, pouring any remaining egg custard over the top.

Cover the pudding tightly with foil and bake on the middle rack for 25 minutes. Uncover, rotate the pan, and bake another 20 minutes (checking after 15), until the pudding is puffy and golden and it begins to pull away from the sides of the pan. Let it cool to room temperature.

While the pudding bakes, make the caramel sauce.

MAKE THE GINGER BOURBON CARAMEL SAUCE: In a small, heavy-bottomed saucepan, swirl the water and sugar over low heat until the sugar is dissolved. Cover the saucepan and raise the heat to medium. Boil, covered, for 3 minutes. Remove the lid and turn the heat to high. When the caramel turns medium amber in color (about 4 minutes), remove it from the heat, swirling the pan carefully to distribute the color evenly (the carryover cooking will result in a deep amber color). Off the heat, and working quickly, whisk in the butter one pat at a time. Whisk in the cream, vanilla, and salt. Let the mixture cool to room temperature, and then add some reserved ginger peach syrup until the caramel reaches a slightly pourable consistency.

TO SERVE: Slice the pudding into nine equal pieces and serve warm, drizzled with caramel sauce.

Sweet Red Pepper Cheesecake with Red Pepper Jam and Corn Cream

MAKES 6 INDIVIDUAL CHEESECAKES

Lauren worked some unforgettable magic melding our perceptions of sweet and savory; her pea custard, Sun Gold tomato tart, and this recipe stand out among them. Some people ordered this as an appetizer (which is fine, if a bit filling for my tastes), but the vast majority of guests enjoyed it as a dessert. In the company of the right wine and the right guests, I would argue that this makes an ideal finale to a grilled meal on a hot summer evening.

One thing to consider when planning to make this recipe: In order to successfully unmold these tarts, they should be made and refrigerated a day in advance, giving them a chance to set up completely.

For the cheesecake
2 red bell peppers
½ cup (80 g) semolina flour
2 tablespoons plus ½ cup (140 g) sugar, divided
2 tablespoons butter, melted
5 ounces (140 g) cream cheese, at room temperature
3 ounces (85 g) whole-milk ricotta cheese
1 egg (50 g liquid egg)
1 egg yolk (18 g)
¼ teaspoon salt

For the Red Pepper Jam
6 large red bell peppers, small dice
1½ cups (340 g) sugar
¼ cup (60 ml) cider vinegar

For the Corn Cream
2 ears sweet corn, shucked
2 tablespoons melted unsalted butter
1 teaspoon salt, divided
1½ cups (355 ml) heavy cream
¼ cup (60 ml) honey
⅛ teaspoon turmeric, for color

MAKE THE CHEESECAKE: Preheat the oven to 450°F (230°C).

Roast the peppers on a baking sheet on the top rack of the oven, turning every 7 minutes, for about 35 minutes total, until the skin has blistered and blackened and the flesh is soft. Remove to a medium mixing bowl, cover tightly with plastic wrap, and let steam for 30 minutes. When the peppers are cool enough to handle, peel them and remove the stems and seeds.

Reduce the oven temperature to 350°F (175°C).

While the peppers are roasting and resting, make the crust: Pan-spray six 4- to 6-ounce (120 to 180 ml) ramekins and place on a flat baking sheet.

Combine the semolina, 2 tablespoons of the sugar, and the melted butter in a medium bowl. Divide the dough evenly among the six ramekins and press down into the bottom and ½ inch (1 cm) up the sides. Bake at 350°F (175°C) for 10 minutes, or until barely golden around the edges. Let cool.

While the crusts are par-baking, puree the peppers in a blender until smooth, scraping down the sides if necessary.

In the bowl of a food processor, blend the cheeses until smooth. Add the remaining ½ cup (115 g) sugar and pulse to combine. Add the egg, yolk, and salt, blend to combine, and scrape down the sides. Add the pepper puree and blend. Strain the mixture into a pitcher or bowl with a pourable spout.

Pour the pepper cheesecake mixture evenly into each crust-lined ramekin. Bake at 350°F (175°C) for about 30 minutes, rotating after 15 and checking for doneness after 25 minutes. The cheesecakes should wobble as a single unit when you shake lightly and should be just

barely firm in the middle when poked gently with a finger. Cool to room temperature and refrigerate overnight.

MAKE THE RED PEPPER JAM: Combine the peppers, sugar, and vinegar in a small, heavy-bottomed pot. Bring to a boil and reduce the heat to a high simmer over medium-low heat. Cook the mixture down until the liquid just barely coats the back of a spoon (it will become thicker as it cools), 25 to 30 minutes. Let it cool to room temperature.

MAKE THE CORN CREAM: Preheat the oven to 400°F (200°C). Drizzle the corn with the melted butter and ½ teaspoon of the salt. Roast, turning once or twice, until the kernels are cooked through and beginning to turn golden brown in spots. Remove the corn from the oven, and when it's cool enough to handle, cut the kernels from the cob and place in a small, heavy-bottomed pot over medium heat with the cream, the honey, and the remaining ½ teaspoon of salt. Bring to just under a boil (watch carefully!), reduce the heat, and simmer about 15 minutes, until the mixture thickens slightly. Remove from the heat and add a tiny pinch of turmeric for color, not taste (optional). Blend the mixture until smooth, cool to room temperature, and refrigerate until you're ready to use it.

TO SERVE: Lightly spread a spoonful of Red Pepper Jam over the top of each cheesecake. Dollop some Corn Cream on a dessert plate. Carefully unmold the cheesecake by running a small offset spatula around the perimeter of the ramekin and shaking it away from the sides. Place the cake on top of the cream sauce. Serve chilled.

CHAPTER SEVEN

EARLY FALL

The Great Bounty

EARLY FALL RECIPES

There is so much to love about the onset of autumn that we New Englanders can only lament the loss of summer for so long. The beauty of late September is almost too much to bear, which is precisely why Josh Jennings, Denise, and I chose to schedule our Heirloom Harvest Barn Dinner on the third Sunday in September, a day that roughly coincides with the equinox.

Since 2009, the Barn Dinner, as it has come to be known, brings our community's most talented chefs together at the stunning Meadow's Mirth Farm barn in Stratham, New Hampshire, where we serve up more than just good local food. We offer guests at the dinner an education about our local farming and fishing communities while enjoying great live music and course after course of innovative dishes that utilize heirloom vegetables and heritage-breed animals. The event sets the finest imaginable dining against the seemingly asynchronous backdrop of a working barn. As the sun sets behind fields of crops viewed from the open barn door, dinner guests behold a portal to something far greater than a good meal in a barn. They experience a kind of enlightenment that can only be achieved through community and solidarity. To be a part of a greater movement, the very premise of which is to change the way our society eats and thinks about food, is to be a Barn Dinner veteran. Whether I play the role of organizer, cook, or emcee, the Barn Dinner will remain one of the most inspiring events I have partaken in.

It is important to note that the individual efforts of countless volunteers and organizations like Chefs Collaborative, Slow Food Seacoast, and Seacoast Eat Local have made both the inception and the perpetuation of the Barn Dinner possible. These are the forces I refer to in this book's introduction, the humble visionaries who have built the scaffolding around the ruins of our food system, so that others may have an easier time making necessary repairs.

Warm Kale Caesar Salad
with Squash Croutons, Bacon Lardons,
and Caesar Aioli

MAKES 10 SALADS

This was perhaps our most popular salad ever. It came about in 2012, at a time when kale everything was sweeping the nation. I love the way this dish coalesces all the adjectives our tongues want: salty, sweet, chewy, tender, crunchy, tangy, and warm. A year later, we replicated this dish with whole brussels sprout leaves, and it was almost as popular, but hitting the kale zeitgeist at its peak made the original the perfect autumn salad in its place and time.

For the Squash Croutons

½ butternut squash, halved, seeds removed, peeled, cut into ½-inch (1 cm) cubes

2 tablespoons olive oil

1 teaspoon salt, divided, plus more for sprinkling

¼ teaspoon pepper

1 cup (120 g) all-purpose flour

2 eggs (100 g liquid egg)

1 cup (50 g) panko or homemade bread crumbs

1 quart (945 ml) canola oil

For the Bacon Lardons

10 ounces (285 g) slab bacon, cut into ½-inch (1 cm) cubes

For the salad

Caesar Aioli (see Tuna Caesar, page 206)

1 tablespoon olive oil

Bacon Lardons

1 head curly kale, stripped of the stalks and chiffonaded

Pinch salt

Pinch black pepper

Squash Croutons

Grated Parmesan cheese

MAKE THE SQUASH CROUTONS: Preheat the oven to 350°F (175°C).

Toss the cubes of squash with olive oil, ½ teaspoon of the salt, and the pepper; spread onto a baking sheet. Par-roast for 20 minutes, until the squash is just beginning to soften.

In a medium bowl, combine the flour with the remaining ½ teaspoon salt. In a second bowl, beat the eggs lightly. Place the bread crumbs in a third bowl. Using standard breading procedure, drop the squash cubes into the flour, tossing to coat evenly. Tap off the excess, and coat with egg. Finally, dip the squash cubes in the bread crumbs, pressing lightly to adhere.

Preheat the canola oil in a small high-sided pot over medium-high heat. When the oil reaches 350°F (175°C), begin frying in small batches so you don't crowd the pan. Deep-fry for 3½ minutes or until the squash cubes are golden brown. Using a slotted spoon, transfer the cubes to a paper-towel-lined plate and sprinkle lightly with salt. Repeat with the remaining squash cubes.

MAKE THE BACON LARDONS: Preheat the oven to 425°F (220°C).

Spread the bacon out onto a parchment-lined baking sheet and bake 25 minutes, until crispy and golden brown. Remove the lardons to a paper-towel-lined plate and set aside.

MAKE THE SALAD: Smear a thin layer of Caesar Aioli dressing on the bottom of all ten salad plates.

In a large wok, carbon-steel, or cast-iron pan over high heat, add the olive oil. When it begins to smoke, add half of the rendered Bacon Lardons and cook, tossing occasionally, for 30 seconds to 1 minute or until golden brown. Set aside a large handful of raw kale and throw the rest in the pan with pinches of salt and black pepper. Cook, tossing, for 30 seconds. Divide the fresh kale evenly among all ten plates and top with the wilted-kale-and-bacon mixture. Sprinkle the Squash Croutons evenly on top of each salad, drizzle with additional dressing, and sprinkle with grated Parmesan cheese. Serve immediately.

Carrot Ginger Harissa Cream

MAKES 1 SCANT CUP (225 ML)

During the Year of the Carrot at Meadow's Mirth Farm, after Farmer Josh had sheepishly approached me citing improbably massive numbers he had estimated for his fall Chantenay carrot crop, I agreed to put his preternaturally succulent heirloom carrots in as many dishes as I could get away with. Carrot Ginger Harissa Cream made a strong comeback that fall, but it was hardly the first time it had graced a Black Trumpet menu.

This popular sauce first appeared on a lamb dish alongside a sirloin steak and shredded braised shank. The creamy and slightly spicy accompaniment went on to seduce many compatible partners on future menus, seemingly without any restraint or discretion, to the point that it developed a reputation for promiscuity. Like all "easy" targets, this sauce soon ingratiated itself to our entire staff, in turn losing our respect. We had to show discipline and distance ourselves from the alluring harlot that had captured our shallow hearts and stomachs, at least for a while. Happily, that window of discipline is behind us, and it is surely time to pay a visit to our flirtatious old friend.

4 Chantenay carrots, peeled, medium dice
½ Spanish onion, medium dice
1 tablespoon clarified butter
1 teaspoon salt
2 tablespoons peeled and grated gingerroot
1 teaspoon minced garlic
¼ cup (60 ml) harissa (page 16)
1 cup (235 ml) heavy cream
1 tablespoon honey

Combine the carrots, onion, clarified butter, and salt in a medium stockpot over medium heat. Cook 4 minutes, stirring occasionally. Add the ginger and garlic and cook 3 minutes. Add the harissa and cream and simmer about 10 minutes. Add the honey, stir, and simmer 1 minute. Remove the pot from the heat, let the sauce cool to room temperature, and add it to the carafe of a blender. Puree until smooth.

Cider-Glazed Carrots

SERVES 6

When our farmers have needed our help moving their carrot surplus, this is another way that Black Trumpet has obliged. Home cooks—especially CSA subscribers—can use this tried-and-true carrot concoction when duty calls. Or just when they want to whip up some carroty goodness. You can find these carrots perched alongside Seared Duck Breast in the photo on page 114.

18 small carrots, scrubbed (unpeeled) and halved lengthwise
4 cups (945 ml) water
1 cup (235 ml) boiled cider (page 17)
6 cardamom pods
1 teaspoon salt
Pinch black pepper
2 tablespoons butter

Preheat the oven to 400°F (200°C). Place the first six ingredients in a large high-sided, oven-safe pan over medium heat. Bring to a boil, reduce to a simmer, cover, and place in the oven. Cook 10 minutes, or until the carrots are fork-tender but still firm. Remove the carrots from the pan, strain and reserve the cooking liquid, and either move on to the next step or let the carrots cool to room temperature and refrigerate until you're ready to use them.

When you're ready to serve, place the carrots and ½ cup (120 ml) of the strained liquid in a large pan over medium-high heat. Bring to a boil and cook 1 minute. Add the butter and a pinch of salt, toss to combine, and remove from heat. Once the butter has melted, serve right away.

These carrots are wonderful as the focal point of a meal, or they can accompany any steak or roast.

Cauliflower and Chickpea Fritter
with Curried Spinach Puree

SERVES 6

A gluten-free cross between falafel and pakora, this fritter wants to be part of a meze served before the rest of dinner, or you can serve it like we did as an appetizer with Curried Spinach Puree and an array of spicy pickled vegetables.

For the fritter

2 cups (450 g) fresh chickpeas
  (if available; if not, increase the
  volume of dried)
1 cup (225 g) dried chickpeas, soaked
  in 4 cups (945 ml) of water overnight
1 small head (about 450 g) cauliflower,
  cut into small florets
1 tablespoon olive oil
1½ teaspoons salt, divided
Pinch black pepper
3 cups (255 g) chickpea flour, sifted
1 teaspoon baking powder
3 tablespoons cumin seed, toasted
  and ground
¼ teaspoon cayenne
6 eggs (300 g liquid eggs)
¾ cup (180 ml) water
Canola oil for frying

For the Curried Spinach Puree

1 tablespoon olive oil
½ Spanish onion, rough-chopped
1 small Yukon Gold potato, ½-inch
  (1 cm) dice
1 small celeriac, peeled, ½-inch
  (1 cm) dice
1 teaspoon rough-chopped garlic
2 teaspoons curry powder,
  as fresh as possible
1 tablespoon honey
1¼ teaspoons salt
¼ teaspoon ground pepper
½ cup (120 ml) vegetable stock
8 ounces (225 g) spinach
  (about 3 bunches)

MAKE THE FRITTER: Combine the fresh chickpeas (if available) and the reconstituted chickpeas with two times their volume of water in a medium pot over high heat. Bring to a boil, reduce to a simmer, and cook until soft but not falling apart, about 25 minutes.

Meanwhile toss the florets with the olive oil, ½ teaspoon of salt, and black pepper, and roast on a baking sheet for about 7 minutes, until beginning to soften and turn pale golden brown. Remove and let cool.

In a medium bowl, whisk together the sifted chickpea flour, baking powder, cumin, cayenne, and 1 teaspoon salt. In a separate bowl, whisk the eggs with the water. Pour the wet ingredients into the dry and stir to combine.

Heat 2 inches (5 cm) of oil in a small, high-sided pot until it reaches 350°F (175°C).

Fold the roasted cauliflower and the chickpeas into the batter with a spatula to combine. In batches, carefully drop tablespoonfuls of the batter into the oil, making sure you don't crowd the pot. Fry for about 4 minutes until golden brown, puffed, and cooked through. Remove to a paper-towel-lined plate and sprinkle with salt. Repeat with the remaining batter. Serve immediately with Curried Spinach Puree.

MAKE THE CURRIED SPINACH PUREE: Add the olive oil to a medium pot over medium-low heat. Add the onion, potato, and celeriac; sweat for about 5 minutes, stirring occasionally, until the potato is just barely tender. The potato pieces tend to stick to the bottom of the pan, so it's important to stir so they don't burn. You don't want any color on the vegetables in this dish. Add the garlic, stir, and sweat 1 minute more. Add the curry powder, honey, salt, pepper, and vegetable stock. Stir to combine. Bring to a boil over medium-high heat, then reduce to a simmer over low heat. Add the spinach and simmer, covered, for 4 minutes. Remove from the heat and let the mixture cool slightly. Puree in a blender until smooth.

Inside-Out Brandade Arancini
with Green Tomato Tartar Sauce

MAKES 20 TO 24 ARANCINI

Brandade and bacalao, variations on salt cod, have appeared on several Black Trumpet menus. When we can keep up with production, we salt our own large cod fillets, but in today's world of diminished wild stocks, such fish are rare. We tried hake and pollock as alternatives to promote other, more sustainable species in our waters, but they just didn't taste the same as salted cod.

Sam Hayward of Fore Street in Portland introduced me to Richard Penfold of Stonington Seafood—a true master of the craft of curing hook-caught large cod—after I tasted Richard's salt cod in a Fore Street brandade cake recipe Sam reproduced on Appledore Island. There was no comparing the delicacy of Richard's salt cod to any other. His attention to detail created something I never knew was possible, and soon all other salt cods faded from my memory.

This recipe turns a popular Italian dish, arancini (so named because the fried rice balls resemble oranges) inside out. Typically, the rice shell of an arancina protects a surprise core, whether it is cheese, meat, or another treat. But in this role reversal, a risotto core lies inside the outer crust of salt cod.

For the Brandade

1 pound (455 g) salt cod
2 cups (475 ml) water, plus more
　for soaking cod
2 cups (475 ml) milk
1 cup (235 ml) heavy cream
6 cloves garlic
4 medium red potatoes, peeled
　and quartered
1 whole egg (50 g liquid egg)
　plus 1 egg yolk (18 g)
1½ teaspoons finely chopped
　fresh rosemary
1½ teaspoons finely chopped
　fresh parsley
Pinch black pepper
Salt to taste
3 cups (335 g) Italian bread crumbs
2 cups (475 ml) vegetable oil,
　for frying

MAKE THE BRANDADE: Soak the salt cod in 2 quarts (1.9 L) cold water overnight, in the refrigerator. Soak again in two more changes of water the following day, each soak lasting at least an hour.

In a 6-quart (6 L) pot over medium heat, combine the salt cod with 2 cups (475 ml) water, milk, cream, garlic, and potatoes. Bring to a high simmer (just before boiling so the pot doesn't overflow) and reduce the heat to low. Simmer 45 minutes, or until the cod is flaky and the potatoes soft. Drain, reserving the liquid, and add the brandade mixture to the bowl of a food processor along with the herbs, salt, and pepper. Blend until smooth, adding up to ¼ cup (60 ml) of the reserved liquid back to the mixture if needed. Brandade can be served cold, like this, or pan-fried with bread crumbs, but for this recipe there are a couple of other steps. First, beat one whole egg and one yolk into the brandade in a standing mixer fitted with the paddle attachment on medium speed. Refrigerate. Next, the risotto:

MAKE THE RISOTTO: Sweat the onion in the clarified butter in a large heavy-bottomed, high-sided pan over medium heat for about 5 minutes. Add the garlic and stir, 30 seconds. Add the arborio rice and toast, stirring often, 3 to 4 minutes. Add the saffron and salt and stir to combine.

For the risotto

1 medium Spanish onion, small dice

2 tablespoons clarified
  (or melted) butter

1 tablespoon minced garlic

4 cups (800 g) arborio rice

¼ teaspoon saffron threads

1 teaspoon salt

1¾ quarts (1.7 L) water, heated to
  just below a boil

¼ cup (25 g) grated Parmesan
  cheese (use the small holes of
  a box grater)

2 tablespoons butter

For the Green Tomato Tartar Sauce

1 tablespoon salt-cured capers

2 medium green tomatoes,
  finely chopped

1 shallot, minced

1 tablespoon olive oil

1 teaspoon salt, plus more to taste

2 egg yolks (36 g)

1 teaspoon Dijon mustard

Juice of 1 lemon

1 tablespoon malt vinegar

1 teaspoon sugar

1½ cups (355 ml) sunflower
  or grapeseed oil

1 teaspoon chopped fresh tarragon

1 kosher dill gherkin, finely chopped
  (optional)

Add hot water, ¾ cup (180 ml) at a time, stirring well every 2 minutes or so. When the rice begins to look dry, add ¾ cup (180 ml) water, repeating until the rice is al dente, about 20 minutes' total cooking time. The rice should be slightly soupy at this point, but not stiff or it will become pasty when you add the cheese. Off the heat, gently fold in the cheese and butter with a spatula, fluffing the risotto in the process. At this point, it should ooze into a bowl, like a stiff porridge. Spread it out on a cookie sheet to stop the cooking process, and let it cool to room temperature.

FORM THE ARANCINI: When the risotto is cool, form into tight 1-ounce (28 g) balls and set aside.

You may want to wear gloves for this next part, because it will otherwise be a gooey mess. Set up a sheet tray lined with parchment. Form the arancini by placing ¼ cup (55 g) brandade in the palm of one hand, flattening it out evenly with your fingertips so that it is about ½ inch (1 cm) thick. Place a ball of risotto in the center of the brandade and wrap the brandade around the ball, covering over any open spots with more brandade. Gently form into a sphere and place on the parchment. Repeat until all the risotto balls are coated with brandade.

Preheat the oven to 400°F (200°C).

Place the bread crumbs in a large mixing bowl and—one by one—roll the arancini in them thoroughly. Return to the parchment sheet.

Set up a paper-towel-lined baking sheet for the finished arancini.

Pour 2 cups (475 ml) vegetable oil into a large, heavy-bottomed saucepan over medium-high heat. When the oil reaches 350°F (175°C), use a slotted spoon to carefully lower the arancini into the oil in a single layer. Fry 2 to 3 minutes, rolling occasionally, until the balls are evenly golden brown. Transfer to the baking sheet. Sprinkle lightly with salt. Fry the remaining cakes, pop them all in the hot oven for 2 minutes, and serve immediately, topped with Green Tomato Tartar Sauce.

MAKE THE GREEN TOMATO TARTAR SAUCE: Soak the capers in ½ cup (120 ml) cold water for 30 minutes. Drain, finely chop, and set aside.

In a small frying pan over medium heat, sauté the green tomatoes and shallot in the olive oil with a pinch of salt for about 3 minutes, until the shallots begin to soften. Remove from the heat and let cool in the pan.

Combine the yolks, mustard, lemon juice, malt vinegar, sugar, and 1 teaspoon salt in the bowl of a food processor; spin until the mixture forms a paste. Stop to scrape down the sides and bottom of the bowl and, with the motor running, add the oil in a slow drizzle to form an emulsion. This should take several minutes. When it's done, the aioli should be thick and shiny. Remove it to a medium bowl and add the tomato mixture, capers, chopped tarragon, and gherkin (if using), folding with a spatula to combine. Adjust the salt to taste and serve or refrigerate until you're ready to use it.

Poblano Goat Yogurt

MAKES ABOUT 1 QUART (945 ML)

This sauce originally accompanied our Moorish Meatballs (page 50). When
you're heating the sauce, do so very gently or it will curdle.

4 poblano peppers
1 tablespoon olive oil
½ medium onion, julienned
1 teaspoon minced garlic
1 teaspoon salt
1 cup (235 ml) goat yogurt (if available;
    if not, plain high-fat yogurt is fine)
1 cup (115 g) fresh goat cheese
1 cup (60 g) loosely packed
    cilantro leaves
1 tablespoon cumin seed, toasted
    and ground
½ teaspoon ground coriander

Roast the poblanos on a gas burner over an open flame. Rotate until
all four sides are thoroughly blackened and blistered, a few minutes
per side. Remove to a mixing bowl and cover tightly with plastic
wrap. Let steam for at least 30 minutes, then stem the peppers and
peel off the skins.

Pour the olive oil into a small pan over low heat. Add the onion
and cook 5 minutes, until it begins to soften. Add the garlic and cook
5 to 7 more minutes, stirring occasionally so the garlic comes into contact with the oil.

Add the poblanos, the onion mixture, and the salt to the bowl of
a blender and puree for 1 minute, until slightly chunky. Add the
yogurt, cheese, cilantro, and spices; spin until smooth. Refrigerate
until you're ready to use it.

Celeriac Brown Butter Whip

MAKES ABOUT 1½ PINTS (710 ML)

One spring, I ate a pile of delicious braised pigtails at the outstanding Cook & Brown in Providence, Rhode Island. Chef Nemo came out after I'd devoured them in all their glazed, sticky goodness. I couldn't stop heaping praise on him for that dish.

All chefs are in some form thieves, or—more generously—we might be called impressionable opportunists. When I returned home from my Providence trip (where I had cooked an annual guest chef event at the spectacular restaurant Gracie's), I began calling around to slaughterhouses to see how I might get hold of some pigtails. Much to my surprise, I came across an abattoir not too far from my home that was willing and able to stockpile tails in their freezer from every pig they butchered. The pigs were USDA processed, so it was all aboveboard. Every couple of weeks, I'd show up at the slaughterhouse to collect my frozen tails. This began the long, slow journey to the plate—one that included curing, smoking, braising, and then refiring each tail smothered in barbecue sauce. *Not very Black Trumpet food*, some guests must have thought, while others—envisioning Heidi or an innocent schoolgirl—may have run screeching at the word *pigtail* on our menu. Those who stuck around and tried the tail enjoyed it immensely. I made any excuse I could to sit down in my own restaurant and eat it while it was on the menu.

Due to the complexity of the dish (and the rarity of the central protein), I have not included the elaborate recipe for pigtails in this volume, but I offer you this rich side dish to accompany any delectably smoky barbecued pig product.

½ cup (120 ml) brown butter (page 18)
3½ cups (340 g) celeriac, peeled, diced into ½-inch (1 cm) cubes
1 cup (235 ml) whole milk
½ cup (120 ml) heavy cream, divided
1 teaspoon salt
¼ teaspoon ground fenugreek seed

In a medium pot over medium-high heat, combine the brown butter with the celeriac, the milk, ¼ cup (60 ml) of the cream, the salt, and the ground fenugreek seed. Stir and bring to a gentle boil. The liquids will curdle slightly because of an enzyme in the celery root. Not to worry. Lower the heat to a low simmer, cover, and cook for 45 minutes, or until the celeriac is very soft.

Transfer the mixture to a food processor and puree until it's fluffy. Scrape down the bottom and sides with a spatula and, with the motor running, add the remaining ¼ cup (60 ml) cold cream to thin and smooth out the puree. Serve immediately or refrigerate and warm slowly over a low flame until heated through.

Delicata Squash Terrine

SERVES 8

One of Denise's favorites, this vegetarian "medium dish" is visually stunning and just the right meeting point between elegant and rustic. It is easier to make than it might seem.

3 delicata squash
½ teaspoon salt, plus more for sprinkling
Pepper, for sprinkling
Olive oil, for roasting
2 cups (300 g) bulgur wheat
3 cups (710 ml) water
1 red onion, minced
1 tablespoon minced garlic
2 quarts (240 g) packed chard, beet tops, turnip tops, or spinach
1 red chile pepper, minced
1 red sweet pepper, minced
1 cup (235 ml) goat ricotta (or substitute cow's milk ricotta)
2 ounces (55 g) feta, crumbled
¼ cup (15 g) loosely packed Italian parsley, chopped
1 teaspoon za'atar (a Middle Eastern spice blend)
1 teaspoon sumac (we forage the seedheads of this native plant locally whenever possible, but the Middle Eastern variety can be found online at stockandspice.com).

Preheat the oven to 350°F (175°C).

Cut off the ends of the delicata squash, then cut them in half lengthwise. Remove the seeds. Sprinkle on salt and pepper and place the squash halves on an oiled sheet tray in the hot oven for 20 minutes. Flip over and bake another 5 to 10 minutes, removing each squash when it is perfectly tender. Let cool.

Bring the bulgur to a boil in 3 cups (710 ml) salted water. Turn off the heat, stir, and let sit on the stovetop over a pilot for 15 minutes. If you're cooking without a gas range, put a lid on the saucepan and leave it on the burner as it cools. After absorption, the bulgur should be tender and there should be no water remaining in the pot.

Meanwhile, sauté the onion and garlic with a little salt until soft. Add the greens and continue to cook over a low flame until they're wilted and tender. Turn off the heat and fold in the peppers, cheeses, parsley, and spices. Transfer to a sheet pan to cool.

In an oil-sprayed terrine mold, layer the roasted squash and the filling to the top. Press down firmly, cover the terrine, and bake at 350°F (175°C) in a water bath for 45 minutes. Remove the terrine from the water bath, empty the water, return the terrine without its lid to the pan, and place a press (we use plastic-wrapped bricks) on top. When cooled to room temperature (about 2 hours later), remove the weight and refrigerate the terrine for 24 hours before unmolding and slicing, ensuring that it is completely firm and cohesive. Slices can be reheated in a 350°F (175°C) oven until warm, and served on their own or, as we did, with a thin pool of Preserved Lemon Crème Fraîche (page 81) and a drizzle of tahini cinnamon honey.

Potato Latkes and Squash Rings

SERVES 6 TO 8

2 russet potatoes (about 10 ounces
   (285 g) each)
2½ teaspoons salt, divided, plus more
   for sprinkling
1 medium delicata squash, scrubbed
2 tablespoons olive oil
1 Spanish onion, julienned
3 tablespoons clarified butter/olive oil
   blend (page 13), divided
Pinch black pepper
2 egg yolks (36 g)

Preheat the oven to 425°F (220°C).

Peel the potatoes and place them in a small pot filled with cold water and 2 teaspoons of the salt. Bring to a boil. Parboil 15 to 20 minutes, until the potatoes start to soften but there's still tension when pierced with a fork. Remove from the water and let cool slightly.

Meanwhile, slice the squash into 1-inch (2.5 cm) rings, carefully removing the inner seeds and membranes with a spoon and discarding the stem and bottom ends. Rub the pieces with the olive oil and a sprinkle of salt; roast on a baking sheet for 20 minutes, turning the pieces and rotating the pan halfway through. The pieces should begin to turn golden brown and soften slightly. Remove from the oven and set aside to cool.

Combine the onion, 1 tablespoon of the butter/oil, and a pinch of salt in a small pan over low heat. Cook, stirring occasionally, until the onion turns translucent and softens but doesn't color, 12 to 15 minutes.

When the potatoes are cool enough to handle, grate on the large holes of a box grater into a mixing bowl. Add the onion, ½ teaspoon salt, a pinch of black pepper, and the egg yolks; mix to combine. Divide the potato mixture evenly among the squash rings, stuffing the middles. Place plastic wrap directly on the rings so the potatoes don't oxidize. The recipe can be made up to this point and held overnight.

When you're ready to serve, preheat the oven to 400°F (200°C) and sprinkle the latkes with salt and pepper. Heat a large nonstick pan over high heat and add the remaining 2 tablespoons butter/oil and the latkes in a single layer. Sear until golden brown, about 1 minute, then flip and remove from the heat. Transfer the latkes to a baking sheet and bake for 6 minutes. Serve immediately with applesauce and sour cream.

Apple Brandy Sour Cream

MAKES ABOUT ¾ CUP (180 ML)

This lovely garnish can be served on Scarlet Turnip Vichyssoise (page 194) or with Potato Latkes and Squash Rings (preceding recipe).

⅓ cup (80 ml) apple brandy
1 tablespoon boiled cider (page 17)
⅔ cup (160 ml) sour cream
¼ teaspoon salt

Make sure your range has sufficient ventilation. Carefully pour the brandy into a small pan over medium-high heat. Let it catch fire and burn for 10 seconds. If you're using an electric stovetop, you will have to ignite the brandy when it is hot with a stick lighter. Remove from the heat. Add the boiled cider to the pan and swirl to combine. Add the sour cream and salt, whisking to combine. Refrigerate until you're ready to serve.

Chicken Change

For many years, small independent restaurants like mine with steadfast local sourcing policies had to answer to the outraged cries of patrons who felt that we were gouging them by charging almost $30 for a half chicken. It is true that national chains might offer a half chicken at less than half that price—and that doesn't even take into account 2-for-1 specials, coupons, or happy-hour incentives. We as a society find ourselves at the beginning of a long learning curve that educates consumers about the real cost of real food. Most people at this point have witnessed (whether in person or via electronic media) the conditions to which conventional farming has subjected our poultry. We know it's messed up, yet we still struggle with the idea of paying more for humanely raised meat. Ultimately, this will have to change, of course. If it doesn't, we will be living shorter lives, malnourished and defenseless, cramped in cubicles under overhead fluorescent lighting, popping prescribed antibiotics to combat the living conditions and weakened immune systems we have created for ourselves. In other words, we will live lives that mirror those of our factory-farmed food, and it will serve us right. We are, after all, what we eat.

Why does local chicken cost so much more? Due to state and federal restrictions, one chicken farmer I have worked closely with, Jeremiah Vernon, has had to truck his birds to a processing facility in Vermont, then to a packaging facility in Connecticut, and then back to New Hampshire, where he sells primarily at farmers markets. All that travel time adds quickly to Jeremiah's costs, which he has to turn around to the buyers of his beautiful birds. Here's another First World problem: No New Hampshire resident wants a poultry-processing facility near their property, so—one by one—major efforts to create more processing centers in the state have fallen by the wayside.

Because of the cost of local chicken, we have had to be disciplined and resourceful with how many orders we get out of a single bird. If I am paying $20 for a chicken, I need to find ways to make that bird go at least four ways. Just like schnitzel and porchetta can stretch a pork loin, the following chicken recipes can make expensive meat go a long way.

Bird Brine

Most home cooks know by now that brining poultry makes for a juicier, more flavorful bird, especially when it comes to the "white meat," which can—especially on a whole roasted bird—come out dry and disappointing. I confess that this is a somewhat exotic brine full of Black Trumpet flavors and hard-to-source ingredients. Don't fret if you can't find them all. All that really matters is that the bird spends some time in a sweet-and-salty bath before it gets cooked.

½ cup (120 ml) preserved lemon liquid
  (page 16)
4 cloves garlic, smashed
½ stick cinnamon
2 cups (475 ml) water
¼ cup (60 ml) honey
1 cup (60 g) chopped fennel fronds
  and stems
1 tablespoon za'atar
2 tablespoons hand-crushed
  avocado leaves
1 bay leaf
1 tablespoon salt
2 boneless breasts from 1 whole local
  chicken (about 8 ounces [225 g]
  each), skin on, tenders removed and
  reserved for chicken leg stuffing
2 bone-in legs from 1 whole chicken
  (about 12 ounces [340 g] each)

Bring all the ingredients (except the chicken breasts and legs) to a boil, stirring to dissolve the spices. Meanwhile, prepare an ice bath. Remove the liquid from the heat and shock it in an ice bath to cool. Strain the liquid into a container for marinating and add the chicken breasts and legs. Refrigerate 3 hours, occasionally checking to make sure the parts are completely immersed in the brine.

Chicken Paillard

SERVES 4

One of our regulars really enjoyed this main course, perhaps because it reminded him a little of his southern upbringing. We served it with Black Olive Salpicon (page 298), and our own Chorizo Meatballs (page 53).

2 boneless breasts (about 8 ounces [225 g] each) from 1 whole chicken, brined (preceding recipe)

¾ cup (90 g) flour

1½ teaspoons Black Trumpet herb mix (page 22)

¼ teaspoon salt

⅛ teaspoon pepper

2 eggs (100 g liquid egg), beaten with 2 teaspoons water

1½ cups (75 g) panko

¾ cup (180 ml) canola or sunflower oil

Preheat the oven to 400°F (200°C).

Remove the breasts from the brine, pat dry, and pound out to ¼ inch (0.5 cm) thick using a meat mallet. Cut each pounded breast in half so you end up with four equal portions.

Place the flour, herbs, salt, and pepper in one bowl, the eggs in a second bowl, and the panko in a third. Using standard breading procedure, coat the first piece thoroughly in flour, tapping to get rid of the excess. Dip to coat in the egg and cover with panko on both sides, patting lightly to adhere. Repeat this with the remaining pieces.

Pour the canola or sunflower oil into a large skillet over medium heat. When the oil is hot (about 3 minutes), add the paillards and pan-fry for 2 minutes, until golden brown and crisp (you may have to do this in two batches). Flip carefully and cook 2 minutes more. Remove to a baking sheet and bake for 6 minutes. Rest for several minutes before slicing and serving.

Stuffed Chicken Leg

SERVES 2

Free-range birds have pretty big legs, and when stuffed as in this recipe, one leg can make a perfectly sufficient meal. The *farce* that fills the leg also tastes great as a stuffing for artichokes in early spring. (Note: If you want to make the legs gluten-free, you can substitute rice for the freekeh.)

2 bone-in brined chicken legs
  (see Bird Brine recipe, page 295)
1½ cups (225 g) freekeh (green wheat,
  described in Spinach Freekeh,
  page 39)
1 tablespoon clarified butter
3 cups (710 ml) poultry, vegetable,
  or rabbit stock
⅓ cup (75 g) medium-diced onion
  (about ½ small onion)
⅓ cup (75 g) medium-diced celery,
  (about 1 stalk)
⅓ cup (75 g) medium-diced carrot
  (about 1 medium)
1 cup (225 g) chicken tenders
  (about 6), reserved from the
  whole-chicken butchery procedure
½ cup (40 g) raw maitake mushrooms
½ teaspoon fennel seed
1 teaspoon minced garlic
½ teaspoon salt
Pinch black pepper
Pinch cayenne pepper
Pinch smoked paprika (sweet, not hot)
Clarified butter/olive oil blend,
  for roasting (page 13)

Preheat the oven to 400°F (200°C).

Working from the side closest to the body of the bird, debone and butterfly the thighs and lay them flat. Leave the bone in on the drumstick portion of the legs. Refrigerate the deboned legs until ready to stuff them.

Toast the freekeh in the clarified butter over medium heat in a 2-quart (2 L) stockpot. Add the stock and bring to a boil. Meanwhile, mince the onion, celery, and carrot in a food processor. Add to the stock when it comes to a boil. Reduce the heat to a simmer, cover, and cook 18 to 20 minutes, until the grains are toothsome. Let cool to room temperature.

In a meat grinder, combine the tenders, mushrooms, fennel seed, and garlic. Place the ground mixture in a medium-sized mixing bowl. Add the salt, pepper, cayenne, paprika, and ⅓ cup (80 ml) of the cooked and cooled freekeh, mixing well with your hands.

Remove the chicken legs from the refrigerator, pat dry, and pound the thighs lightly with a mallet to make sure the thigh meat is an even thickness. Add ⅓ to ½ cup (80 to 120 ml) stuffing to the center of the pounded thigh meat (depending on the size of the leg). Starting from the outer flap of meat, wrap it up around the stuffing, molding it back into the shape of a leg and wrapping as much skin around it as possible. Starting at the drum end, tie with chicken twine, making ties about 1 to 1½ inches (2.5 to 4 cm) apart up the length of the leg (three or four ties total).

Rub the legs with butter/olive oil blend, salt, and pepper, place them on a baking sheet or small roasting pan, and slide into the oven.

Bake for 25 minutes, until golden brown and cooked through.

Black Olive Salpicon

MAKES 2½ CUPS (590 ML)

One summer our menu featured the Chicken Paillard recipe on page 296—a twist on fried chicken that people really enjoyed—with this salpicon. A Mediterranean hybrid of tapenade and guacamole may seem odd at first, but the way the sharp and briny olives interact with the creamy avocado works really well as a foil for the fried chicken.

You can prepare this salsa a few hours in advance, but it will turn gray overnight as the black olive juice leaches into the avocados, so it's best to serve right away.

2 chipotles (canned in adobo work well in this recipe), chopped

1 cup (140 g) pitted black oil-cured olives, chopped

1 medium red bell pepper, small dice (about 1 cup [225 g])

1 small red onion, small dice (about 1 cup [225 g])

2 ripe avocados, medium dice

1 orange, segmented

Combine all the ingredients in a medium bowl. Toss lightly to combine. Serve immediately.

The Mole Chronicles:
A Fight, A Woman's Honor,
and a Backpack Bomb

When I worked in Mexico, my kitchen staff was almost entirely women. One of my cooks was a woman who had culinary training, strong opinions, and a mouth to go with them. She was called Bochis. Her teenage niece, Pecas (whose name translates to "freckles" in English), also cooked with us. The two of them flirted with me like coquettish high school girls, but they also cooked with an urgency I have rarely encountered in American cooks. I have been known to say that, in my perfect world, I would staff my kitchen with only Mexican women. Further commentary on this matter might induce mutiny among my male cooks, so I will stop right there for now.

One of the great gifts these Mexican women gave to me was a recipe for mole (pronounced *MOE-lay*), the enigmatic family of Mexican sauces that can be traced primarily to the regions of Oaxaca and Puebla. Moles have their roots in the oldest civilizations of Mesoamerica, and they contain ingredients that American cooks might not consider putting in the same meal, never mind the same sauce. I can't say that I love all moles, but I can say that I have the utmost respect for their tradition and their idiosyncrasy.

Before our move to Mexico in 2001, I had been inspired to create an Easter menu for Ciento, the restaurant in which I was then cheffing. In what proved to be an unpopular decision, I put together a special I called Chocolate Bunny that substituted delicious rabbit for chicken in the traditional Oaxacan *pollo con mole* dish. You cannot imagine how good braised rabbit tastes with the right mole sauce. Two people ordered that dish on a busy night, and several commented that they found it offensive. Sense of humor on menus is a slippery slope. That time proved to be a loser, although I stand by my inspiration, because flavor overrides aesthetic, concept, and even opinion, in my book.

Bochis is a marvelous and spirited cook who took a shine to me when I assumed the reins of her kitchen. In the pecking order of the twelve or so female cooks, she was the alpha hen for sure. After I earned her respect,

she taught me a few things every chef should know. One of those things was that great dishes must not fall prey to substitution or shortcut. The other was *Sopa del día de hoy, salsa del día mañana*, a mantra for waste prevention that translates, "Today's soup is tomorrow's sauce." Using the reflexive axiom, I would argue that the opposite is also true, and this mole makes a fine flavor enhancement and thickener for rich winter soups and stews.

In this book, I suggest shortcuts and substitutions where I deem them appropriate, or even necessary, but the words of Bochis echo in my mind every time: Why would you want to change what took hundreds of years to perfect?

This recipe is so coveted that, when Bochis was making a batch of her famed and sought-after mole, I—her boss—had to take a number to get a 1-gallon (3.8 L) plastic bag, half full of the indescribably rich and delicious sauce, tied off in the quick knot all Mexicans seem to be able to tie blindfolded. There were others who put their names in before me, so I knew she was keen on me when she slipped the murky bag in my backpack at the end of the day, the majority of which she had spent making only that recipe.

Since I was about ten years old, I have kept two things close to me at all times: a bag and a notebook. The bag has changed shape and size over time, migrating from ratty school backpack to stylish shoulder bag. But regardless of its design, I have always needed such a vessel for collecting my notes, scraps, sundries, objets d'art, totems, and ephemera. In other words, junk. In my fertile imagination, in this junk lie pearls in waiting. Recipes, writings, scribbles, sketches, and scrawls. Doodles, lyrics, poems, lunatic rants. Drunken philosophy. These are the tools of an attention-deficit-afflicted writer and chef. These are the domain of the self-proclaimed quixotic warrior working at a fever pitch to conquer every known windmill in his path. I salute the bag and the notebook, for they are the weapons and the shields I have built in my arsenal, to protect me from the unknown, to give me strength. Yet in the end, they are the same devices that can be used to expose my weakness. I never fully grasped that concept until the day I left work with that unknown gift, a bag of Bochis's mole, tucked into my bag.

So much irony weighs on this tale, I have a hard time recanting it without giggling. But it was a serious moment, leavened by a trifle of ignorance, that made this yarn so vivid.

On that afternoon, as dusk approached, the grackles had descended like locusts on the town square, as they were wont to do, creating the guttural steampunk harangue of squawks and whistles that few avian species can achieve. As always, I marveled at the cacophony and wondered how many people, other than me, were in the square dreading a Hitchcockian guano blizzard.

In the sfumato shadows of the picturesque *jardín*, as I walked below the elevated central square, I glimpsed Pecas (Bochis's niece) being accosted by a young man and his accomplice, right there in broad twilight, separated from my position by an 8-foot (2.4 m) stone wall and 20 or so level feet (6 m) of concrete and paving stones. I struggled to gauge the situation as the man appeared to be pushing her and grabbing her bag while the man next to him laughed and cajoled. I yelled her name. No response. So I sprang heroically into action, hurling my backpack over the tall wall onto the concrete-and-fieldstone terrace above. In short order, I had scaled, perhaps awkwardly (although I remember it

differently), the tall wall and now found myself hurdling my bag to get to the scene of the perceived crime. And there in the dying light was Pecas, innocent, adorable Pecas, laughing—not crying or screaming—at her attackers as though she knew them. Which, I quickly learned, she did. As I prepared to engage in my first-ever firefight in defense of a woman's honor, Pecas informed me that the two would-be assailants were in fact her brother and his friend, and that they were merely teasing her, as any brother is encoded to do. She introduced me to the two gentlemen, and I shook their hands and mumbled a winded "*Mucho gusto.*"

When I returned to my bag, lying there on its side where it had landed, I found it wet and warm, with a brown stain expanding on the outside. I opened the bag, squinting with trepidation. The mess inside was a sort of paper dysentery that left no hope of ever being undone. Bochis's bag of mole had exploded on impact, taking no prisoners. Every note and doodle, every business card and notebook page, had been instantly stained for life, cohering in a glop that smelled so good I could have sat there in the dark and sucked on every piece of paper, calling it a fine picnic in the park.

The next day, I explained to Bochis that I had lost everything in my bag while trying to save her niece from an innocent brother, and after an initial five minutes or so of laughter, she not only gifted me another bag of sacred mole, but she gave me something far greater. The recipe!

Bochis's Mole

MAKES JUST OVER 2 QUARTS (2 L)

Like most moles, this one has a bajillion ingredients. I suggest following the advice of Bochis and avoid omissions and substitutions if at all possible. This means spending some time sourcing the right products. *¡Buena suerte!*

8 fresh bay leaves (or 1 teaspoon ground bay leaf)
2 tablespoons peanut oil
8 Oaxacan pasilla chiles
8 ancho chiles
8 cascabel chiles
1½ Spanish onions, julienned
2 red Fresno or red jalapeño peppers, stemmed and coarsely chopped
1½ tablespoons minced garlic
3 ounces (85 g) unsalted peanuts
½ Granny Smith apple, rough-chopped
1 large tomato, coarsely chopped
6 tomatillos, husks removed and fruit halved (about 10 ounces [285 g])
1 quart (945 ml) chicken stock
2 cups (475 ml) vegetable stock
1½ teaspoons fresh marjoram
8 sprigs thyme
1 stick Mexican, or Ceylon, cinnamon
2 ounces Abuelita Mexican chocolate, round disks quartered
2 tablespoons sugar
½ banana
2 ounces (55 g) stale baguette
1 stale corn tortilla
1 tablespoon plus 2 teaspoons salt

Preheat the oven to 300°F (150°C).

Place the bay leaves on a cookie sheet and dry them in the oven for 10 minutes.

Remove, let cool, and grind to a powder in a spice grinder.

In a 5- to 6-quart (5 to 6 L) nonreactive pot over medium heat, cook the oil and the chiles, stirring frequently, until the chiles smell like they are beginning to toast. Reduce the heat to low and add the onions and fresh red peppers, stirring to combine. Cook for 2 minutes and add the garlic, cooking about 1 minute more. Add the peanuts, apple, tomato, and tomatillos, and simmer 15 minutes, until the fruits and vegetables begin to break down and release their juices. Increase the heat to medium-high and add the stocks. Bring the liquids to a boil, then reduce to a simmer and add the herbs, spices (including the ground bay leaves), chocolate, sugar, and banana. Stir to combine, cover, and simmer over low heat for 15 minutes. Add the baguette and tortilla and simmer 5 minutes.

Remove the pot from the heat and remove the cinnamon stick. Transfer the mole to a blender and blend in batches. Add salt to taste and additional stock if it seems too thick. Cool the mole to room temperature and refrigerate. The flavors improve with time and the sauce can be held in the refrigerator for up to a week. Reheat slowly over a low flame when you're ready to serve.

Braised Pork Shank with Mashed Turnips and Long Beans

SERVES 8

A hearty autumn dish that makes good use of seasonal ingredients, this main course is always a hit among carnivores. We have grown a number of heirloom varieties of long bean over the years. I have a fondness for the Liana and Red-Seeded Asparagus bean varieties, but any long bean works just as well. In fact, good old-fashioned green beans can sub in just fine if long beans prove to be a long shot.

For the braise

8 pork shanks
2 tablespoons salt
1 tablespoon pepper
2 tablespoons olive oil (or lard, if you have it)
1 small onion, medium dice
2 carrots, peeled, medium dice
2 stalks celery, medium dice
1 Pasilla de Oaxaca, seeds and stems removed, torn into pieces
2 tablespoons minced garlic
1 cup (235 ml) tomato puree
¼ cup (60 ml) sherry vinegar
4 cups (945 ml) water
2 cups (475 ml) veal or pork stock
½ cup (120 ml) maple syrup
8 dried apricots
1 teaspoon cumin seed
1 stick Ceylon cinnamon

For the Mashed Turnips

1 Gilfeather turnip or rutabaga, peeled, chopped into 1-inch (2.5 cm) pieces
2 pounds (910 g) scarlet turnips, washed, not peeled
3 cups (710 ml) vegetable stock
5 tablespoons (140 g) unsalted butter
¼ cup (60 ml) heavy cream
½ teaspoon ground fenugreek seed
1 teaspoon salt

BRAISE THE PORK: Preheat the oven to 325°F (165°C).

Coat the shanks evenly with the salt and pepper. Heat a large oven-safe, high-sided skillet with oil or lard over high heat until it begins to smoke. Add the shanks, searing until golden brown on all four sides, about 10 minutes. Remove the shanks from the pan and add the next five ingredients, stirring to combine. Cook 5 minutes. Add the tomato puree and reduce for 3 minutes. Deglaze with the vinegar, cooking for 1 minute. Add the remaining ingredients and bring to a boil. Transfer the mixture to a deep roasting pan or 6-quart (6 L) Dutch oven, cover, and bake for 3 to 3½ hours, until the meat is pulling away from the bone.

Remove from the oven and let cool. If you're serving right away, transfer the shanks to a separate pan and hold in a low oven. Meanwhile, strain the braising liquid through a china cap, pressing on the solids to express all the juices from the contents of the pan. Give the strained braising liquid 5 minutes to settle, then skim the fat off the top. If you're serving right away, remove the shanks from the low oven and plate them with the turnips and beans, pouring the braising liquid over the top to glaze the meat and pool on the plate. Shanks and sauce can also be refrigerated at this point and held in a refrigerator, then reheated in a 350°F (175°C) oven for 12 minutes and served.

MAKE THE MASHED TURNIPS: Combine all the ingredients in a large, heavy-bottomed pot over high heat. Bring to a boil, then reduce the heat to a simmer. Cover and simmer 25 minutes over a very low flame, until the vegetables are soft. Transfer the mixture to a food processor and puree until smooth. Serve right away, or reheat with the shanks at a later time.

For the Long Beans

24 red or green Chinese long beans,
  stump ends removed
1 tablespoon butter
Salt and pepper to taste

MAKE THE BEANS: Bring a large pot of heavily salted water to a boil over high heat. Prepare an ice bath. Blanch the beans for 1 minute and shock them in the ice bath. When you're ready to serve, reheat them in a small pan with a pat of butter and a sprinkle of salt and pepper to taste.

TO SERVE: Place a healthy dollop of mashed turnip on each plate and, using a spatula and tongs to hold the meat on the bone, carefully place each shank portion on top of the turnip. Encircle the turnips and shanks with three long beans. Pour the braising liquid over the top of everything and serve right away.

Terroirism

There has been a lot of talk about terroir. It started in the wine world, which is rife with French-language terminology for things we don't have words for in English. Even if we do have equivalent words in English, we use the French words to sound more sophisticated. This should probably tell us something, but Anglophiles also borrow language we need to describe terms we don't fully comprehend. *Terroir* means, essentially, "sense of place," and it refers to the effects (flavors) a single environment will bring to bear on what is grown or raised there.

So, for example, a Charolais steer raised on Kimmeridgian-soil-fed grass in the oenocentric region of Bourgogne will have a certain *je ne sais quoi* (to borrow another French phrase we can't exactly translate) that differentiates it from other kinds of beef around the world. Kobe beef, a supreme Japanese tradition, comes from steers that are treated to a select diet that includes booze. Each animal is handled by a personal massage therapist and essentially allowed to live the good life before it goes to slaughter, so that humans can share in good living by ingesting the royally treated animal's meat.

Like all powerful words of language, *terroir* has gone from a little known French wine word to a widely used food descriptor that encompasses any attempt to explain the connection between environment and flavor. In fact, a few years ago the Slow Food movement coined the term *merroir*, which is a sort of contraction of the French words for "sea" and "sense of place." This term was apparently created to underscore the importance of eating seafood from nearby as opposed to seafood from really far away.

I think my first terroir awakening happened in Sardinia. Denise and I were on an epic honeymoon that began in Rome and descended the west coast of the boot, hopping over to Capri and then the volcanic Aeolian Islands, then Sicily, and—finally—Sardinia. A close friend's mother lived outside Sardinia's capital, Cagliari, and had issued us an open invitation to visit while we were in Italy. We accepted, perhaps to the surprise of the woman who made the generous offer, and set up camp there for ten days while we explored the island. On an ill-fated day trip in a modest *deux chevaux* rental, we ascended the mountain goat paths near Oristano until our vehicle became lodged on a narrow path that towered (without guardrails, of course) over a rocky gorge. Goat country. We got out of the car to ponder our next move, and as we walked, our footfalls summoned a heady waft of wild herbs. We survived that day trip, ate grilled horse and donkey that evening, and returned to Cagliari in a very banged-up car. The next day, we bought a cheese made in the region where we had been lost, and the same aromatics that had wafted from our footfalls the day before were present in the cheese. It was an uncanny example of how terroir might insinuate itself into the food we eat.

About Sardinia, I will say this: It is a gigantic island of many mysteries, undiscovered by Americans for the most part. The most beautiful beach I have ever had the pleasure of visiting, aside from my perennial New England favorites, is in Pula, which lies on the rectangular island's southwest corner. The beach we visited at Pula showcased all the sensuous summertime S's: sand, sun, sea, and the often overlooked S, a seductive, sexy supermodel who was being photographed topless for a photo shoot right next to where we had laid down our towel. Denise thinks the last of the S's has swayed my opinion of the beach at Pula, but I assure her—and you, the reader—that this was not the case at all.

Marinated Grassfed Steak with Black Trumpet Mushroom Cream Sauce

SERVES 6

We usually, although not always, have a steak dish on our menu. Our first few Black Trumpet menus featured hanger steak, a particularly delicious cut that only yields a few pounds per ½ ton of meat on a single animal. Not the poster cut of sustainable meat, to say the least. Over time, as we began to shrink the greater pasture from which we sourced our meat, we had to move away from putting single cuts of meat on the menu. In order to work closely with local cattle farmers, we had to commit to one animal at a time and work our way through it, braising, grinding, and searing as the muscle type called for.

In late summer and early fall, this simple steak lover's dish can be whipped up in no time. Be sure to support your local grassfed beef program when shopping for steak cuts.

2 pounds (910 g) grassfed beef, cut into even 1-inch (2.5 cm) thick steaks weighing a little over 5 ounces (140 g) each
2 tablespoons minced garlic
1 teaspoon chopped fresh rosemary
1 teaspoon chili powder
1 tablespoon mustard
½ cup (120 ml) olive oil
1 teaspoon salt, divided
1 teaspoon black pepper, divided
2 tablespoons clarified butter/olive oil blend (page 13)
1 shallot, julienned
6 ounces (170 g) fresh black trumpet mushrooms, picked through carefully to remove forest floor fodder
1 ounce (30 ml) sherry
½ cup (120 ml) veal demi-glace (page 16)
½ cup (120 ml) heavy cream

Marinate the steaks in the next five ingredients for 4 or 5 hours. Remove them from the marinade, pat them dry, and preheat the oven to 450°F (230°C).

Season the steaks on both sides with half of the salt and pepper. In a skillet on the stove, heat the butter/oil blend over a high flame and, when the pan is smoking, add the steaks and sear well, 2 minutes on each side. Remove the steaks to a baking sheet and put in the oven for 2 minutes (for medium rare). Meanwhile, add shallot and mushrooms to the steak searing pan, sautéing over a medium flame for 2 minutes. Add the remaining salt and pepper, and deglaze the pan with the sherry. Add the demi-glace and bring to a boil. Stir in the cream and reduce in the pan for 3 minutes while the steaks are resting at room temperature. Serve with old-fashioned mashed potatoes slathered with the sauce for a comforting crowd pleaser.

Baked Apples Stuffed with Cheddar and Calvados-Soaked Sultanas

SERVES 8

One fall, someone introduced me to McDougal Orchards, which is only a few miles from my house but had somehow eluded my attention for years. The endless sprawl of apple trees on the McDougal property impressed me immediately upon first inspection, but a deeper exploration yielded something akin to heirloom Narnia. In one relatively tiny corner of the extensive orchard, I came across a few rows dedicated to heirloom strains of apple. I ate through them with a querulous anxiety, amazed at the variety of flavors, shapes, textures, and colors those few rows possessed. It was there and then that I became enamored of the Blue Pearmain, a gigantic heritage apple with tremendous density and great flavor.

Whether you're following this recipe or any other that calls for whole baked apples, I highly recommend Blue Pearmains over other varieties that can lose flavor or turn to moosh.

½ cup (75 g) sultanas (golden raisins)

½ cup (120 ml) calvados (apple brandy from Normandy is ideal), or other apple brandy

8 Blue Pearmain apples, peeled and center-cored with an apple corer (apple left whole)

½–1 cup (115–225 g) brown sugar (depending on size of apples)

1 tablespoon plus 1 teaspoon cold unsalted butter, diced into 8 pieces

4 ounces (115 g) cheddar cheese, diced into 16 cubes

1 cup (235 ml) apple cider

Preheat the oven to 350°F (175°C).

Place the raisins and calvados in a small pan over medium-low heat. When the calvados is warm to the touch, remove from the heat and let sit 1 hour. Strain the liquid from the raisins and set aside.

Meanwhile, rub each apple with 1 to 2 tablespoons of brown sugar, depending on size. Place each in an oven-safe ramekin or cast-iron crock with one cube of cold butter and 2 tablespoons water per ramekin. Place the ramekins on a baking sheet and slide into the oven. Bake 15 minutes, rotate the pan, and flip each apple (carefully, they're hot!). Bake for another 5 minutes, checking periodically to make sure they are not getting too soft.

Remove from the oven and flip again so the top side is up. Let the apples cool to room temperature. Stuff each apple with two cubes of cheddar cheese and 2 tablespoons soaked raisins.

At this point, the stuffed apples can be refrigerated until you're ready to serve.

When you're ready to reheat the stuffed apples, heat up the cider and place the apples, right side up, on a baking sheet. Spoon 1 tablespoon of hot cider into the center of each apple and bake at 400°F (200°C) for about 4 minutes. When the cheese is fully melted, remove from the oven and serve right away, preferably with leaves of phyllo sprinkled with cinnamon sugar.

Brown Butter Chocolate Bites with Chile Marshmallow

MAKES 48 SMALL BITES

I don't attend a lot of potluck events, not because I don't support them 100 percent, but because I tend not to have time to cook something in my home kitchen and then attend an event the same day. If the stars line up and I can pull it off, maybe in retirement, I will someday bring these infectious treats to a potluck. They are the perfect two-bite morsels of party food, somewhere between a s'more and a s'gone.

For the cookie layer

1 cup (120 g) flour

½ teaspoon salt

¼ teaspoon baking powder

¼ teaspoon baking soda

¼ cup plus 2 tablespoons (85 g) brown butter (page 18), in solid form but softened

¼ cup (55 g) brown sugar

¼ cup (55 g) sugar

1 egg (50 g liquid egg)

½ teaspoon vanilla extract

For the chocolate layer

12 ounces (340 g) chocolate (I prefer the producers El Rey and Tcho, but they are pricey and hard to find)

2 tablespoons brown butter (page 18)

2 tablespoons corn syrup

½ teaspoon salt

½ cup (120 ml) whole milk

4 egg yolks (72 g)

1 cup (235 ml) heavy cream, whipped to soft peaks

For the chile marshmallow

4 egg whites (120 g)

1 cup (225 g) sugar

1 teaspoon cream of tartar

2 teaspoons ancho chile powder (or other medium-hot chili powder)

¼ cup (28 g) powdered sugar

MAKE THE COOKIE LAYER: Preheat the oven to 350°F (175°C).

In a small bowl, combine the flour, salt, baking powder, and baking soda.

Combine the butter and sugars in the bowl of a stand mixer fitted with the paddle attachment. Beat on medium-high speed until light and fluffy, 4 or 5 minutes. Stop to scrape the bottom and sides of the bowl with a spatula and add the egg and vanilla extract, whisking until fully incorporated. Add the dry ingredients and mix just until incorporated.

Spread the batter evenly in the bottom of a sprayed 13 × 9 inch (33 × 23 cm) pan (it should be about ¼ inch [0.5 cm] thick) and bake on the middle rack of the oven for about 30 minutes, or until just golden and set.

Let cool completely before proceeding to the next step.

MAKE THE CHOCOLATE LAYER: Pour 2 inches of water into a 4-quart (4 L) pot and bring up to a high simmer. Combine the chocolate, brown butter, syrup, and salt in a medium bowl and set over the simmering pot of water. Melt the chocolate, stirring occasionally with a rubber spatula to incorporate the ingredients. Set aside.

In another medium bowl, whisk together the milk and egg yolks. Place over the double boiler, stirring often with a rubber spatula until the mixture thickens enough to coat the back of a spoon, 8 to 10 minutes. Be careful not to get the mixture too hot or the eggs will curdle. If this happens, strain the egg mixture.

Slowly drizzle the eggs and milk into the chocolate mixture, folding gently but constantly with a spatula until well incorporated. Gently fold the whipped cream into the mixture until it's fully incorporated. The mixture should be smooth and fluffy.

Spread evenly over the cooled cookie base and chill until set, at least 4 hours and up to a day. When set, trim the edges (if desired) and slice into forty-eight small squares.

MAKE THE CHILE MARSHMALLOW: Hand-whisk the egg whites, sugar, and cream of tartar in the bowl of a stand mixer for about 1 minute. Place the bowl over the existing simmering water bath and hand-whisk continually, until the sugar dissolves and the mixture warms slightly, about 2 minutes. Attach the bowl to the stand mixer and, using the whisk attachment, whip on high speed for 5 minutes, until the mixture is thick and light. Fold in the chile powder. Spread the marshmallow evenly about a half inch thick on a piece of oil-sprayed parchment. Dust the top of the marshmallow with powdered sugar and let cool.

Serve the marshmallow alongside the Brown Butter Chocolate Bites.

CHAPTER EIGHT

LATE FALL
The Final Forage

LATE FALL RECIPES

Late fall represents the gray-scale transition between the glorious tapestry of autumn foliage and the peaceful and pristine white backdrop of fresh snowfall. In this "shoulder" season, with November at its heart, the last foraging runs yield handfuls instead of bagfuls, and the last chances to can and preserve garden harvests go full tilt. Kale abounds, as do roots, and Black Trumpet pasta dishes take a heartier turn, as the recipes in this chapter demonstrate.

Foraging has been a pastime of mine since 1993, when I turned a lifelong penchant for bird-watching into an obsessive desire to identify mushrooms. After spotting some magnificent boletes while on a hike, I bought my first field guide and was on my way. About seven years later, after having caused more than one domestic disturbance with foraged samples that began to decompose or even crawl off the kitchen counter, I began eating the mushrooms I foraged. It took that long for me to have confidence in my ability to positively ID the specimens I found. In my house, foraging has been a family activity since my kids were knee-high (which actually gave them an altitude advantage when we went

mushroom hunting). The recipes included here span the course of many years of playing with wild food and charting a course that has offered Black Trumpet patrons a walk on the wild side.

One caveat: Most communities have regulations about whether or not restaurants can legally serve wild foraged foods. It is fair to say that most health departments choose to overlook the responsible foragers, but most communities are only one fatality away from pursuing new laws prohibiting the use of wild foods in professional kitchens. Some European countries, which have all spent a few more centuries thinking about these matters, have resolved to have foragers bring their harvests to a central location to be approved by an expert or authority. I would prefer to continue foraging without an intervening agency to answer to, but I worry about the less experienced foragers out there who may not know the difference between, say, a chanterelle (delectable) and a galerina (deadly). So much of our farmed food is unjustly subjected to excessive scrutiny, it does seem strange that wild harvests of potentially lethal fungi make it to our plates without any verification.

The Matsutake Mother Lode

One of my favorite foraging anecdotes is the one where a local guy—down on his luck—stumbles on a gold mine of matsutake mushrooms at the same time a horrible nuclear accident in Japan has rendered that entire nation's population of sacred matsutake mushrooms inedible.

I should preface this by saying that this is a very true story, and the protagonist is a mushroom forager and grower with whom I continue to work closely. His name is Dennis Chesley, and his business is called New Hampshire Mushroom Company. Dennis is as charming and witty a forager as you are likely to meet. He says likably off-color things like, "I'm as happy as a warm fart in January," and "I've been busier than a cat trying to bury a turd on a frozen lake in Maine." His PG-13 similes are his trademark, but his mushroom growing and hunting prowess have built his reputation as New England's foremost mushroom purveyor. Today the New Hampshire Mushroom Company grows a wide variety of mushrooms, including lesser-known varieties like chestnut and bear's head, and every so often, if I'm lucky, Dennis might sneak a few wild matsutakes or chanterelles into my delivery.

In March 2011, the Fukushima nuclear accident in Japan led to what many experts believe was the worst environmental disaster in history. I share the belief articulated by Greenpeace in the aftermath that we need no better evidence than Fukushima of how the same technology that humans have created to overcome

the elements has made our race more vulnerable *to the* elements! Hundreds of thousands of human lives were affected by the radiation contamination that ensued when a tsunami breached the nuclear facility on that fateful spring day.

A few months later, across the globe in the foothills of New Hampshire's White Mountains, a royal flush of Japan's most coveted (and pricey) mushroom species was discovered by none other than Dennis Chesley. According to Dennis, he and his young partners were "just starting to get our foot in the door" of Portsmouth restaurants at the time. For a few months, I had been buying from Dennis and his partners boxes of the most beautiful cultivated oyster mushrooms I had ever seen. I had also been reading with horror how the half-life of nuclear waste from the accident had rendered matsutakes on all of Honshu—Japan's main island—highly toxic for a very long time.

When Dennis asked me what he could do with thousands of pounds of matsutakes, I immediately thought of a forager named Ben Maleson I had met a decade earlier when I was a food writer in Boston. Like Dennis (and most foragers for that matter), Ben Maleson was a spirited eccentric with a reputation for sometimes vanishing from the grid. If Dennis's trademark was his cornball humor, Ben Maleson's was surely his pants. Back in the 1990s, long after the MC Hammer harem style had died off, Maleson would show up at the kitchen doors of New England's most reputable restaurants wearing brightly patterned culottes and bearing a basket of fungi. The other thing about Ben was that he was very good at marketing his foraging services. Back then, few chefs bought wild mushrooms, but those who did bought from Ben. He had made inroads into the restaurant industry, and those who knew him marveled at his foraging (and networking) skills.

I had heard something about Ben developing a market in Asia for his mushrooms, so I sent Dennis to talk to him about the matsutake mother lode he had discovered. After a conversation with Ben, in a few days of mad foraging ("busier than a one-armed paper hanger"), Dennis was able to gather up hundreds of pounds of choice matsutakes and ship them to a Japanese market bereft of the sacred species. His profit from the single sale of those mushrooms essentially jump-started his small business, a fact that Dennis Chesley will never let me forget. You might say he was luckier than two rabbits wearing horseshoes who stumble on a patch of four-leaf clovers on the first day of the month.

When asked about the success of his business, Dennis describes the restaurant scene in the New Hampshire Seacoast (his primary client base) as a mycelium. I have also used this term—which describes the subterranean, finely filamented, fabric-like root system of many mushrooms—to describe our community. It is not visible to the naked eye, but the network of local-food-based businesses in the Portsmouth area has created many success stories like that of New Hampshire Mushroom Company, and in the process we have attracted plenty of new business opportunities.

How Black Trumpet Got Its Name

There is something Zen-like about the desultory perambulations of a forager. At first glance, an onlooker might question the sanity of the hunched-over, slow-moving stalker in the woods, but—despite being prone to eccentricity—most foragers are just lovable geeks with a bent for nature. Our purpose may be invisible to the naked eye, yet the first sign of the bounty we seek brings an excitement to the fore that is usually found only in children at holiday time. Upon finding a choice edible, we may dance or, worse, we may let out a caterwaul to celebrate our eureka moment. I have been known to take a knee, genuflecting to Mother Nature in thanks for her gifts. It was exactly this kind of moment of ecstatic discovery that gave Black Trumpet its name.

In the summer of 2006, after having foraged pretty extensively for over a decade, I was comfortable picking a dozen or so species on a regular basis for my personal consumption and, after years of testing and retesting, to cook and serve in my restaurant. Of all the species of edible foods, the black trumpet mushroom (*Craterellus cornucopioides*) had bewitched me unlike any other. Its versatility, its abundance, its long season all contributed to my unrequited love for the species with the seemingly conflicting nicknames "horn of plenty" and "trumpet of death."

One morning in late August 2006, my family and I set out on a hike at a nearby mountain. One of my children—then six years of age—was on foot. The other—only three at the time—was alternating between a backpack I was wearing and a footloose scramble up the rocks. I had packed a yummy lunch in another backpack, which my wife was kind enough to bear. We were just shy of the summit when I stumbled on an out-of-place meadow with some older fruit trees.

Our serendipitous detour to the meadow revealed a long seam in the ground, the flanks of which bore an extraordinarily dense profusion of black trumpets. I fell to my knees and declared religious faith in nature's unexpected bounty. Then, in a poor parenting moment, I began to unpack the backpacks of food and provisions, and promptly started picking mushrooms and stuffing them into the bags. Agile and energetic as a young mountain goat back then, I loped down the mountain with my fateful winnings, secure in the knowledge that I finally had a name for my restaurant. Anticlimactically (and somewhat guiltily), I then reascended the trail to ensure that my children had food and water.

Ethics, Etiquette, and Ecology

I think it is worth noting that wild food foraging has evolved into a growth sector of our country's food system. This bodes well for our health (if the obvious, sometimes fatal risks of uneducated foraging are erased from the picture), because properly handled wild foods often supply us with nutrients and even curatives our bodies need.

Among veteran foragers, there remain a few unspoken laws that may be best summed up by the name of the Massachusetts lake my mother taught me to say when I was a child: Char-gogg-a-gogg-man-chaugg-a-gogg-chau-bun-a-gung-a-maugg. Loosely translated from the Nipmuc, this means, "You fish on your side, I fish on my side, and nobody fishes in the middle."

Foragers stake their claims and, in most cases, recognize and respect the territories of others. Although I have little issue trespassing if I think there lies a bed of ramps or a cluster of chanterelles on the other side of the property line, I will avoid going where I know another forager already goes. This is a common courtesy that may be falling by the wayside in today's world, where rookie foragers run amok, making the shared, peaceable foraging kingdom a thing of the past.

When foragers do discover a patch, if they are wise, they will nurture it much as any gardener might do with planted crops. Obviously, watering and fertilizing are out of the question, but sustaining these wild harvests year after year can happen through responsible stewardship of the land. The rules for this are simple. Don't take everything. Leave as much as you can. Tread lightly and harvest with a porous basket that will disseminate spores or seeds. Proper foraging demands respect for nature!

Legal Fermentation Practices, from the Offices of Garum, Garen, and Katz

The ancients harnessed the natural act of fermentation to preserve food. I have always marveled that that learning process back then was most likely deadly. Salt and other antiseptic agents, when added to the decomposition of food ingredients, can transform those ingredients into something intensely flavorful and, oftentimes, healing. This scientific reality makes our sterilized American food culture very squeamish. But that is changing, thank goodness.

It is easy to understand how alcohol ferments came into popularity, but it seems to me a little more arbitrary how some other ferments (black peppercorns, pickled cucumbers, sauerkraut, and soy sauce) made it into most American households, while Vietnamese fish sauce, Korean black garlic, and Mediterranean black lemon still live on the outer fringes of culinary awareness. Blessedly, today's food-centric culture is pulling those esoteric fermentations in from the periphery, employing things like kombucha, kimchi, and fish sauce

more regularly in home kitchens. American chefs have only recently delved into the alchemic craft of fermentation (much to the chagrin of health departments everywhere), and regulation is still a little nebulous in most places, but I think it's safe to say that fermentation is here to stay.

Garum, the fermented juice of salted and pressed Mediterranean anchovies, may be the oldest intentional food fermentation on Earth. It is believed to date back at least twenty-five hundred years. The Roman naturalist Pliny the Elder himself defined garum as "the guts of fish and the other parts that would otherwise be considered refuse . . . soaked in salt, so that garum is really liquor from the putrefaction of these matters." Mmmmm, putrefaction! Garum was a condiment back then. In my kitchen, it's an additive, like its Asian cousin fish sauce, that can turn most mundane broths, dressings, and sauces into an umami party. Garum can be found online or at specialty food shops.

Not to be confused with garum, my farmer friend Garen, back in the dismal winter of 2009, brought me a recipe for lactofermented beets that I made into a tequila-based cocktail that, at the time, was too weird for restaurant-goers. The liquid from that ferment—at once tangy, bubbly, and creamy—was a hot-pink stomachic that looked and acted not unlike Pepto-Bismol, but its sweet and earthy beet flavor made the perfect midwinter refreshment, with or without the tequila. I resolved to enjoy its merits unto myself.

One year just before first frost, using our garden's spiciest chile peppers and a score of unripe tomatoes, I made a hybrid of piccalilli (an old New England green tomato pickle) and Serbian tursija (a recipe I gleaned from Sandor Katz, whom I met shortly after the publication of his great book, *The Art of Fermentation*). For

reasons I cannot explain, and much to the horror of my friends and family, over the course of the next two winters I took a 1-ounce (30 ml) shot of the incendiary liquid from this ferment whenever I felt a cold coming on. Not once during that two-year period did a single cold or flu symptom last more than a few hours in my body. I have Mr. Katz, with whom I have spoken at more than one Chefs Collaborative Summit, to thank for my conversion into the misunderstood netherworld of fermentation.

Apple Kimchi

MAKES ABOUT 4 GLASS 1-QUART (1 L) JARS

Denise gave me a 5-gallon ceramic "rot pot" for my birthday one year. I made my favorite crock pickle recipe from our garden's bounty of heirloom cukes. Then came more complex ferments. Soon, I came to realize that fermentation is not as scary as it seems. I went through a two-year phase of fermentations for home before I came up with one I liked enough to try at the restaurant. Our staff went nuts for Apple Kimchi. It was like cuckoo for Cocoa Puffs, but with a really healthy result.

1 head napa cabbage, outermost leaves removed, quartered lengthwise, core removed, and chopped crosswise in ¼-inch (0.5 cm) ribbons

1 head red cabbage, outermost leaves removed, quartered lengthwise, core removed, and chopped crosswise in ¼-inch (0.5 cm) ribbons

1 large Spanish onion, julienned

1 large carrot, grated

8 ounces assorted fresh chiles, rough-chopped, with seeds intact

1 head garlic, cloves peeled and thinly sliced

1 thumb gingerroot, peeled and sliced (1½ tablespoons)

12 cups (2.8 L) water

1 cup (235 ml) cider vinegar

6 apples, preferably a dense heirloom variety like Blue or Gray Pearmain

1¼ cups (185 g) salt

⅓ cup (80 ml) maple syrup

1 stalk Mexican mint marigold (can substitute tarragon or fennel frond)

Mix the first seven ingredients in a large bowl, then pack in a 5-gallon (20 L) ceramic fermenting jug. On the stove, bring the six remaining ingredients to a boil, stir to ensure that the salt is fully dissolved, let cool, and pour into the fermenter, placing a plate or weight on top to fully submerge the veggies. Don't worry if, at first, the vegetables are not fully submerged. They will be after a few hours of being pressed. In 3 days, the fermentation process will be under way. Remove the weight and inspect the top for any signs of mold. If there is mold forming, remove the surface vegetables that are hosting the mold and then—with clean tongs—stir the contents of the pot, replacing the weight and letting the ferment sit for another 3 days. Repeat the inspection process and let sit for 4 more days. After this 10-day period, the ferment should be sour, lightly effervescent, and full of intense flavor.

At this point, you can choose to let it go longer for more intense flavor or pack the kimchi into sterilized quart jars, filling up each jar to the very top with the fermenting liquid, then tightly lidding the jars before refrigerating. I have kept ferments of this nature in my refrigerator for over a year, but you may want to err on the side of caution and consume it over a shorter time frame.

Potato Bread

MAKES 1 LOAF

Everyone likes this bread, and no Wonder! It is the healthy, craft version of Wonder bread. Filling yet neutral enough in flavor to appeal to the masses, this bread will please even the most finicky kids and adults alike.

1 medium russet potato, peeled and quartered

2 quarts (1.9 L) cold, unsalted water

1⅛ teaspoons active dry yeast

3 tablespoons sugar

¼ cup (55 g) butter, melted but not hot

2 tablespoons milk

2 eggs (100 g liquid egg), divided

¾ teaspoon salt

2 cups (240 g) bread flour or sifted all-purpose flour

Place the potato in a medium pot with the water. Bring to a boil and cook until the potato is fork-tender. Drain the water, reserving ½ cup (120 ml). Cool the potato and cooking water to lukewarm. Place the potato water in a large mixing bowl. Sprinkle the yeast over the top and let sit 5 minutes. Whisk in the sugar, butter, milk, and one egg until combined. Mash the potato with a fork until it's soft and add ½ cup (115 g) of the mash, along with the salt, to the mixing bowl, whisking to combine. (Save any leftover potato for another use.) Add the flour and mix by hand until a soft dough forms. Cover with a clean, damp towel and let rise 1 hour.

Turn the dough out onto a floured board and roll into an oval loaf. Place the loaf into a sprayed 9 × 5 × 3 inch (23 × 13 × 7.5 cm) loaf pan and let rise 30 minutes.

Preheat the oven to 350°F (175°C).

Fork-beat the remaining egg with a teaspoon of water in a small bowl. Brush the top of the loaf with the egg wash and slide the loaf into the oven. Bake 40 minutes, or until golden brown and cooked through, rotating once halfway through baking. Remove the loaf from the oven, let it cool in the pan for about 10 minutes, remove to a cooling rack, and cool to room temperature before slicing.

Sesame Lavash

MAKES 3 LARGE SQUARES OF LAVASH

We created this classic Middle Eastern flat bread recipe to give people an appropriate vehicle for eating Muhammara (page 328).

Gingelly oil is a West African sesame oil that can be purchased online at www.idhayam.com. Lightly toasted sesame oil is a good substitute, but avoid traditional Japanese sesame oils that are dark-roasted, as this can make the baked crackers taste burned.

3⅓ cups (395 g) all-purpose flour
1 teaspoon salt
½ teaspoon sugar
⅔ cup (160 ml) water
1 egg (50 g liquid egg)
¼ cup (55 g) butter, melted and
   cooled slightly
Clarified butter, for brushing
6 tablespoons gingelly oil
1 tablespoon coarse sea salt

Place the flour, salt, and sugar in a medium bowl and whisk to combine. In another medium bowl, whisk together the water, egg, and butter. Add the egg mixture to the dry ingredients and stir just until the dough comes together. Knead five or six times in the bowl. Turn the dough out onto a clean work surface and divide into thirds. Cover with a damp towel or spritz the tops with water and let rest 30 minutes.

Preheat the oven to 425°F (220°C).

Turn three 14 × 16 inch (35 × 40 cm) baking sheets over and brush the bottoms with clarified butter. Roll the dough into balls and flatten with the palm of your hand. Gently stretch the dough out to ⅛ inch (0.3 cm) thick and drape over the upturned baking sheets. Make sure the edges of the dough drape over the edges of the pans—this will hold the dough in place while it bakes. Brush the tops evenly with 2 tablespoons gingelly or sesame oil and sprinkle each with 1 teaspoon coarse sea salt. Place the baking sheets on other, larger sheets to prevent dripping and bake on the top rack of the oven for 4 minutes. Rotate the pans and bake 3 to 4 minutes more, until crispy and golden brown in spots.

Let cool completely on the baking sheets, break into pieces, and serve or store in an airtight container.

Pretzel Rolls

MAKES ABOUT 40 ONE-OUNCE (28 G) ROLLS

Our first pastry chef and baker, Jasmine Inglesmith, came up with this recipe, which was an instant hit. Before long, most of our staff began complaining about weight gain they attributed exclusively to snacking on Pretzel Rolls.

This may seem like a lot of Pretzel Rolls for a single recipe, but you would be amazed at how quickly they disappear. Any dinner party that features these addictive little buns should take into account that guests' appetites will be ruined from pretzel overconsumption. Therefore, I'd recommend serving a bowl of these rolls with a side of Mustard Butter (recipe follows), a soul-warming winter soup or stew, and maybe a light, refreshing salad.

For the dough
2 cups (475 ml) warm water
1¼ teaspoons active dry yeast
1 tablespoon sugar
5½ cups (600 g) all-purpose flour
1 tablespoon salt

To make the pretzels
1 gallon (3.9 L) water
¼ cup plus 1 tablespoon (90 g)
  baking soda
1 egg (50 g liquid egg) beaten
  with 1 teaspoon water
Kosher salt or pretzel salt,
  for sprinkling

MAKE THE DOUGH: Combine the water and yeast in a large bowl and let sit 5 minutes. Mound the sugar and flour in the bowl, adding the salt last so it doesn't come into direct contact with the yeast. Stir to combine. When the flour is mostly incorporated, turn the dough out onto a clean work surface and knead until it's smooth and tacky but not sticky, about 5 minutes total. Clean the mixing bowl and rub with oil or pan spray. Add the dough to the bowl and cover with a clean towel. Let rise in a warm, dry place until doubled in size, about 1 hour.

MAKE THE PRETZELS: Preheat the oven to 450°F (230°C).

Punch down the dough and quarter it. Divide each segment into ten 1-ounce (28 g) pieces, forty total. Round each piece into a ball and let rest on a sprayed baking sheet for 20 minutes. While the dough rests, heat a gallon (3.9 L) water with the baking soda in a nonreactive pan over high heat just until it reaches a boil. Reduce the heat to medium-low to maintain a high simmer.

Working with ten rolls at a time, plunge them into the simmering water and cook 1 minute, flipping each occasionally to ensure equal cooking time on both sides. Using a slotted spoon, remove the rolls to a baking sheet sprayed with pan spray. Repeat with the remaining balls.

Brush the rolls with egg wash and sprinkle each liberally with kosher or pretzel salt. Bake on the top rack of the oven for 8 minutes, rotating once after 4 minutes, until the rolls are deep golden brown and spring back when poked gently with a finger.

Let cool for a few minutes and serve with Mustard Butter.

Mustard Butter

MAKES ABOUT ¾ CUP (180 ML),
ENOUGH FOR ONE BATCH OF PRETZEL ROLLS

This butter is a great accompaniment to the Pretzel Rolls, but it can also be used to finish meat-based pan sauces that go with pork, sausage, or sweetbreads.

2 tablespoons house mustard (page 21)
¾ cup (180 ml) whole unsalted butter
1 teaspoon salt

Whip the ingredients in a stand mixer using the paddle attachment, until fully combined. Refrigerate until you're ready to use it.

Acorn Vinaigrette

MAKES ENOUGH FOR 12 SALADS

This unusual dressing has a slight bitterness to it that I like (my aging palate also gravitates toward bitters-laced cocktails), but because I suggest tossing hearty, late-fall greens with it, a salad made with this dressing should also contain sweet dried fruits or berries.

I also need to credit my son and his schooling at White Pine Programs in York, Maine, for introducing me to the acorn as human food. Like most people, I had once thought the ubiquitous nut to be suitable only for squirrels.

2 cups (260 g) acorns
1 quart (945 ml) water
¼ cup (60 ml) olive oil
1 shallot, chopped
1 egg yolk (18 g)
1 tablespoon Dijon mustard
Zest of 1 orange
3 tablespoons honey
¾ cup (180 ml) sunflower oil
¼ cup (60 ml) peanut oil
½ teaspoon salt

Preheat the oven to 400°F (200°C).

Crack the acorns with a large chef's knife blade pressed flat against the nut. If the inside of the nut is black or dirty, throw it out. Boil the cracked acorns in the water for 3 minutes. Using a fork or paring knife, remove the meats from the shells. Toss the acorn meats with the olive oil and bake for 4 minutes.

Spin the roasted acorns, shallot, egg yolk, and mustard in a food processor until fairly smooth. Add the zest and honey and spin again, gradually adding the oils until emulsified. Season with salt and spin to combine. Use immediately or refrigerate.

Levant-Spiced Pumpkin Soup

SERVES 8

Depending on what types of storage squashes we have on hand in the late fall from our heirloom garden, this soup may vary slightly in thickness and flavor. Red Kuri works as well as Small Sugar pumpkin, which is more readily available. For testing the recipe, we used Upper Ground Sweet Potato Squash, and it came out great, if a bit paler than the pumpkin version. The year we successfully grew Sweet Potato Squash, and we also trained a few other sweet heirlooms, including a bumper crop of Green Striped Cushaw (depicted in the photo), courtesy of Josh Jennings's and Jenna Darcy's brilliant innovation: In place of a trellis, they affixed a lengthy arcade of excess hog fencing. That was our best squash year ever. Coincidence? I don't think so!

One 4- to 5-pound (1.8–2.3 kg) Small Sugar pumpkin
2 tablespoons olive oil
Pinch plus 1 tablespoon salt
4 cloves garlic
3 tablespoons clarified butter/olive oil blend (page 13)
½ cup (115 g) medium-diced onion
½ cup (115 g) medium-diced carrot (about 1 medium)
½ cup (115 g) medium-diced celery (about 1 small stalk)
1½-inch (4 cm) thumb gingerroot, peeled and minced (2 tablespoons minced)
½ teaspoon allspice
¼ teaspoon ground nutmeg
¼ teaspoon ground cinnamon
¼ teaspoon ground turmeric
¼ teaspoon cayenne pepper
¼ teaspoon ground coriander
1½ quarts (1.4 L) vegetable stock
1 cup (235 ml) cider

Preheat the oven to 350°F (175°C).

Cut the pumpkin down the middle, vertically from stem to bottom end, being careful to make a straight cut so the pumpkin will lie flat and create a seal when roasted cut side down. Scoop out the seeds and fibers, rub the flesh with the olive oil, and sprinkle with a pinch of salt. Place two cloves of garlic on a baking sheet under each dome of pumpkin and roast until the pumpkin flesh is soft, 1¼ to 1½ hours. Scoop out the flesh when it's cool enough to handle, and set aside, along with the garlic cloves.

Meanwhile, place a large pot over medium heat. Add the clarified butter/oil blend, the vegetables, ginger, and remaining tablespoon of salt; stir to combine. Cook until the vegetables begin to soften, about 5 minutes. Add the spices and stir to combine. Deglaze the pot with the stock and add the roasted pumpkin flesh, garlic, and cider. Bring to a simmer over medium heat and cook a few minutes, until the flavors have combined. Remove from the heat and let cool slightly. Carefully transfer to the bowl of a blender and puree until smooth. Serve immediately or cool to room temperature and reheat slowly over low heat.

Brown Butter Fettuccine Tossed with Kale, Pecans, and Roasted Beets over Carrot Sour Cream Sauce and Topped with a Farm Egg

SERVES 8 TO 10

Usually, I'm not a fan of menu items that read like a paragraph, but here's an exception. The phrasing really sold this dish, so our servers never had to explain to people what it was all about. This also marks one of the few times a menu item showed pity for what our servers have had to go through to explain dishes tableside. I'm sorry about that. But also not sorry.

Because this recipe has a lot of moving parts and requires a more than passing knowledge of cooking, it is wise to read through the manifold recipes below before embarking on making the dish from scratch. Shortcut options are permissible—cooking store-bought fettuccine and omitting the fried egg, for example—but, as is often the case, the result will not be the same.

For the Brown Butter Fettuccine
(makes 1½ pounds [680 g])
3 cups (360 g) all-purpose flour, sifted
¼ teaspoon salt
1 egg (50 g liquid egg)
2 egg yolks (36 g)
½ cup (120 ml) brown butter, melted
  but not hot (page 18)
½ cup (120 ml) warm water

To roll and cook the fettuccine
½ gallon (1.9 L) water
1½ teaspoons salt
Flour, for rolling
Semolina flour, for sprinkling
Olive oil

For the Roasted Beets
4 small red beetroots, scrubbed
2 teaspoons olive oil
Pinch salt
Pinch black pepper

MAKE THE BROWN BUTTER FETTUCCINE: Pour the flour and salt into the bowl of a stand mixer. Make a deep well in the middle and pour in the egg and yolks. Fit the mixer with the hook attachment and run on medium speed until the wet ingredients are just barely incorporated into the dry. With the motor running, add the brown butter and water in a slow trickle. Increase the speed slightly and mix just until combined, about 1½ minutes. Turn the dough out onto a floured work surface and knead for about 2 minutes, while it's still tepid (unlike other dough). Wrap the dough tightly in plastic wrap and refrigerate at least 1 hour, or up to 2 days.

ROLL AND COOK THE FETTUCCINE: Set the water to a boil with 1½ teaspoons salt.

Roll out the pasta by dividing it into four even pieces. Flatten the first piece with the palm of your hand and sprinkle with flour. Using a pasta sheeter, roll out the dough on the widest setting. Make a gate fold by folding one side of the dough to the center, folding the other half to the center, and then folding in half so the dough makes a narrow rectangle. Flatten with the palm of your hand and roll through the widest setting again. Move down two settings, sprinkle the dough with semolina flour, and roll through the sheeter. Decrease two more settings, sprinkle with semolina flour, and sheet again. At this point, you want to be on the third-narrowest setting. If not, move down

**For the Carrot Sour Cream Sauce
(makes 1 cup [235 ml])**

6 ounces (170 g) carrots (about 4
   small ones), peeled and roughly but
   evenly chopped
8 cloves garlic
2 teaspoons olive oil
Pinch plus ¼ teaspoon salt, divided
3 tablespoons heavy cream
¼ cup (60 ml) vegetable stock
½ cup (120 ml) sour cream
Black pepper to taste

For the final dish

4 Roasted Beets, peeled and quartered
1 tablespoon clarified butter/olive oil
   blend (page 13)
1 bunch kale, stems removed, washed,
   rolled, and sliced into ribbons
1½ cups (175 g) raw pecans,
   rough-chopped
Salt
Pepper
Brown Butter Fettuccine
1 cup (235 ml) vegetable stock
2 tablespoons butter
1 cup (235 ml) Carrot Sour Cream Sauce
8–10 fresh local farm eggs

until you reach this setting and sheet again. Sprinkle the dough with flour and roll through the fettuccine attachment or hand-cut. Place the cut pasta on a baking sheet sprinkled with semolina flour.

When the water is just under a boil, add the pasta and cook 2 minutes, until al dente. Drain and toss lightly with olive oil to prevent sticking. Spread it out on a baking sheet and "fluff" with your fingers so it doesn't stick together. This can all be done up to a day in advance and stored in a refrigerator, if necessary.

MAKE THE ROASTED BEETS: Beautiful beets, when roasted in oil, salt, and pepper, take on a depth of character that other vegetables dream of. We roast small beets whole with the skins on at 400°F (200°C) until they are fork-tender and then, when cool, we peel the skins off. Some people like the bitter, earthy flavor of the roasted skins, but I find them to be a leathery distraction from the pure, sweet essence of the beet. Moreover, I have found that too much grit can adhere to the skins, even after washing the beetroots.

For this recipe, after peeling the beets, quarter and store them until you're ready to execute the final dish.

MAKE THE CARROT SOUR CREAM SAUCE: Preheat the oven to 425°F (220°C).

Toss the carrot chunks and garlic cloves with olive oil and a pinch of salt and roast on a baking sheet for about 15 minutes, or until they are just beginning to color and soften. Remove to a small pan and add the cream and stock. Simmer, covered, over low heat until soft, stirring occasionally, 7 to 10 minutes. Remove to the carafe of a blender, add the sour cream, and puree until smooth. Fold in the remaining ¼ teaspoon salt and black pepper to taste. Refrigerate until you're ready to use it.

PLATE THE FINAL DISH: Heat the oven to 400°F (200°C). Reheat the beets in the oven for 5 minutes.

Meanwhile, in a wok or large sauté pan, heat the butter/oil blend. Add the kale and the pecans, sprinkle with a pinch of salt and pepper, and sauté for a minute. Then add the pasta and stir with tongs until everything in the pan is combined and the noodles are starting to brown. Add the vegetable stock, another pinch of salt and pepper, and the butter, stirring everything to coat the pasta well. When the butter is completely melted, transfer the contents of the pan to a large mixing bowl. Add the Carrot Sour Cream Sauce to the pan and heat very quickly. Spoon 2 tablespoons of the sauce onto plates or bowls and spread it out so that it covers a large area. Using tongs, twist the pasta up and place on top of the carrot sauce. Add two quarters of roasted beet to each plate. When each plate is ready, fry up the eggs and serve sunny-side up on top of the pasta. (For a simpler, less rich version, grated Parmesan or Grana Padano cheese can be substituted for the fried egg.)

Muhammara

MAKES 3 CUPS (710 ML)

I just love this all-purpose Turkish dip for more reasons than I can cite here. One of my favorite Chef's Meze Plates included baked local chèvre, Muhamarra, and Cherry Tapenade (page 351). I highly recommend that you try the same thing, especially if you have lots of lavash or pita kicking around, to scoop up the goodness.

6 red bell peppers
1 tablespoon olive oil
1 red onion, julienned
2 teaspoons salt, divided, plus more
   to taste
1 cup (130 g) whole shelled walnuts
1¼ teaspoons sumac
¼ teaspoon black pepper
Juice and zest of ½ orange
1 teaspoon pomegranate molasses
¼ teaspoon cayenne pepper

Preheat the oven to 450°F (230°C).

Place the peppers on a baking sheet on the top rack of the oven and roast, turning every 7 minutes, until every side begins to blister and blacken, about 35 minutes total. Remove to a bowl and cover tightly with plastic wrap. Allow the peppers to steam for 30 minutes. Remove the plastic wrap and, when the peppers are cool enough to handle, destem them and peel their skins. Squeeze out the seeds, using as little water as possible to remove them. Set aside.

Add the olive oil to a 10- or 12-inch (25 to 30 cm) pan over low heat. Add the onion and 1 teaspoon salt and sauté, stirring occasionally, until the onion begins to caramelize, about 15 minutes. Increase the heat to medium and add the walnuts, sumac, and black pepper. Toast the nuts for 8 to 10 minutes, stirring occasionally. Deglaze the pan by adding the orange juice and scraping up the browned bits. Add the zest and the molasses and stir to combine.

Scrape the walnut mixture into the bowl of a food processor and pulse several times until the mixture is chunky but not yet forming a paste. Squeeze out the peppers to remove any remaining water and add to the bowl with the walnuts. Add the cayenne and spin until the mixture forms a smooth paste, stopping once or twice to scrape down the bottom and sides of the bowl, about 1 minute total. Add the remaining 1 teaspoon salt, or to taste, and serve.

Rabbit Agnolotti with Pecans, Broccoli, and Oven-Dried Tomato

SERVES 8 (MAKES ABOUT 4 DOZEN AGNOLOTTI)

Like the previous pasta recipe, this dish looks simple on the plate, but a good amount of work goes into its preparation. For the home cook, anytime there is leftover braised meat (in this case rabbit) kicking around, consider it a pasta filling at the ready. A spring version of this with broccoli rabe in place of broccoli also hits the spot. The flank meat and legs of rabbit eat best when slow-cooked, while I prefer to quickly fry or roast the saddle or loin.

For the braised rabbit filling

Forelegs, hind legs, and flank meat
   from 2 rabbits
1 tablespoon salt
1 teaspoon black pepper
1½ tablespoons olive oil
1 small Spanish onion, medium dice
2 stalks celery, peeled, medium dice
3 carrots, peeled, medium dice
2 bay leaves
1 teaspoon chopped fresh thyme
2 tablespoons minced garlic
2 quarts (1.9 L) rabbit stock (can substitute chicken stock)
1 tablespoon chopped fresh herbs
   (equal parts rosemary, thyme,
   oregano, and chives)

For the agnolotti

1 batch plain pasta dough (page 18)
Flour, for rolling
1 egg (50 g liquid egg) beaten with
   1 teaspoon cold water
2 cups (455 g) shredded braised
   rabbit meat
Semolina flour, for sprinkling

MAKE THE BRAISED RABBIT FILLING: Preheat the oven to 325°F (165°C).

Season the rabbit legs with the salt and pepper. In a large pan over high heat, add the olive oil and sear the legs on all sides until golden brown, 7 to 8 minutes total. Add the veggies, bay leaves, thyme, garlic, and stock, and bring to a boil. Immediately reduce the heat to a simmer and transfer the ingredients to a roasting pan. Slide the pan onto the middle rack of the oven and braise, uncovered, for 90 minutes. Remove from the oven and strain the meat, reserving the liquid and veggies for another use. Let cool, and shred the rabbit.

Combine the shredded rabbit with the chopped herb mixture and set aside.

FORM THE AGNOLOTTI: Remove the prepared pasta dough from the refrigerator and divide into three equal pieces. Wrap two pieces loosely in plastic wrap. Flatten the third piece slightly with the palm of your hand and roll through the pasta maker at the widest setting. Make a gate fold by folding a third of the dough to the center, then the other third to the center, and folding again in half (so you have one narrow rectangle). Flatten slightly with the palm of your hand and roll the dough through the widest setting on the machine one more time. Lightly flour your work surface and pat the dough lightly with flour on both sides. Move down two settings on the pasta maker (to level 5 on my machine) and guide the dough through the machine. Brush both sides of the dough lightly with flour, move down two more levels (to level 3), and guide the dough through the machine. Move down one level (to level 2) and flour both sides of the dough. Pass it through the machine and lay the sheet of dough out on a lightly floured work surface. (This depends on how many settings your pasta maker has. You want to end on the second-narrowest setting.)

For the final presentation
Uncooked agnolotti
Olive oil, for tossing
½ cup (115 g) unsalted butter
½ cup (85 g) dried tomatoes, julienned
    (we oven-dry ours, but sun-dried
    work just fine)
½ cup (60 g) toasted pecans,
    coarsely chopped
1 cup (200 g) broccoli florets,
    chopped small
Shredded Parmesan, for serving

Using a knife or pasta cutter, slice the sheet of dough in half horizontally so you have two long, narrow strips of dough. Make an egg wash by beating the egg in a small bowl with 1 teaspoon water.

Make 2-teaspoon heaps of filling and place them along the top half of both sheets of pasta. You should have seven to nine piles of filling per sheet, evenly spaced about ½ to ¾ inch (1 to 2 cm) apart. Place the filling just above the midline of the dough, but not near the top.

Square off the ends of the dough, and brush egg wash along the top, on the two ends, and in between each pile of filling (don't brush it along the bottom of the dough). Fold the dough down over the filling on both sheets, and, using a sharp knife or pasta cutter, cut between each pile of filling. Each agnolotto should be about 3 inches (7.5 cm) wide. Using a crimper or a fork, crimp each of the agnolotti on the three cut sides and place on a sheet tray covered with semolina flour.

Repeat the entire process with the remaining two disks of dough. There should be fourteen to eighteen agnolotti per disk of dough, or forty-two to fifty-four total.

Store the agnolotti on the semolina-dusted sheet trays at room temperature for 30 minutes, until somewhat dry, then refrigerate or freeze.

ASSEMBLE THE DISH: When you're ready to serve, bring a large pot of heavily salted water to a boil. In batches of twelve or so, drop the agnolotti into the pot and boil 2½ minutes, until the dough is tender and the filling warmed through. Strain and spread the agnolotti out onto a baking sheet, tossing with olive oil to prevent sticking. Repeat with the remaining agnolotti.

Place a large cast-iron or other heavy pan over high heat. When the pan is very hot, add the butter. Immediately add the agnolotti and cook in batches, undisturbed, for about 20 seconds per batch, until golden brown and beginning to crisp. Flip over and cook for an additional 20 seconds. Add the julienned tomato, pecans, and broccoli florets; toss to combine. Turn the pan off and let the mixture sit for 1 minute to finish heating through.

To serve, arrange six to eight agnolotti, plus about 1 tablespoon each of the julienned dried tomato, broccoli, and pecans, on each plate. Top with a few slivers of shredded Parmesan. Serve immediately.

Cider-Braised Pork Osso Buco

SERVES 8

Similar in many ways to the Pork Shank with Mashed Turnips and Long Beans (page 302), this smaller, crosscut portion of pork cooks slowly in a complex late fall admixture of aromatic spices. The braising liquid that results, when reduced, tastes like the perfect welcome to the oncoming chill of winter.

Eight 3-inch (7.5 cm) crosscut pork hind shanks
1 tablespoon salt
1 teaspoon black pepper
½ cup (120 ml) rendered leaf lard (substitute bacon fat or canola oil)
1 Spanish onion, medium dice
2 large carrots, medium dice
3 stalks celery, medium dice
12 cloves garlic
1 thumb gingerroot, peeled and minced
1 stick cinnamon
1 dried chipotle pepper, torn into pieces
2 star anise
½ teaspoon ground allspice
½ teaspoon cumin seed
2 cups (475 ml) tomato puree
1½ cups (355 ml) apple cider
½ cup (120 ml) apple cider vinegar
½ cup (120 ml) honey
6 cups (1.4 L) pork stock or other meat stock

Preheat the oven to 325°F (165°C).

In a large mixing bowl, combine the hind shanks with the salt and pepper, tossing to coat evenly.

Place a 12-inch (30 cm) high-sided, heavy-bottomed skillet (sauteuse) over high heat. When it just barely begins to smoke, add the lard and half of the meat in a single layer. Cook the shanks, undisturbed, until they turn golden brown, 2½ to 3 minutes. Flip and repeat on all sides, about 15 minutes total. You may need to reduce the heat to medium-high to prevent scorching. Remove the meat to a roasting pan with the widest mouth of the marrow bone facing up so the marrow doesn't leak into the braise. Repeat with the second batch of shanks.

Remove all but ¼ cup (60 ml) pork fat from the pan. Reduce the heat to medium, add the onion, carrots, and celery, and cook 1 minute. Add the garlic and cook, stirring, 1 minute more. Add the ginger and spices and cook 1 minute, stirring to combine.

Add the tomato puree, and deglaze the pan by scraping up the browned bits stuck to the bottom. Cook 2 minutes, until the tomato reduces slightly. Add the cider, cider vinegar, and honey; cook 3 minutes, continuing to scrape the bottom of the pan as you stir. Add the stock and bring the mixture to a boil over high heat. Pour the liquid over the shanks in the roasting pan, cover with foil, and slide into the oven. Braise for about 2½ hours, checking for doneness after 2 hours. When the meat is starting to fall away from the bone at the center, let the pan cool with the meat and liquid in it until the shanks can be removed with your bare hands. Also remove the star anise and cinnamon stick, skim the fat from the surface of the braising liquid with a ladle, and puree the braising liquid in a blender until smooth. If the resulting liquid is too thick, add a little stock or cider to thin it.

Serve right away, pouring the liquid over the shanks, or as we do at the restaurant, refrigerate and reheat.

Lady Apple Chutney

MAKES 1 QUART (945 ML)

We served this chutney on two very different dishes, with equally tasty results. The first, pan-fried trout on a mushroom-and-pecan risotto, relied on Carolina-farmed trout that is no longer available, but with a burgeoning local steelhead program, this dish may stage a comeback . . . you never know. The second, a braised pork osso buco, stuck around for quite a while. That recipe precedes this one.

Although crab apples work well as a substitution in this recipe, the skins of Lady apples have a unique aromatic quality, and the flesh is more substantial than crab apples, so I prefer to cook with this small, ancient heritage variety whenever it's available.

1½ cups (355 ml) sherry vinegar

1½ cups (340 g) sugar

½ teaspoon dried red pepper flakes

10 Lady apples (or crab apples), cored and quartered

1 large red onion, julienned

1 ounce (28 g) gingerroot, peeled and minced

1 tablespoon honey

Zest and juice of 1 orange

Juice of 1 lemon

1 tablespoon pomegranate molasses

1 teaspoon rose water

¼ teaspoon salt

In a heavy-bottomed pot or large saucepan, bring the vinegar, sugar, and pepper flakes to 225°F (110°C) over medium-high heat (10 to 12 minutes). Reduce the heat to medium and add the apples, onion, and ginger. Cook until the apples are soft, 12 to 15 minutes. Add the honey, citrus, pomegranate molasses, and rose water; cook until the apples are mushy but still intact, about 5 minutes more. Add the salt, stir to combine, and allow the mixture to cool in the pan. Refrigerate until ready to eat.

Potatoes:
From Peru to Pierogi

I have always said, perhaps with perceived airs I don't wish to possess, that I should have been a food anthropologist. I did badly enough in college to eliminate any hope of finding a challenging curriculum that might support this aspiration. Alas, I now have no academic degree to stand on, but I do have a lust for knowledge about the origins of food ingredients, how they evolved and came to be what we cook with today, and a nagging desire to share that awareness with unsuspecting restaurant patrons.

A good example of my passion for tracing foods to their source came during two trips to Peru in 1994. I was traveling on business, at that time working for a consultant who mediated corporate mergers and acquisitions all over the world. At the same time that I was lugging flip-chart pads and other rudimentary conference materials through airports for him, I was writing a dining column for an alternative newspaper in Boston. I took other side jobs and writing gigs for the money, but I mostly split my time between doing odd jobs for an odd guy on the fringes of Corporate America while honing my skills as a young food critic.

These weeks-long adventures in Peru included plenty of conference administration and corporate drudgery followed by days of hell-bent exploration into the unknown elements of the Andes. The first trip included memorable dinners in Lima followed by hikes to sacred sites in Ica, Cuzco, Machu Picchu, and Lake Titicaca. In one conference I was laboriously recording, my role included reading aloud from a text in Spanish to a roomful of Peruvian secretaries who worked for the big bosses of some of the world's most prominent copper mining corporations. My first day on that particular job, weary from a missed connection in Miami, I did my best to read in a language I did not speak (this was not an abnormal expectation of me in those years). I read the words in front of me at the end of every page, which instructed me to tell the audience to turn the page to follow along. In Spanish, as I learned years later, the word for "turn" is *volver*. Conjugating that verb still causes me a few difficulties. But more important, the word for "page," *pagina*, and the word for "vagina," *vagina*, are—well—perilously similar on the sloppy, lax tongue of an inexperienced American lad. Suffice to say that, at the end of that day's conference, I was mortified to learn from one of the secretaries that I had not been asking them to "turn the page."

I was joined on some of these adventures by the patient and querulous traveler who would later become my wife. Denise and I traversed the awe-inspiring Inca Trail in four long days, highlighted by a final ascent and Hollywood-worthy passage through the "Gates of the Sun," where we looked down—as so many others have—at the resurrected lost city of the Inca, jaws grounded. Such a spectacle, and such a gift for the hikers who make the long trip to get there the hard way. As the Inca would have wanted it!

Back in Cuzco, where we began our trek, we visited another ruin, Sacsayhuaman, where we learned from our guide that the Inca—light-years ahead of the rest of the world in terms of selective breeding—had developed more than a thousand varieties of potato. And that was over a thousand years ago. Since then, farmers have expanded on that number somewhat, bringing today's total number of varieties to over four thousand (this statistic varies wildly, because many potato varieties have never been introduced to the greater marketplace).

On my second trip to Peru, I journeyed alone, taking a bus from Lima to Huaraz, a very small city in the midst of the very large Cordillera Blanca range. There, on a solo hike up over 13,000 feet (3,962 m), I got lost. The narrowing trail I had been ascending all day dumped me out—just before sunset—at a cultivated summit plateau, where a silhouetted man with a pickax was wrapping up his workday on a potato farm. I was weak, exhausted, and very hungry. He saw me teetering at the edge of his field and approached me, the ax slung over his shoulder. Although he wasn't much more than 5 feet (1.5 m) tall, he hefted the heavy pickax like an Olympian. He introduced himself as Ciruhuamanca, a name I will never forget. I spoke no Spanish, and he spoke only Quechua, the native tongue of the Andes. I motioned that I was hungry and thirsty, and he led me by the arm across the field and down a narrow path to a small hut. As the sun went down behind the Andes, Ciruhuamanca and a very old woman who must have been his mother sat me down inside their hut and fed me a memorable bowl of guinea pig and potato soup . . . from a guinea pig they had me pick from the herd scuttling about the dirt floor. Ciruhuamanca and the old woman may have saved my life. I have never looked at a potato (or a guinea pig, for that matter) the same since.

Potato and Cheese Pierogi with Blueberries, Kale, and Smoked Corn Bisque

SERVES 8

Although Black Trumpet has employed several Polish-Americans over the years, it was French-Canadian sous chef Carrie Dahlgren who turned this dish into an instant Black Trumpet classic. In fact, after she moved on to other pastures, Carrie continued to prepare these pierogi with farmer pal Garen Heller at our local winter farmers market.

The inspiration for the corn broth used to make the bisque sauce came from Brazilian cooks I worked with in Cambridge, Massachusetts, years ago, who used to make tea out of the husks and drink it as a refreshing beverage. So many corn husks get discarded here in America, but in Latin America they are put to good use. When you consider the staggering statistic that food hub advocates bandy about—that 40 percent of all food grown in this country never gets eaten—it makes sense for all of us to reconsider food waste.

While I have always made a point of whole animal utilization—whether through buying whole animals, smart freezer management, charcuterie, or simply working with purveyors to order cuts for my menu that no one else was buying—I didn't start thinking about whole plant utilization until embarrassingly late in my career. The use of husks in making a sweet corn broth—and in our boom stock—was an early exception.

For the pierogi dough
2 cups (240 g) flour
1 teaspoon salt
4 egg yolks (72 g)
2 tablespoons sour cream
½ cup (120 ml) hot water

MAKE THE PIEROGI DOUGH: Preheat the oven to 400°F (200°C).

Combine the dry ingredients in a medium bowl. In another small bowl, whisk together the egg yolks and sour cream. Add the hot water in a slow drizzle, to temper the eggs so they don't scramble. Turn out the dry ingredients onto a clean work surface. Make a deep well in the

For the pierogi filling

4 russet potatoes, scrubbed but
  not peeled
2 tablespoons olive oil
½ teaspoon salt, plus more
  for sprinkling
½ cup (60 g) grated Comté cheese
  (or any substitute Gruyère)
¼ cup (25 g) grated Parmesan cheese
¼ teaspoon pepper
1 egg (50 g liquid egg), fork-beaten
  with 1 teaspoon water

For the corn broth

Leaves from 6 ears of corn
3 quarts (2.8 L) water
1 Spanish onion, rough-chopped
2 tablespoons sugar
4 makrut lime leaves (available in
  some Asian markets, also marketed
  as kaffir lime)
1 stalk lemongrass, chopped
2 bay leaves
2 tablespoons whole black
  peppercorns

For the Smoked Corn Bisque

½ cup (85 g) applewood chips
2 ears corn, shucked
1 leek, white part only, cut into quarter
  moons ¼ inch (0.5 cm) thick
2 tablespoons clarified butter
½ teaspoon salt
½ cup (120 ml) corn broth or
  vegetable stock
1½ cups (355 ml) heavy cream

To finish the dish

2 tablespoons clarified butter/olive oil
  blend (page 13)
Salt and pepper, for sprinkling
8 leaves dinosaur (aka lacinato) kale,
  stacked, rolled up, and sliced in a
  chiffonade
1 pint (340 g) blueberries

center and add the wet ingredients. Stir carefully from the inside of the well out to combine. Assemble the dough into a craggy ball and knead several times until it becomes smooth, about 1 minute. Form the dough into a disk, wrap tightly in plastic, and refrigerate at least 30 minutes.

MAKE THE PIEROGI FILLING: Rub the potatoes with the olive oil and a sprinkling of salt. Roast on the top rack of the oven until soft, about an hour. When they're just cool enough to handle, peel the potatoes and put them through a potato ricer or food mill into a medium bowl. Add the cheeses, ½ teaspoon salt, and pepper to the bowl; mix to combine. Set aside while you sheet the dough.

PREPARE THE PIEROGI: Remove the dough from the refrigerator, divide it into two sections, and flatten one of them with the palm of your hand. Using a pasta sheeter, roll out the dough on the widest setting. Repeat. Move down two settings and roll out once. Move down two more settings and roll out once. The sheeter should now be on the second- or third-narrowest setting. Spread the sheeted dough out onto a clean work surface and cut out circles with a 2¼- to 2½-inch (5.5 to 6 cm) biscuit cutter or a widemouthed mason jar lid. Repeat with the remaining dough. When all the circles are formed, place 1½ tablespoons of filling in the middle of each.

With a brush or fingertip, rub the perimeter of each disk with the egg wash. Fold the top over the bottom and crimp the edges with your fingertip. Repeat with the remaining pierogi. These can be stored for a short period of time in the refrigerator if necessary.

MAKE THE CORN BROTH: Press the corn leaves down firmly in a large 5- to 6-quart (5 to 6 L) stockpot. Add the remaining ingredients and bring to a boil over high heat. Reduce the heat to low and simmer 40 minutes. Let cool to room temperature, strain through a chinois or fine-mesh strainer, and use to make Smoked Corn Bisque.

MAKE THE SMOKED CORN BISQUE: Form a small, shallow bowl with a 9-inch-square (23 cm) piece of foil. Place the wood chips in the bowl and place the bowl in a small, high-sided pot. Nestle a steamer insert over the foil bowl and place the corn on the steamer insert. Cover the pan tightly with foil, poke a small hole in the foil, and turn the burner on high heat. (Be sure to do this in a well-ventilated kitchen.) Smoke for 6 minutes, until smoke is billowing out of the small hole in the foil. Turn off the heat and smoke an additional 10 minutes (without disturbing the foil cover).

Remove the corn from the smoker, cut the kernels from the cobs, and discard the cobs. Set the kernels aside.

Sauté the leek in the clarified butter and salt in a medium sauté pan over medium-low heat for about 10 minutes, or until soft. Add the smoked corn and stir to combine. Add the broth and heavy cream and simmer 6 minutes over low heat. Let the mixture cool and puree in a blender.

PLATE THE PIEROGI: Heat a large nonstick pan with a tablespoon of oil. Sprinkle the pierogi with salt and pepper and assemble in the pan in a single layer (you'll need to do this in batches). Carefully brown them on one side, flip, and transfer to a baking sheet. Brown the remaining pierogi and pop the baking sheet in the oven for 4 minutes.

Add 1 tablespoon butter/oil blend to the same pan and place it over a high flame. Add the kale ribbons and, within seconds, as they begin to crisp in the pan, sprinkle with salt and stir in the blueberries. Toss to combine and remove the pan from the heat.

Divide the kale and blueberries evenly among eight plates and top with the hot pierogi. Drizzle about ¼ cup (60 ml) Smoked Corn Bisque over the top of each plate and serve right away.

Ostrich, Emu, and Elk, Oh My!

These three animals—one of them is not like the others, but we have treated them more or less the same—have all appeared on Black Trumpet menus over the years. For reasons I don't fully understand, these meats have become harder to source in recent years, whether that means fewer farmers are dabbling in more exotic meats, or the importation laws have changed. Either way, when I have been able to find New England farms raising these animals, I am always quick to try to source the lean, delicious meat from them. One steady supplier is Velvet Pastures Elk Ranch in Lee, New Hampshire. Jim and Lou Ann Griswold raise beautiful elk, the meat of which tastes superior, in my opinion, to both white-tailed and red deer.

When local sources dry up, my fallback is a game meat fantasyland in Texas called Broken Arrow Ranch. On a plot of land that is larger in size than most major cities, Broken Arrow Ranch releases a number of species—wild boar, axis deer, and blackbuck antelope, to name a few—that live on the vast prairie as they would in the wild, foraging food and water alongside native species. Routine culling of the herd is done by marksmen in helicopters. A USDA-certified mobile processing unit follows the helicopters on land and butchers the animals on the spot.

When I have a dinner that calls for game, I make a call to Broken Arrow, and the hunt begins. This is not too far afield from the way I think meat sourcing should go.

Ostrich Fan Fillet with Concord Grape Demi-Glace

SERVES 6

Here is a dish that sold very well for us, much to my surprise at the time. The beauty of this recipe—lest home cooks feel intimidated—is that pretty much any cut of any game meat can be substituted for the ostrich fan fillet.

A quick note about demi-glace: Some butcher shops and supermarkets sell this deep-amber magic, which chefs use to thicken and enhance the flavor of sauces like the Concord Grape Demi-Glace in the ostrich recipe. *Demi* means "half," but in our kitchen, stock is reduced by quite a bit more than that, as occurs in this recipe.

For the ostrich
One 1-pound (455 g) ostrich fan fillet
2 tablespoons juniper berries
2 tablespoons black peppercorns
1 tablespoon pink peppercorns
1 tablespoon salt
1 tablespoon dried rosemary
1 teaspoon dried sage
1 teaspoon granulated garlic
1 teaspoon chili powder
1 teaspoon fennel seed
Zest of 1 orange
2 tablespoons olive oil

For the Concord Grape Demi-Glace
1 shallot, minced
2 cloves garlic, minced
1 tablespoon olive oil
½ cup (120 ml) red wine
1 quart (945 ml) meat stock
   (veal, beef, or pork)
½ cup (115 g) Wild Grape Preserves
   (page 352)
Juice and zest of 1 orange
5 juniper berries, bruised with a knife
1 sprig rosemary

PREPARE THE OSTRICH: Preheat the oven to 400°F (200°C).

Slice the ostrich into 2½-ounce (70 g) pieces.

Combine the next ten ingredients in a spice grinder and grind to a fine powder.

Rinse the ostrich and pat dry. Rub liberally on all sides with the spice rub and let sit up to 1 hour, but no longer. Heat a large frying pan over high heat and, when it begins to smoke, add the olive oil and the meat. Sear 20 seconds on all sides, then pop into the oven for 1 minute. Remove from the oven, flip the meat, and let cool in the pan for 40 seconds. Remove from the pan, let cool for 2 more minutes, slice, and serve.

PREPARE THE CONCORD GRAPE DEMI-GLACE: Combine the shallot, garlic, and olive oil in a 2-quart (2 L) pot over medium heat. Cook 3 minutes, until the vegetables begin to soften. Deglaze with the wine, cooking 2 to 3 minutes, or until the scent of alcohol wears off. Add the remaining ingredients and bring to a boil over medium-high heat. Reduce the heat to maintain a low boil and reduce by three-quarters, until the mixture coats the back of a spoon, about 1 hour. Remove from the heat and strain the solids through a fine-mesh strainer. Serve immediately, drizzled over the ostrich, or cool to room temperature and refrigerate.

Mountain Paella

SERVES 4

4 one-ounce (28 g) Chorizo Meatballs (page 53) *or* 4 ounces (115 g) Spanish-style chorizo, quartered lengthwise and chopped into ½-inch (1 cm) pieces
1 red bell pepper, medium dice
8 large chanterelles
½ cup (40 g) wild or domestic mushroom mix
½ Spanish onion, small dice
1 teaspoon minced garlic
1½ teaspoons plus a pinch of salt, divided
Pinch black pepper
1 cup (200 g) Calasparra rice
2 cups (475 ml) stock (any meat or poultry stock will do)
8 Braised Burgundy Snails (page 98)
4 braised rabbit hind legs (braising recipe from Rabbit Agnolotti on page 329)
¼ cup (60 ml) rabbit braising liquid
Pinch Red House Pepper Blend (page 22)
Pinch mixed herbs (page 22)

Preheat the oven to 450°F (230°C).

Heat a 14-inch (36 cm) paella pan over a medium flame. Add the meatballs (or chorizo) and render, stirring, for 2 minutes. With a slotted spoon, remove to a paper-towel-lined plate. If the pan starts to smoke, remove from the heat until it cools slightly. Add the pepper and mushrooms and cook, undisturbed, for 30 seconds. Add the onion, garlic, 1½ teaspoons salt, and pepper, stirring well to incorporate, about 30 seconds. Reduce the heat to low and add the rice. Cook 1 minute, shaking the pan often to toast evenly. Increase the flame to medium-high and add the stock, stirring to incorporate. Carefully arrange the chorizo, meatballs, snails, braised rabbit legs, and rabbit braising liquid in the pan and cook 5 minutes. Transfer to the oven and cook 15 minutes more until you achieve the pega (until there's no visual liquid and the edges have turned golden brown; see the "Pega" sidebar on page 219). Sprinkle Red House Pepper Blend and fresh herbs on the top and serve on a trivet with a serving spoon and four plates.

Pear Crème Brûlée with Pear Chutney and Ginger Tuile

MAKES 12 FOUR-OUNCE (115 G) INDIVIDUAL PORTIONS

4 large Bartlett pears, peeled and chopped off the core into 4 pieces
1 cup (235 ml) white wine
½ stick cinnamon
1 vanilla bean, split
3 star anise
2 cups (455 g) sugar, divided, plus more for brûléeing the tops of the custards
9 egg yolks (160 g)
3 cups (710 ml) heavy cream
Hot tap water

Combine the pears, wine, cinnamon stick, vanilla bean, star anise, and 1½ cups of the sugar in a large pot. Bring to a boil and reduce to a simmer, stirring to dissolve the sugar. Poach 40 minutes, until the pears are soft. Remove the pears, strain the solids from the syrup, and continue reducing the syrup until it's slightly thickened but still liquid, about 30 minutes.

Place the pears and ⅓ cup (80 ml) syrup in a food processor and puree until mostly smooth (some small chunks are okay). Reserve the rest of the syrup for Pear Chutney (recipe follows).

Preheat the oven to 325°F (165°C).

In a large mixing bowl, whisk the egg yolks with the remaining ½ cup (155 g) sugar. Add the cream and the pear puree; whisk gently to combine (so as not to add too many air bubbles). Strain the mixture into a pitcher. Set up a water bath by placing twelve ramekins in a large roasting pan, and placing the roasting pan on a flat baking sheet. Carefully pour the brûlée mixture into each ramekin (just over three-quarters full) and carefully pour hot water down the side of the roasting pan, so it comes halfway up the sides of the ramekins. Cover the roasting pan with foil and slide into the oven. Bake about 30 minutes (depending on the width and depth of your ramekins), or until the middle is set (the custard should wobble as a single unit when shaken gently). Begin checking for doneness after about 25 minutes, as you don't want the mixture to overcook and the eggs to curdle.

Remove from the oven and let the custards cool to room temperature, uncovered, in the water bath. Remove and refrigerate until chilled and ready to serve.

TO SERVE: Sprinkle 1 to 2 tablespoons sugar evenly over the top of each ramekin and torch so the sugar melts, turns golden brown, and becomes smooth as ice. Serve immediately.

Ginger Tuile

MAKES ½ CUP (120 ML) BATTER, OR ABOUT 10 TUILES

3 tablespoons unsalted butter,
  at room temperature
½ cup (28 g) powdered sugar
1 egg white (30 g)
¼ cup (30 g) all-purpose flour
¾ teaspoon cornstarch
¾ teaspoon ground ginger
¼ teaspoon heavy cream
¼ teaspoon vanilla extract

Cream the butter and sugar with a hand mixer on medium speed for about 5 minutes. Add the egg white and mix until fully incorporated. Combine the flour, cornstarch, and ginger in a small bowl, whisking to combine. Add the dry ingredients to the wet, whisking just until combined. Add the cream and vanilla extract and mix just until combined. Refrigerate the batter until chilled, about 1 hour.

Preheat the oven to 400°F (200°C).

Line a baking sheet with a Silpat or other nonstick surface. Spread 1 tablespoon of tuile batter on the Silpat using a small, offset spatula. Spread to about ⅛ inch (0.3 cm) thick, about 2 inches (5 cm) wide, and 2 inches (5 cm) long. Repeat with the rest of the dough, working in batches if necessary.

Slide the baking sheet into the oven and bake 3 minutes. Rotate 180 degrees and bake 3 more minutes. Remove when the edges are golden brown and the cookie is crisp. Wait 10 seconds, then, using the offset spatula, carefully flip the cookie onto a French rolling pin. Working quickly, roll the tuile around the pin, let it sit 30 seconds, until hardened and cooled, and carefully slide off. Store immediately or hold for up to 1 day.

Pear Chutney

MAKES ABOUT 1 CUP (235 ML)

2 pears, peeled and cored, small dice
⅔ cup (150 g) sugar
1 small thumb gingerroot, peeled and
  minced (about 2 teaspoons)
Zest and juice of ½ orange, zest
  removed with a peeler and sliced
  into long, thin strips
1 star anise
1 stick cinnamon

Place all the ingredients in a small heavy-bottomed pot over medium heat, stirring well to combine. Bring up to a simmer, then reduce the heat to low to maintain. Simmer 45 minutes, until the pears are soft and the liquid is syrupy but only slightly thickened. Remove from the heat and let cool to room temperature (the mixture will thicken significantly as it cools). Refrigerate. Serve with the Pear Crème Brûlée and Ginger Tuiles, both recipes preceding.

BEST SUPPORTING ROLES

SUPPORTING RULES
RECIPES

Some aspects of our menu don't fit into any seasonal grouping or sequence. Yet the sourcing and preparation of these outliers follow the same strict rules as the rest of the menu. This chapter calls Black Trumpet miscellany into the spotlight.

Charcuterie and Cheese Slates

Slate has always played an important role in the Black Trumpet motif. When we first opened, we bought antique chalkboard scraps and used them to make our front door sign and the board of daily additions to the menu. As serendipity would have it, we had to do some reconstruction in the front of the restaurant that required matching the existing slate floor tiles. When I saw the 12 × 6 inch (30 × 15 cm) rectangular slate slabs left over from construction, I knew we had to use them as "slate plates" on which we could write the names of the featured cheeses or meats. What I couldn't have anticipated was that the slates would stand the test of time, outlasting every other plate in the building.

The cheeses and meats, whether cured in-house or elsewhere, that have adorned these slates over the years, have been accompanied by condiments, pickles, mustard, and toasts made from leftover bread. Below are some of the most versatile condiment pairings, most of which found their way onto the main menu in other supporting roles.

Apricot Pine Nut Conserve

MAKES ABOUT 2½ CUPS (590 ML)

This conserve makes a particularly fine match with aged goat cheeses and soft, triple-cream cow's milk cheeses.

½ cup (70 g) pine nuts
2 cups (255 g) dried apricots, julienned
½ cup (75 g) minced shallot (about 1 medium)
½ cup (120 ml) sherry
½ cup (120 ml) sherry vinegar
1¼ cups (285 g) sugar
⅛ teaspoon salt

Place the pine nuts in an 8-inch (20 cm) dry pan over medium heat. Stir and flip them often until they toast to an even golden brown, about 5 minutes. Watch them closely because they burn easily.

In a small 1- to 2-quart (1 to 2 L) pot, combine the remaining ingredients over high heat. Bring the mixture to a boil, reduce the heat to a simmer, and cook until the mixture is thick and syrupy, about 1 hour. Allow the mixture to cool partially, about 10 minutes, and fold in the pine nuts. Let the mixture cool to room temperature and refrigerate until you're ready to use it.

Smoked Almond and Arugula Pesto

MAKES ABOUT 1 PINT (475 ML)

This is a delicious pesto that pairs so well with scallops and chanterelles, you might think, as I do, that the three were destined to find one another. The recipe appears here because it also makes a fine pairing with cured meats and hard cheeses. Veteran Black Trumpet bartender Sara Hamilton, herself a pesto master, really liked this one.

1 cup (170 g) apple- or hickory wood chips
½ cup (70 g) blanched whole almonds
1 clove garlic
4 ounces (115 g) arugula
Juice of ½ lemon (about 1 tablespoon)
½ cup (120 ml) olive oil
3 tablespoons freshly grated Parmesan cheese
1½ teaspoons salt, or to taste

MAKE THE SMOKED ALMONDS: Form a small, shallow bowl with a 9-inch-square (23 cm) piece of foil. Place the wood chips in the bowl and place the bowl in a small, high-sided pot. Place a steamer insert on top of the foil bowl and scatter the almonds on the steamer insert. Cover the pan tightly with foil and poke three small holes in it. Turn the burner on high and heat until smoke starts billowing out of the foil holes, about 5 minutes. (Be sure to do this in a well-ventilated kitchen.) Reduce the heat to low and smoke for 5 minutes without disturbing the cover. Remove from the heat, still covered, and let cool.

ASSEMBLE THE PESTO: Add the almonds to the bowl of a food processor and pulse until the nuts are reduced to small chunks but the mixture isn't pasty, seven to ten pulses. Add the garlic and pulse until it is minced, three or four pulses. Add the arugula and lemon juice and pulse until the arugula is minced. Scrape down the bottom and sides of the bowl and, with the motor running, add the olive oil in a slow and steady stream. Stop the motor, scrape down the sides and bottom of the bowl, add the cheese, and pulse to combine. Taste for seasoning, adding up to 1½ teaspoons salt, as needed.

Bacon Pomegranate Jam

MAKES ABOUT 1½ CUPS (355 ML)

½ pound (225 g) bacon, large dice
1 cup (235 ml) pomegranate juice
¾ cup (170 g) sugar
Juice of ½ orange
1 tablespoon pomegranate molasses
¾ cup (170 g) pomegranate seeds (from 1 pomegranate)

Slowly render the bacon in a large, heavy-bottomed frying pan over low heat, about 30 minutes. Drain the fat, add the pomegranate juice, sugar, and orange juice, and simmer, covered, for about 45 minutes, until the mixture is thick and foamy.

Add the molasses and pomegranate seeds and simmer, uncovered, for 15 minutes. Let the mixture cool slightly off the heat; remove it to the bowl of a food processor and pulse eight to ten times, until you see uniform small chunks of bacon. Let it cool to room temperature and refrigerate until cold.

Date Orange Molasses

MAKES 1½ CUPS (340 G)

This a delectable deep-winter condiment that we have paired with foie gras, lamb burgers, duck breasts, and pungent cheeses.

12 Medjool dates, pitted (always pit them yourself; if you buy pitted dates, they have a tendency to be dried out and stale)
¼ cup (55 g) packed brown sugar
2 cups (475 ml) water
1 bay leaf
1 star anise
Zest and juice of 1 orange
3 tablespoons molasses
2 tablespoons minced peeled gingerroot
¼ teaspoon salt

Combine all the ingredients in a small heavy-bottomed pot and cook over medium heat for 8 minutes. Reduce the heat to low, cover the pot, and simmer until the star anise is soft, about 45 minutes. Remove the bay leaf, let the mixture cool, and puree it in a food processor until it's relatively smooth.

Rhubarb Catsup

MAKES 1½ QUARTS (1.4 L)

To produce this condiment, we used pulp from a cocktail syrup that made a pint of by-product from hanging a muslin bag of stewed rhubarb and sumac. That rhubarb-tinged Moscow Mule was delicious and popular, but I would argue the catsup made from its refuse was even better!

If you aren't making rhubarb mules anytime soon, simply add to this recipe 3 cups (360 g) chopped rhubarb, 1 tablespoon sumac, and an extra cup (225 g) brown sugar.

½ Spanish onion, rough-chopped
1 teaspoon minced garlic
2 tablespoons olive oil
2 pounds (910 g) rhubarb, ends removed, rough-chopped
2 cups (475 ml) rhubarb sumac pulp (from cocktail prep, or see note above)
2 cups (475 ml) tomato puree
2 tablespoons honey
1 tablespoon pomegranate molasses
1 tablespoon salt
1 thumb gingerroot, peeled and minced
2 teaspoons garam masala

Sweat the onion and garlic in the olive oil over medium-low heat for 3 to 5 minutes. Add the remaining ingredients and simmer over medium heat until the rhubarb is soft and the mixture has reduced and thickened, about 45 minutes. Stir occasionally, scraping up the browned bits on the bottom.

Let the mixture cool slightly and puree in a blender. Adjust the seasoning, let the mixture cool to room temperature, and refrigerate until you're ready to use it.

Cherry Tapenade

MAKES 1 CUP (235 ML)

This neoclassic spread makes a great meze item on its own, thrives in the company of good goat cheese, and also played a significant role in a Black Trumpet dish with zucchini carpaccio, chèvre, and fried squash blossoms.

1½ teaspoons olive oil
½ red onion, minced
¼ pound (115 g) Bing cherries, pitted
¼ pound (115 g) Kalamata olives
1½ teaspoons minced garlic
1½ teaspoons chopped mixed fresh herbs (page 22)
¼ teaspoon sherry vinegar

Pour the olive oil into an 8- or 10-inch (20 or 25 cm) pan over medium heat. Add the onion and sweat until soft, about 10 minutes. Remove from the heat and let cool.

Meanwhile, combine the rest of the ingredients in a food processor and spin until chunky, stopping once to scrape down the sides and bottom of the bowl. Remove the mixture to a bowl, fold in the onion, and refrigerate until you're ready to use it. This will hold in the refrigerator for up to 10 days.

Wild Grape Preserves

MAKES 5 CUPS (1.2 L)

When the season is good, we may forage as much as 100 pounds (45 kg) of Concord grapes. In years when I don't have time to forage, we will buy from other pickers and process less than half that volume. Either way, these intense clusters of Indian-summer fruit give us a sweet dose of summer that can last well into the winter.

In addition to pairing this preserve with cheese and charcuterie, we also use it as a base for a demi-glace that we serve with ostrich and game meats later in the season (chapter 8).

2 pounds (910 g) wild Concord grapes
1 tablespoon elderflower liqueur
1 cup (235 ml) white wine
2 cups (455 g) sugar
2 sprigs rosemary
Pinch salt
½ cup (120 ml) water
1½ tablespoons gelatin powder (about 2 envelopes)

Remove the woody stems and wash the grapes. Bring the first six ingredients to a boil over high heat in a nonreactive, heavy-bottomed pot. Reduce the heat to a high simmer over medium heat and thicken for about 10 minutes. Pour the mixture through a mesh strainer, gently pressing the solids to release all the liquid.

Pour the water into a small bowl and sprinkle the gelatin evenly over the top, allowing it to bloom for 5 minutes. Add 1 cup (235 ml) of the hot grape liquid to the bowl and whisk to dissolve the gelatin. Add the mixture back into the larger bowl of grape preserves and stir to combine. Pour into pint or quart containers, cover, and either process for canning or let cool to room temperature and refrigerate. Refrigerate for at least a day before serving. If canned, this preserve will last through the winter.

Candied Crab Apples

SERVES 10

Store-bought crab apples, if you can find them, are quite a bit larger than most wild varieties, and quite a bit easier to work with. If you're using wild crab apples, you might consider quadrupling the number of apples. Coring the little ones is also a challenge, so I have candied wild crab apples whole as a cocktail garnish, but the seeds—which contain innocuous traces of cyanide—can be a nuisance.

These syrupy little jewels make the perfect pairing with aged Vermont cheddar.

½ cup (120 ml) boiled cider (page 17)
½ cup (120 ml) cider vinegar
1 cup (235 ml) water
1½ cups (340 g) sugar
1 small stick cinnamon
10 crab apples (about 1½ inches [4 cm] in diameter), rinsed, cored, and held in lemon water until ready to cook

Bring all the ingredients but the crab apples to a boil in a medium nonreactive pot over high heat. Skim the scum that rises to the top of the pot, add the crab apples, and reduce the heat to a low simmer (if the flame is too high, the delicate apples will crack).

Cook 25 to 28 minutes, remove the apples from the liquid, and continue reducing the liquid over low heat (so it doesn't cloud) until it thickens, about 30 minutes total.

Off the heat, add the apples back to the liquid, cool to room temperature, and refrigerate until you're ready to use it. Canny canners can can these for later use!

Oil Drill

Here is an alphabetical list of all the oils we have worked with at Black Trumpet, with applications for each.

- **ALMOND OIL:** A strong oil used sparingly in dressings and desserts.
- **ARGAN OIL:** A strong nutty aroma and tangy flavor—used in Moroccan dishes and dressings.
- **AVOCADO OIL:** High smoke point, distinct flavor.
- **BERGAMOT OIL:** This is the only infused oil we have come back to over time, because there is nothing quite like it.
- **BLACK OLIVE OIL:** Castelas brand presses oil from cured black Spanish olives; great for anywhere your dish wants deep, roasty olive flavor without the salt or brine.
- **CANOLA OIL:** Canola oil got its name, which is a contraction of *Canada* and *oil*, from plant breeders looking to refine an oil for cooking. So it is a GMO (genetically modified organism) and is grown widely in the United States and Canada for oil production. Most restaurants use some form of canola oil, and we have always used it in our little fryolator whenever our menu calls for deep-frying. Coppal House Farm in nearby Lee, New Hampshire, is producing some canola oil that is not derived from GM plants.
- **COCONUT OIL:** A panacea for pantry and pharmacy alike, trending heavily these days.
- **GRAPESEED OIL:** Loved by many for its neutrality, sweetness, and brightness, as well as its high smoke point, grapeseed oil (which is a smart by-product of the winemaking industry) is indeed a delicious and healthy alternative to heavier, stronger oils. We use it in vinaigrettes and pestos.
- **HAZELNUT OIL:** This oil can overpower just about anything, so we add mere drops to finish fall and winter soups.

- **OLIVE OIL, EXTRA-VIRGIN:** Strictly a finishing oil, used in some vinaigrettes. For years we used only OLEA, my friend Steve's uncle's oil produced from his groves in Sparta that we visited.
- **OLIVE OIL, PURE:** We use more of this than any other oil because it has a neutral flavor and decent smoke point. Everything we sauté or pan-fry during service is fired in a combination of pure olive oil and clarified butter. Generally speaking, it is our go-to cooking oil.
- **PEANUT OIL:** Because of the increase in peanut allergies, it doesn't make sense to use this oil in a small kitchen like ours—the risk of cross-contamination is too great. But I do believe that peanut oil makes the best Cajun roux, which we use to make gumbo and shrimp Creole, two mainstays throughout Black Trumpet's life span.
- **SESAME/GINGELLY/BENNE OIL:** This oil has roots in southern cooking, although toasted sesame oil is more frequently associated with Asian cuisines. We dabble in both but use very little sesame oil as a rule.
- **SUNFLOWER OIL:** Nearby Coppal House Farm produces an award-winning example of this underappreciated oil. It is almost too sacred to cook with, so we generally use it as a light but flavorful finishing oil.
- **WHITE TRUFFLE OIL:** Beware the impostors on the market. The good stuff is worth the extra money, and the in-your-face burning rubber aromatics of the more common, artificially flavored varieties will turn you off truffle oil for life.

We also cook with rendered animal fats like pork lard, bacon fat, and beef tallow, but that's a whole other thing entirely.

Top Stock + Spice Blends

When we opened Stock + Spice next door to the restaurant, we wanted to sell lots of preserved ingredients gleaned from local farms to diminish the ratio of wasted produce from those farms. (I remain astonished at the amount of edible human food that never gets eaten by humans.) Alas, when we discovered the number of agency hoops we would have to jump through, we tacked a little from the plan, focusing on shelf-stable, dry ingredients that did not require certification. Before long, the people spoke, and soon our little shop specialized in proprietary spice blends.

These are some customer favorites we sell:

- Pork Rub
- Steak Seasoning
- Tabil
- Kharcho
- Berbere
- Garam Masala
- Baharat
- Yucatan
- Great Bay
- Ras el Hanout
- Tuscan
- Jerk Seasoning

Cocktails

A lot has happened to cocktail culture during the height of the Good Food Revolution. Our country went from favoring margarita-style fruit puree drinks, to reliving the upside of Prohibition, to our current drinkscape, where mixologists and bartenders put every bit as much creative effort into drink menus as chefs do into their food menus. I have even known a few good cooks who have gone from behind the stove to behind the bar.

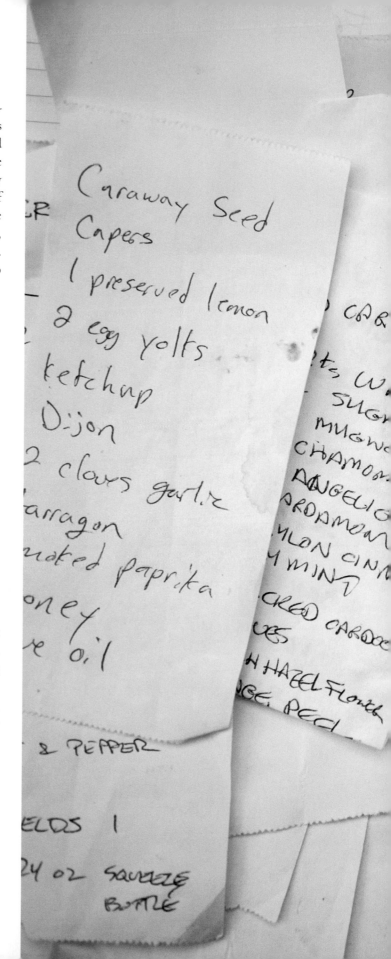

Black Trumpet has followed this curve to some extent, although throughout its course, I have always tried to infuse the drink menu with my own chef instincts, and in recent years I have pursued my mad scientist leanings with wild abandon, crafting bitters, infusions, shrubs, cordials, syrups, and all manner of bar additives for our drink program.

Rudyard Tippling

SERVES 1

2 ounces (60 ml) Prairie Organic gin
¼ ounce (7.5 ml) fresh lime
½ ounce (15 ml) curry/cardamom Tippling Syrup
½ ounce (15 ml) Cocchi Americano
1 fresh curry leaf

In a glass, stir all the ingredients with a bar spoon. Muddle the fresh curry leaf in the glass. Fill the glass three-quarters full with ice cubes and continue to stir gently with the spoon. Strain through a cocktail strainer into a martini glass. Garnish with fresh curry leaf and serve ice cold.

Tippling Syrup

MAKES ABOUT A PINT (475 ML)

10 green cardamom pods
2 cups (455 g) sugar
2 cups (475 ml) water
20 curry leaves, crumpled

Simmer the cardamom, sugar, and water, stirring occasionally, for 5 minutes. Add the curry leaves and simmer 3 more minutes. Turn off the heat, make sure the leaves are submerged, and let the mixture cool. Strain when completely cooled.

Visigoth

SERVES 1

1½ ounces (45 ml) calvados
¾ ounce (22 ml) blood orange juice
½ ounce (15 ml) Vermut (Spanish vermouth)
½ ounce (15 ml) Fabrizia (New Hampshire blood orange liqueur)
⅛ ounce (1 teaspoon) Luxardo Maraschino
½ ounce (15 ml) Bulleit Rye
2 dashes citrus bitters

Stir everything in a cocktail shaker or pint glass over ice, strain into a coupe glass, and serve with a cherry garnish.

Frank Shirley's Temple

SERVES 1

Talk about worshiping false idols . . . Named after Clark Griswold's boss in the Chevy Chase vehicle *National Lampoon's Christmas Vacation*, this pink drink is hardly stingy on flavor and refreshment.

4 whole cranberries, plus more for garnish
2 ounces (60 ml) Bully Boy white whiskey
½ ounce (15 ml) fresh lime juice,
  plus lime peel for garnish
¾ ounce (22 ml) Canton ginger liqueur
½ ounce (15 ml) Chartreuse, infused for 24 hours
  with 1 bruised Thai chile
Cranberries and lime peel, for garnish

Muddle four cranberries in a Collins glass and add all the other ingredients. Transfer to a shaker and shake with ice. Pour back into the glass over fresh ice, top off with soda, and stir with a spoon.

Garnish with more cranberries and a lime peel.

The Wanderer

SERVES 1

2 ounces (60 ml) bourbon
¾ ounce (22 ml) maple syrup
¼ ounce (7.5 ml) cider vinegar
1 eyedropperful of dandelion bitters
  (we use my homemade "backyard bitters")
4 ounces (120 ml) pale ale

Shake everything except the ale with ice and strain over fresh ice. Top with ale, stir, and serve.

"Encore" Apple Sangria

MAKES ABOUT 1½ GALLONS (5.7 L),
WHICH SERVES AROUND 40 PEOPLE

This autumnal sangria recipe was first concocted for an off-site wedding event, and we couldn't get over how delicious it came out. So naturally, we put it on

the drink menu shortly thereafter. Fear not how much this makes. If you omit the sparkling cider from the recipe and add it as needed, this "sangria" can last a long time in the fridge.

3 quarts (2.8 L) apple cider
1 bottle (750 ml) Flag Hill Josiah Bartlett apple brandy
½ bottle (375 ml) Orleans Bitter
½ bottle (180 ml) boiled cider (page 17)
1½ cups (340 g) sugar
4 apples, rough-chopped
1 orange
1 stick cinnamon
1 bottle (750 ml) Farnum Hill Extra Dry
  sparkling cider

Stir all the ingredients together, except the sparkling cider. Store for 3 days. Strain and serve over ice. Top off with a splash of sparkling cider, stir, and serve.

Lava Lamp

SERVES 10

3½ tablespoons pomegranate molasses
1 bottle (750 ml) Spanish cava sparkling wine
1 pomegranate

Carefully drizzle the molasses around the inside of ten champagne flutes. Pour cava almost to the top of the glasses and then drop a dozen pomegranate seeds into each drink. If the Lava Lamp does its job, these seeds will move around in the glass, resembling the cocktail's psychedelic inspiration.

The Roots of a Signature Cocktail

Denise and I knew when we were looking to build our nest that we wanted some land for our kids to carry out their daily adventures, because, in my mind, that is the best part of being a kid. For financial reasons, we had to stray from the immediate environs of Portsmouth, and when we spotted the 11-acre (4.5 ha), mostly wooded parcel in southern Maine, we knew we had found our spot. Although we eventually lost some of that (prime

foraging) land to a power company under the laws of eminent domain, we continued to find two delectable species of fruit in abundance. Blackberries and elderberries grow on or near our property in effusions so dense that, under certain summer conditions, our hands and shoes get stained magenta.

The road we live on was once called Blackberry Hill Road, so named for a hummock of brambles very near our house that keeps on giving from late July well into August. These wild berries are sometimes seedy, a little tart, and rarely as plump as the farmed variety that graces supermarket shelves. In other words, they are perfect for jams, jellies, cordials, and wine. I would love to boast that Black Trumpet's signature namesake cocktail came from the bounty of berries that grow on or near our house, but the reality is much less quaint. The fact is, in our early days as a restaurant, there were a few attempts at creating the "Black Trumpet," including one particularly regrettable admixture of black Sambuca and a brand of vodka that came in a trumpet-shaped bottle. Through a collaboration process that was clouded perhaps by the effects of its research, we eventually came

up with this perfect concoction that can be enjoyed all year round (if you can find blackberry puree or are lucky enough to be able to make and freeze your own).

Black Trumpet Cocktail

MAKES 5 COCKTAILS

½ cup (115 g) sugar
1 pint (340 g) fresh blackberries
Zest and juice of 1 orange
1 vanilla bean, split
1 tablespoon turbinado sugar
   (also sold as Sugar In The Raw)
1 teaspoon ground black pepper
3 halved limes, one half reserved to rim the glasses
   and the rest juiced and refrigerated
1¼ cups (295 ml) vodka
5 ounces (150 ml) limoncello

Prepare the syrup ahead of time. In a stainless saucepan, stir the sugar, blackberries, juice and zest of the orange, and scraped seeds and pod of the vanilla bean. Simmer, stirring occasionally, for 10 minutes. Remove the vanilla pod and puree the mixture in a blender for 10 seconds. Strain through a fine-mesh strainer and let cool. This should yield about 7.5 ounces (220 ml) Black Trumpet cocktail syrup.

Refrigerate the syrup.

Meanwhile, mix the turbinado sugar with the black pepper. Rub the rim of five martini glasses with the lime half and then roll the rims in the pepper/sugar mix. Fill the glasses with ice cubes and let them sit while you shake the cocktail.

In a cocktail shaker, place ice cubes, syrup, lime juice, vodka, and limoncello. Dump the ice out of the glasses and pour the cocktail into them, using a cocktail strainer to catch the ice. Serve immediately.

My Top Ten Most Life-Changing Bites of Food

Like most chefs, I am often asked what the best meal I have ever had was. Honestly, I have had very few meals in restaurants that have blown me away. I find that the lofty cost of dining at Michelin restaurants is never met by the flavors on the plate. The visuals may be stunning, but when I eat, I want flavor to win out, and that doesn't always happen at those fine-dining destination restaurants. So when held at knifepoint to answer this question, I flip through a Rolodex of flavors that have changed the very fabric of my thinking about food. Often, these flavors have been augmented by a sense of place, evoking more than mere taste. These are my top ten such moments of food epiphany.

1. Chile relleno in the Jalapa market
2. Ravioli in Anacapri
3. Ham, Banon cheese, epi, fresh fig, walnut mustard, in a rental car zooming down the autopiste in Provence
4. Bluefin toro salad in my kitchen at home
5. Carnitas at Santa Rosa de Jauregui
6. Street pizza in Piazza di Campo dei Fiore, Rome
7. Olives and almonds at Lucques
8. Leftover turkey, blue cheese, and cranberry sandwich at the summit of Pawtuckaway
9. Bannock bread with wild arctic char at the foot of Mount Pelly, Nunavut
10. Green apples, Camembert, and Sancerre on Chappaquiddick Island

The Bitter Truth

One of the assets an evolved cocktail program has brought to our restaurant (and the hospitality community at large) is what can only be called a Renaissance of cocktail bitters. Not long ago, our country could only claim a small handful of bitters producers. Today, bitters are everywhere, and the spectrum of flavors and aromatics they represent is so diverse, entire books have been written on the subject.

When I traveled to Italy for Slow Food's Terra Madre Conference with my friends John Forti and Jean Pauly, John brought back a copper pot still that we proceeded to set up in the front of the Black Trumpet dining room. John taught me how to produce distillations from herbs that he had grown and berries he had foraged.

The rather complicated process of small-batch distillation would test anyone's patience. I determined quickly that I required more immediate gratification, so I began making bitters, cordials, amaros, and decoctions on the stovetop with less refined, but equally tasty, results.

In the ensuing years, we began planting herbs, spices, flowers, and fruits for bitters production. At the same time, our gardener (who also happens to be a world-class forager), Jenna Darcy, started bringing us wild treats like spruce tips, chaga, witch hazel, and autumn olives—ingredients better known for their medicinal properties than their comestible applications.

My mad-scientist tendencies really kicked in at this point, resulting in dozens of different cocktail additives that we have used intermittently ever since. We now use bittering agents like cardoon and horehound from our garden, and wild mountain ash fruit and dandelion from the wild, to create a base that we can apply to any other aromatics we choose to play with.

horehound
parsley
MINT   14°°

ADD
to 1/2 bottle
of mix   CHILE

WINTER BI
lack walnut, blood or
innamon, fennel, clo
+ cardoon

How to Get Our
Culture Back on Track

Thank goodness that, one family at a time, we are as a culture gradually hopping off the crazy train of irresponsible food production and consequent dietary mistakes, potentially reversing the damage that industrialized agriculture and processed food have done to our minds, bodies, and souls. The track we should be on lies in plain sight, yet still too few Americans are able to hop on board. Time may not be on our side when we talk about climate change or many of the other environmental hazards that lie ahead for our population, but there is time to act now and make measurable change in the way we treat our crops, livestock, wild foods, and the environment that sustains them. I believe with all my heart that my children's children will live in a world with different values, having witnessed the damage shortsighted thinking will have wrought on our fragile food system.

As long as I can grip a whisk or type coherent sentences, I will continue to be a part of this Good Food Revolution, in part because it is a tastier place to be, but also because I believe positive change is happening now, all around the world, to correct what has been broken. I am optimistic that we are moving the dial, if painstakingly slowly, in the direction of enlightenment.

We have stopped what Wendell Berry calls "exploiters" from turning the last wild stock of sockeye salmon into a remote mining enterprise.

We have raised awareness of the critical decline in wild fish stocks, and have seen more and more people selecting sustainable fish species for dinner.

We have seen an explosion in so-called farm-to-table restaurant business models, the majority of which are actively changing the public perception of local food and its importance.

We have begun to question chemical inputs and unnatural genetics in our food by demanding transparency in food packaging and labeling.

But those steps are just the beginning. We have to reboot our thinking and begin shopping for ingredients rather than boxes and cans. We have to meet our farmers, fishermen, and food producers so we have a better understanding of how a holistic agrarian system can feed not only our people, but our economy and our heritage. In my fantasy world, real food is everyone's birthright. Currently, most everyone has access to "food" made from genetically altered plants and animals, packaged and promoted to appeal to our most urgent need for convenience, but few people have access to real, whole ingredients devoid of chemical and biological inputs.

We have to recognize that food is more than sustenance. It is community, relationships, culture, and heritage. And it is central to our lives. Therefore, we need to give it as much thought as any other aspect of living. I hope this book has lent some weight to this conviction, and that our greater community will continue to strive for growth and enlightenment, one delicious bite at a time.

GLOSSARY AND SOURCING INFORMATION

"00" FLOUR: A fine soft-wheat pasta flour used by many authentic Italian restaurants for pizza and pasta dough. It can be sourced online or found in Italian specialty markets.

ALARIA: A variety of sea vegetable, *Alaria esculenta*, that grows in relative abundance on the rocky coast of Maine. A healthy food ingredient eaten primarily in Northern Europe, alaria is starting to get some attention from chefs and foragers on our shores.

ALEPPO: A uniquely warm, but not overly hot, red pepper that is named after the war-ravaged Syrian city of its origin. Aleppo has the distinction of being the first seed to be withdrawn from the "doomsday" Arctic seed vault. Efforts to reintroduce the pepper plant on a global scale are under way.

ARK OF TASTE: Slow Food International created this program to expose geographically specific food-ways and food ingredients at risk of disappearing. We hosted the Ark of Taste nominating committee in 2009.

AVOCADO LEAVES: An ingredient that can add flavor to broths and soups, easily sourced online.

BACALAO/BACALHAU: The Spanish/Portuguese word for "salted cod."

BAY SCALLOPS: These sweet pearls of goodness can be found fresh from November through March (most years) at some New England fishmongers but can also be shipped direct to you from my personal favorite scalloper, Jeff at Salty Balls on Nantucket (508-280-1542).

BLUE STRAWBERY: The name of the influential and long-lived restaurant that occupied the space at 29 Ceres Street where Black Trumpet now resides.

BOILED CIDER: I get mine from Provisions International, Ltd., a wonderful purveyor out of Vermont, but this New England delicacy may also be purchased from Woods Cider Mill at woodscidermill.com.

BRANDADE: A Provençal dish (its full name is brandade de morue) that involves reconstituting and boiling salt cod with garlic and potatoes to make a delicious spread.

BRIX: The scientific measurement for the sugar content in plants, frequently used by farmers and winemakers.

CALVADOS: A type of apple brandy native to Normandy, France, that has its own appellation.

CBOOB: Clarified butter/olive oil blend, used at Black Trumpet and throughout this book.

CHEFS COLLABORATIVE: A nationwide organization (of which I have been a board member) of chefs and stakeholders in the food industry whose vision is to make sustainability second nature for every chef in America (chefscollaborative.org).

CHERMOULA: A marinade/sauce/dressing that hails from North Africa yet bears a striking resemblance to salsa verde from the Americas.

CHESTNUT FLOUR: A fine, sweet, and nutty flour that we use in the depth of winter to enrich pastas, sauces, and desserts. Order online or from Provisions International, Ltd.

CHIFFONADE: The technique of rolling up leaves such as basil or spinach and slicing them into very thin ribbons.

CIENTO: The short-lived but much-loved Spanish-themed tapas bar opened in Portsmouth by the founders of Lindbergh's Crossing.

DULSE: A type of sea vegetable (*Palmaria palmata*) celebrated worldwide for its health benefits, often sold dried and used in many cuisines ranging from Japanese to European.

EPAZOTE: A plant in the Amaranth family, native to Mexico and Central America, that has a distinct flavor and also aids in the digestion of legumes.

FISH PEPPER: An important heirloom chile that was first brought to the Americas in the 1800s by African-Americans in the Chesapeake Bay area.

FISHCHOICE.COM: One of the two resources I stand by to get information about the sustainability of wild fish stocks and the species that are seasonally available and relatively abundant.

FREEKEH: Also known as green wheat, this grain, harvested before ripening on the plant, is used in cuisines ranging from Persian to Cajun.

GARDEN SEEDS: I recommend finding a seed house from your region that features organic, GMO-free heirloom seeds. An heirloom garden will bring all the usual pleasures of a culinary garden, plus the added benefit of helping ensure that our regional foodways and plant biodiversity remain intact.

GARUM: An ancient fermented juice made by pressing cured anchovies. We use it to add Mediterranean umami to dressings and sauces, much as Southeast Asian cooks might use fish sauce.

GOAT MEAT: You might be surprised at how many goat farms are out there these days. Look around for one that is raising heritage-breed meat goats. We use Riverside Farm in Lee, New Hampshire, for this purpose, but I also recommend finding a butcher shop or market that sells Vermont Chevon goat, a cooperative of goat farms that produce consistently clean and delicious goat meat (vermontchevon.com).

GRAINS OF PARADISE: Also known as malagueta pepper, this aromatic grain gained attention in the United States when Samuel Adams brewer Jim Koch first marketed Sam Summer Ale, which uses grains of paradise as one of its refreshing aromatics. We use it in pickling spices and other blends to add a floral aroma and minor kick of heat.

GRUIT: A beer style that predates the use of hops, often incorporating herbs that were grown in colonial times for apothecary gardens. Portsmouth's Earth Eagle Brewings has helped bring this historical beer style back to the mainstream.

HARRY B'S: The Cajun-themed restaurant where I cooked in San Miguel de Allende, Mexico, from 2001 to 2003.

KATA'IFI: Shredded phyllo dough that can be used for both savory and sweet applications, found online or frozen in Middle Eastern specialty markets.

KEFTA: Also known as kofta in some circles, this North African meat dish appeared on early Black Trumpet menus as three meatballs bathed in a spicy tomato sauce with an egg baked on top.

LARDO: Cured pork fatback that, in Italy (and now various American salumerias), is served sliced very thin with bread. We incorporate the fat into sausages and various other recipes.

LEAF LARD: The pure white fat that surrounds the kidneys and other organs in most mammals. Leaf lard from a pig is particularly succulent and, when rendered, makes a wonderful substitute for butter in savory pastry production.

LINDBERGH'S CROSSING: The restaurant at 29 Ceres Street that Denise and I purchased in 2007. I had worked as the executive chef there for four years and learned invaluable lessons from its two generous and kind owners, Tom and Scott.

LYCOPERSICONS: The fancy Linnean name for tomatoes (*Lycopersicon lycopersicum*).

MAGHREB: The region of North Africa that includes Morocco, Tunisia, Libya, and Algeria, the collective cuisine of which has made a name for itself stateside in recent years.

MAILLARD REACTION: The conversion of starch to sugar that results from high heat, often creating a "caramelization" process.

MARFAX: An heirloom bean from northern Maine that almost became extinct. Restored to the collective conscience of New Englanders by a handful of bean growers and seed houses, this brown bean was once the staple of Maine's signature baked bean dish.

MECO CHIPOTLE: A pale variety of dried jalapeño chile from Oaxaca with a concentrated flavor and mellow heat.

MEZCAL: A distillation of the blue agave plant related to, but tasting very different from, tequila. Mezcal can be dark and brooding, always slightly smoky, and—at its best—comparable to fine Scotch. It can be found in most liquor stores, but be wary of brands that contain the "worm" or *gusano*, a marketing gimmick that usually accompanies mezcales of the lowest grade.

MICROPLANE: One of the commercial kitchen's favorite tools, this perforated blade removes the outer zest of citrus in no time without taking any of the bitter white pith.

MIREPOIX: Described in this book's "Building Blocks" section (page 13), *mirepoix* is the French term for the combination of carrots, celery, and onions used in making most stocks, soups, and sauces.

MOLCAJETE: A Mexican mortar made of lava rock that is used to grind chiles, corn, and spices as well as serving as a vessel to serve hearty stews in central Mexico.

MONSANTO: A multinational corporation I have alluded to in this book whose track record includes a number of lobbying efforts that have undermined the goals of the Good Food Revolution. In addition to the ubiquitous herbicide Roundup, Monsanto has developed a number of genetically modified foods that imperil the future of biodiversity on Earth, not to mention the damage GM foods have done and will continue to do to our planet and our bodies.

PAELLA: A classic Spanish rice dish that has graced almost every Black Trumpet menu in some form.

PAILLARD: A thin, pounded fillet, usually of meat. Also known as escalope.

PATLICAN SALATASI: A Turkish eggplant salad, our version of which can be found on page 239.

PEGA: The Spanish term for the caramelized, stuck-on reduction of stock-infused rice that adorns the bottom and edges of a cooked paella.

POMEGRANATE MOLASSES: Now found in many specialty shops, this is a crucial ingredient in lots of Middle Eastern dishes.

RAS EL HANOUT: Literally translated from the Arabic as "head of the shop," this spice mix traces its roots to the Spice Route that brought exotic spices to Europe via North Africa's Barbary Coast.

ROBOT COUPE: The invaluable food processor brand we use for everything from aioli to mixing dough.

RONDEAU: A large, heavy pan used to brown meat before stewing or braising.

SALMOREJO: A garlicky soup from Spain that is related to gazpacho, used sometimes at Black Trumpet as a sauce.

SALPICON: Any thick combination of finely chopped meats and vegetables, often used for stuffing.

SALT COD: Ask your fishmonger to source this for you, or track down Richard at stoningtonseafood.com. His is the supreme example of what salt cod is capable of.

SALT-CURED CAPERS: A more intense and flavorful caper than the ones sold in brine, this great culinary treat can be found online at moulinsmahjoub.com.

SAN MIGUEL DE ALLENDE: The hopelessly picturesque colonial city in Mexico where we lived for almost two years.

SAUTEUSE: A large, heavy pan used to sauté a large volume of food.

SCOVILLE UNITS: Named after Wilber Lincoln Scoville, this is the commonly accepted scale—ranging from 0 to 2.2 million units—that measures and charts the heat of chile peppers.

SEA LETTUCE (*ULVA LACTUCA*): One of my favorite sea vegetables, sold dried but common in Gulf of Maine waters. Sea lettuce can be ordered from Browne Trading Company.

SEAFOOD WATCH: Monterey Bay Aquarium's groundbreaking rating system for seafood species has led the way in getting information about sustainable (and not-so-sustainable) species to the chef and consumer.

SHAKSHUKA: An Israeli dish of eggs baked in a piquant tomato sauce.

SLOW FOOD USA: The American branch of the international nonprofit organization founded by Italian politician Carlo Petrini in the late 1980s whose ambitious vision is restoring old regional foodways while expunging the industrialized global food production and distribution system.

SMELT: A delicious small forage fish found in both salt and fresh water in northern regions of the world.

SOCCA: A leavened chickpea pancake.

SPICES: We opened our store Stock + Spice in 2014 to offer Black Trumpet customers and other passersby an opportunity to buy hard-to-find spices and culinary crafts. Visit stockandspice.com to source any spices and proprietary blends.

SUGAR KELP (*SACCHARINA LATISSIMA*): A rugged sea vegetable that can grow to dozens of feet in length whose population is susceptible to warming oceans and whose underwater "forests" play a key role as habitat for many aquatic species.

SULFAR BEAN: Sometimes referred to as the sulfur bean, this heirloom variant of the China Yellow bean boasts a thin skin and a rich, buttery flavor. The more common cannellini makes a fine substitute.

SUMAC: A tangy "spice" used widely in Mediterranean and Middle Eastern cuisines, these dried flowers from the bright-red spikes of the common sumac shrub may be foraged with great care and dried at home.

TAMIS: A French screen-like tool used to separate clumps and impurities from pureed or mashed foods.

TOGARASHI: A somewhat trendy Japanese seasoning blend that includes sesame seeds, dried seaweeds, and a variable smattering of spices. Can be found in Japanese markets or online.

TOMATO VINEGAR: If you don't want to make your own, here is the best of the best: A l'Olivier Tomate Basilic (alolivier.com).

TUNISIAN COUSCOUS: My favorite "gauge" of couscous, this intermediate size is versatile and delicious, often packed with chile peppers to lend heat to the finished dish. It can be found online at moulinsmahjoub.com, the same place we source salt-cured capers.

TZATZIKI: A common Middle Eastern and Greek yogurt-based dipping sauce.

URFA PEPPER: This dried mild brown pepper from Turkey is versatile and possesses a rich toasty flavor.

VERJUS: Produced since ancient times, this juice of unripe grapes makes a softer substitute for vinegar in sauces and dressings.

VITAMIX: A revolutionary blender that enables any cook to produce a refined puree worthy of the finest dining establishments.

ZA'ATAR: A Middle Eastern spice blend, the constituents of which vary from country to country, and even from household to household.

SUGGESTED MENUS

Early Winter

Scallops with Couscous and Cider Cream Sauce

Paired with Catarratto or Farnum Hill Cider

Warm Spinach Salad with Duck Confit

Paired with Austrian Pinot Noir

Valencian Orange Curd with
Thyme Shortbread and Toasted Meringue

*Paired with Moscato d'Asti
or Ancestral sparkling Malvasia*

Late Winter

Octopus Strata with Chorizo Puree

*Paired with rosé of Grenache (Garnacha)
or Belgian dubbel ale*

Sautéed Calamari with
Harissa, Celery, and Preserved Lemon

*Paired with Tempranillo
or pilsner beer*

Winter Flounder Roulades Stuffed
with Rouille, and Yankee Collard Greens

Paired with Southern Rhône White Blend

Banana Cake

*Paired with Papa's Pilar brand rum
(or other sipping rum)*

Early Spring

Fried Almonds, Olives, and Garlic

Paired with Oloroso sherry or vin jaune du Jura

Pork Schnitzel with Pretzel Spätzle

Paired with Kolsch or dry Riesling

Olive Oil Cake with Prune Jam
and Whipped Ricotta

Paired with Cardamaro or espresso, or both

Late Spring

Rhubarb Chlodnik
with Spice-Roasted Strawberries,
Crème Fraîche, and Caviar

*Paired with Champagne
or Cava Rosado*

Fried Rabbit Loin with
Cheesy Polenta Pudding and Rhubarb Salsa

Paired with Txakolina

English Pea Panna Cotta

Paired with mint julep

Early Summer

Ceviche with Pico de Gallo

*Paired with Albariño
or Barranco Jefe Weiss Beer*

Seafood Paella

*Paired with Assyrtiko white
or Mencia red wine*

Red Quinoa Coconut Milk Pudding
with Rhubarb Compote, Hibiscus Whip, and Kata'ifi

Paired with good sake or Vieux Macvin du Jura

Late Summer

Meze of Falafel, Patlican Salatasi,
and Tzatziki with Pita Bread

Paired with Vinho Verde

Sockeye Salmon
with Chile Fettuccine, Bacon, and
Chanterelles in Gin Tomato Cream Sauce

*Paired with Oregon Pinot Gris
or Pinot Noir*

Corn Mousse with Fresh Summer Fruit

*Paired with Muscat (Moscato)
or Vouvray*

Early Fall

Warm Kale Caesar Salad
with Squash Croutons, Bacon Lardons,
and Caesar Aioli

Paired with brown ale

Chicken Paillard
with Black Olive Salpicon

Paired with Rhone Syrah

Brown Butter Chocolate Bites
with Chile Marshmallows

Paired with Uruguayan Tannat dessert wine

Late Fall

Levant-Spiced Pumpkin Soup
with Potato Bread

Paired with dry sparkling cider

Cider-Braised Pork Osso Buco
with Lady Apple Chutney

Paired with Cabernet Franc

Pear Crème Brûlée with
Pear Chutney and Ginger Tuile

Paired with Italian brandy

RECIPE INDEX BY COURSE

Pumpernickel Pudding   39
Sautéed Calamari with Harissa, Celery,
    and Preserved Lemon   99
Scallops with Couscous and Cider Cream Sauce   41
Stuffed Squid with Sulfar Beans   101
Vuelve a la Vida with Totopos   102

Salads

Asian Seaweed Salad   253
Beet Tortellini with Raisin Pine Nut Salad   65
Bistro Bean Salad   256
Coban Salad   157
Smoked Eggplant Salad   240
Stone Fruit Salad   260
Tuna Caesar with Parmesan Tuiles
    and Caesar Aioli   206
Warm Kale Caesar Salad with Squash Croutons,
    Bacon Lardons, and Caesar Aioli   281
Warm Spinach Salad with Clementines,
    Goat Cheese, and Pickled Shallots   31

Soups

Baked Stuffed Quahog Chowder   210
Beef and Beet Borscht with Nigella and
    Preserved Lemon Crème Fraîche   81
Black Beluga Lentil Soup   88
Chanterelle Corn Bisque   245
Chilled Cucumber Soup   193
Chilled Zucchini Soup   261
Garden Tomato Soup with Shellfish and
    Saffron Cream   217
Levant-Spiced Pumpkin Soup   324
Rhubarb and Chicken Dumpling Soup with Crottin
    Brûlée and Shaved Artichokes   170
Rhubarb Chlodnik with Spice-Roasted Strawberries,
    Crème Fraîche, and Caviar   169
Rhubarb Tomato Soup   192
Scarlet Turnip Vichyssoise   194
Smoked Eggplant Soup with Falafel and Tzatziki   241
Summer Squash Bisque   212

Main Courses

Baked Chestnut Gnocchi   58
Braised Beef Short Rib   77

Braised Pork Shank with Mashed Turnips
    and Long Beans   302
Brown Butter Fettuccine Tossed with Kale, Pecans,
    and Roasted Beets Over Carrot Sour Cream Sauce
    and Topped with a Farm Egg   326
Chicken Paillard   296
Cider-Braised Pork Osso Buco   334
Duck Leg Confit on a Bistro Bean Salad Tossed
    in Apricot Sherry Vinaigrette   256
Gruit-Braised Goat   48
Jacketed Sweet Potato with Lentil Dal, Feta,
    and Blood Oranges   62
Marinated Grassfed Steak with Black Trumpet
    Mushroom Cream Sauce   306
Moroccan Chicken   115
Mountain Paella   342
Ostrich Fan Fillet with Concord Grape
    Demi-Glace   341
Pheasant Two Ways: Roulade and Leg Stewed
    with Prunes   69
Potato and Cheese Pierogi with Blueberries, Kale,
    and Smoked Corn Bisque   337
Pretzel- and Chestnut-Crusted Meat Tarts   59
Quail Adobado with Quince Hash   70
Rabbit Agnolotti with Pecans, Broccoli, and
    Oven-Dried Tomato   329
Rabbit Fricassee   73
Risotto-Stuffed Tomato with Summer
    Squash Bisque   212
Seafood Paella   218
Seared Duck Breast   110
Shakshuka with Duck Eggs and Herbed
    Semolina Dumplings   56
Sockeye Salmon with Chile Fettuccine, Bacon, and
    Chanterelles in Gin Tomato Cream Sauce   265
Spring Mushroom and Fiddlehead Paella
    with Saffron Rice, English Peas, Peppers,
    and Spring Garlic   176
Stuffed Chicken Leg   297
Tea-Smoked Young Chicken   145
Twice-Baked Eggplant Markeb   263
Winter Flounder Roulades Stuffed
    with Rouille   116
Winter Root Veggie Potpie   74

Vegetables, Grains, and Legumes

Sauces, Dressings, Condiments, and Accoutrements

INDEX

Note: Page numbers in *italics* refer to photographs.

ABOUT THE AUTHOR

Chef Evan Mallett's path to professional cooking has been a sinuous one, wending its way from Washington, DC, up the coast to Boston, and eventually to the small seaport city of Portsmouth, New Hampshire.

In 2007, Evan and his wife, Denise, bought what would become Black Trumpet, taking over a historic restaurant location—an old ship's chandlery that first opened in 1970 as the legendary Blue Strawbery, an early pioneer of New American cuisine.

Evan is a three-time James Beard semi-finalist for Best Chef, Northeast. He is actively involved in and sits on the boards of Chef's Collaborative, Slow Food Seacoast, and the Heirloom Harvest Project, an initiative that brings together farmers, chefs, and educators to identify and restore a food system native to the greater New England Seacoast region.

He lives with his family in southern Maine.